Allied Artists
Horror, Science Fiction
and Fantasy Films

ALSO BY MICHAEL R. PITTS
AND FROM MCFARLAND

*Columbia Pictures Horror, Science Fiction
and Fantasy Films, 1928–1982* (2010)

Western Film Series of the Sound Era (2009)

*Poverty Row Studios, 1929–1940:
An Illustrated History of 55 Independent Film Companies,
with a Filmography for Each* (1997; paperback 2005)

*Charles Bronson: The 95 Films and the 156
Television Appearances* (1999; paperback 2003)

Horror Film Stars, 3d ed. (2002)

*Western Movies: A TV and Video Guide to
4200 Genre Films* (1986; paperback 1997)

*Hollywood and American History: A Filmography of Over
250 Motion Pictures Depicting U.S. History* (1984)

Allied Artists
Horror, Science Fiction and Fantasy Films

Michael R. Pitts

McFarland & Company, Inc., Publishers
Jefferson, North Carolina, and London

LIBRARY OF CONGRESS CATALOGUING-IN-PUBLICATION DATA

Pitts, Michael R.
Allied Artists horror, science fiction and fantasy films / Michael R. Pitts.
    p.   cm.
Includes bibliographical references and index.

ISBN 978-0-7864-6046-5
softcover : 50# alkaline paper ∞

1. Allied Artists Pictures Corporation — Catalogs.   2. Motion pictures —
United States — Catalogs.   3. Horror films — United States — Catalogs.
4. Science fiction films — United States — Catalogs.
5. Fantasy films — United States — Catalogs.   I. Title.
PN1999.A4P58 2011   791.430973 — dc22   2011006773

BRITISH LIBRARY CATALOGUING DATA ARE AVAILABLE

© 2011 Michael R. Pitts. All rights reserved

*No part of this book may be reproduced or transmitted in any form
or by any means, electronic or mechanical, including photocopying
or recording, or by any information storage and retrieval system,
without permission in writing from the publisher.*

On the cover: Poster art from the 1959 film *The Giant Behemoth*,
originally titled *Behemoth, the Sea Monster* (Allied Artists/Photofest)

Manufactured in the United States of America

*McFarland & Company, Inc., Publishers
Box 611, Jefferson, North Carolina 28640
www.mcfarlandpub.com*

For my grandson,
Jacob Michael Cruz

Table of Contents

Preface 1

FEATURE FILMS 3
TELEVISION FEATURES 181
REISSUES 227

Theatrical Films in Chronological Order 233

Bibliography 235

Index 237

Preface

When Screen Gems released its "Shock!" and "Son of Shock!" packages of old Universal and Columbia horror films to television in the late 1950s, it opened a floodgate of popularity for horror, science fiction and fantasy films that has yet to abate. Living in Central Indiana, I was able to see these wonderful movies on WISH-TV, Channel 8, when they were presented by the hugely popular horror host, Selwin. From 1958 to 1961 the classic movie monsters were seen each Friday night until Selwin began showing Tarzan and Bomba movies on an afternoon show called *Selwin on Saturday*. In the spring of 1962 he was back on late Fridays wearing a silver spacesuit purchased from the Captain Company and presenting a new flock of scary movies, this time from Allied Artists. It was evident these more modern fright fest offerings were of a different (lesser) breed than the monster movies of yore, but they had a lure of their own. Many a baby boomer got hooked on horror movies watching these Allied releases and after nearly a half century they retain a place in the hearts of genre followers.

From 1952 to 1978 Allied Artists Pictures Corporation released over 80 feature films in the horror, science fiction and fantasy film categories. Like most of the studios' product, they were mainly average outings but there were some top-notch productions like *House on Haunted Hill, Invasion of the Body Snatchers, Macabre, The Maze, Not of This Earth* and *World Without End*. At the other end of the spectrum, the company was responsible for the release of movies like *The Bride and the Beast, The Disembodied, Frankenstein Meets the Space Monster, From Hell It Came* and *Mission Mars*. Somewhere in the middle come such favorites as *Attack of the 50 Foot Woman, The Atomic Submarine, The Bat, Black Zoo, Daughter of Dr. Jekyll, The Giant Behemoth, Queen of Outer Space* and *The Strangler*. For traditionalists there is John Carradine in *The Cosmic Man*, Lon Chaney in *Indestructible Man* and *The Cyclops* and Boris Karloff in *Frankenstein 1970* and *The Sorcerers*. One of the studio's most popular series was "The Bowery Boys" and several of their entries involved horror, sci-fi or fantasy. Allied also imported the genre features *Blood and Black Lace, Caltiki the Immortal Monster, Crow Hollow, Island of the Doomed, The Magic Weaver* and *Moonwolf*. There were even some sex horror imports, including *Blood Rose* and *Eugenie*.

Allied Artists' history goes back to the silent days when W. Ray Johnston started Rayart Productions in 1924; it became Syndicate Film Exchange in 1928. With the coming of sound there were a few releases under the banners Continental Talking Pictures and Raytone, and then in 1931 the company became Monogram Pictures. In 1935 Johnston and Trem Carr, who was in charge of production, merged Monogram with several other studios (Mascot, Majestic, Liberty) and Consolidated Film Industries to form Republic Pictures Corporation. In 1937 Johnston re-started Monogram and the company returned to motion picture production. Among its product was some horror movies, including some with Bela Lugosi in the 1940s. In 1946 Johnston became chairman of the studio's board and general sales manager Steve Broidy succeeded him as Monogram's president. Since Monogram was associated with program pictures, Broidy formed Allied Artists Productions in 1946 to make prestige productions. By 1953, Allied Artists Pictures Corporation completely phased out Monogram. For the next 13 years Allied Artists continued to make and/or distribute a variety of films, including the big-budget items *Friendly Persuasion* (1956), *Love in the Afternoon* (1957), *The Big Circus* (1959) and *55 Days at Peking* (1963). Two of the studio's biggest moneymakers were producer-director William Castle's initial "gimmick" productions *Macabre* (1958) and *House on Haunted Hill* (1959).

In 1965 Broidy left Allied Artists and was succeeded by Claude A. Giroux. The company went into television and quit making films in 1966. Two years later, Emanuel L. Wolf took over the company and for the next several years Allied mainly released imports before resuming film production with the big-budget affairs *Cabaret* (1972), *Papillon* (1973), *The Man Who Would Be King* (1975) and *The Betsy* (1978). With dwindling revenue, Allied Artists joined Kalvex, Inc./PSP, Inc., to form Allied Artists Industries in 1976 but declared bankruptcy three years later. In 1980 Lorimar Productions purchased the company's film library; Time Warner bought Lorimar in 1988. Today most of the Allied Artists film library is under the control of Warner Bros. Entertainment, Inc.

Allied was one of the first to go into TV distribution with its Interstate Television Corporation, a subsidiary that released most of the old Monogram product to television stations. As Allied Artists Television Corporation, the studio had nearly 400 feature films available to television stations in 14 different packages, plus an additional 135 Monogram westerns in five more packages, in the mid–1970s. Twenty-two of these movies, although released theatrically by other companies, are discussed in this volume since it was Allied that made them available to the small screen. In one case, *Hand of Power*, this proved to be the movie's first U.S. showing. Also included in the text is Allied's 1963 double-bill reissue of the Jack H. Harris productions *The Blob* and *Dinosaurus!*

In the summer of 1978, the studio formed Allied Artists Video Corporation, a subsidiary that planned to release some 500 titles on video. Thus Allied became the first major studio distributor to tap the VCR market. It released over 100 titles in both the Beta and VHS formats before being shuttered by Lorimar in the fall of 1980.

This volume takes a look at the genre films of Allied Artists between 1952 and 1978, along with the already noted TV releases and the two 1963 reissues. I have tried to give balanced coverage of these films, including both personal and critics' comments as well as detailed plot synopsis, casts and credits. Films are in black and white unless otherwise noted. I have a special fondness for the Allied product, especially those from the 1950s into the mid–1960s, and I hope this work will encourage others to take a look at these entertaining movies. Thanks to the video market, most of them are available for viewing.

Some sources list *Queen of Spades*, a 1948 British film, as a 1950 Allied release but it was issued under the Monogram banner in the U.S. Another alleged Allied release is the 1976 West German production *Superbug*, but it was issued stateside by Scorpio International and Central Park Films. Included in the TV section is the 1962 film *This Is Not a Test* which at least one source claims to be an Allied release but its only theatrical showings seem to have been through Modern Films.

I would like to thank Len D. Martin, Gary Kramer, Ray White and James Robert Parish for their help with this book.

While Allied Artists was not in the top echelon, the studio kept up a steady program of popular low-budget movies and many of their horror, science fiction and fantasy films have more than stood the test of time. Most important, they continue to entertain. I hope you enjoy reading about them.

Feature Films

The Atomic Man (1956; 78 minutes)

Producer: Alec C. Snowden. Director: Ken Hughes. Screenplay: Charles Eric Maine, from his novel *The Isotope Man*. Photography: A.T. Dinsdale. Editor: Geoffrey Muller. Music Director: Richard Taylor. Art Director: George Haslam. Sound: Ronald Abbott. Production Manager: Jim O'Connolly. Makeup: Jack Craig. Wardrobe: June Kirby. Continuity: Marjorie Owens. Assistant Directors: Denis Johnson and Ted Sturgis.

CAST: Gene Nelson (Mike Delaney), Faith Domergue (Jill Rabowski), Donald Gray (Robert Maitland), Joseph Tomelty (Detective Inspector Cleary), Leonard Williams (Detective Sergeant Haines), Barry MacKay (Inspector Hammond), Peter Arne (Dr. Stephen Grant Rayner/Jarvis), Martin Wyldeck (Dr. Preston), Mary Jones (Sister Brown), Philip Dale (Dr. Peters), Carl Jaffe (Dr. Marks), Patricia Driscoll, Phillipa Hiatt (X-Ray Assistants), Gordon Bell (Assistant Surgeon), Ian Cooper (Anesthetist), Vanda Godsell (Stenographer), Launce Maraschal (Editor Alcott), Charles Hawtrey (Office Boy), Vic Perry (Emmanuel Vasquo), Paul Hardmuth (Dr. Bressler), Dervis Ward (Allegan), Anthony Woodruffe (Nuclear Physicist), Brian O'Higgins (Barman Pat).

When an unconscious man is pulled from the Thames River near Duggan's Wharf in London and sent to a hospital, his photograph is familiar to science writer Mike Delaney (Gene Nelson). With his girlfriend, news photographer Jill Rabowski (Faith Domergue), Mike comes to believe the man is Dr. Stephen Rayner (Peter Arne) of the Brandt Nuclear Research Institute. A world-renowned physicist, Rayner is known as the Isotope Man because of his work with atomic energy.

Mike and Jill go to the hospital where the man is pronounced dead following an operation to remove a bullet from his back. The operation was performed by Dr. Preston (Martin Wyldeck). After a shot of adrenalin, the patient revives. Mike shows his picture to the doctor and Inspector Cleary (Joseph Tomelty) and both agree there is a resemblance to the scientist. A check at the institute by Sergeant Haines (Leonard Williams) proves that Rayner is there. At the hospital, Jill takes a picture of the revived man. The next day Mike goes to visit his old friend Robert Maitland (Donald Gray), Brandt's director. He also meets Rayner, who shows no interest in the photograph of the man in the hospital and mentions that he is working on a project that could have worldwide effects. Mike's editor (Launce Maraschal) orders him to quit the Rayner case and stick to scientific writing. After noticing that all the photos of the revived man have the same foggy glow, Mike goes back to see Maitland, who says the effect might be caused by static electricity. Since the man in the hospital complains of headaches and has a high fever, Dr. Preston orders an x-ray be taken but there is a malfunction due to radioactivity in the room. Mike and Preston talk to the revived man but he only rambles and mentions "Vasquo" and UTC. Mike and Jill go to Rayner's residence where she takes his photograph. As they leave, Mike is intrigued to see a hat with the initials EV which came from Buenos Aires. Rayner, whose real name is Jarvis, meets with Dr.

Bressler (Paul Hardmuth), the plastic surgeon who made him look like Rayner. Jarvis tells his employer, Argentine businessman Emmanuel Vasquo (Vic Perry), that a test of the new formula will result in an explosion that will destroy the institute and its inhabitants. Jill reveals that the man pretending to be Rayner is a fake because the photo she took of him has no glow. Mike is fired by his editor for working on the Rayner case and not the assignment given to him. Mike gets permission from Dr. Preston to question the man in the hospital but his responses make no sense until Jill transcribes them to show that he answers questions before they are asked. Preston tells them that the man's heart stopped for seven or eight seconds before he was revived. They learn the wounded man had been abducted by Vasquo's operatives. Mike deduces that Rayner developed a formula for synthetic tungsten and Vasquo wants it destroyed since his company, United Tungsten Corporation (or UTC), controls two-thirds of the world's supply of that mineral. Jarvis goes to the institute and plants a plutonium bomb in the nuclear reactor but is distressed to learn that the scheduled test will be delayed several hours. That night someone shoots at Mike in front of his apartment building. When Jill goes there the next morning, she finds him with Inspector Haines, who is questioning him about the attack. Delaney goes with Haines to see Inspector Cleary and there he meets Dr. Marks (Carl Jaffe), a psychoanalyst who says that when Rayner's heart stopped, his brain continued to function and when revived his consciousness was 7.5 seconds ahead of his physical self. He theorizes that this happened due to the scientist's long involvement with radioactivity. Jill borrows an ice pick from a barman (Brian O'Higgins) and breaks into the Argentine's UTC office. Vasquo learns from an informant (Vanda Godsell) at the hospital that Rayner has been given an antidote that has brought him back to real time and that he recalls his kidnapping. Vasquo orders Bressler to kill Rayner but the surgeon cannot make himself commit the crime. Bressler leaves behind a syringe filled with poison. Mike, Cleary and Dr. Marks go to see Rayner and when they pass Bressler in the hall, Marks recognizes him. Mike finds out that Bressler tried to get rid of Rayner and tells Cleary. A police dragnet is launched for Vasquo and the fake Rayner as the plastic surgeon is brought in on a stretcher after having committed suicide by jumping in front of a car. Jill calls Mike to tell him she found photographs of Rayner in Vasquo's office but the crook and his henchman (Dervis Ward) show up. Arriving at the Argentine's office, Mike finds it empty but answers the telephone and is told to go to Duggan's Wharf, where a boat is waiting. There he discovers Jill is a prisoner at a warehouse. During a shootout, Vasquo is accidentally killed by his henchman, who is then shot by Delaney. Jill informs Mike that Vasquo planned to blow up the institute and they take Jarvis to the site just in time to have Maitland halt the test. Cleary shows them the plutonium bomb found there by his men. Mike and Jill decide to carry out their own experiments in romance.

The sci-fi element of *The Atomic Man* deals with Rayner's mind jumping 7.5 seconds into the future following the stoppage of his heart for that length of time. Outside of the sequence of his answering questions before they are asked and the use of a tape recorder to match his answers with previously asked queries, the feature is basically an anemic espionage thriller, slow-moving and methodical. Produced in England at Merton Park Studios, it was issued in that country in 1955 by Anglo-Amalgamated Film Distributors as *Timeslip* with a 93-minute running time. When Allied Artists released it in the U.S. as *The Atomic Man* in March 1956, it was cut by thirteen minutes. In some stateside venues it was double-billed with *Invasion of the Body Snatchers* (q.v.).

David Quinlan reported in *British Sound Films: The Studio Years 1928–1959* (1984), "For [the] unlikely plot to succeed, [the] film has to be fast and exciting: it is." Donald C.

Willis in *Horror and Science Fiction Films: A Checklist* (1972) opined, "No story to go with the intriguing central gimmick." Ed Naha agreed in *Horrors: From Screen to Scream* (1975) when he wrote, "[T]his production presents an interesting premise that doesn't get a full plot treatment." *VideoHound's Sci-Fi Experience* (1997) noted, "Preposterous but intriguing idea is wasted in this dull, talky British feature."

The same year *The Atomic Man* debuted in its homeland as *Timeslip*, Faith Domergue also starred in *It Came from Beneath the Sea*, *Cult of the Cobra* and *This Island Earth*. Her later genre efforts were *Voyage to the Prehistoric Planet* (1965), *Legacy of Blood* and *The House of Seven Corpses* (both 1972). Best known as a movie dancer, top-billed Gene Nelson turned to directing and helmed *Hand of Death* (1962). Director Ken Hughes also directed *The Brain Machine* (1954), a segment of *Casino Royale* (1967), the fantasy *Chitty Chitty Bang Bang* (1968) and the slasher thriller *Night School* (1981). The feature's production manager, Jim O'Connolly, went on to write the well-liked sci-fier *The Night Caller* (1965), released stateside as *Blood Beast from Outer Space*; he directed the topnotch Joan Crawford thriller *Berserk!* (1967) and the entertaining *The Valley of Gwangi* (1968), as well as serving as producer-director on *Horror on Snape Island* (1971), also known as *Tower of Evil* and *Beyond the Fog*.

The Atomic Submarine (1959; 72 minutes)

Producers: Alex Gordon and Henry Schrage. Associate Producer–Screenplay: Orville H. Hampton. Producer Associates: Irving Block and Jack Rabin. Director: Spencer G. Bennet. Photography: Gilbert Warrenton. Editor: William Austin. Music: Alexander Laszlo. Art Directors: Don Ament and Daniel Haller. Sound: Ralph Butler. Sets: Harry Reif. Production Manager: Edward Morey, Jr. Makeup: Emile Lavigne. Special Effects: Irving Block, Louis DeWitt and Jack Rabin. Wardrobe: Norah Sharpe and Roger J. Weinberg. Assistant Director: Clark Paylow.

CAST: Arthur Franz (Lieutenant Commander Richard "Reef" Holloway), Dick Foran (Commander Dan Wendover), Brett Halsey (Dr. Carl Neilson, Jr.), Tom Conway (Sir Ian Hunt), Paul Dubov (Lieutenant David Milburn), Bob Steele (Chief Petty Officer "Griff" Griffin), Victor Varconi (Dr. Clifford Kent), Joi Lansing (Julie), Selmer Jackson (Commander Terhune), Jack Mulhall (Secretary of Defense Justin Murdock), Jean Moorhead (Helen Milburn), Richard Tyler (Carney), Sid Melton (Chester Tuttle), Ken Becker (Powell), Frank Watkins (Watkins), Everett Creach (Seaman), Edmund Cobb, Frank Lackteen (Strollers), John Hillard (Alien Voice), Pat Michaels (Narrator).

Nostalgia fans like the films of producer Alex Gordon, if for no other reason than he stocked his movies with old-time players. After working as one of

Dick Foran, Arthur Franz and Paul Dubov in *The Atomic Submarine* (1959)

the founding producers of American International Pictures, Gordon came to Allied Artists with *The Atomic Submarine*, which the studio released late in 1959. True to form, it was loaded with veteran players: Dick Foran, Tom Conway, Bob Steele, Victor Varconi, Jack Mulhall, Selmer Jackson, Edmund Cobb and Frank Lackteen. In fact, the familiar faces were the highlight of this science fiction effort that offered Electro-Sonic music, grainy stock footage and rather unconvincing miniatures. The alien creature in the feature is an H.P. Lovecraft–like monstrosity, a dark squid-type creature with tentacles and a huge eye. The production moves at a fairly steady clip and, while obviously made on a low budget, it probably did not disappoint viewers upon its initial release.

The depths of the Arctic Circle corridor are closed by the military after ships and submarines are blown up by an unknown force. After the atomic submarine *Sturgeon* is destroyed, a meeting is called at the Pentagon by Bureau of Arctic Defense head Admiral Terhune (Selmer Jackson). There he introduces Dan Wendover (Foran), commander of the atomic submarine *Tiger Shark*, to Secretary of Defense Justin Murdock (Mulhall), Nobel Prize–winning scientist Sir Ian Hunt (Conway) and his colleague Dr. Clifford Kent (Varconi). Wendover is told that his sub will be equipped with ultra-modern tracking devices, warheads and the Lung Fish, a diving bell. His mission is to find and stop whatever is destroying the seagoing craft. Lieutenant Commander Richard "Reef" Holloway (Franz), Wendover's executive officer, is on shore leave making love to beautiful blonde Julie (Lansing) but is interrupted by a telegram telling him to immediately report for duty. At the Bremerton Navy Yard he finds Chief Petty Officer "Griff" Griffin (Steele) screening the men who are returning to the vessel. On board he is upset to find that he is bunking with Dr. Carl Neilson, Jr. (Brett Halsey), the son of his mentor. He dislikes the young scientist, who developed the Lung Fish with his father, because Carl's pacifistic views caused the elder Neilson to resign his Navy commission and concentrate on scientific work. Also on board the submarine are Hunt, Kent and two frogmen, Carney (Richard Tyler) and Powell (Ken Becker). The submarine heads under the North Pole. Carl gets a telegram saying his father has sufficiently recovered from a heart attack to join the mission but the young man refuses to sacrifice his dad's health and announces he will carry on in his place, much to Reef's chagrin. As the two men are arguing, the craft is hit by a freak electrical storm and a strange craft is seen speeding away. Hunt draws a picture of the mystery vessel and Kent announces that it looks similar to a photograph he has of a flying saucer. Since the alien ship was topped with a light that looked like an eye, Hunt begins referring to it as the Cyclops. As reports come in of further attacks on U.S. vessels, Hunt theorizes that the craft operates on a magnetic field and it has to return to the North Pole to be re-energized. Wendover conceives a plan to have the *Tiger Shark* wait at a point where the saucer may next strike and then attack it with nuclear warheads. With the submarine on silent running, the men wait for the UFO to appear. When it does, the commander orders the warheads fired. One warhead misses the

Arthur Franz in *The Atomic Submarine* (1959)

craft and the other is stopped by a jelly-like substance emitted by the flying saucer. Over Carl's objections, Wendover orders the sub to ram the UFO. In doing so, it pierces and becomes locked into the craft. Both the flying saucer and the sub then sink to a depth of 1,200 feet. Reef suggests the Lung Fish be used to transport him, Lieutenant Milburn (Paul Dubov) and the frogmen to the craft; once inside they might be able to dislodge the sub with blowtorches. Carl pilots the four men to the UFO. Reef, Milburn and the frogmen enter the alien ship through a portal and find that it contains oxygen. As they work to free the submarine, it is noted that radiation levels are rising. Hunt theorizes that the spaceship is returning to "life" and moving toward the Pole. Reef hears a voice calling to him and he and Milburn follow it. Frogman Powell is burned to death by a ray, and in trying to get back to the diving bell Carney is crushed by the closing door of the portal. Reef is told to come alone to an opening and there he sees a giant one-eyed monster with tentacles that communicates with him through thought waves. The alien says it is exploring various worlds for possible habitation. When Milburn tries to shoot the being, it kills him with a death ray. Reef is told that he will return with the alien, along with other specimens, for study. Reef shoots out the monster's eye and runs back to the diving bell. He tells Wendover to pull the *Tiger Shark* out of the saucer and he and Carl return to the submarine in the Lung Fish. As the flying saucer speeds back to the North Pole, Reef warns that the world is doomed if the alien is allowed to escape. Their one hope lies in converting the last warhead into a guided missile. After it is readied, the crew waits until the UFO breaks through the ice and rises into the sky. Wendover orders Griff to fire the missile and it destroys the flying saucer. Back at the navy yard, Reef and Carl agree they can work together to stop the aliens if they ever return.

Filmed by Gorham Productions in the summer of 1959, *The Atomic Submarine* has had mixed reviews. Steven H. Scheuer in *Movies on TV 1975–76 Edition* (1974) said it "leaves one cold." In *The Phantom of the Movies' Videoscope* (2000), Joe Kane wrote, "Aside from its nostalgia value, the pic generates genuine suspense...." Ed Naha in *Horrors: From Screen to Scream* (1975) noted, "A favorite of TV viewers, this delightfully inept film is fascinating fun to behold.... Brings back fond memories of those great Saturday afternoon matinees." Writing on more of a highbrow level, Welch Everman in *Cult Science Fiction Films* (1995) saw a deeper meaning to the production when he referred to it as "another threat-of-invasion movie from the fifties, a period during which Americans expected a nuclear attack from the Soviet Union any day. Movies such as this one spoke directly to our nation's most pressing fears." In regards to the plot's hawkish attitude toward alien invaders, he said that the feature demonstrates "there is no question that atomic submarines and nuclear weapons are good things, and the ending of the film tells us that, as long as science and the military can resolve their differences and work together, everything will be ok—an idea that got harder and harder to swallow as the 1960s wore on."

Attack of the Crab Monsters (1957; 63 minutes)

Producer-Director: Roger Corman. Associate Producer–Screenplay: Charles B. Griffith. Photography: Floyd Crosby. Editor: Charles Gross. Music: Ronald Stein. Makeup: Curly Batson. Assistant Directors: Maurice Vaccarino and Lindsley Parsons, Jr.

CAST: Richard Garland (Dale Drewer), Pamela Duncan (Martha Hunter), Russell Johnson (Hank Chapman), Leslie Bradley (Dr. Karl Weigand), Mel Welles (Jules Deveroux), Richard H. Cutting (Dr. James Carson), Beach Dickerson (Ron Fellows), Tony Miller (Jack Sommers), Ed Nelson (Ensign Quinlan), Maitland Stuart (Mac), Charles B. Griffith (Tate), Robin Riley, Doug Roberts.

The setting is a small Pacific Ocean atoll that had been the site of fallout from an

H-bomb test. Navy Ensign Quinlan (Ed Nelson) brings a scientific team to the locale to study the effects of radiation and also try and find their missing predecessors led by Dr. McLean. The head of the group is Dr. Karl Weigand (Leslie Bradley), a nuclear physicist, and joining him are biologists Dale Drewer (Richard Garland) and Martha Hunter (Pamela Duncan); electronics expert Hank Chapman (Russell Johnson); geologist James Carson (Richard H. Cutting); French botanist Jules Deveroux (Mel Welles); and two Navy demolition men, Ron Fellows (Beach Dickerson) and Jack Sommers (Tony Miller). Deveroux notices the lack of insect noises and jokingly says they may soon hear the voices of the ghosts of McLean and his crew. A seaman falls from a boat while unloading supplies and while he is underwater his head is severed from his body. While getting settled in the house on the atoll, the group is subjected to an earthquake followed by an avalanche. Later they watch as Quinlan's seaplane takes off; it explodes and Quinlan and his men are killed. In the laboratory in the house, Hank is unable to make radio contact with the mainland due to a powerful storm. Weigand reads from a journal left by McLean which ends abruptly with a description of finding a portion of a giant worm. After another earthquake, Martha does some underwater exploring and is joined by Dale. When they return to land, Weigand and Carson take them to a deep pit which has just been formed. During the night, Martha hears a voice claiming to be McLean. When she investi-

Poster for *Attack of the Crab Monsters* (1957)

gates she is joined by Carson and the two go to the pit. Carson climbs down just as another tremor is felt and he falls while Martha passes out. The remaining men find the young woman and hear Carson calling to them from the bottom of the pit saying he has a broken leg. As Dale takes Martha back to the house, the rest of the group go through a series of tunnels in hopes of locating Carson. Back at the house, Dale and Martha hear a strange noise and when Dale goes into the lab he is attacked by a large claw. When the other men cannot find Carson, they return to the lab to see it wrecked, food taken and their radio destroyed. Going back to continue to search for Carson, the group is beset by another tremor and Deveroux's right hand is severed by a falling rock. As Martha tends to Deveroux at the house, Fellows and Sommers play cards in their tent and are attacked by an unseen (by the audience) monster. That night the voices of the two seamen call to Deveroux and he goes to the edge of the pit where he is killed by the claw. Awakened by the botanist's screams, the others soon hear him talking to them only to find his room is deserted. The next night, Deveroux calls out to the team and asks them to join him in the caves. Weigand, Dale and Hank go there only to be attacked by a giant crab. Bullets and hand grenades fail to stop the creature but it is killed when a huge stone falls on it. Weigand severs one of the beast's claws. As the trio is about to leave, they are attacked by a second huge crab which Dale delays with a grenade. After examining the severed claw, Weigand concludes that the giants have been created by radiation poisoning; after devouring the brains of their victims, they take on their intelligence and are able to project thoughts in the dead men's voices. He also states the remaining giant crab is slowly sinking parts of the island by emitting an arc of heat. Martha examines a photo of the surviving crab and it says it is about to give birth. Hank uses electricity to disintegrate the severed claw and Weigand orders him to set up a ray that they will use to kill the second crab. After Hank and Martha place electrical devices in the cave in order to kill the creature, they are chased by the monster but escape by swimming underwater. More landslides take place and the island continues to get smaller. Hank successfully rebuilds a new radio and Martha tells him that she and Dale are going to be married. Weigand and Dale, exploring what is left of the island, see an oil spill and take separate paths trying to find its origin. The physicist goes into the cave where he is stunned by setting off the ray and is devoured by the monster. Seeing his demise, Dale, Martha and Hank go back to the lab. Deveroux's voice tells them they will soon be absorbed and the giant crabs will continue to attack humans. As a huge earthquake nearly demolishes the atoll, the three survivors make it to a rock jutting into the ocean, where the radio tower still stands. When they fail to stop the beast with their remaining hand grenades, Hank rushes the creature and is injured. As Dale and Martha try to fight off the giant crab, Hank climbs the radio tower and brings it down on the monster with both of them being electrocuted.

Made on a $70,000 budget late in 1956 as *Attack of the Giant Crabs*, the feature was the first made by producer-director Roger Corman that used market research to give a film its title. Allied Artists released it on a double bill with *Not of This Earth* (q.v.) in February 1957 and the combo went on to gross over one million dollars at the box office. Actor Ed Nelson, along with fellow performer Beach Dickerson and key grip Chuck Hanawalt, operated the crab monster that was made of Styrofoam and was moved by one of the men sequestered in the hollowed-out area behind its face. Running slightly over one hour, *Attack of the Crab Monsters* moved at a fast clip as most of the cast are devoured by the mutated creatures.

The Hollywood Reporter called it "average" and noted that the film "suffers from a limited budget." According to *Variety*, "It isn't believable, but it's fun...." Mark Thomas McGee in *Roger Corman: The Best of the Cheap Acts* (1988) noted, "There are moments when *Crab Monsters* takes on the characteristics of an old fashioned ghost story when the voices of the victims call to their friends." In *Sleaze Creatures* (1995), D. Earl Worth compared the feature to another Corman production: "In many respects, *Attack of the Crab Monsters* was a carry over from *Day the World Ended*. Both began with heady anticipation of nuclear spectacle. Aftermaths of the explosions were commented on by similar celestial voices. The characters lived in isolated but comfortable homes. Most sections of their environments looked normal but felt strange. In various ways, the mutants were travesties of people."

Parts of the film's score appears on the compact disc *Not of This Earth! The Film Music of Ronald Stein* (Varese Sarabande VSD-5634), released in 1995. The CD has scores from seven of Stein's films including *Not of This Earth* and *Attack of the 50 Foot Woman* (1958) [q.v.].

Attack of the 50 Foot Woman (1958; 65 minutes)

Producer: Bernard Woolner. Executive Producer–Photography: Jacques Marquette. Director: Nathan Hertz [Juran]. Screenplay: Mark Hanna. Editor: Edward Mann. Music: Ronald Stein. Sound: Philip Mitchell. Makeup: Carlie Taylor. Props: Richard Rubin. Assistant Director: Ken Walters.

CAST: Allison Hayes (Nancy Archer), William Hudson (Harry Archer), Yvette Vickers (Honey Parker), Roy Gordon (Dr. Cushing), George Douglas (Sheriff Dubbitt), Ken Terrell (Jess Stout), Otto Waldis (Dr. Heinrich Von Loeb), Eileen Stevens (Nurse), Michael Ross (Bartender Tony/Giant Alien), Frank Chase (Deputy Sheriff Charlie), Thomas E. Jackson (Prospector), Dale Tate (TV Newsman).

One of the true joys of 1950s bad science fiction is *Attack of the 50 Foot Woman*, a film so beloved by genre fans that it was remade in 1993 as a TV movie with Daryl Hannah. The update went in for a tongue-in-cheek approach and was nowhere near as entertaining as the original that played it straight, making it the far more amusing of the two. The 1958 version does have its share of comedy, mainly supplied by a bumbling deputy sheriff (Frank Chase), and the sorry-looking giant hand belonging to the title character and a space alien. Filmed as *The Astounding Giant Woman*, the Allied Artists release also sported shoddy special effects, especially in the long shots of the alien and giant woman. Much of the time the two titans are transparent. Best of all, the movie features two sexy leading ladies, Allison Hayes and Yvette Vickers, and both make the most of their scenes; the former as a drunk, neurotic heiress who is losing her husband to

Yvette Vickers and William Hudson in *Attack of the 50 Foot Woman* (1958)

William Hudson and Allison Hayes in *Attack of the 50 Foot Woman* (1958)

the latter. Vickers gives a classic portrayal of a cheap slut — the same type of character she played to perfection in another "attack" movie, *Attack of the Giant Leeches* (1959).

Director Nathan Juran helmed *Attack of the 50 Foot Woman* using only his given and middle names, Nathan Hertz, apparently hoping to avoid association with such a cheap outing. (He did the same with 1958's *The Brain from Planet Arous* [q.v.], a Howco International release that Allied Artists included in a 1970s TV package.) Scripter Mark Hanna also wrote *Not of This Earth* [q.v.], *The Undead*, *The Amazing Colossal Man* (all 1957) and *Terror from the Year 5000* (1958).

A television reporter (Dale Tate) relates sightings of a huge glowing sphere being seen in the skies near the Bering Sea, Egypt, South Africa and New Zealand, and he predicts the orb will soon be over Southern California. Beautiful Nancy Archer (Hayes), heiress to the $50 million Fowler fortune, is driving through the desert on her way home after arguing with her husband Harry (William Hudson) over his attentions to redhead Honey Parker (Vickers) while they were dining at Tony's Bar. She is stopped by a large glowing object in the roadway. A bald giant (Mike Ross) emerges and tries to take the priceless Star of India diamond she is wearing. Back at the bar, Harry romances Honey who wants him to leave Nancy. He tells her he cannot afford to desert his rich wife. The distraught Nancy runs into town and demands to see Harry. Sheriff Dubbitt (George Douglas) tells his deputy Charlie (Chase) to fetch Harry, but Harry bribes the lawman to say he has gone home. Nearly hysterical, Nancy tells the skeptical law enforcers about her experience on the highway, and they go with her to search for the alien but only find her abandoned car. Later that night, Nancy calls Harry a gigolo and a miserable parasite but confesses she still loves him. Harry tells her to get some rest and gives her sleeping pills and then returns to the bar to see Honey. There he informs his young mistress he will try to get his wife returned to the sanitarium where she once was committed for emotional problems. In doing so he will be able to get control of her estate. To convince Honey of his intentions, he shows her the Star of India diamond. Harry calls in Nancy's physician Dr. Cushing (Roy Gordon); Harry is disappointed when the medical man refuses to re-commit Nancy. Nancy again confronts Harry about his relationship with Honey and accuses him of wanting to put her back in the sanitarium. While watching television she hears a news report about her supposedly seeing a flying saucer and in anger she smashes the TV screen. She then tells Harry he will go with her into the desert to search for the UFO; she takes along a pistol belonging to her loyal butler, Jess (Ken Terrell), who does not like Harry. After driving most of the day, Nancy sees the flying saucer at twilight. When they approach the orb, the giant comes out. Harry shoots at it and drives away, leaving the screaming Nancy behind. Harry goes back home and starts to pack. When Jess wants to know what happened to Nancy, the two men fight and Harry hits Jess with a bottle. Harry goes to Honey's hotel room and orders her to quickly pack so they can get out of town. Charlie stops the two lovers and takes them to the sheriff's office and the next morning they learn that Nancy has been found unconscious on the roof of her pool house. Suffering from burns and scratches around the neck, she is treated by Dr. Cushing and a nurse (Eileen Stevens). After Honey hears Cushing tell the nurse to be careful not to give Nancy an overdose of her medication, she convinces Harry to get rid of his wife by that method. That night Harry sneaks into Nancy's bedroom to kill her but the nurse follows him and when she turns on the light she becomes hysterical because Nancy has greatly increased in size. A specialist, Dr. Von Loeb (Otto Waldis), is brought in by Cushing and the two men have the unconscious Nancy chained and give her huge amounts of morphine. The sheriff and his deputy find large footprints on the estate. Dubbitt and Jess follow the tracks into the desert and come upon the UFO. They enter the craft and find a room in which precious gems, including Nancy's diamond, are apparently used to power the craft. The giant chases them out and destroys their car but returns to the orb when Dubbitt uses hand grenades. The spaceship takes off and the two men start to walk back to town. Nancy wakes up and calls for her husband. Harry refuses to allow her any other medical treatment although Von Loeb wants to operate on her in hopes of reversing the growth process. The two doctors use an elephant syringe to give Nancy more drugs but she comes to and breaks through the roof and sets out to find Harry. Cushing, Von Loeb and the nurse drive back to town and along the way pick up the sheriff and Jess as Nancy frightens an old prospector (Thomas E. Jackson). She destroys the hotel where Honey rooms and then tears the roof of the bar where Harry and Honey have been drinking. Harry shoots at Nancy. A huge beam falls on the table under which Honey is hiding, crushing her. Nancy picks up Harry and begins walking away as the sheriff fires at her with a shotgun. The giant woman walks into some power lines and Dubbitt shoots at them, causing an explosion that electrocutes Nancy, who falls to the ground, holding her dead husband.

Dennis Fischer wrote in *Science Fiction Film Directors, 1895–1998* (2000), "Despite its shoddy effects such as its see-through double exposed space giant, or maybe because of them, *Attack of the 50 Foot Woman* retains its appeal due to a sly sense of humor, the pulchritudinous appeal of its star Allison Hayes, and some fine supporting performances." In *Science Fiction* (1984), Phil Hardy noted, "The corniness of Hanna's screenplay and Juran's plodding direction.... The special effects are dire...." Bill Warren in *Keep Watching the Skies! The 21st Century Edition* (2009) said, "Some people consider this to be one of the great inadvertent comedies of the 1950s.... The film's own screwy logic is relentless, there are several scenes which couldn't have been more outrageous if they had been designed to be, and the special effects are jaw-droppingly awful."

Portions of Ronald Stein's score are included in the compact disc *Not of This Earth!: The Film Music of Ronald Stein* (Varese Sarabande VSD-5634), issued in 1995.

The Bat (1959; 80 minutes)

Producer: C.J. Teylin. Director-Screenplay-Story: Crane Wilbur. From the play by Mary Roberts Rinehart and Avery Hopwood. Photography: Joseph Biroc. Editor: William Austin. Music: Louis Forbes. Song: Alvino Rey. Art Director: David Milton. Sound: Ralph Butler. Sets: Rudy Butler. Production Manager: Edward Morey, Jr. Makeup: Kiva Hoffman. Wardrobe: Norah Sharpe and Roger J. Weinberg. Continuity: Virginia Mazzuca. Props: Ted Mossman. Assistant Director: Clifford Broughton.

CAST: Vincent Price (Dr. Malcolm Wells), Agnes Moorehead (Cornelia Van Gorder), Gavin Gordon (Lieutenant Andy Anderson), John Sutton (Warner), Lenita Lane (Lizzie Allen), Elaine Edwards (Dale Bailey), Darla Hood (Judy Hollander), John Bryant (Mark Fleming), Harvey Stephens (John Fleming), Mike Steele (Victor "Vic" Bailey), Riza Royce (Jane Patterson), Robert B. Williams (Detective Davenport), William Janssen (Bank Clerk), Virginia Linden (Bank Customer), John Lomma (Voice of the Bat).

One of the chestnuts of the 20th century stage, *The Bat* had its basis in Mary Roberts Rinehart's novel *The Circular Staircase*, published in 1908. Under that title it was filmed by Selig Pictures in 1915 by director Edward J. Le Saint, starring Guy Oliver, Edith Johnson, Stella Razetto, Eugenie Besserer and Bertram Grassby. Five year later Rinehart and Avery

Agnes Moorehead and Lenita Lane in *The Bat* (1959)

Agnes Moorehead, Lenita Lane and Vincent Price in *The Bat* (1959)

Hopwood collaborated on a stage version, *The Bat*, which debuted at Broadway's Morosco Theatre on August 23, 1920, and had a run of 867 performances. The cast included Effie Ellser, Edward Ellis, Anne Morrison and May Vokes. Two years later it was staged in London and in its cast were Claude Rains, Arthur Wontner (a future screen Sherlock Holmes), and Eva Moore; it ran for over 300 performances. Mary Pickford produced the first screen adaptation of *The Bat* (United Artists, 1926) featuring her younger brother Jack Pickford along with Jewel Carmen, Louise Fazenda, Emily Fitzroy, Robert McKim, Sojin, Eddie Gribbon and Tullio Carminati. It was adapted to the screen and directed by Roland West, who also did the same chores for the first sound version of the vehicle, *The Bat Whispers*, which was produced by Art Cinema Corporation and issued by United Artists in late November 1930. Chester Morris, Una Merkel, William Bakewell, Gustav von Seyffertitz, Richard Tucker, Grayce Hampton and Maude Eburne headed the cast. May Vokes repeated the role of Lizzie in the 1937 Broadway revival of *The Bat* which also featured Minnette Barrett, Herman Lieb, Linda Lee Hill and Robert Ober. The production had a brief run on Broadway early in 1953 with Lucille Watson, ZaSu Pitts and Shepperd Strudwick. At the end of that year it was presented on the syndicated *Broadway Television Theatre* program, starring Estelle Winwood, Alice Pearce and Jay Jostyn. In March 1960, "The Bat" was an episode of NBC-TV's *Dow Hour of Great Mysteries* and its cast included Helen Hayes, Jason Robards, Shepperd Strudwick, Bethel Leslie and Margaret Hamilton.

Eight months before the NBC-TV program, Allied Artists released a screen version of

Gavin Gordon, Lenita Lane (in background), Vincent Price, Agnes Moorehead, Riza Royce and Elaine Edwards in *The Bat* (1959)

The Bat with the advertising pitch, "When the Bat flies, someone dies." Silent screen star Crane Wilbur adapted the Rinehart-Hopwood play and also directed the film for Liberty Pictures. He previously wrote *House of Wax* (1953) and *The Mad Magician* (1954), both vehicles for Vincent Price, who headlined this third version of *The Bat* in the expanded role of Dr. Malcolm Wells. Despite top billing, Price had less screen time than co-star Agnes Moorehead, who dominates the proceedings as mystery writer Cornelia Van Gorder. Some publicity was generated for the movie by including Darla Hood, once the little darling of the "Our Gang" comedies, in what would be her final film. Gavin Gordon, as Lieutenant Anderson, and John Sutton, playing Warner the butler, were featured although the film would have benefited if they had swapped roles. *Variety* called the production "sluggish." In *Theatre: Stage to Screen to Television* (1981), William Torbert Leonard noted it had "overactive performances and a lack of definition both in characterization and incident, and one is left caring as little about the victims as about the identity of [the Bat]." Filmed in the spring of 1959, the production is definitely the least of the three screen versions of the highly successful mystery play but it is not without merit and overall is a well-made and fairly entertaining horror-mystery. Of particular interest is the underplayed friction between the characters of Dr. Wells, Lieutenant Anderson and Warner the butler.

Best-selling mystery writer Cornelia Van Gorder (Moorehead), along with rough-hewn Lizzie Allen (Lenita Lane), her companion, lease a remote mansion called the Oaks so she can concentrate on writing a new novel. Once they are settled, Lizzie complains that the servants want to leave because a series of murders were committed in the area by a hideous cloaked maniac known as "The Bat." She also claims there are rumors the madman has released rabid bats in the locale. Going to the local bank, the two women meet Vic Bailey (Mike Steele), the vice-president, and his pretty bride Dale (Elaine Edwards). Vic says he is surprised that his boss, bank president John Fleming (Harvey Stephens), who built the Oaks, had rented it and she informs him the transaction was handled by insurance man Mark Fleming (John Bryant), John's nephew. Cornelia and Lizzie are also introduced to Police Lieutenant Andy Anderson (Gordon). After they leave, Vic and Dale tell the law officer that the bank has been robbed of over one million dollars in bonds and securities. Anderson wants to call in the bank president but he is out of town on a hunting trip with the local doctor, Malcolm Wells (Price). At their remote cabin, John Fleming informs the physician that he embezzled the money from the bank and offers him one-half of it if he will stage a false death for him by killing their guide Sam. When Wells hesitates, Fleming threatens him. Fleming's attention is diverted when he notices the woods are on fire, and Wells shoots him. Several days pass and Cornelia and Lizzie read in the newspaper that Vic Bailey is in jail accused of embezzlement. The novelist refuses to believe he is guilty. All of their servants except chauffeur Warner (Sutton) quit and Cornelia promotes him to butler. That night a terrible thunderstorm erupts and as Cornelia is about to latch the front door Lizzie screams as a clawed hand reaches for her boss. The hand disappears. A figure in black breaks into the house and releases a bat through a bedroom transom. It bites Lizzie before Cornelia traps it in a closet. Cornelia calls Wells, whom Anderson spies experimenting on a bat in his home laboratory. After Wells leaves, the policeman searches the lab as the doctor goes to the Oaks and examines Lizzie. He takes the bat with him for an examination but tells the women he thinks it is not rabid. As the physician leaves the house, Anderson shows up and tells the women the culprit is the Bat and that he will have the place watched. Worried about the savings he had in the bank, Anderson goes to see Mark and tells him he feels Vic is innocent and that John Fleming (whose body has been brought home and buried) robbed the institution and hid the money at the Oaks. Mark informs him that Judy Hollander (Hood), his uncle's secretary, plans to testify for Brady at his trial. Judy and Dale are invited by Cornelia to stay at the Oaks. Also living in the house is Jane Patterson (Riza Royce), the new cook. Cornelia confides to the women she thinks John Fleming embezzled the bank's money which is hidden in the house and the Bat is trying to find its location. She has Dale telephone Mark to inquire if he has the plans for the edifice and he says he thinks they may be there and he will come search for them. After dinner, Cornelia announces she will write a mystery novel about the missing money and the Bat and she asks Dale to be her secretary. Mark secretly enters the house and locates a small closet behind a clock. There he finds the plans but he is attacked by the Bat and killed. When the women hear the clock striking, something it has not done before, they investigate and find the murdered Mark hanging in the closet. The police and Wells are called. When the physician shows up, Anderson questions him but is told it was his night off. Later the butler follows the police lieutenant when he roams around the grounds. During the night, the dark figure cuts the telephone lines and goes to the third floor and begins removing part of a wall. The noise awakens Judy and Dale who investigate. The Bat kills Judy on the stairway as he makes his escape. Anderson shows up and Mrs. Patterson tells him that Warner is absent. The unkempt butler arrives and says he was struck on the head while trailing the policeman around the estate. Since Cornelia hit the escaping Bat with a poker on the side of the head, Anderson accuses Warner of being the madman. The doctor suddenly returns to the Oaks, claiming he was in a car accident, and Anderson also suspects him of the crimes. Detective Davenport (Robert B. Williams) is assigned to guard the house but during the night he is drugged. Cornelia goes back to the third floor and finds a secret room, containing a locked safe, behind a fireplace. She gets locked in the room while the Bat surprises Wells in his laboratory and kills him. Lizzie revives Davenport and the two locate Cornelia who is about to suffocate in the closed room. When they see the garage is ablaze, Cornelia realizes that the Bat set the fire to get them out of the house. The trio waits for the killer. The Bat shows up and tries to open the safe where the stolen money is hidden; as he is about to murder the two women, he is shot in the back by Warner who unmasks the madman. Cornelia has the stolen money returned to the bank. Vic Bailey is freed and Cornelia finishes her latest thriller about the Bat.

Beast from Haunted Cave (1959; 72 minutes)

Producer: Gene Corman. Associate Producer: Charles Hanawalt. Director: Monte Hellman. Screenplay: Charles B. Griffith. Photography: Andrew Costikyan. Editor: Anthony Carras. Music: Alexander Laszlo. Sound: Charles Brown. Production Coordinator: Beach Dickerson. Technical Advisors: Ed Keene and Birdie Arnold.

CAST: Michael Forest (Gil Jackson), Sheila [Noonan] Carol (Gypsy Boulet), Frank Wolff (Alexander "Alex" Ward), Wally Campo (Byron Smith), Richard Sinatra (Marty Jones), Linne Ahlstrand (Natalie), Christopher [Chris] Robinson (Creature/Bartender), Kay Jennings (Jill Jackson), Imelda (Small Dove).

At a remote lodge in the Black Hills of South Dakota, Alex Ward (Frank Wolff) takes ski lessons from instructor Gil Jackson (Michael Forest), who also runs a bait shop with his sister Jill (Kay Jennings). Alex has come to the area with his heavy drinking girlfriend Gypsy (Sheila Carol) and two cohorts, taciturn Marty (Richard Sinatra) and goofy Byron (Wally Campo), to rob the local bank. Alex hires Gil to take the group on a two-day skiing trip to his cabin in the forest and he orders Marty to plant dynamite in a mine. He plans to use the explosion as a cover when they rob the bank. That evening Gypsy drinks too much and makes a pass at Gil. Marty talks barmaid Natalie (Linne Ahlstrand) into going with him to the mine. There he sets the explosives to go off at nine the next morning and he also sees fragments of what appears to be a giant egg. As he begins to make love to Natalie, a tall, web-covered monster (Chris Robinson) attacks the girl. Marty returns to the hotel-bar and tells Alex what happened but his boss thinks he is crazy. To get Gil out of town, Alex has Gypsy meet him at the ski lift as Alex, Marty and Byron hear the mine explosion and then break into the bank, where each of them takes two gold bars. The trio heads to the trailhead where they meet with Gil and Gypsy and head cross-country to Gil's cabin, where Alex plans to rendezvous with a pilot who will fly the robbers to Canada. That night they stop along the trail to sleep and Marty says he thinks they are being followed. While standing guard he hears strange noises and, going to investigate, he finds Natalie in a cocoon in a tree. Marty becomes distraught but refuses to talk. The next day, Gil spots unknown animal prints in the snow. Arriving at the cabin, the skiers meet Gil's housekeeper Little Dove (Imelda), whom Byron thinks wants to scalp him. Rather than returning to the lodge, Alex suggests they stay the night at the cabin. Over the radio they hear about the bank robbery and the explosion that killed one of the miners. The news of the man's death causes Gypsy to drink more and she kisses Gil who is then forced to fight Alex and Marty but is stopped at gunpoint by Byron. Alex slaps Gypsy who later meets outside with Gil and tells him she stays with Alex because he saved her from an unsavory past. The monster shows up outside the cabin and attacks Marty but he scares it away. The next morning, while Gil chops wood, he is told by Gypsy that Alex plans to murder him. When Gil tells her he will ski back to town and get the law, she asks to go with him. Marty locates a cave that he thinks houses the monster. Alex confides to Byron he plans to kill Gil and Small Dove (even though Byron has grown fond of the Indian woman), and that he wants to get rid of Marty who is no longer trustworthy due to his maniacal desire to kill the mystical beast. When Alex later inquires about Gil's whereabouts, Gypsy tells him he has gone deer hunting. When she goes outside, she is followed by Byron who sees her depart on skis. The monster attacks Byron, who throws a torch at it. The fleeing creature carries off Small Dove. Gil waits for Gypsy on the trail and the two begin skiing back to the lodge. Marty tells Alex about seeing the egg shell in the mine and theorizes that the monster hatched out of it. Byron sneaks out of the cabin in search of Small Dove. Going to the cave, he finds Natalie and the Indian woman encased in webs along a wall. As he is about to free them, the monster attacks him. Gil and Gypsy arrive at the cave to get out of a coming blizzard. Leaving Gypsy at the entrance, Gil explores the cavern and sees Byron, Natalie and Small Dove in their cocoons as the beast tries to kill him. Gil shoots at the creature and Gypsy arrives and begins throwing rocks at it. Gil yells to Gypsy to run away. As she does so, she meets Alex and Marty, who have come armed with weapons and flare guns, and she tells Alex that Gil is inside the cavern, unarmed. The monster kills Alex and fatally wounds Marty who, before dying, shoots one of the flare guns, setting the beast on fire and destroying it. Gil and Gypsy embrace and escape from the cave of horror.

Cult director Monte Hellman made his debut with *Beast from Haunted Cave*, which was filmed on location in Deadwood, South Dakota, by the Filmgroup, a company owned by the Corman brothers, Roger and Gene. Seeking new locales, the producers decided on South Dakota since it was a non-union state; the money they saved by not dealing with unions was used to make a second feature. Gene and Hellman filmed *Beast* for two weeks and then Roger produced and directed *Ski Troop Attack* in the following fourteen days. Charles B. Griffith wrote both scripts and Michael Forest, Frank Wolff, Wally Campo, Richard Sinatra and Sheila Carol appeared in both. Roger was the uncredited executive producer on *Beast*. He and Gene asked Paul Blaisdell to create the title monster but when he wanted too much money they assigned the task to Chris Robinson, who not only appeared as the creature but also had a small role as the bartender at the ski resort town's bar-hotel. He made the beast out of plywood covered by chicken wire to which he attached putty and angel and crepe hair. Robinson later starred in the horror film *Stanley* (1972).

The Beast has often been described as a spider-like creature but it has a more ghostly appearance, sort of a tall emaciated corpse covered with webs. For the most part the Beast is only seen fleetingly, thus heightening the fright value of the creature. The film itself is a somber affair, its main locales being the bar-hotel, the remote cabin and the cave. Even in the outdoor scenes there is no sunlight, the shooting apparently taking place under overcast conditions. The characters differ drastically: Gil, the hero, is almost intolerably dull, while the sadistic Alex is a thug, girl-shy Marty is psychotic and his pal Byron is almost brain dead. The most interesting of the lot is Gypsy, a drunken hooker, nicely enacted by Carol, who reforms at the finale and wins the hero's love. As Sheila Noonan, Carol appeared the same year in producer-director Jerry Warren's vapid *The Incredible Petrified World*. Richard Sinatra, who played Marty, was the son of bandleader Ray Sinatra, the first cousin and musical mentor of Frank Sinatra. While trying to romance Gil's sister Jill, Marty's character reverts to hip talk, and throughout the feature the characters of Alex and Gypsy refer to each other as "Charles." When the film was scheduled for TV release it proved to be a bit short and director Hellman filmed a couple of additional minutes with his wife Jaclyn doubling in the role of Jill Jackson.

Although cheaply made and given only quick playoff (and, like most of the Filmgroup product, not even copyrighted), *Beast from Haunted Cave* leaves a somewhat positive impression with the viewer, something not always accomplished by late 1950s sci-fi–horror efforts. In fact, its main assets may very well be its impoverished look, unusual locations, a set of diverse characters and a genuinely scary monster. It got quick theatrical playoff by Allied Artists, on a double bill with Roger Corman's *The Wasp Woman* (q.v.), in the late summer and fall of 1959.

Beyond Love and Evil (1971; 89 minutes; Color)

Producer: Roland de Nesle. Director: Jacques Scandelari. Screenplay: Jean-Pierre Deloux, Jacques Scandelari and Jean Stuart. Story: Jean Stuart, from the novel *La Philosophie dans le Boudoir* (The Philosophy of the Boudoir) by Marquis de Sade. Photography: Jean-Marc Ripert. Editor: Roger Ikhlef. Music: Jean-Claude Pelletier. Production Design: Michel Lablais. Sets: Quassar. Makeup: Jean d'Estree. Special Effects: Kalinowksy. Costumes: Jean Bouquet. Assistant Directors: Jose Pinheiro and Jean Stuart.

CAST: Souchka (Xenia), Lucas de Chabanieux (Zenoff), Fred Saint-James (Yaid), Marc Coutant (Young Man), Sabry (Sabrina), Serge Halsdorf (Varlac), Michel Lablais (Ladies' Man), Milarka Nervi (Pisces), Doris Thon (Panther Woman), Nadia Kempf (Lolita), Ursuel Pauly (25-Year-Old Woman), Nicole Huc (Fleeing Woman), Jean-Christophe Vouvet (The Grand Minister).

Just how much the grip of censorship had weakened by the early 1970s is exemplified by Allied Artists releasing this dubbed French import to theaters, despite its heavy doses of nudity and near XXX sexual shenanigans. Made by Comptori Francais du Film Production in 1969, it was shown in its homeland as *La Philosophie dans le Boudoir* (The Philosophy of the Boudoir) and had its plot origins in the 1795 novel by the Marquis de Sade. Its alternate French titles were *Decameron Francese* and *De Sade 76*. U.S. outings were trimmed by three minutes. For horror fans the plot includes a torture dungeon in an old chateau inhabited by a huge ape man called Varlac (Serge Halsdorf), who delights in ravishing nubile young women.

After a skeleton on a cross is set on fire, a young man, Zenoff (Lucas de Chabanieux), travels at night to the chateau of Xenia (Souchka), the woman he loves. He is unaware she belongs to a sex cult led by Yald (Fred Saint-James), whom she intends to marry. The two announce their wedding plans at a dinner party at which the guests engage in body painting. Yald tells the group they can have sex with his bride but only after he has consummated their marriage. Zenoff is quite upset and doubts that the betrothed are truly in love. When a young woman (Nicole Huc) is accused of breaking the cult's rules, she is thrown out of the castle, given a head start and then pursued through the woods. As she is about to escape through a fence, she suddenly stops and lets herself be captured. For the evening's entertainment, Yald releases Varlac (Halsdorf), an ape-like man, who pursues the runaway and rapes her in his cell as the cultists watch and then engage in a orgy. The next day, another young woman (Doris Thon) is sent into the woods and hunted by the cultists who capture and beat her. Zenoff tries to get Xenia to run away with him but ends up having sex with her. Later the cultists watch as Xenia and Yald consummate their marriage. Zenoff is shocked by the proceedings. He and Yald agree to a contest in which the winner gets Xenia if she can be picked out of all the women wearing masks. Yald wins but during their second game with knives he is stabbed by Zenoff. Xenia becomes the cult leader. Following another orgy, she has the young man engage in the flogging of a girl and then he goes with Xenia to her bedroom. There she has one of the cultists beat him before Xenia throws Zenoff out of the chateau, despite his begging her to let him stay.

The previous year Allied Artists released another European production based on DeSade's novel *Eugenie... The Story of Her Journey Into Perversion* (q.v.).

Black Zoo (1963; 88 minutes; Color)

Producer: Herman Cohen. Director: Robert Gordon. Story-Screenplay: Aben Kandel. Photography: Floyd Crosby. Editor: Michael Luciano. Music: Paul Dunlap. Song: Robert Marucci and Russell Faith. Art Director: William Glasgow. Sound: John Bury, Jr. Makeup: Philip Scheer. Production Manager: Edward Morey, Jr. Special Effects: Pat Dinga. Wardrobe: Jack Masters. Optical Effects: Howard Anderson Co. Assistant Director: William McGarry.

CAST: Michael Gough (Michael Conrad), Jeanne Cooper (Edna Conrad), Rod Lauren (Carl Conrad), Virginia Grey (Jenny Brooks), Jerome Cowan (Jerry Stengel), Elisha Cook, Jr. (Joe), Marianna Hill (Audrey), Oren Curtis (Radu), Eilene Janssen, Eric Stone (Newlyweds), Dani Lynn, Susan Slavin (Art Students), Edward Platt (Detective Rivers), Douglas Henderson (Lieutenant Mel Duggan), Jerry Douglas (Perkins), Claudia Brack (Carl's Mother), Daniel Kurlick (Carl as a Child), Byron Morrow (Coroner), Michael St. Angel (Officer Donovan), Joseph Mell (Frank Cramer), Warrene Ott (Mary Hogan), George Barrows (Victor the Gorilla), Herman Cohen (Guided Tour Member).

Twenty-seven years before the formation of People for the Ethical Treatment of Animals (PETA), *Black Zoo* contained a similar organization, the True Believers. This group, however, believed in the migration of animal souls and one of its members, zoo owner Michael Conrad (Michael Gough), used his "pets" to get rid of those who got in his way. In *The Encyclopedia of Horror Movies* (1986), Phil Hardy wrote, "Ineptly scripted, ploddingly directed, wildly overacted by Gough ... it has nowhere near the same charge as the very similar *Murders in the Zoo* (1933). But [Floyd] Crosby's camerawork is excellent, and no film that has the wit to include a scene in which Gough ushers a lion, tiger, a black panther and a cougar into his sitting-room, installs them on couches and easy chairs, and solemnly indulges them with a lullaby on the organ, can be all bad."

Released by Allied Artists in May 1963 and also called *Horrors of the Black Zoo*, the feature was the last of three horror outings Gough headlined for producer-writer Herman Cohen, preceded by *Horrors of the Black Museum* (1959) and *Konga* (1961). The actor went on to appear in two Cohen horror films with Joan Crawford, *Berserk* (1967) and *Trog* (1970). Among Gough's other genre efforts are *Horror of Dracula* (1958), *The Phantom of the Opera* (1962), *Dr. Terror's House of Horrors* (1965), *They Came from Beyond Space* (1967), *Crucible of Horror* (1970), *Horror Hospital* (1973), *Satan's Slave* (1976), *The Serpent and the Rainbow* (1988) and *The Haunting of Helen Walker* (1985). He is probably best remembered as butler Alfred Pennyworth in *Batman* (1989), *Batman Returns* (1992) and *Batman Forever* (1995).

Herman Cohen (1925-2002) produced and often co-wrote a number of other genre efforts, including *Bela Lugosi Meets a Brooklyn Gorilla* (1952), *Target Earth* (1954) [q.v.], *I Was a Teenage Werewolf*, *I Was a Teenage Frankenstein*, *Blood of Dracula* (all 1957), *The Headless Ghost* (1959), *A Study in Terror* (1965), *Craze* (1974) and *Watch Me When I Kill* (1977). The director of *Black Zoo*, Robert Gordon, also helmed *It Came from Beneath the Sea* (1955). The same year he co-starred in *Black Zoo*, Rod Lauren appeared in *Terrified* and *The Crawling Hand*. Virginia Grey was also in Cohen's *Target Earth*, *House of Horrors* (1946), *Who Killed Doc Robin? Unknown Island* and *Jungle Jim* (all 1948). Jerome Cowan's genre credits include *Fog Island*, *The Crime Doctor's Courage* and *The Jungle Captive* (all 1945), *Night in Paradise*

Rod Lauren, Jeanne Cooper and Michael Gough in *Black Zoo* (1963)

and *Flight to Nowhere* (both 1946), *Night Has a Thousand Eyes* (1948), *Have Rocket, Will Travel* (1959), *Visit to a Small Planet* (1960) and *The Gnome-Mobile* (1967).

In the Westwood section of Los Angeles, a young woman (Warrene Ott) is mauled to death by a tiger while walking home. The next day Michael Gordon (Gough), the owner of Conrad's Animal Kingdom, shows off his prize animals, including a tiger, lion, black leopard, cougar and Victor (George Barrows), a huge gorilla, to a tour group. The audience is also treated to a chimp show given by Gordon's wife Edna (Jeanne Cooper). Verbose developer Jerry Stengel (Cowan) comes to see Gordon and offers to buy his land for a housing project he wants to build but the zookeeper refuses to sell and orders the obnoxious businessman off his property. Gordon chews out mute animal keeper Carl (Rod Lauren) for not keeping the animal cages clean and then orders him to bring the big cats to his study where he plays the organ and lectures them about greedy men who want their land and how he will always protect them. The next day Stengel returns and promises to zone off the area as a residential district, close the zoo, have Conrad's license revoked and the animals condemned. Gordon then agrees to the deal. That night Carl drives him to the developer's home but before signing the contract, Conrad lets in King, a lion, who kills Stengel. The day after the developer's death is reported, Gordon is contacted by the police to see if any of his animals have escaped. Three pretty art students (Marianna Hill, Dani Lynn, Susan Slavin) get the owner's permission to sketch his animals. One of them, Audrey (Hill), is attracted to Carl and they start to become friends. That evening, Edna's drinking upsets Gordon and they argue over Carl because she wants the young man to be sent to a special school where he will get an education. Gordon slaps his wife but then apologizes. While feeding Baron, a tiger, zookeeper Joe (Elisha Cook, Jr.) torments the animal and it claws him. Joe shoots the big cat. When Gordon finds out, he beats the worker until Edna begs him to stop. Sending his wife back to their house, Gordon and Carl throw Joe into the lion's cage where he mauled to death. Under cover of night, the Gordons and Carl bury Baron in an old cemetery. Gordon attends a meeting of the True Believers, an animal lovers' cult, where he is consoled and given a tiger cub. The group performs a ceremony that passes the soul of Baron into the body of the young cat. Edna's former agent and friend, Jenny Brooks (Grey), convinces her to accept an offer to star with her chimp act in the Madison Circus for a year. When Gordon finds out about the agreement, he and Carl take Victor to the agent's garage and when she returns home it kills her. During a police investigation, the coroner (Byron Morrow) informs Lieutenant Duggan (Douglas Henderson) that the woman was done in by a tremendous blow to the head that was not administered by a human. Police Chief Rivers (Edward Platt) refuses to believe the death was caused by an animal until a laboratory technician (Jerry Douglas) confirms that hair found in Jenny's hand was not human. Edna becomes upset when she learns of her friend's death. After Gordon leaves to attend a meeting of the True Believers, Edna hears on the radio that Jenny was murdered by an animal and she comes to realize that her husband is behind the killing. After forcing Carl to reveal that he drove Gordon to Jenny's house the night before, she tells the young man they will leave that night and he can become her assistant in the chimp act. As they are about to depart during a thunderstorm, Gordon returns and Edna accuses him of causing Jenny's death. As Gordon begins to beat his wife, she begs Carl to help her and he says the young man is his son. Carl remembers that as a child (Daniel Kurlick) he witnessed his father murder his mother (Claudia Brack) and the shock caused him to lose his voice. When Gordon orders Carl to open the lion's cage so he can dispose of Edna, the young man rebels and the two men fight in the rain. Gordon calls for the big cats to help him as Carl strangles his father.

Black Zoo is highlighted by the reverent burial of the tiger in a spooky cemetery while its ravaged slayer is unceremoniously disposed of off-camera, and the chimp act sequence when one of the participants is urged to smoke a cigarette.

The year of the film's release, Charlton Publications, who did *Horror Monsters* and *Mad Monsters* magazines, issued a comic book made up of photographs from the film. Titled *Horror Monsters Presents Black Zoo*, it was billed as "A Picture by Picture Chiller Mag."

Blood and Black Lace (1965; 84 minutes; Color)

Producers: Massimo Patrizi and Alfredo Mirabile. Director: Mario Bava. Screenplay: Marcello Fondato. Story: Giuseppe Barilla, Mario Bava and Marcello Fondato. Photography: Ubaldo Terzano. Editor: Mario Serandrei. Sound: Vittorio Trentino. Sets: Arrigo Breschi. Production Managers: Benito Caripi, Armando Govoni and Franco Grifeo. Makeup: Emilio Trani. Assistant Directors: Priscilla Contardi and Cristina Grieco.

CAST: Cameron Mitchell (Max Martan), Eva Bartok (Countess Christina Como), Thomas Reiner (Inspector Sylvester), Arianna Gorini (Nicole), Dante De Paolo (Frank Sacalo), Mary Arden (Peggy), Franco Ressel (Marquis Richard Morell), Claude Dantes (Tao-Li), Luciano Pigozzi (Cesare Losarre), Lea Kruger (Greta), Massimo Righi (Marco), Francesca Ungaro (Isabella), Giuliano Raffaeli (Zanchin), Harriet White Medin (Clarise), Mara Carmosino, Heidi Stroh, Nadia Anty (Models), Enzo Cerusico (Service Station Attendant).

During a storm, model Isabella (Francesca Ungaro) meets with drug addict Frank Sacalo (Dante De Paolo) and promises to get him a fix. After leaving Christina's, the high-class fashion salon where she works, the young woman is stalked by a masked figure in black who kills her and drags her body to a secluded area. As Countess Christina Como (Eva Bartok), the owner of the establishment, closes for the night, she threatens to fire Isabella for being absent during the evening, and later finds her corpse in a clothes closet. Inspector Sylvester (Thomas Reiner) talks with Christina and co-owner Max Martan (Cameron Mitchell), who tells him to contact the dead woman's roommates Nicole (Arianna Gorini), Peggy (Mary Arden) and Greta (Lea Kruger), models for the salon. Dress designer Cesar Losarre (Luciano Pigozzi) informs Sylvester that Isabella's lover was antique dealer Sacolo. The inspector calls on Sacolo and says cocaine was found in Isabella's home. During a showing at the salon, Nicole finds a diary that belonged to the murdered model. She tells Christina that she will turn it over to the police the next day. She then telephones Frank who asks her to come to his shop. When she does, the masked maniac torments her before killing her with a metal hand with knife-like fingers. When the murderer fails to find the diary in her purse, he drives off in her car. Peggy and Marco (Massimo Righi) meet at her home where they are greeted by housekeeper Clarise (Harriet White Medin). After she leaves, Marco tells Peggy he loves her. Peggy gets a telephone call from Reiner informing her that her car, which Nicole had borrowed, has been found abandoned. The officer says he is coming to see her and Marco leaves. Peggy reads part of the diary and then burns it in a fireplace. When she answers the door, the hooded fiend drags her back into the apartment. After he beats her, she informs him that she burned the diary. When he hears the police arriving he knocks her out and carries her away. Sacolo comes to the villa Christina shares with Marquis Richard Morrell (Franco Ressel) and tells them he found Nicole's murdered body in his shop. He suggests they each give the other an alibi. When Morell refuses, Frank reminds him he signed IOUs to Isabella for several thousand dollars he could not repay. Bound and gagged, Peggy is kept in a dank cellar by the killer. As he beats and tortures her she rips off his mask, and he drives her face into a hot stove. Reiner questions Frank about Nicole's murder and accuses him of being a drug addict. At police headquarters, the inspector asks Clarise to identify any of the suspects she saw driving Peggy's car, and Marco accuses Cesare of being the murderer. Marco suffers an epileptic fit and is taken to the hospital. Reiner informs Max, Frank, Cesare and the marquis they are all suspects in the killings and has them placed under arrest. That night at the salon, Greta is afraid to go home alone but she is sent away by Christina who drives to the chateau where she discovers the body of Peggy in the trunk of her car and drags it inside. Someone moves the corpse and tries to

Advertisement for the Allied Artists double bill of *Blood and Black Lace* and *Young Dillinger* (1964)

smother Christina, who survives to call the police. Reiner is forced to release the five suspects. Model Tao-Li (Claude Dantes) comes to Max and tells him she plans to fly to Paris the next day. After she leaves, he uses a secret passage behind a bookcase to go into the cellar where Peggy was held hostage. Christina shows up and tells him she killed Greta in the house the models rented. He informs her that the police think the murderer is a sex maniac. Lovers Max and Christina blame Isabella for all their troubles since she blackmailed them over the suspicious car accident that killed the countess' husband. Max tells Christina they must place the blame on someone else for the police. She drowns Tao-Li in her bathtub and then slits the dead woman's wrist to make it look like suicide. As Christina attempts to flee from the murder scene, she climbs along a balcony but slips and falls off a ledge. At the salon, Max opens a strongbox filled with jewels but is confronted by the badly injured Christina. She tells him she realizes he only wanted her wealth. When he embraces and kisses her, she shoots him. Christina calls the police and then dies holding her lover.

In 1960 Allied Artists released the Italian production *Caltiki the Immortal Monster* (q.v.), photographed by Mario Bava, who was also the feature's uncredited co-director. Following the success of Bava's first official directorial assignment, *Black Sunday* (1960), which American International Pictures released in the U.S., Allied went on to issue Bava's *Blood and Black Lace* in the spring of 1965. Its pre-release title was *Fashion House of Death* and in a few locales it got distribution by Woolner Bros. A co-production of France, Italy and Monaco, the film was released in Italy in 1964 as *Sei Donne per l'Assassino* (Six Women for the Killer) at 88 minutes, four minutes more than its stateside showings. The film was dubbed by Allied Artists with Paul Frees supplying most of the male voices, including that of top-billed Cameron Mitchell. Its thin story of a stocking mask–wearing maniac in black murdering various women in gruesome ways was typically enhanced by Bava (some sources claim that he was also the film's co-photographer), with terrific visuals that included mostly night and inside locales, rain-swept terrain and dark shadows. *John Stanley's Creature Feature Movie Guide Strikes Again* (1994) noted, "Bava uses primary colors to psychological effect, creating the paradox of a beautiful-looking movie about death."

Castle of Frankenstein #8 (1966) said the film was a "[m]inor Italian-made chiller ... Mostly whodunit fare, but director Mario Bava adds horrific overtones." James O'Neill in *Terror on Tape* (1994) felt that "Bava's neon-colored atmosphere paved the way for the lush cosmopolitan thrillers of Dario Argento and has violence, which, though not overly gory, is still pretty strong stuff.... Only the poor dubbing detracts from the overall effect." *Video Hound's Complete Guide to Cult Flicks and Trash Pics* (1996) reported, "The story is violent and suspenseful, and Bava brings to it his trademark atmospheric cinematography, careful use of color, and perverse manipulation of characters." In *Spaghetti Nightmare* (1996), Luca M. Palmerini and Gaetano Mistretta called *Blood and Black Lace* the "[f]oundation stone of the Italian thriller."

Blood Rose (1970; 91 minutes; Color)

Producer: Edgar Oppenheimer. Director: Claude Mulot. Screenplay: Claude Mulot, Edgar Oppenheimer and Jean Larriaga. Photography: Roger Fellous. Editor: Monique Kirsanoff. Music: Jean-Pierre Dorsay. Production Manager: George Dyerman. Unit Director: Hubert Bausmann. Makeup: Nicole Felix. Special Effects: Guy Delecluse. Assistant Director: Jean Larriaga.

CAST: Philippe Lemaire (Frederic Lansac), Anny Duperey (Anne Lansac), Howard Vernon (Dr. Romer), Elisabeth Teissier (Moira), Olivia Robin (Barbara), Michelle Perello (Agnes), Valerie Boisgel (Catherine), J.P. Honore (Paul Bertin), Gerard Huart (Wilfried), Jacques Seiler (Inspector Dorte), Michel Charrel, Veronique Verlhac (Gallery Clients), Roberto (Igor), Johnny Cacao (Olaf).

Starting with *Les Yeux Sans Visage* (The Eyes Without a Face), a 1959 French release issued in the U.S. three years later as *The Horror Chamber of Dr. Faustus*, there were a number of feature films about mad scientists trying to restore disfigured young women's scarred faces with skin grafts. Others in the canon include Spain's *Gritos in la Noche* (Cries in the Night) (1962), released stateside in 1965 as *The Awful Dr. Orloff*, the British production *Corruption* (1967) and the 1970 film *La Rose Ecorchee* (The Burnt Rose) from France. Allied Artists issued the latter that October in the U.S. as *Blood Rose*; it got an R rating. It was billed as "The First Sex-Horror Film Ever Made" although that claim probably goes to director Jess Franco's 1967 production *Succubus*. Franco directed *The Awful Dr. Orloff* starring Howard Vernon in the title role and the actor was also in *Succubus* as well as having special billing in *Blood Rose*.

La Rose Ecorchee ran 95 minutes when it was shown in France but its Allied Artists stateside version was minus four minutes of lesbian scenes. In Italy it was shown as *Tre Gocce di Sangue per una Rosa* (Three Drops of Blood for a Rose). When it was issued in Great Britain in June 1970 by S.F. Distributors at 88 minutes, it was titled *Ravaged* and was assigned a Certificate X. It had limited release in West Germany as *Die Geschaendete Rose*.

At a remote chateau, Frederic Lansac (Philippe Lemaire) and his friend and business partner Wilfried (Gerard Huart) await a doctor's verdict on the condition of Frederic's wife Anne (Anny Duperey), who has been badly burned in a fire. Frederic, a famous portrait painter as well as a botanist and beauty salon owner, recalls how he rejected the advances of his former girlfriend Moira (Elisabeth Teissier) after hiring beautiful Anne as his new model. He falls in love with Anne, who has inspired his best paintings, and takes her to his old country castle where she tells him she wants to live. They are tended by two dwarfs, Igor (Roberto) and Olaf (Johnny Cacao), who have been at the chateau since Frederic was a boy. To celebrate their marriage, Anne gives an outdoor costume party. When Moira arrives, the two women have words and Anne backs into a bonfire with her dress catching fire. As a result, Anne can never walk again, her eyesight is somewhat blurred and her face is terribly disfigured. She insists her death be announced and lives at the chateau hidden away from the world. The institute Frederic operates with Wilfried hires Dr. Romer (Vernon) to work on a formula extracted from a poisonous plant. Since Frederic can no longer paint because of what happened to his wife, Wilfried, who has to go away for a time, suggests he take over running the institute. Agnes (Michelle Perello) is hired to take care of Anne as Frederic brings home one of the deadly plants to study. Anne becomes jealous of Agnes. After the blonde nurse becomes Frederic's lover, Anne induces her to touch the plant, causing the nurse to die. Anne informs her husband she caused the girl's death because she was too beautiful. That night Frederic and the dwarfs bury the victim. At the institute, Frederic overhears Romer talking about performing facial surgery at his home and that night he follows him there and confronts his employee. Romer admits he lost his medical license after the failure of a skin graft technique he developed and that he was sent to prison. After being freed, he was forced to change the facial features of criminals and took the institute job to put that in his past. Frederic takes Romer to examine Anne but he says it is hopeless since he would need a living woman's face to replace hers and the donor would die in the process. Anne dreams that her beauty is restored but she is haunted by the visage of Agnes' resurrected corpse. Frederic opens a letter from Agnes's sister Barbara (Olivia Robin) telling her that she and Paul (J.P. Honore) plan to marry. After a number of young women are judged, Frederic orders Romer to take Catherine (Valerie Boisgel) to the chateau for the skin graft surgery. At the chateau, the two dwarfs sexually assault and kill Catherine, causing the now mad Anne to beat them. Pretending to be a writer researching an article on old chateaus, Barbara arrives and is asked to stay the night by Frederic after a terrible storm erupts. Finding a photograph of herself with Agnes, the young woman explores the castle and sees Catherine's corpse. Frederic realizes Barbara's true identity and has her put in a dungeon. When Igor tries to molest her, Barbara knocks him out with a water pitcher and runs away but is recaptured by Frederic. Police Inspector Dorte (Jacques Seiler) confronts Romer after a gangster with a changed face is found murdered. The doctor denies any knowledge of the event. After he gets a call from Frederic ordering him to come to the chateau to perform the skin graft, he sneaks out of his apartment building and eludes the watchful policeman. Barbara begs Romer, who feels the graft will not be successful, to let her go. Romer hangs himself. Anne wakes up to find him dead and blames Frederic and the dwarfs for her being unable to have a new face. The dwarfs drag her into the hall and kick Anne to death. As Frederic tries to cut Barbara free, Igor attacks him. The two fight with Frederic being badly wounded. Barbara kills Igor with a scalpel. She tries to help Frederic but Paul arrives and she makes him drive her away from the chateau. The dying Frederic phones the police and tells them he killed his wife and a servant and that two women are buried on the chateau grounds. As Olaf mourns Igor's death, Frederic tries to finish his portrait of Anne.

Blood Rose contains quite a bit female nudity and its leisurely paced story is enhanced by surreal atmosphere and a dream-like staging technique. A great asset is the huge old chateau where most of the action takes place. Donald C. Willis wrote in *Horror and Science Fiction Films* (1972), "Lush music, weird little atmospheric bits, and senseless bursts of brutality, all of which adds up to nothing but a small bore." In *Film Review 1971–1972* (1971), F. Maurice Speed dubbed the film a "chiller-diller." Michael J. Weldon noted in *The Psychotronic Encyclopedia of Film* (1983), "This strange, atmospheric production is more warped than usual, thanks to two dwarf servants who wear animal skins, are sexually active, and generally get underfoot." When the feature was issued on video in Germany as *Horrormaske* (The Mask of Horror), *Video Watchdog* #12 (July-August 1992) said, "The film is an early example of the combination of horror and nudity, typical for the work of French filmmakers in the '70s."

Bluebeard's Ten Honeymoons (1960; 92 minutes)

Producer: Roy Parkinson. Director: W. Lee Wilder. Screenplay: Myles Wilder. Photography: Stephen Dade. Editor: Tom Simpson. Music: Albert Elms. Songs: Albert Elms and Josephine Caryll. Sound: George Adams. Makeup: George Partleton.

CAST: George Sanders (Henri Desire Landru), Corinne Calvet (Odette), Jean Kent (Julienne Guillin), Patricia Roc (Vivienne Dureaux), Greta Gynt (Jeanette), Maxine Audley (Cynthia), Ingrid Hafner (Giselle), Selma Vaz Dias (Madame Boyer), Peter Illing (Lefevre), George Coulouris (Lacoste), Sheldon Lawrence (Pepi), Paul Whitsun-Jones (Station Master), Keith Pyott (Estate Agent), George Melford (Concierge), Robert Rietty (Bank Clerk), Mark Singleton (Advertising Clerk), Milo Sperber (Librarian), C. Denier Warren (Neighbor), Harold Berens (Jeweler), Ian Fleming (Attorney), Dino Galvani (Hardware Store Proprietor), John Gabriel (Barber).

In 1901, French film pioneer George Melies made the short *Barbe-Bleue* (Bluebeard) based on a story by Charles Perrault about a man who marries and murders women for their money. Bluebeard became a term synonymous with bigamist killers and was the nickname of Henri Desire Landru (1869–1922), the famous French serial killer. John Carradine played the title role in *Bluebeard*, a 1944 PRC production directed by Edgar G. Ulmer; three years later Charles Chaplin wrote, directed, composed the music and starred in United Artists *Monsieur Verdoux*, a comedy melodrama based on a story by Orson Welles about the Landru

Spanish lobby card for *Bluebeard's Ten Honeymoons* (1960), picturing George Sanders and Patricia Roc

case. In 1963 Charles Denner had the title role in the French production *Landru*, released as *Bluebeard* by Embassy Pictures in the United States. Richard Burton starred in the 1972 release *Bluebeard*, directed by Edward Dmytryk. Sandwiched between the Chaplin film and the 1963 French production was *Bluebeard's Ten Honeymoons*, which Allied Artists issued in the spring of 1960.

Filmed in France and at England's Elstree Studios, *Bluebeard's Ten Honeymoons* was directed by W. Lee Wilder and written by his son, Myles Wilder. The elder Wilder was the brother of Billy Wilder. W. Lee and Myles Wilder had earlier collaborated on *Phantom from Space* (1953), *Killers from Space*, *The Snow Creature* (both 1954), *Fright* (q.v.) and *Manfish* (both 1956) before the son began working exclusively in television. W. Lee Wilder went on the make *The Man Without a Body* (1957), *Caxambu* (1967) and *The Omegans* (1968); his best film was his directorial debut, the taut *film noir* melodrama *The Glass Alibi* (1946), which he remade in 1955 as a shallow imitation called *The Big Bluff*. He also produced *The Great Flamarion*, a 1945 Republic release.

The title role of Landru in *Bluebeard's Ten Honeymoons* was played by suave George Sanders, who was also no stranger to horror, sci-fi and fantasy films. Among his many genre credits are *The Man Who Could Work Miracles* and *Things to Come* (both 1936), *Rebecca* and *The House of the Seven Gables* (both 1940), *The Lodger* (1944), *Hangover Square*, *The Picture of Dorian Gray* and *The Strange Affair of Uncle Harry* (all 1945), *The Ghost and Mrs. Muir*

(1947), *From the Earth to the Moon* (1958), *Village of the Damned* (1960), *The Jungle Book* (1967; voice only), *The Body Stealers* (1969) [q.v.], *Future Women* (1970), *Endless Night* (1971), and *Doomwatch* and *Psychomania* (both 1972). The brother of actor Tom Conway, Sanders (who was once married to Zsa Zsa Gabor and was later her brother-in-law) committed suicide in Spain in 1972 at age 66.

Paris antique furniture store owner Henri Landru (Sanders) becomes infatuated with cabaret singer Odette (Corinne Calvet) and she takes him to her apartment thinking he is rich. The young woman's lover, Pepi (Sheldon Lawrence), calls her and she informs Landru that her mother needs five thousand francs for an operation. After giving her two thousand francs and promising the rest, Landru stays the night with Odette but the next day she will have nothing to do with him when he cannot come up with the rest of the money. Wanting to win back Odette, Landru agrees to help Vivienne Dureaux (Patricia Roc) sell some furniture. He is introduced to her sister Giselle (Ingrid Hafner). Vivienne is attracted to Landru who is unable to sell the furniture to another dealer, Lacoste (George Coulouris). When he finds out that the woman has sold the furniture, Landru, who has told her he is a retired army colonel, tries to persuade her to let him invest the proceeds. When she refuses, he pushes her off a bridge and steals her money, ring and keys. Going to her apartment, Landru sells the dead woman's possessions and gives the money to Odette, who takes him back. Changing his name and shaving his beard, Landru answers a newspaper advertisement placed by Julienne Guillin (Jean Kent). He tells her he is a diplomat and takes her for a weekend at a remote villa he rented near the village of Gambais in Austria. There he proposes marriage and she accepts, giving him access to her bank account and apartment. Landru murders Julienne and cuts up her body, burning it in the villa's large game roasting stove. After getting the murdered woman's funds, Landru asks Odette to marry him but she refuses. He continues to obtain money by romancing a quartet of rich widows whom he murders for their savings. His next victim, Jeanette (Greta Gynt), is murdered in Paris and her body is buried in two suitcases at a building site after which he pretends to be her husband and raids her bank deposit box. While at the bank he meets Madame Boyer (Selma Vaz Dias) and finds out that her husband deserted her two years before and left for Africa. Landru pretends to know her husband and claims he is owed a gambling debt. He fleeces the woman out of the money and takes it to Odette but overhears her and Pepi deride him. Later Landru asks Odette to join him at the Austrian villa and tries to poison her. When the singer realizes her benefactor is trying to kill her, she mocks him and his habit of recording all purchases, including the weapons he used to murder his victims. Landru beats Odette to death and burns her remains. Giselle, who has located the man who bought her sister's furniture and through him gets Landru's name, tells the police what she has learned and goes to Gambais. Landru is about to leave the village when the station master (Paul Whitsun-Jones) informs him of Giselle's arrival. He goes back to the villa where he finds her searching the place. He tries to kill her but is interrupted by the police and runs into the forest where he is captured after being attacked by Julienne's cat Max, who he let run wild after her murder. Landru is tried and convicted of his many offenses and is guillotined.

Eugene Archer wrote in the *New York Times*, "Under W. Lee Wilder's melodramatic direction, the suave matrimonial criminal is neither a figure of dark comedy nor an anarchistic symbol of the post-war devaluation of human life. He is merely a not-too-bright 'con man' who stumbles into his murderous career.... George Sanders half-heartedly tries to inject an occasional note of jocularity ... but he soon surrenders to occupational fatigue." *Variety* also found fault with Sanders who the reviewer said "is completely bogged down by his material." Regarding the overall production, the British *Monthly Film Bulletin* complained, "Period, background and mood all fluctuate maddeningly." Co-star Corinne Calvet gave a deft performance as the seductive, two-timing Odette.

The Body Stealers (1969; 89 minutes; Color)

Producer: Tony Tenser. Director: Gerry Levy. Screenplay: Michael St. Clair. Photography: John Coquillon. Editor: Howard Lanning. Music: Reg Tilsley. Art Director: Wilfred Arnold. Sound: Hugh Strain. Production Manager-Assistant Director: John Workman. Special Effects: Tom Wadden. Wardrobe: Frank Vinall.

CAST: George Sanders (General Armstrong), Maurice Evans (Dr. Matthews/Marthos), Patrick Allen (Bob Megan), Hilary Dwyer (Dr. Julie Slade), Lorna Wilde (Lorna), Neil Connery (Jim Radford), Robert Flemyng (Wing Commander W.C. Baldwin), Allan Cuthbertson (Hindesmith), Carl Rigg (Pilot Officer Briggs), Sally Faulkner (Joanna), Michael Culver (Lieutenant Bailes), Shelagh Fraser (Mrs. Thatcher), Steve Kirby (Driver), Leslie Schofield (Gate Guard), Max Latimer (Guard Sergeant), Ralph Carrigan (Military Policeman), Johnny Wade (Orderly), Edward Kelsey, Dennis Chinnery (Control Officers), Michael Warren (Harry), Arnold Peters (Mr. Smith), Clifford Earl (Laboratory Sergeant), Larry Dann (Jeep Driver), Michael Goldie (Dispatch Driver), Wanda Moore (Blonde Secretary), Jan Miller (Sally), Derek Pollitt (Dr. Davies), Carol Hawkins (Paula), Colin Rix (Control Sergeant), Michael Graham, Brian Harrison (Pilots).

Made at Shepperton Studios in England by Tigon Pictures and Sagittarius Productions, *The Body Stealers* was issued in the U.S. in the spring of 1969 by Allied Artists. It received an R rating due to brief nudity. In its homeland it was called *Thin Air*; some stateside release prints carried the title *The Invasion of the Body Stealers*, apparently an attempt to confuse the public into thinking the feature was akin to *Invasion of the Body Snatchers* (1956) [q.v.]. Despite a top-notch cast and more than passable production values, the feature is a drawn-out affair. *Films and Filming* declared, "[D]espite the efforts of Patrick Allen, George Sanders and, in particular, Hilary Dwyer, disbelief is not suspended for one moment of the film's seemingly lengthy ninety minutes." Top-billed Sanders also headlined Sagittarius' *The Candy Man* the same year.

NATO representatives General Armstrong (Sanders), Lieutenant Bailes (Michael Culver) and parachute designer Jim Radford (Neil Connery) observe a test flight in which a trio of pilots try out Radford's new suits. During the demonstration, the men disappear into a red cloud and only the parachutes reach the ground. At an air show, three skydivers also disappear in a red cloud and the next day it is revealed that a total of eleven men went missing while using parachutes. Jim suggests to Armstrong that his friend Bob Megan (Patrick Allen), a veteran skydiver, be hired to investigate since bureaucrat Hindesmith (Allan Cuthbertson) demands immediate results. Bob agrees to do the job for $25,000. That night, while walking along a beach, he meets beautiful Lorna (Lorna Wilde), who runs away when he tries to make love to her. The next day Bob meets with the area's space research laboratory director, Dr. Matthews (Maurice Evans), and is attracted to his lovely assistant, Dr. Julie Slade (Hilary Dwyer). As he looks at the recovered parachutes and checks the reports, Dr. Matthews suggests to Bob that he not keep his queries earthbound and have an open mind. Armstrong and Megan request that Hindesmith halt all military maneuvers since the missing men had space conditioning. The general is informed that one of the men has been found but he is dying. He and Bob rush to the research lab where Dr. Matthews says that the man has died, but not from injury, disease or exposure. Armstrong telephones Hindesmith who agrees to the grounding order. That night Bob again meets Lorna on the beach and they have sex. Later, when the young woman sees Jim taking pictures of her, she runs away and Bob follows but loses her. Back at his hotel, Bob gets a call from Julie that is abruptly cut off. He drives to the lab where he finds her recovering from being knocked out. She informs him she was hit from behind; the parachutes are missing. Julie also says that test results show the dead man was changed as his organic cells were so altered he was no longer human and he was also radioactive. Dr. Matthews theorizes that the man was changed for another environment or atmosphere. When General Armstrong reveals that Lieutenant Bailes has been found murdered, Bob calls Jim at the hotel and asks him to bring a link hook he found at the airfield to the lab; it proves to be radioactive. Hindesmith is told by Armstrong that Bob will make a parachute jump wearing a radiation-proof suit. Jim shows Armstrong the photos he took the night before of Bob and a young woman but only his friend is visible in the pictures. Just before the jump, Bob is visited by Lorna who begs him not to go through with it. He makes a date with her for that night. At the airfield, Jim spots Lorna; when she sees him she runs away. He follows her into a wooded area where he is murdered. During the jump, Bob is engulfed in a red cloud and disappears but soon reappears and pulls his parachute cord, landing unconscious. He is taken to the lab where he revives and hears Armstrong say that Jim has been killed. Finding out that a scarf he got from Lorna is radioactive, Bob sends Julie to find Dr. Matthews as he heads for his date. Julie drives to her boss' home and there she finds his body and faints. As Bob meets Lorna at the beach, Armstrong learns that Dr. Matthews took control of the parachutes and decides to investigate. Bob returns Lorna's scarf and demands to know where she came from, causing her to run away. He follows her to Matthews' house where he finds the scientist's dead body and Julie unconscious. He is held at gunpoint by what appears to be Matthews' double but the being turns out to be Marthos (Maurice Evans), an alien from the planet Mygon. He informs Bob that he took the scientist's form upon arrival on Earth seeking men to help repopulate his plague-decimated planet. He says the fliers were chosen because they could adapt to a new atmosphere. Lorna begs Marthos not to kill Bob and Julie. When the two try to escape, he starts to shoot at them but is stunned by Lorna's space gun. Bob tells her that if she lets the captives go, he will try to organize volunteers to help repopulate her planet. As they walk outside and say goodbye, a huge spaceship materializes and Lorna vanishes. The airmen revive and Armstrong arrives at Matthews' house. Hindesmith tells the general that the incident "officially" never occurred as Bob and Julie fly away in his private plane.

The producer of *The Body Stealers*, Tony Tenser, did more than a dozen horror and science fiction films, including *The Black Torment* (1964), *The Projected Man* (1966), *The Sorcerers* (1968) [q.v.], *The Blood Beast Terror*, *Witchfinder General (Conqueror Worm)* and *Curse of the Crimson Altar (The Crimson Cult)* (all 1968), *Zeta One* and *The Haunted House of Horror (Horror House)* (both 1969), *The Beast in the Cellar* (1970), *Blood on Satan's Claw* (1971), *Doomwatch* (1972), also with George Sanders, *The Creeping Flesh* (1973) and *Frightmare* (1974).

The Bowery Boys Meet the Monsters (1954; 65 minutes)

Producer: Ben Schwalb. Director: Edward Bernds. Screenplay: Elwood Ullman and Edward Bernds. Photography: Harry Neumann. Music Director: Marlin Skiles. Editor: William Austin. Art Director: David Milton. Sound: Ralph Butler. Production Manager: Allen K. Wood. Sets: Joseph Kish. Makeup: Edward Polo. Wardrobe: Bert Henrikson. Special Effects: Augie Lohman. Continuity: John L. Banse. Assistant Director: Edward Morey, Jr.

CAST: Leo Gorcey (Terence Aloysius "Slip" Mahoney), Huntz Hall (Horace Debussy "Sach" Jones), Bernard Gorcey (Louie Dumbrowski), Lloyd Corrigan (Anton Gravesend), Ellen Corby

(Amelia Gravesend), John Dehner (Dr. Derek Gravesend), Laura Mason (Francine Gravesend), Paul Wexler (Grissom), David [Gorcey] Condon (Chuck), Bennie Bartlett (Butch), Rudy Lee (Herbie Wilkins), Norman Bishop (Gorog the Robot), Paul Bryar (Officer Martin), Jack Diamond (Skippy Biano), Pat Flaherty (Officer O'Meara), Steve Calvert (Cosmos the Gorilla).

Between 1946 and 1952, Monogram Pictures released twenty-eight "Bowery Boys" features, the series being a derivative of earlier juvenile pairings like "Dead End Kids," "Little Tough Guys" and "East Side Kids." Allied Artists became the releasing company for the series in 1953 and until 1958 churned out another twenty "Bowery Boys" adventures. Several of the comedies had the boys involved with the supernatural. Huntz Hall played the none-too-bright Sach Jones in all the films while Leo Gorcey headlined as smart-talking, English-language mangling Slip Mahoney until 1956 when he was replaced in the final seven outings by Stanley Clements, playing Stanislaus "Duke" Coveleskie. James Robert Parish wrote in *The Great Movie Series* (1971), "*The Bowery Boys* have had enormous popularity both in theatrical release and in constant television syndication ... (they) have always had an indefinable appeal, stemming from the lower comic sense of slapstick and corny punning dialogue which fills their pictures."

In an interview with Ted Okuda in *Filmfax* #9 (February–March 1988), the director and co-writer of *The Bowery Boys Meet the Monsters*, Edward Bernds, said the feature was the biggest moneymaker of the series, adding that all of the "Bowery Boys" movies turned a profit. "Something about the juxtaposition of the Bowery Boys and a bunch of monsters appealed to audiences," he said. Bernds also noted that the feature used material from *Dopey Dicks* (1950), a two-reel Three Stooges short he directed for Columbia.

Released in June 1954, the comedy horror programmer begins at Louie Dumbrowski's (Bernard Gorcey) sweet shop in New York's Lower East Side where street urchins break one of his windows with a baseball. Since the boys have no place to play baseball, Slip Mahoney (Leo Gorcey) and Sach Jones (Hall), two denizens of Louie's place, decide to lease a local vacant lot next to the Acme Warehouse as a playground. A family named Gravesend owns the property so Slip and Sach drive to their spooky mansion to propose a business deal. There they find the family members and their household to be something out of the ordinary, being made up of siblings Anton (Lloyd Corrigan) and Dr. Derek Gravesend (John Dehner), their sister Amelia (Ellen Corby) and beautiful niece Francine (Laura Mason). All the family members take an intense interest in Slip and Sach. The brothers show the boys their labs where Derek runs a test on Sach's brain and finds it is perfect for a gorilla's head. Slip and Sach are invited to spend the night so the family lawyer can attend to the details of the rental agreement the next day. When the boys cannot sleep, Slip goes for a snack but it is nearly consumed by Amelia's giant carnivorous plant, Igapanthus. Anton uses a microphone to control his robot Gorog (Norman Bishop), accidentally ordering it to kill Sach. The metal man breaks into Sach's bedroom but the brothers hear the noise and Anton recalls the robot. When Slip returns with more food, Sach thinks he is the giant and knocks him out. Anton concocts a formula that is supposed to transform anyone into a beautiful being but when he gets the family's sinister butler, Grissom (Paul Wexler), to drink it he briefly turns into a monster. Derek decides to transplant Sach's brain into the head of his gorilla Cosmos (Steve Calvert). When Slip and Sach do not return to the sweet shop, Louie and their pals Chuck (David Condon) and Butch (Bennie Bartlett) go looking for them. At dawn, Slip and Sach are held at bay by gun-carrying Derek who tells them they are about to be used for the sibling's experiments to create a new, peaceful race of beings. Just as the brothers are about to commence their experiments on Slip and Sach, Grissom informs them that they have visitors. Derek tells Louie, Chuck and Butch that their friends left the night before. Slip saws through the wall of the closet in which he and Sach have been locked and the two find themselves in the gorilla's cage. When Louie, Chuck and Butch hear their cries, they too are locked away, although Amelia and Francine want them for their own purposes. Grissom ties Slip to Anton's operating table while Derek straps Sach to the one in his laboratory. Cosmos breaks out of the closet, knocks out Anton and frees Slip, who takes the microphone and activates Gorog, who fights with the gorilla. Slip tries to get away but runs into Amelia, who attempts to feed him to her plant. Francine frees Sach but Derek tries to stop her as he gets away from them only to be chased by both Gorog and Cosmos. Slip tries to find Sach while Anton orders Grissom to get him a head. The plant nearly eats Sach, who is saved by the butler, who then takes him to the brothers. Louis manages to get free of his bonds but runs into Cosmos who is chased off by Gorog. Anton calls the robot back to the lab. Slip finds Louie and they free Chuck and Butch, who have been frozen. Derek locks Cosmos in his cage and Anton places Gorog in the closet and the brothers continue to fight over who will have Sach's head. Slip has Louie call the police as Sach throws him the microphone through a transom and Slip orders Gorog to break out of the closet and attack the brothers. Anton cuts off the robot's power source and the brothers and Grissom prepare to operate on Sach, who accidentally drinks the elixir concocted by Anton and turns into a hideous monster. He beats up the siblings and the butler and then attacks his pals before returning to normal. Slip gets the groggy Derek to sign the lease on the lot. Back home, the boys find more of Louie's windows have been broken, this time by the batting of the Bowery Tigers' new star, Gorog.

Phil Hardy wrote in *The Encyclopedia of Horror Movies* (1986), "Not very amusing, but with [Huntz] Hall turned into a sort of werewolf, there isn't really leisure to be bored." In *Horrors: From Screen to Scream* (1975), Ed Naha opined, "This one can mercifully termed 'unique.'" David Hayes and Brent Walker said in *The Films of the Bowery Boys* (1984), "*The Bowery Boys Meet the Monsters* has a funny script and the best supporting cast in the series' history. It is replete with puns, horror house clichés and talent." *Variety* noted that the film "goes overboard on the malapropisms which generally give zest to the series.... [It] is on the weak side, not up to the usual standard, with appeal even for followers of the series apt to be limited."

Bowery to Bagdad (1955; 64 minutes)

Producer: Ben Schwalb. Director: Edward Bernds. Story-Screenplay: Elwood Ullman and Edward Bernds. Photography: Harry Neumann. Editor: John C. Fuller. Music Director: Marlin Skiles. Art Director: David Milton. Sound: Ralph Butler. Production Manager: Allen K. Wood. Sets: Joseph Kish. Makeup: Edward Polo. Special Effects: Augie Lohman. Wardrobe: Bert Henrikson. Continuity: John L. Banse. Assistant Director: Edward Morey, Jr.

CAST: Leo Gorcey (Terence Aloysius "Slip" Mahoney), Huntz Hall (Horace Debussy "Sach" Jones), Bernard Gorcey (Louie Dumbrowski), Joan Shawlee (Velma), Eric Blore (The Genie), Jean Willes (Claire Culpepper), Robert Bice (Duke Dolan), Richard [Dick] Wessel (Gus), Michael Ross (Tiny), Rayford Barnes (Canarsie), Rick Vallin (Selim), Paul Marion (Abdul), David [Gorcey] Condon (Chuck), Bennie Bartlett (Butch), Charles Lung (Caliph Hamud), Leon Burbank (Guard).

Centuries pass after Aladdin's magic lamp is stolen. Selim (Rick Vallin) and Abdul (Paul Marion) arrive in New York City under orders from the caliph (Charles Lung) of Bagdad to locate it. Finding the lamp in a thrift shop, Sach Jones (Huntz Hall) buys it as a gift for sweet shop owner Louie Dumbrowski's (Bernard Gorcey) birthday. His overbearing pal Slip Mahoney (Leo Gorcey) makes fun of Sach for buying junk as hoodlums Tiny (Michael Ross) and Canarsie (Rayford Barnes) try to strong arm Louie into selling his lease to their boss, gangster Duke Dolan (Robert Bice). Sach accidentally rubs the lamp and a genie (Eric Blore), the slave of the lamp, appears and grants his wish for six malted milk shakes. Tiny sees what happened and reports to Duke whose underling Gus (Dick Wessel) urges him to obtain the magic lamp after reading a similar story in *The Arabian Nights*. The two Arabs fight over the lamp but drop it and run away when the boys interrupt them. Slip throws the lamp in the trash since he does not believe Sach's story about the genie. Slip later rubs the lamp and when the genie appears he and Sach fight over him until they agree to own the lamp jointly. Slip tells the genie to only take orders from him and Sach together and the boys ask for a million dollars which they get in gold bars. Slip and Sach argue over the money and Sach accidentally wishes away the gold and the lamp. Tiny and Canarsie take the lamp at gunpoint but are followed by Selim and Abdul. After Duke gets the lamp, his moll Velma (Joan Shawlee) rubs it. When the genie appears, he says he cannot grant them any wishes; they try to beat him up and he disappears. Duke tells Velma to go to Louie's place and bring the boys back to his penthouse at the Winthrop Towers. She pretends to be Southern Belle Cindy Lou Calhoun and vamps Sach, but Slip will not let him go with her unless he too has a date, so Velma gets Claire Culpepper (Jean Willes), Canarsie's girlfriend, to pretend to be her cousin. At the penthouse, Claire flirts with Slip while Velma lures Sach to Duke who orders him to make the genie do his bidding. Slip manages to make a getaway as the genie informs Duke he can only take orders jointly from Sach and his pal. Selim and Abdul put Slip in a pantry as the genie tells Sach to get away from Velma by pretending to make love to her. Slip and Sach's pals Chuck (David Condon), Butch (Bennie Bartlett) and Louie arrive at the penthouse looking for them. Gus and Canarsie get Slip out of the pantry as Louie finds the lamp with Selim pretending to be the genie. Tiny and Canarsie knock out the Arabs, and the genie sends Selim and Abdul back to Bagdad. Louie tells Chuck and Butch to go for the police and ends up in the pantry where he gets drunk with the genie. Fed up with constantly being hit on the head, Duke tells his men to shoot Slip and Sach as they try to escape on a window ledge so he can be the genie's master. Sach rubs the lamp and the genie grants their wish to be taken home but they end up in Bagdad, his home, where they are attended to by beautiful harem girls. The caliph orders Slip and Sach decapitated and they agree to free the genie in order to return to the Bowery. They find themselves back on the window ledge and about to be shot by the gangsters when Chuck and Butch show up with the police, who arrest Duke and his gang. Back at the sweet shop, the genie reappears and grants Slip and Sach one final wish. When Slip tries to monopolize the opportunity, Sach asks for the courage to punch out his pal. This accomplished, Sach escapes before Slip revives.

The film's director and co-writer, Edward Bernds, told Ted Okuda in *Filmfax* #9 (February-March 1988) that *Bowery to Bagdad* was his favorite of the eight "Bowery Boys" features he helmed. He also noted that the movie was influenced by *Three Arabian Nuts* (1951), a Three Stooges short he directed for Columbia Pictures. Overall, the feature is only an average series entry, albeit a fast-paced fantasy comedy highlighted by Eric Blore's amusing portrayal of the jovial genie. The funniest scene came in the sweet shop when bungling Sach gives Slip a cup of paint instead of coffee and Slip throws a piece of pie at him in retaliation and hits vamping Velma.

The Bride and the Beast (1958; 78 minutes)

Producer-Director-Story: Adrian Weiss. Screenplay: Edward D. Wood, Jr. Photography: Roland Price. Editor: George M. Merrick. Music: Les Baxter. Production Design: Edward Shiells.

Sets: Harry Reif. Makeup: Harry Thomas. Special Effects: George Endler. Production Supervisor: Louis Weiss. Assistant Directors: Harry L. Fraser and Harry S. Webb.

CAST: Charlotte Austin (Laura Carson Fuller), Lance Fuller (Dan Fuller), Johnny Roth (Taro), William Justice (Dr. Carl Reiner), Gil Frye (Captain Cameron), Jeanne Gerson (Marka), Steve Calvert (Spanky the Gorilla), Slick Slavin (Messenger), Jean Ann Lewis [Eve Brent] (Stewardess), Shogwah Singh (Native), Bobby Small (Gorilla).

Filmed early in 1957 as *Queen of the Gorillas*, this pedestrian jungle melodrama was released theatrically in February 1958 by Allied Artists. Since the 1980s it has come into favor with schlock cinema fans because it was written by Edward D. Wood, Jr.

Outside of the heroine wearing an angora sweater and her surname Fuller (the same as leading man Lance Fuller and also that of Wood's long-time girlfriend Dolores Fuller), the script shows little of the loony plotting and stilted dialogue associated with Wood, the producer-director-writer of such cinema fare as *Bride of the Monster* (1955), *Plan 9 from Outer Space* (1958) and *The Sinister Urge* (1961). Laced with lots of jungle stock footage (much of it from Universal's *Man Eater of Kumaon* [1948]), *The Bride and the Beast* is basically a plodding, uninteresting affair outside its having the beautiful heroine brush off her stoic husband in favor of cohabitating with a gorilla.

The film was a family affair production-wise with Adrian Weiss producing and directing, as well as writing the story on which Wood's script was based; Louis Weiss serving as production supervisor and Samuel Weiss the assistant editor. Louis Weiss produced Wood's initial directorial effort *Glen or Glenda?* (1953). The assistant directors for the feature were Hollywood Poverty Row oldtimers Harry L. Fraser, a veteran writer-director, and Harry S. Webb, the one-time operator of such studios as Biltmore, Metropolitan and Reliable Pictures.

Big game hunter Dan Fuller (Lance Fuller) and his new bride Laura (Charlotte Austin) arrive at his home during a thunderstorm. Caged in the basement is Dan's pet gorilla Spanky (Steve Calvert),

Poster for *The Bride and the Beast* (1958)

who fascinates Laura since she grew up with a pet monkey. When she gets too close to Spanky's cage, he grabs her wrist and caresses her hair and angora sweater, but she talks him into letting her go. When she leaves, the gorilla goes berserk and tears up his cage. Laura dreams of the beast and then, unable to sleep, she gets up as Spanky breaks out of his cage and comes into her bedroom. The gorilla again caresses Laura and tears her nightgown as Dan wakes up and kills him with a pistol. Laura tells Dan she was unafraid of the creature and felt a kinship with him. Going back to sleep, Laura has a recurring dream of living in a jungle; when she sees her reflection in a pool of water, she wakes up screaming since she saw a gorilla's face. Dan goes to town the next day and brings back Dr. Carl Reiner (William Justine). Reiner, who has known Laura for many years, suggests trying regression deep sleep therapy to bring an end to her nightmares. He places her under a hypnotic spell and takes her back in time with Laura remembering a previous life as a gorilla. Dan is unconvinced but Dr. Reiner suggests to him the newlyweds postpone their upcoming trip to Africa. They ignore his advice and along with houseboy Taro (Johnny Roth) fly to Africa, take a cattle boat to a port town and then go by truck into the jungle. Captain Cameron (Gil Frye), the local game warden, checks Dan's papers and gives him permission to capture animals for his employer, a stateside zoo. Laura loves being in the jungle as her husband and his native workers snare a leopard, zebra, rhino and giraffe. Cameron consults with Dan since two killer Indian tigers are loose in the area after being set free by a shipwreck; he asks Dan's help in finding them. The hunt takes the Fullers and their party into gorilla country where one of the tigers killed a native. When camp cook Marka (Jeanne Gerson) is attacked and mauled by one of the beasts, Dan wounds it but the tiger escapes. The other tiger falls into a pit dug by Dan's bearers and he waits for its mate to return. Laura finds that her husband is gone and goes searching for him. The tiger attacks Dan but runs away when he shoots at it. The big cat then chases Laura, causing her to fall off a precipice and be knocked out. As the tiger is about to pounce on his wife, Dan comes to her defense and is badly scratched when he kills the beast with a knife. Dan asks Taro to go for a doctor. As Dan tends to his own wounds, Laura comes to and leaves her tent and is carried off by a gorilla who knocks down her husband when he tries to intervene. Dan follows his wife and the gorilla to a cave where he kills one of the beasts but is left unconscious when he fights his wife's abductor. Laura then willing leaves with the gorilla. Back home, Fuller tells Dr. Reiner he did everything he could to find his wife, and the medical man says he believes Laura went back to where she came from.

Outside of beautiful Charlotte Austin, the daughter of crooner Gene Austin, *The Bride and the Beast* has little to recommend it, even for the most rabid of bad movie lovers. The same year she was in *Frankenstein—1970* (q.v.) after having previously appeared in *Gorilla at Large* (1954) and *The Man Who Turned to Stone* (1957). Leading man Lance Fuller was also in *This Island Earth* (1955), *The She-Creature* (1956) and *Voodoo Woman* (1957). The title beast was played by Steve Calvert who wore the gorilla outfit, which he bought from Ray "Crash" Corrigan in the early 1950s, in numerous films and TV programs.

Caltiki the Immortal Monster (1960; 76 minutes)

Producers: Bruno Vallati and Samuel Schneider. Directors: Robert Hamton [Riccardo Freda] and (uncredited Mario Bava). Screenplay: Philip Just [Filippo Sanjust]. Photography: John Foam [Mario Bava]. Editor: Salvatore Billitteri. Music: Robert Nicholas [Roberto Nicolosi] and Roman Vlad. Sound: Lee Kresel and Maurice Rosenblum. Special Effects: Mario Foam [Mario Bava]. Choreographer: P. Gozlino.

CAST: John Merivale (Dr. John Fielding), Didi Sullivan [Dide Perego] (Ellen Fielding), Gerald Haerter [Gerard Herter] (Max Gunther), Daniela Rocca (Linda Gunther), Giacomo Rossi-Stuart (Laboratory Assistant), Daniele Vargas (Bob), Victor [Vittorio] Andre (Professor Rodriguez), Arturo Dominici (Nieto), Black Bernard [Nerio Bernardi] (Police Chief), Gay Pearl (Dancer), Deirdre Sullivan (Jenny Fielding), Tom Felleghy (Astronomer).

Made in Italy as *Caltiki — I Monstro Immortale* (Caltiki — The Immortal Monster), this combination horror–sci-fi outing was set in Mexico and its credits claimed it was "Based on an Ancient Mexican Legend." Released in the U.S. in the summer of 1960 by Allied Artists as *Caltiki the Immortal Monster* and also called *Caltiki the Undying Monster*, it was a staple of mid–1960s television, where it got its reputation as an out-of-the-ordinary scare production with visuals a notch above most imports of its ilk. The dubbed U.S. version was produced by Titra Sound Corporation. Later it was learned that the director, Robert Hamton, usually spelled Hampton, was really Riccardo Freda, who abandoned the project, with cameraman John Foam finishing the production. It was revealed that Foam was Mario Bava, later the cult director of such genre fare as *Black Sunday* (1960), *Evil Eye* (1962), *Black Sabbath* (1963), *Blood and Black Lace* [q.v.] and *Planet of the Vampires* (both 1965), *Kill Baby Kill* (1966), *Danger: Diabolik* (1967), *Hatchet for a Honeymoon* (1969), *Baron Blood* (1972) and *Shock* (1976). The film is highlighted by Bava's photography with much of the production done in dark or semi-lit locals with very few outdoor scenes. The title monster is a blob-like creature capable of rending itself to multiply. It is said to have been made of cow entrails.

At the site of the abandoned Mayan city of Tekal, 300 miles south of Mexico City, Nieto (Arturo Dominici) runs screaming "Caltiki" into an archaeological expedition camp. Leaving his wife Ellen (Didi Sullivan) to look after the hysterical man, Dr. John Fielding (John Merivale) and co-workers Max Gunther (Gerald Haerter) and Bob (Daniele Vargas)

Didi Sullivan and John Merivale in *Caltiki the Immortal Monster* (1960)

go to the cave where Nieto and another expedition member, Almer, were exploring. They find an opening in the cave wall caused by the recent eruption of a nearby volcano and they descend a flight of stone stairs taking them to an underground temple with a lake and a statue of the goddess Caltiki. Their Geiger counter picks up radiation near the lake and John suggests they explore its bottom; they go back to camp for diving equipment. That night John and Ellen argue over the expedition as the local Indians dance to ward off evil spirits. Max tells Ellen he is attracted to her but she rejects his advances. The Indians halt their dance when they see Bob filming the ceremony. John and Ellen make up the next morning and he tells her to return to Mexico City with Linda (Daniela Rocca), Max's beautiful half-breed wife. At the temple, Bob dives into the lake and finds the bottom strewn with skeletons and lots of gold ornaments, some of which he brings back to the surface. Over John's objections, Bob goes back into the lake and, while picking up more treasure, he is attacked. When John and Max bring him up, they see his face has been dissolved. A giant blob-like creature rises from the water and chases them out of the cavern. Max goes back to get the treasure and the thing takes hold of his arm; John chops off part of its flesh as the two men escape. John drives their truck into the mouth of the cave, causing an explosion that destroys the monster. Back in Mexico City, Professor Rodriguez (Victor Andre) informs John that an unknown substance from the creature ate away the flesh, and the poison from the organism will soon enter Max's bloodstream and go to his brain. Max overhears the two men. John tries to figure out what caused the abnormal development that destroys any living thing with which it comes in contact. Wanting to help Max, John decides to use radioactivity on a section of the creature. Cutting it in half, he uses beta-tron rays, causing the thing to activate, grow and multiply. Max becomes deranged and tells Linda he plans to get revenge against John and Ellen; that night he kills a nurse and escapes from the hospital. Linda becomes upset because Max wants Ellen. Linda gets a telephone call asking them to come to the hospital. There they find the nurse has been murdered and Max is missing. The police begin searching for Max as Rodriguez and John discuss the Mayan prophecy that a comet will give the goddess Caltiki ultimate power over the world. After Rodriguez leaves, John receives a telephone message saying the alien flesh has started to grow and multiply and he orders it destroyed by fire. After he leaves for the laboratory, Max breaks into the house and cuts the telephone wires. Rodriguez consults an astronomer (Tom Felleghy) who informs him a comet last seen on Earth in 607 A.D., the year of the mysterious Mayan evacuation of Tekal, is due in the heavens. The doctor realizes that all specimens of the creature must be destroyed but he is unable to reach John by telephone. Driving back to

A nurse (actress unidentified) is attacked by a man (Gerard Haerter) in *Caltiki the Immortal Monster* (1960).

John's house, the doctor's car careens off a cliff and crashes. Later the doctor's assistant (Giacomo Rossi-Stuart) tells John about the comet and he requests the military bring flame throwers to his house to destroy the last sample of the monster. Linda takes Max food as the part of the creature in the laboratory begins to grow and breaks out of its glass container. Max tries to attack Ellen; when Linda attempts to stop him, she shoots her. Hearing noises in the laboratory and thinking it is John, Max opens the door and is devoured by the monster. Ellen runs upstairs and, taking her little daughter Jenny (Dierdre Sullivan), she tries to escape from the house by a balcony but the creature has multiplied to the point they cannot get to the ground. Speeding toward home, John is picked up by the police and put in a cell but manages to escape as the lawmen pursue him. As John arrives home, he is followed by the police and the military. He orders them to set off the flame throwers which consume some of the blobs. Ellen and Jenny are trapped in a bedroom. John climbs a ladder to get them but the blob nearly knocks it over before the trio fall back to the ground on the ladder and escape the monster. The soldiers then release the full force of the flame throwers, completely destroying Caltiki.

Despite the movie's popularity, especially with Baby Boomers, reviews of *Caltiki the Immortal Monster* have been a mixed bag. Luca M. Palmerini and Gaetano Mistretta in *Spaghetti Nightmares* (1996) called it a "[v]ery inventive and enjoyable 'fanta-horror' films, excellently made and with an skillful use of black and white photography." In *Terror on Tape* (1994), James O'Neill said it was a "[p]assable spin-off of *The Blob* and *The Creeping Unknown* ... Visually imaginative ... but this otherwise routine, with silly special effects." Danny Peary in *Guide for the Film Fanatic* (1986) declared, "Undeniably silly, but still it's one of my favorite low-budget horror films.... Film contains one genuinely spooky sequence in which a diver explores a deep, uncharted mountain pool and finds out too late that he's not alone. It will remind some of the scene in *Alien* in which John Hurt comes across the alien hatchery." In *Science Fiction* (1984), Phil Hardy said, "A minor outing, this was one of the earliest Italian films to be aimed at the American market.... Though the acting is routine and the script leaden, Bava injects a few stylish flourishes." Donald C. Willis in *Horror and Science Fiction Films: A Checklist* (1972) felt it was "[r]ather tame after an eerie beginning."

Golden Era released the feature in Great Britain in 1961 as *The Immortal Monster*. The same year, the French company Star-Cine Cosmos published a photo novel of the film entitled *Le Monstre Immortel* (The Immortal Monster).

Arturo Dominici, who had the small role of Nieto, the next year portrayed the resurrected Javuto in Bava's classic gothic horror thriller *Black Sunday*. Vittorio Andre, who portrayed Dr. Rodriguez in the production, also supervised its voice dubbing for the English language version released by Allied Artists.

Communion (1976; 108 minutes; Color)

Producer: Richard K. Rosenberg. Director: Alfred Sole. Screenplay: Rosemary Ritvo and Alfred Sole. Photography: John Friberg. Editor: Edward Sailer. Music: Stephen Lawrence. Sound: Mark Salwasser. Production Design: John Lawless. Sets: Stephen Finon. Makeup: Anne Paul and Karen Sole. Production Manager: Rosemary Rivto. Wardrobe: Lenora Guarini. Costumes: Michelle Cohen. Assistant Director: Adrienne Hamalian.

CAST: Linda Miller (Catherine "Kay" Spages), Mildred Clinton (Mrs. Tredoni), Paula Sheppard (Alice Spages), Niles McMaster (Dominick "Dom" Spages), Jane Lowry (Annie DeLorenze), Rudolph Willrich (Father Tom), Michael Hardstark (Detective Mike Spina), Alphonso DeNoble (Mr. Alphonso), Gary Allen (James "Jim" DeLorenze), Brooke Shields (Karen Spages), Louisa

Spanish lobby card for *Communion* (1976)

Horton (Dr. Whitman), Tom Signorelli (Detective Ray Brennan), Lillian Roth (Pathologist), Patrick Gorman (Father Pat), Kathy Rich (Angela DeLorenze), Ted Tinling (Detective Cranston), Mary Boylan (Mother Superior), Peter Bosche (Monsignor), Joseph Rossi (Father Joe), Marco Quazzo (Robert "Bob" DeLorenze), Dick Boccelli (Hotel Clerk), Ronald Willoughby (Funeral Home Director), Sally Anne Golden (Policewoman), Lucy Hale (Church Soloist), Libby Fennelly (Nun), Maurice Yonowsky, Beth Carlton (Children's Shelter Attendants), Drew Roman (Policeman), Antonino Rocca, Michael Weil (Funeral Home Attendants), Dr. Leslie Feigen (Doctor).

Filmed in Patterson, New Jersey, by Harristown Funding, *Communion* was issued to theaters in November 1976 by Allied Artists. The R-rated production drew little box office response and quickly faded but was reissued by Allied in 1978 as *Alice, Sweet Alice* due to the presence of Brooke Shields, who made her debut in the film. That year she had caused a sensation as a child prostitute in *Pretty Baby* and the studio took advantage of her newfound popularity to try and breathe life into *Communion*. The ploy was not very successful. In 1981 Citadel Films tried again, releasing the production for a third time theatrically (this time as *Holy Terror*), with ten minutes shorn from its running time. Overlong, slowly paced and Catholic-baiting, *Communion* lost what little punch it had by revealing the identity of the killer too soon. It constantly shows holy images contrasted with acts of violence, the best staged being the stabbing of the aunt on a staircase, the action being right out of a playbook by Alfred Hitchcock or William Castle. The cast also includes Lillian Roth in her penultimate film role and a fleeting bit by wrestling great Antonino "Argentine" Rocca.

Catherine Spages (Linda Miller), a divorcee with two young daughters, Alice (Paula Sheppard) and Karen (Shields), goes to the rectory of St. Michael's Catholic Church where nine-year-old Karen is soon to receive first communion. Karen is a favorite of the priest, Father Tom (Rudolph Willrich), who gives her a crucifix that belonged to his mother. Jealous of her sister and the priest's affinity for her, Alice dons a shiny, grinning face mask and deliberately scares the rectory housekeeper, Mrs. Tredoni (Mildred Clinton), and is chastised by her mother. Taking her younger sister's doll, Alice later lures her to an abandoned warehouse where she frightens Karen with the mask and pushes her into a storage room. Letting her out, Alice warns Karen not to tell their mother or she will get rid of the doll. Back at their apartment building, Alice has a confrontation with the landlord, Mr. Alphonso (Alphonso DeNoble), a huge, bald, unkempt man she calls Fatso. At the communion ceremony, Catherine's sister Annie DeLorenze (Jane Lowry) sends her overweight daughter Angela (Kathy Rich) to find the absent Alice as Karen checks on a noise in a nearby room and is strangled from behind with a large candle by someone dressed in the fright mask and a bright yellow school raincoat. Karen is placed in a chest, the crucifix is ripped from her neck and her body is set on fire. Alice shows up wearing a bridal dress and carrying a school raincoat and attempts to receive communion when a nun (Libby Fennelly) screams after finding Karen's body. Catherine learns of her daughter's murder and is consoled by the priest and her sister as Alice hides Karen's communion veil. Police detectives Spina (Michael Hardstark), Brennan (Tom Signorelli) and Cranston (Ted Tinling) investigate as Dominick "Dom" Spages (Niles McMaster), Catherine's ex-husband and the girls' father, arrives for the funeral. Afterward, Annie announces she plans to stay with Catherine in her time of grief, and a belligerent Alice is told she will have to return to school. Alice hates her aunt and the two argue; Annie thinks her niece deliberately dropped a glass of milk and implicates her in the crime, saying she had Karen's veil in her pocket. Dominick goes to see Brennan who wants to talk with Alice but he refuses after Cranston tries to implicate her in the killing. Cranston informs Brennan that school officials wanted Alice to see a psychiatrist. When Alice gives Mr. Alphonso the rent check, she deliberately crumples it; he tries to grope her and she retaliates by strangling his beloved cat. Going to the basement of the apartment building, Alice wears the mask and feeds cockroaches she keeps in a jar. As Annie leaves the building, a figure in mask and raincoat stabs her several times in the feet and legs. After she is taken to the hospital, Dominick finds Alice in the basement and she tells him that Karen attacked Annie. Dominick and Father Tom go to the hospital to see Annie. Cranston arrives to question her but she only wants her milquetoast husband Jim (Gary Allen). She tells him her assailant was Alice but Catherine calls her a liar and questions where her daughter Angela was at the time of Karen's murder. After failing a lie detector test and telling the police that Karen attacked Annie, Alice is placed in a children's shelter where Dr. Whitman (Louisa Horton) informs her parents that the young girl needs psychological help. Back home, Dominick tells Catherine he thinks Angela may have murdered Karen but she disagrees. The two start to make love when his wife calls. Catherine tells her ex-husband to stop playing detective and go home but he vows to find his daughter's killer. Later he gets a telephone call from Angela who says she has Karen's crucifix and he agrees to meet her at a waterfall near an abandoned warehouse. Seeing someone he thinks is Angela, he follows her into the building and is stabbed in the left shoulder and then knocked out with a brick and bound with rope. As he is about to be pushed out a third floor window, Dominick finds out his assailant is Mrs. Tredoni. Almost caught when returning to the church, the housekeeper hides in a confessional where she tells Father Tom she has sinned for being impatient with the parish's now addled monsignor (Peter Bosche). When Dominick does not return, Catherine goes to the rectory to see Father Tom. Mrs. Tredoni offers her coffee and says her own little girl died on the day of her first communion and that little children have to pay for the sins of their parents. Father Tom returns and tells Catherine about Dominick being found murdered. At the autopsy, the pathologist (Roth) finds a crucifix lodged in his throat. As a result, Catherine and Father Tom go to the children's shelter and bring Alice home but she is not informed of her father's murder. The next day Alice places a jar filled with cockroaches on the huge stomach of the sleeping Mr. Alphonso. After she and her mother leave for mass, Mrs. Tredoni, dressed in the mask and yellow raincoat, shows up to kill them. Mr. Alphonso wakes up screaming when he finds the insects crawling over him and runs into the hallway where she sees Mrs. Tredoni. Thinking she is Alice, he grabs her and the woman stabs him to death and runs from the apartment building. She is followed by Spina, who has been trailing her. Before the church service begins, Father Tom tells Spina he will turn Mrs. Tredoni over to the police when she attempts to get communion. Rushing to the altar, Mrs. Tredoni is denied communion by the priest and she stabs him in the neck. In front of the horrified congregation, Mrs. Tredoni hugs Father Tom as Alice leaves the church in a dazed state, carrying the killer's shopping bag and bloody knife.

Communion is populated by unlikable characters, some of them eccentric, like the grotesque landlord and the shrewish aunt. Surprisingly, the title character, Alice, has almost no redeeming qualities. She is a nasty, self-centered brat whose mental state is certainly questionable. Phil Hardy, in *The Encyclopedia of Horror Movies* (1986) tries to analyze the heroine's actions by saying she is "[m]enaced on the one hand by a Church in its dotage urging submission on pain of hellfire, and on the other by a corrupt society assuming eagerness to participate in its secret vices" so she "almost inevitably takes over where her predecessor left off."

No doubt due to Brooke Shields' involvement in the production, *Communion* received considerable coverage for a not very good slasher feature, with both adherents and foes. *The Phantom's Ultimate Video Guide* (1989) termed it "a wonderfully perverse low-budget *Bad Seed*–type tale.... The best Catholic-themed *verite* ever lensed in New Jersey...." *Video Hound's Complete Guide to Cult Flicks and Trash Pics* (1996) said the feature is a "shocking, suspenseful horror thriller, full of bizarre images and sudden violence." Mike Mayo went even further in *Videohound's Horror Show* (1998), calling it a "complex indictment of Catholicism" and adding, "The film's influence on various slasher films of following decades, particularly the Italians, is obvious. Despite a modest budget, it's aged better than many more expensive productions of the same era. The ending's terrific." In *Guide for the Film Fanatic* (1986), Danny Peary opined, "Cult horror film is guaranteed to keep you tense. The attack scenes are not for the faint-hearted.... Picture is full of offbeat touches and characters. Well made, but beware." Far more on the mark was Donald C. Willis in *Horror and Science Fiction Films II* (1982) when he wrote, "A gallery of psychological grotesques in a very loud, crude slash-and-stab horror thriller. Gross and unpleasant."

Confessions of an Opium Eater (1962; 85 minutes)

Producer-Director: Albert Zugsmith. Screenplay: Robert Hill, from the novel *Confessions of an English Opium Eater* by Thomas De Quincey. Photography: Joseph F. Biroc. Editors: Roy V. Livingston and Robert S. Eisen. Art Director: Eugene Lourie. Sound: Ralph Butler. Sets: Joseph Kish. Production Manager: Lonnie D'Orsa. Costumes: Norah Sharpe and Roger J. Weinberg. Makeup: Bill Turner. Continuity: Eylla Jacobs. Assistant Director: Lindsley Parsons, Jr.

CAST: Vincent Price (Gilbert "Gil" De Quincey), Lindo Ho (Ruby Low/Ling Tang), Philip Ahn (Ching Foon), Richard Loo (George Wah/Old Man), June Kim (Lotus), Yvonne Moray (Child), Alicia Lu (Ping Toy), John Mamo (Auctioneer), Arthur Wong (Kwai Tong), Jo Anne Miya,

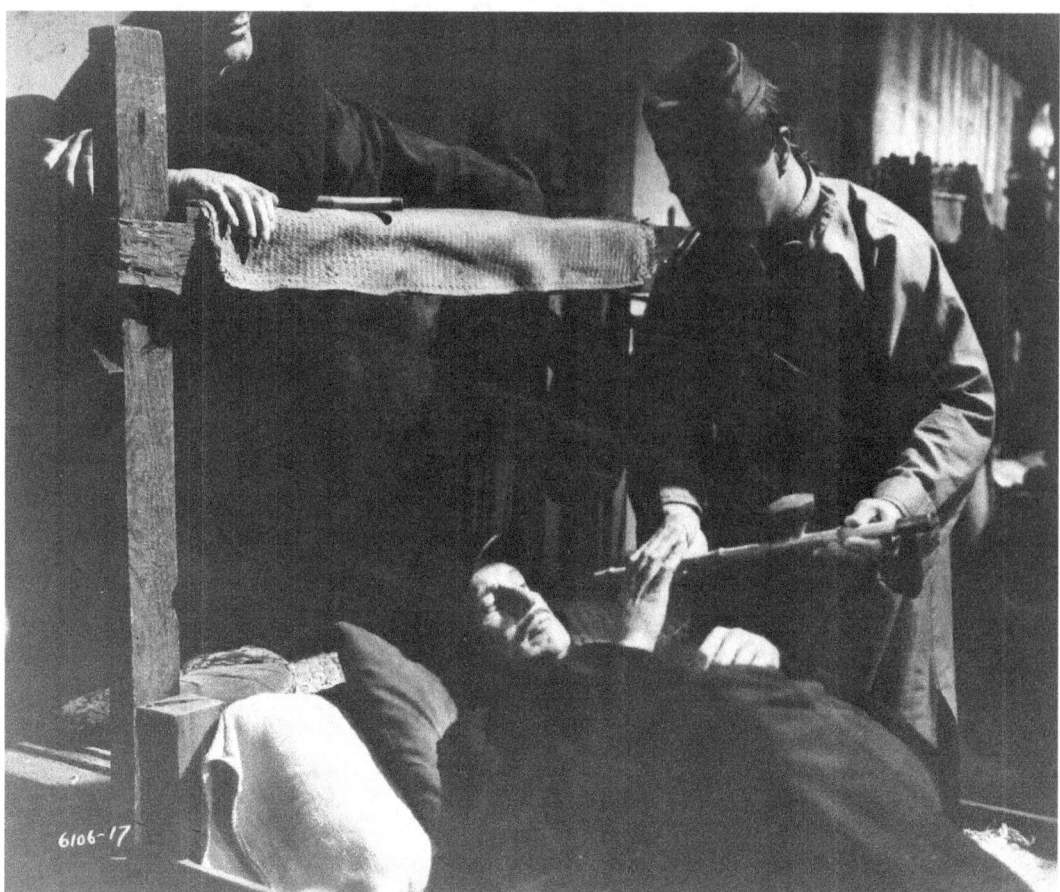

Terence De Marney, Vincent Price and Arthur Wong in *Confessions of an Opium Eater* (1962)

Geri Hoo, Keiko [Nishimura] (Dancing Girls), Carol Russell (Slave Girl), Terence de Marney (Opium Den Customer), Vincent Barbi (Captain), Caroline Kido (Lo Tsen), Gerald Jann (Fat Chinaman), Vivianne Manku (Catatonic Girl), Miel Saan (Look Gow), Victor Sen Yung (Wing Young), Ralph Ahn (Wah Chan), Richard Fong (Bidder), Roy Jenson, Charles Horvath (Boat Crewmen), Angelo Rossitto (Newspaper Seller), David Chow (Opium Eater).

In the fall of 1958 Allied Artists announced it was going to film the 1821 work *Confessions of an English Opium Eater* by Thomas De Quincey and it would be made in color in Japan by producer-director William Castle. Nothing came of the project but it was revived two years later by producer-director Albert Zugsmith Photoplay Associates with Vincent Price starring as a descendant of De Quincey and the action set in San Francisco in 1902. Released in the summer of 1962, the feature was shown in the United Kingdom as *Evils of Chinatown* and was reissued as *Secrets of a Soul* and *Souls for Sale*. Zugsmith, who had produced *The Tarnished Angels* (1957), *Touch of Evil* (1958) and *Imitation of Life* (1959), also wrote, produced and directed *Sex Kittens Go to College* (1960) [q.v.] and *Dondi* (1961) for Allied. In 1966 he directed another drug-themed feature, *Movie Star American Style, or, LSD I Hate You* for his Famous Players company.

A shipment of Chinese women arrives on the California coast but one of the captives, 17-year-old Lotus (June Kim), manages to escape. George Wah (Richard Loo) is injured fighting her captors. Adventurer Gilbert "Gil" De Quincey (Price) arrives in San Francisco and visits the antique shop of Ching Foon (Philip Ahn). A Tong war takes place over the murder of Wah, the editor of the *Chinatown Gazette*. Foon sends Gil to Ruby Low (Linda Ho), who is mourning the death of Wah although he was her enemy, with his exposés of the selling of imported slave girls to Tong members. Ruby is the mistress of elderly Ling Tang, the head of the slavery operation. After getting caught in the middle of a Tong fight, Gil breaks into the newspaper office and hears Foon talking with Lotus. Gil later questions Lotus, who tells him she was abducted from her homeland and brought to San Francisco to be sold into sexual slavery. When attackers break into the room, Gil spirits Lotus into an elevator that leads them to the sewers. As they try to escape they are attacked by four men, and the girl is carried away by them. Gil follows but is knocked out. When he comes to, he is confronted by several men wearing masks, one of whom is Foon who, like De Quincey, has the tattoo of Ling Tang. Breaking free of his bonds, Gil enters a cellar where he finds Ping Toy (Alicia Lu), diminutive Child (Yvonne Moray) and a dying girl (Vivianne Manku) in cages. Child, who is really a small adult and once the consort of Ling Tang, tells him they are being starved instead of killed outright so their ghosts will not haunt their former owners. Gil sets them free and they lead him to another room where he jumps onto a hanging cage that carries him to a balcony where he finds a passage that leads to an opium den. There he smokes an opium pipe and has terrible visions and weird dreams of attackers and monsters. Awaking, De Quincey jumps out of a window and goes into a building where he hears someone crying for help. Pursued by men with weapons, he falls from a balcony and wakes up when Ruby Low throws water on him. They are in her apartment where she reveals a secret room containing the vast treasure of Ling Tang which she plans to use to rule a province in China. They kiss and she knocks him out. Gil is placed in a cage in a room next to the area where the slave auction is being held. He also finds Child and Ping Toy have been recaptured. As young women are forced to dance for Tong members who bid for them with opium, Gil manages to get out of his cage and sets Child and Ping Toy free. He leads them to Ruby Low's apartment where they find firecrackers; he shows them how to empty gunpowder out of the fireworks and spread it throughout the building. When one of the girls proves to be bald, the Tong buyers squabble, and Ling Tang appears to arbitrate the matter. Lotus is made to dance and is purchased by an old man (Loo) for fifteen head of opium. After being given a signal by Gil, Ping Toy lights the gunpowder as the old man is revealed to be George Wah, whose death was staged so he could infiltrate the Tongs. Pandemonium erupts as the girls try to escape. Gil joins Wah in fighting their captors. Gil, Wah, Lotus, Ping Toy and Child run out of the burning building but are pursued by the Tong members. They escape through a manhole but Gil is knocked out and Child is killed. Falling into the sewer, Gil is attacked by the masked Ling Tang who turns out to be Ruby Low. He pulls her into the rapidly flowing water and they drown together.

Confessions of an Opium Eater is a confusing affair that hints that the character of Gilbert De Quincey, a descendant of Thomas De Quincey, may have some prior knowledge of the slave trade and came to San Francisco to aid Wah and his men in the Tong war — but this is not delineated in the script. The film is padded with drawn-out sequences of the captured girls dancing at the slave auction. Its only real horrific parts came at the beginning with a couple of scenes of a rotting corpse on a beach and De Quincey's later confused dream after smoking opium. The latter was mainly made up of clips from such American International features as *Invasion of the Saucer Men* and *Voodoo Woman* (both 1957) and *Earth vs the Spider* (1958).

Vincent Price is miscast in the leading role, a part better suited to any number of action stars. The feature was not popular with critics with the *Monthly Film Bulletin* referring to it as a "crude piece of claptrap." James Robert Parish and Steven Whitney in *Vincent Price Unmasked* (1974) called the film "a tattered, exploitation presentation," adding, "Price's exaggerated performance and his nonheroic demeanor were hardly an intrinsic asset to this warped–low budget offering." Michael Weldon in *The Psychotronic Encyclopedia of Film* (1983) referred to it as an "[i]ncredible, trashy drug adventure" and noted, "In the late '60s this Albert Zugsmith epic was a favorite of drugged patrons at midnight shows."

About the only highlight in this mundane adventure feature is the work of midget Yvonne Moray as Child. Her lively and ingratiating work helped provide some amusement in an otherwise drab affair. Moray's film career dated back to the mid–1930s; the actress, who was sometimes called a little Garbo, also appeared in *The Wizard of Oz* (1939).

The Cosmic Man (1959; 73 minutes)

Producer: Robert A. Terry. Associate Producer: Harry Marsh. Director: Herbert Greene. Story-Screenplay: Arthur C. Pierce. Photography: John F. Warren. Editors: Richard C. Currier and Helene Turner. Music: Paul Sawtell and Bert Shefter. Musical Director: Lou Kosloff. Sound: Philip Mitchell. Production Supervisor: Lester D. Guthrie. Special Effects: Charles Duncan. Assistant Director: Richard Del Ruth.

CAST: John Carradine (The Cosmic Man/The Stranger), Bruce Bennett (Dr. Karl Sorenson),

Paul Langton and Bruce Bennett in *The Cosmic Man* (1959)

Angela Greene (Katherine "Kathy" Grant), Paul Langton (Colonel Mathews), Scotty Morrow (Ken Grant), Lyn Osborn (Sergeant Gray), Walter Maslow (Dr. "Rich" Richie), Herbert Lytton (General Knowland), Ken Clayton (Major), Alan Wells (Sergeant), Harry Fleer (Park Ranger Bill), John Erman (Corporal), Dwight Brooks (Radar Operator), Hal Torey (Dr. Steinholtz).

Forest rangers report a UFO has landed in Stone Canyon and General Knowland (Herbert Lytton) of Air Force Intelligence orders Colonel Mathews (Paul Langton) to investigate. He also consults with astrophysicist Dr. Karl Sorenson (Bruce Bennett), who agrees to go the site. Mathews arrives at Stone Canyon with Sergeant Gray (Lyn Osborn) and they are taken to the UFO by a park ranger (Harry Fleer) and find Karl testing the area for radioactivity. The craft is a large egg-shaped sphere hovering above the ground. While the scientist theorizes the object is some type of probe, the colonel feels it might be hostile and notes that finding out how it works could give the country space supremacy. Kathy Grant (Angela Greene) and her son Ken (Scotty Morrow), who cannot walk, drive to the area to check out the local gossip about a flying saucer landing in the area, since Ken wants to be an astronomer. Kathy owns Grant's Lodge and the colonel makes a deal with her to use the facility to house his men. While she and Ken get acquainted with Karl, Mathews radios the general and questions Karl's loyalty. Knowland says the scientist, who Mathews believes is anti-military, is a major general in the reserves and one of those responsible for the atomic bomb. At his laboratory at Pacific Technical University's Science Department, Karl describes the object to his assistant, Dr. Richie (Walter Maslow), who resents the international barriers that prevent them from discussing the matter with other scientists. Richie also expresses his frustration at not being able to successfully complete a photon chamber diagram. A sergeant (Alan Wells) makes sure the landing site is well guarded and goes to the lodge where he has the feeling of an unseen presence, not realizing a light from the craft followed him. At the lodge, Mathews shares a drink with Kathy who tells him her husband was a Korean MIA and that Ken has only six months to a year to live. When the colonel leaves the room to take a telephone call from the general, Kathy is frightened by a man in black who quickly disappears. That night the town is disturbed by the presence of the black-caped shade. The next day, Richie informs Karl that all their tapes have been demagnetized and someone has made the proper corrections to the photon chamber diagram. This convinces Karl that the area is being visited by an alien. He later learns that the colonel plans to move the UFO to the local military post for inspection. When Karl leaves to go to the landing site, a stranger (John Carradine) wearing a hat, long coat and thick glasses requests a room that will provide him with privacy. At Stone Canyon, the Air Force men are unable to move the sphere with a net attached to a truck nor can it be breached with a torch. Karl determines that the object can turn light into energy and use it to emit powerful sonic blasts. This causes Mathews to demand the object be taken apart. After he arrives at the lodge, the general agrees after Karl suggests the landing site may have been chosen because it is near plants working with ion propulsion and radiation. As Mathews announces that Dr. Steinholtz (Hal Torey) is due to arrive from Washington D.C. to look into the matter, the lights go out and a powerful voice informs those present that he is an alien who has come to Earth to gain knowledge for the inhabitants of other planets; he also praises the work of Karl and his colleagues. As the alien starts to leave the room, Mathews fires at him but to no avail. Ken tells Karl about the strange man staying at the hotel and the general issues an order for the alien's capture. When Karl objects, he is placed under protective custody and told by Mathews that various weaponry plants have suffered sabotage. Karl finds out that Steinholtz plans to place a magnetic field around the UFO to stop the alien from returning to the craft. During the night,

Kathy awakens to find the stranger playing chess with her son. The man later enters the boy's room, telling him not to be afraid. The next morning Kathy finds out that Ken is missing. Karl and the sergeant, his guard, drive to the landing site over a little-used mountain path, followed by Kathy and Richie. After they arrive at the sphere, the stranger shows up carrying a sleeping Ken and puts him on the ground. He tells the military men to shut down the magnetic field so he can return to the craft since his mission is completed. The apparatus is stopped but Steinholz wants to study the alien and turns it back on, causing the Cosmic Man to collapse. Karl then turns it off as Ken wakes up and walks to his mother. A light from the craft disintegrates the space man as Ken bids him farewell. Karl announces that the alien will someday return.

The only production of Futura Pictures, *The Cosmic Man* was filmed early in 1958 and purchased by Allied Artists as a companion feature for *House on Haunted Hill* (q.v.), with theatrical issuance in February 1959. In the United Kingdom it was released by Associated British-Pathé. Despite budget limitations, it is a fairly well-made and well-acted production that is too talky and action-less. The UFO looks like a huge suspended egg and the title character, mostly shown in a negative image, is not frightening and has little screen time, despite being portrayed by top-billed John Carradine. No doubt audiences expecting a monster and a few scares were sadly disappointed. Although the sci-fier has a heartwarming ending with the paraplegic boy being cured by the Cosmic Man, the feature simply lacks the thrills its title promised. It does provide a hint of romance with Kathy being attracted to both the cerebral Karl and visceral Mathews.

Donald C. Willis in *Horror and Science Fiction Films: A Checklist* (1972) judged it "Poor" and *Castle of Frankenstein* #8 (1966) called it "[r]outine grade-B science-fiction." Ed Naha wrote in *Horrors: From Screen to Scream* (1975), "Childish romp with good intentions and fairly nice results if you don't take it too seriously…. John Carradine as the interplanetary peacemaker brings the film much more dignity than it warrants." In *Science Fiction* (1984), Phil Hardy noted, "One of a series of films of the fifties infected with the general fear of nuclear war, this engaging, low-budget oddity, like Robert Wise's far more assured *The Day the Earth Stood Still* (1951), explores the idea of a benevolent alien trying to set Earth to rights…. The film's optimistic ending has a certain naïve power."

Crashing Las Vegas (1956; 62 minutes)

Producer: Ben Schwalb. Director: Jean Yarbrough. Story-Screenplay: Jack Townley. Photography: Harry Neumann. Editor: George White. Music: Marlin Skiles. Art Director: David Milton. Sound: Joe Edmondson. Sets: Victor Ganelin. Production Manager: Allen K. Wood. Makeup: Frank McCoy. Special Effects: Ray Mercer. Wardrobe: Bert Henrikson. Production Assistant: Rex Bailey. Continuity: Richard Chaffee. Assistant Director: Edward Morey, Jr.

CAST: Leo Gorcey (Terence Aloysius "Slip" Mahoney), Huntz Hall (Horace Debussy "Sach" Jones), Mary Castle (Carol LaRue), Don Haggerty (Tony Murlock), David [Gorcey] Condon (Chuck), Terry Frost (Sergeant Kelly), Jimmy Murphy (Myron), Mort Mills (Oggy), Jack Rice (Wiley), Nicky Blair (Sam), Doris Kemper (Kate Kelly), Don Marlowe, Dick Foote (Policemen), Jack Grinnage (Bellboy), Robert Hopkins (Quiz Show Host), John Bleifer (Joe Crumb, Man in Seat 62), Emil Sitka (Man in Seat 87), Frank J. Scannell (Croupier), Joey Ray (Floor Manager/Dream Judge), Jack Chefe, Cosmo Sardo (Waiters), Frank Hagney (Guard), Speer Martin (Elevator Operator), Jimmy Brandt (Usher), Minerva Urecal (Woman), Alfred Tonkel (Man).

After starring as Slip Mahoney in 41 "Bowery Boys" programmers, Leo Gorcey called it quits with *Crashing Las Vegas*, released to theaters in the spring of 1956. The reason Gorcey gave for leaving was the death of his father Bernard Gorcey, who played the part of sweet shop owner Louie Dumbrowski for a decade. Other sources claim Leo was terminated because of excessive drinking; in some scenes in *Crashing Las Vegas* he does appear inebriated. Filmed in Las Vegas, the production has a tacky look with little of the glitter of the gambling capitol rubbing off on the tired proceedings. Huntz Hall as Sach dominates the action but his character is less appealing than usual, making the outing a chore to watch. In *The Films of the Bowery Boys* (1982), David Hayes and Brent Walker opined, "*Crashing Las Vegas* tries to spoof television game shows and gambling systems. It succeeds at doing the first, but the Las Vegas footage is comprised of just standard 'B' film plottage." *Variety* declared, "*Crashing Las Vegas* may not be the best in this long series of 'Bowery Boys' films, but has plenty of laughs.... This is Hall's film all the way, and Leo Gorcey is just shadow dressing." The film's minor link to sci-fi and fantasy deals with Sach's getting an electric shock that enables him to pick winning numbers.

Although they have no money, Slip Mahoney (Gorcey) and Sach Jones (Hall) vow to help their landlady Mrs. Kelly (Doris Kemper) when she cannot meet her mortgage payment. Sach accidentally gets shocked by an electric outlet and then goes with Slip, Chuck (David Condon) and Myron (Jimmy Murphy) to a TV quiz program with the four hoping to hit the jackpot for Mrs. Kelly. Slip manages to predict the winning number in a wheel of fortune spin, getting a month's vacation in Las Vegas. When Slip, Chuck and Myron complain, the show makes it a week for four in the glitter capitol. After getting settled in their hotel, Sach wins a big stake at another wheel of fortune game but loses it by leaving the table. Accepting a loan from Mahoney, Sach piles up another win and gets noticed by beautiful blonde gold digger Carol LaRue (Mary Castle) and her partners, Oggy (Mort Mills) and Sam (Nicky Blair). The crooks think Sach has a system and Carol plays up to him, even letting Sach believe he saved her life when she pretends to drown in the hotel swimming pool. Carol tells Sach she wants to win enough money to pay for an operation for her mother and he takes her money and promptly loses it at roulette. Carol walks out on Sach who admits to Slip that with her around he cannot think of numbers — and then proceeds to shut down the roulette wheel when he wins with his predictions. The three crooks enlists the aid of their pal Tony Murlock (Don Haggerty) and set out to fleece Sach of his gambling winnings. After Carol calls to apologize to Sach, he informs Slip they have enough money to rescue Mrs. Kelly but Slip wants him to continue gambling to pay for their retirement. After a newspaper story about Sach's luck is published, none of the gambling houses will let them play. That night Sach goes off with Carol. His pals think he has been abducted and call the police. Carol takes Sach to her apartment house and he is tricked into thinking her room is on the twenty-first floor although they never leave the ground floor. When Carol gets too friendly with Sach, Tony, who claims to be her husband, shows up and the two men get into a shoving match with Tony going out a window. As Oggy pretends to call the law, saying Sach murdered Tony, Sach rushes out of the apartment and ends up in a police car where he hears a radio call looking for him. Not realizing that it deals with his pals saying he was kidnapped, Sach thinks he is a wanted man and runs back to the hotel and takes refuge in a closet. After hearing Slip, Chuck and Myron talk about a murder, Slip passes out and dreams that he and his friends have been sentenced to the electric chair. The boys hear his cries and get him out of the closet. When Sach tells him about Tony's death, Slip realizes his pal has been framed to get his money and decides to get him a lawyer. After he leaves, Carol and Oggy show up and demand to know Sach's gambling system. Sach tells them he does not have a system but gives them his suitcase filled with the money he won and they depart. When Slip returns, Sach informs him what happened and is told there has been no murder. The boys goes to Carol's apartment and search the place as Tony, Oggy and Sam arrive with the suitcase and they all get into a fistfight. Sach and the crooks end up being knocked out. When Sach comes to, he switches on a fan that blows the money out a window. Unplugging the fan, Sach gets a shock that cancels out his powers of predicting correct numbers. The dejected boys go back to their hotel but get a telephone call from Mrs. Kelly, who has followed them to Las Vegas. They set out to find her room, but Sach guesses the wrong number and is throttled by Slip.

Huntz Hall was promoted to top billing in the "Bowery Boys" series following Leo Gorcey's departure and Stanley Clements was brought in as his replacement, playing the character Stanislaus "Duke" Coveleskie. Seven more series outings were released from 1956 to 1958, including *Hold That Hypnotist*, *Spook Chasers* and *Up in Smoke* (all 1957) [qq.v.].

Crow Hollow (1952; 69 minutes)

Producer: William H. Williams. Director: Michael McCarthy. Screenplay: Vivian Milroy, from the novel by Dorothy Eden. Photography: Robert Lapresle. Editor: Eric Hodges. Art Director: George Haslam. Sound: Sidney Rider. Production Manager: Adrian Worker. Production Supervisor: Leslie Sinclair. Makeup: Jack Craig. Wardrobe: Elsie Curtis. Continuity: Betty Harley. Assistant Director: Kenneth Rick.

CAST: Donald Houston (Dr. Robert "Bob" Amour), Natascha Parry (Ann Amour), Pat [Patricia] Owens (Willow), Esma Cannon (Aunt Judith), Nora Nicholson (Aunt Opal), Susan Richmond (Aunt Hester), R. Meadows White (Dexter), Melissa Stribling (Diana Wilson), Penelope Munday (Cass), Ewen Solon (Sergeant Jenkins), Denis Web (Police Inspector York), Georgie Herschel (Nurse Baxter), Gordon Bell (Alec), Janet Barrow (Mrs. Wilson), Norman Claridge (Hospital Doctor), Doris Yorke (Hospital Nurse).

In London, beautiful Ann Amour (Natascha Parry) awakens her roommate Cass (Penelope Munday) to tell her that she is going to marry Dr. Robert Amour (Donald Houston), whom she has known for only a week. At their wedding reception, he informs their friends that he and Ann plan to live at his family's house at remote Crow Hollow. Before leaving, the newlyweds visit Mrs. Wilson (Janet Barrow), a terminal case and an old family friend of the groom. She tells Ann that her new husband is an orphan and becomes agitated at the mention of his three aunts who live at Crow Hollow and begs the young woman not to go there. When they arrive at Crow Hollow, Bob introduces Ann to his maiden aunts, Judith (Esma Cannon), a naturalist who collects rare insects; Hester (Susan Richmond), who makes soup for invalids; and Opal (Nora Nicholson), who is greatly attached to their maid-companion, Willow (Patricia Owens). The newlyweds are given the room where the aunts' mother died forty years before. The next morning Ann meets the beautiful Willow, who brings her breakfast, but they immediately mistrust each other. Ann inspects the grounds and looks at Judith's insect collection but is frightened when she sees a large poisonous spider that has just arrived from Australia. She also meets the gardener, Dexter (R. Meadows White), who warns her not to be dominated by the three old women. After becoming upset when she finds Willow trying on her clothes, Ann drives into town with Hester and has lunch with her husband, telling him that life for her at Crow Hollow is a useless existence and she wants them to have their own home. He tries to cheer her up by saying they will attend a local dance but on the day of the festivities, when Willow is doing her hair, the poisonous spider falls on Ann's shoulder and is killed by Bob. Judith questions how the spider got out of its box; Ann contends it was not an accident. At the dance, Robert introduces her to Diana Wilson (Melissa Stribling), the daughter of the dying woman she met in London. Ann asks Diana why her mother warned her not to come to Crow Hollow and she is told that Mrs. Wilson trained Willow and was unhappy when the aunts bribed the young woman to work for them. When Ann again asks to leave, Robert tells her he promised his grandfather that his aunts would always have a home at Crow Hollow. Dexter informs Ann that the aunts were not happy when Robert married a stranger and they had felt the same way when his father, their half-brother, married the doctor's late mother Marguerite, who died 25 years before under vague circumstances. Ann visits Marguerite's grave at the local churchyard but a storm ensues and she comes down with chills and a fever. When Ann begins to recover, Hester brings her soup; when the young woman eats it she becomes deathly ill and tells Bob she was poisoned. She recovers as Judith searches for a large deadly toadstool that Dexter found for her but she only locates a bottle of strychnine, which Hester uses to poison rabbits raiding her garden, and gives it to Willow. After a 20-year absence, crows return to the property as Ann packs and informs Willow that she is going away for a time. Getting a ride to the train station, she begins to feel weak and runs into Diana and goes to her house. There Diana informs Ann that her mother felt the aunts wanted Robert to marry Willow. Diana takes Ann back to Crow Hollow where she finds Willow has been stabbed while sitting at Ann's dressing table. Ann tells Bob that she was the intended victim. She is questioned by Police Inspector York (Denis Webb) and finds out from him and Sergeant Jenkins (Ewen Solon) that the murdered girl had been adopted, her father being a gardener for Mrs. Wilson two decades before; her unknown mother may have come from a prominent family. Realizing that she is the main suspect, Ann tells the police she had left a hat on her bed before she departed and that Willow had probably tried it on; since she was stabbed from the back, the murderer mistook the maid for Ann. The inspector agrees this might be the case and he leaves a policeman at Crow Hollow and asks Diana to stay for a few days. That night Bob is called out on a case and he takes Ann to Diana's room and both women realize they did not hear the telephone ring. Ann runs to Bob, who is in the kitchen with Opal, who offers both of them coffee. They refuse to drink the brew, realizing it might be poisoned. Opal admits that Willow was her daughter and that she tried to kill Ann with Judith's spider and Hester's soup. She killed her own daughter thinking she was Ann. As the newlyweds leave to call the police, the woman drinks the coffee she planned to use to poison them. Robert tells Ann he will apply for the position of a house surgeon in Middlesex but she wants to remain at Crow Hollow.

Allied Artists released the British import *Crow Hollow* in the U.S. in 1952 following Eros Pictures debuting it in its homeland that August. Made by Bruton Film Producers at Merton Park Studios, it was called *La Isla de la Muerte* (The Island of the Dead) in Spain. Based on Dorothy Eden's 1950 novel, it is a compact and moderately entertaining psychological horror film highlighted by beautiful Natascha Parry as the heroine in harm's way. It is best remembered for providing Melissa Stribling's film debut; she later portrayed Mina in *Horror of Dracula* (1958). Patricia Owens, who played the lovely Willow, was the wife of the scientist in *The Fly* (1958). Top-billed Donald Houston was also in *Maniac* (1963), *A Study in Terror* (1965), *Tales That Witness Madness* (1973) and *Clash of the Titans* (1981), and a regular on the 1973 British sci-fi TV series *Moonbase 3*.

In *British Sound Films: The Studio Years 1928–1959* (1984), David Quinlan called it a "[g]loomy yarn, poorly made, performed without conviction. Best thing's the title."

Curse of the Voodoo (1965; 73 minutes)

Producer: Richard Gordon. Executive Producer: Kenneth Rive. Director: Lindsay Shonteff. Screenplay: Tony O'Grady [Brian Clemens] and Leigh Vance. Photography: Gerald Gibbs. Editor:

Barry Vince. Music: Brian Fahey. Art Director: Tony Inglis. Sound: Jock May. Production Executive: Fred Slark. Makeup: Gerry Fletcher. Wardrobe: Mary Gibson. Assistant Director: Bill Snaith.

CAST: Bryant Halliday (Michael "Mike" Stacey), Dennis Price (Major Lomas), Lisa Daniely (Janet Stacey), Ronald Leigh-Hunt (Doctor), Mary Kerridge (Janet's Mother), John Wittey (Police Inspector), Jean Lodge (Beva Lomas), Danny Daniels (Simbaza Chief), Dennis Alaba Peters (Saidi), Tony Thawnton (Mr. Radlett), Michael Nightingale (Second Hunter), Nigel Feyisetan (London Simbazan), Louis Mahoney (African Expert), Valli Newby (Pickup), Andy Meyers (Tommy Stacey), Jimmy Feldgate (Barman), Bobby Breen Quintet (Night Club Musicians), Beryl Cunningham (Dancer).

British film producer Richard Gordon made a number of popular genre efforts, including *Fiend Without a Face* and *The Haunted Strangler* (both 1958), *First Man into Space* (1959), *The Projected Man* and *Island of Terror* (both 1966), *Tower of Evil* (1971), *Horror Hospital* (1973) and *Inseminoid (Horror Planet)* (1981). *Curse of the Voodoo*, however, is not a high water mark in his career, since it is a boring, slow-moving and cheaply made production with an unlikable lead character. It also has a number of drawn-out sequences, such as a silly night club dance and the "hero" being stalked by vengeful natives. Filmed at Shepperton Studios in England, the film was released in that country in 1965 as *Curse of Simba*, running 61 minutes. Allied Artists issued it on the bottom half of a double bill the same year in the U.S. with *Frankenstein Meets the Space Monster* (q.v.) which probably made cinema customers want their money back. It also had some stateside showings as *Voodoo Blood Bath*. The Bobby Breen Quintet, which provided music in a night club sequence, was a black band.

During a safari in Simbaza country in Africa, Radlett (Tony Thawnton) wounds a lion but does not kill it. Simba is a lion god to the natives and the penalty is death for anyone who kills one of the beasts. Big game hunter Mike Stacey (Bryant Halliday) goes into the brush with bearer Saidi (Dennis Alaba Peters) and finishes off the wounded lion. Later, in camp, the Simbaza chief (Danny Daniels) throws a sword in front of Stacey, placing him under a black magic curse. The leader of the safari, Major Lomas (Dennis Price), orders everyone, including Mike, who was injured by the lion, to return home. On the trip back, Saidi tries to stab Mike but is stopped by Lomas and runs away. In Johannesburg, Mike learns that his wife Janet (Lisa Daniely) has taken their small son Tommy (Andy Meyers) and returned to live with her mother (Mary Kerridge) in England. Mike takes the advice of Lomas' wife (Jean Lodge) and follows Janet back to England where he meets her at his mother-in-law's country home and gives his son a stuffed lion. Mike makes a date with Janet for that evening so they can discuss a reconciliation but when she does not show up he goes home with a young woman (Valli Newby) he picks up in a bar. During the night he dreams that Saidi has been captured by the natives and when he is tortured, Mike feels the pain. He leaves the woman and walks through a wooded area where he thinks he hears a lion roar and then goes to see a doctor (Ronald Leigh-Hunt) who treats his re-opened wound. He returns to the woman who tells him he had a bad nightmare before he awoke. When he mentions hearing a lion nearby, she says a zoo is only a few blocks away. When Janet comes to see him, Mike asks her to return to Africa with him but she refuses. When he thinks he sees a Simbaza native (Nigel Feyisetan) he follows the man but loses him on a bus. That night Mike shoots at the native when he tries to break into his room. The police investigate and an inspector (John Wittey) takes his gun. When he is walking in the country, Mike sees two Simbaza natives coming at him with spears and he runs from them and wakes up to the doctor giving him a shot. The medical man says Mike's arm is infected and not healing properly. Janet, who has come to help her husband, asks about his hallucinations; the doctor thinks they may be due to his excessive drinking. Mike tells Janet the Simbazas are after him. After three days the doctor says his condition is worsening and the trouble is in his mind. Mike awakes and sees the native at his window and hears his son call for help. Janet goes to see an expert (Louis Mahoney) in African lore who tells her that anyone who kills a lion may be put under a curse by the Simbaza tribe and the only way to break the spell is to return to Africa and kill the man who placed him under a curse. After she tells him what the expert said, the weak Mike announces he plans to go back to Africa and asks her to contact Lomas to make the arrangements. In Africa, Mike tells Lomas to stay with Janet as he drives a Jeep into Simbaza country where Saidi is still being tortured. He rescues his bearer and pursues the chief on foot but runs out of ammunition. Feeling weak, Mike goes back to his Jeep and uses it to run down the chief. Relieved of the curse, Mike sets out with Saidi to return to Janet.

The same year he produced *Curse of the Voodoo*, Richard Gordon made *Devil Doll*, which also starred Bryant Halliday and was directed by Lindsay Shonteff.

The Cyclops (1957; 66 minutes)

Producer-Director-Screenplay-Special Effects: Bert I. Gordon. Associate Producer-Production Manager: Henry Schrage. Assistant Producer: Flora M. Gordon. Photography: Ira Morgan. Editor: Carlo Lodato. Music: Albert Glasser. Sound Effects: Douglas Stewart. Makeup: Carlie Taylor and Jack H. Young. Assistant Directors: Harry O. Jones [Harry L. Fraser] and Ray Taylor, Jr.

CAST: James Craig (Russ Bradford), Gloria Talbott (Susan Winter), Lon Chaney, Jr. (Marty Melville), Tom Drake (Lee Brand), Duncan [Dean] Parkin (The Cyclops — Bruce Barton), Vicente Padula (Governor), Marlene Kloss (Newsstand Girl), Manuel Lopez (Police Officer), Paul Frees (Voice Effects).

Lon Chaney, James Craig and Gloria Talbott in *The Cyclops* (1957)

Producer, director, writer and special effects artist Bert I. Gordon is best known for his sci-fi productions with giants: humans, animals and insects. Thus he has been nicknamed "Mr. BIG," relating his initials to his screen reputation. After making TV commercials and editing TV movies, Gordon's first directing effort was the wretched *King Dinosaur* (1955); next he made *The Cyclops*, the first of several films featuring human giants. *The Cyclops* was made in 1955 and was sold to RKO Radio which planned to release it on a double bill with the British import *X—The Unknown* (1956), but the studio went out of business and Gordon's film went to Allied Artists and was issued with *Daughter of Dr. Jekyll* (q.v.) in July 1957. Both features starred Gloria Talbott.

In Guayjorm, Mexico, Susan Winter (Talbott) meets with the local governor (Vicente Padula) in an attempt to obtain a permit to fly inland in search of her fiancé Bruce Barton, who disappeared during a solo plane flight three years before. The official does not trust her traveling companions, bacteriologist Russ Bradford (James Craig), who was a close friend of Bruce and now is in love with Susan; uranium hunter Marty Melville (Lon Chaney, Jr.), and pilot Lee Brand (Tom Drake), and denies her request. He also demands one of the men remain in town while a police officer flies home with them. The next day Marty knocks out the officer (Manuel Lopez) and the four take off for the interior despite being warned of downdrafts. Marty's uranium detector picks up signs of the mineral but he panics when the flight gets bumpy and knocks out Brand, causing the craft to nosedive. Susan manages to wake Lee, who lands the plane in the area where Bruce's craft may have crashed. Upon landing, Marty realizes the area is rich in uranium and wants to return immediately to Guayjorm to file a claim which will make him millions. The others refuse to leave until they find out what happened to Bruce. Looking over the area, Russ spies a dinosaur-size lizard but it quickly disappears before the others can see it. Susan and Russ search for Bruce's plane and he tells her he loves her and is tired of contending with a dead man for her affections. They hear a loud noise and see a giant hawk devour a rodent as big as a dog. They return to the plane, which Lee and Marty have turned around for takeoff, and Susan asks Russ to take possession of its keys. The four then set out to search the area and see a fight between a giant iguana and a lizard. Marty insists they return home and Russ agrees but first he takes a skin sample from the mortally wounded iguana. At their camp he determines that its cells are multiplying at a fantastic rate. He theorizes that the creatures were originally normal size but radioactivity caused them to mutate and become giants. Russ warns the same thing can happen to humans. While the men sleep, Susan searches for her fiancé's plane and, seeing

Gloria Talbott is astounded to see *The Cyclops* (1957).

something towering over her, she screams. The others locate her in a cave which also contains airplane parts. As Russ tries to calm her, a 25-foot-tall giant (Duncan Parkin) with a disfigured face and one eye blocks the cave entrance with a huge rock. Russ theorizes that the Cyclops' is due to radiation and he hopes to be able to communicate with him although all the creature does is emit loud roars. As the group sleeps, Marty takes Russ' gun. The creature returns and Russ suggests that Susan try to talk to it. As she is doing so, Marty shoots at the giant, who kills him, picks up the young woman and sets her on the boulder. She screams when she sees a gigantic snake which the Cyclops eventually subdues. Russ and Lee climb out of the cave and the trio set out for their landing site. As they stop to rest, Russ convinces Susan that the giant is Bruce. The trio creep past the sleeping Cyclops and get back to the plane. The craft will not start. When they see the Cyclops approaching, the three run into the hills. Afraid the creature will wreck the plane, Russ lures him away. Climbing into some rocks, he ties dry grass onto the end of a long stake, sets it on fire and throws it into the giant's eye, causing him to collapse. Susan, Russ and Lee get back in the plane which Lee gets started. Just as they take off, the giant returns but the plane flies over him and out of the area. As they head home, Susan looks down to see the man she once loved dead on the ground.

Filmed at Griffith Park and Bronson Caves, *The Cyclops* has been criticized for tacky special effects and an arid plot. For Baby Boomers watching it for the first time on TV in the 1960s, it was more than passably good entertainment, with a hideous monster, giant wildlife and an over-the-top performance by genre star Lon Chaney, Jr., who earlier had the title role in Allied's *Indestructible Man* (1956) [q.v.].

The film was no critical success, although it fared well at the box office. Regarding the title monster, the *Monthly Film Bulletin* opined, "The Cyclops, revoltingly ugly and emitting horrible noises, does not survive searching close-ups, but despite this limitation he makes an unusually grim addition to the gallery of screen monsters." *Castle of Frankenstein* #8 (1966) called it a "[d]ismal low-grade adventure.... Inept special fx by Bert I. Gordon." Dennis Fischer wrote in *Science Fiction Film Directors, 1895–1998* (2000), "The effects consist of bad superimpositions and awkwardly staged split screen shots. The plot is rambling and practically non-existent, with only Albert Glasser's score and some hamming from the usually drunk Chaney maintaining any interest whatsoever." In *Horror and Science Fiction Films: A Checklist* (1972), Donald C. Willis termed the feature "[c]lumsy and boring." Steven H. Scheuer's *Movies on TV, 1975–76 Edition* (1974) concurred, calling it a "[h]umdrum thriller."

Daughter of Dr. Jekyll (1957; 70 minutes)

Producer-Screenplay: Jack Pollexfen. Associate Producer: Ilse Lahn. Director: Edgar G. Ulmer. Photography: John F. Warren. Editor: Holbrook N. Todd. Music Supervisor: Melvyn Lenard. Art Director: Theobold Holsopple. Sound: Fred Kessler. Sets: Mowbray Berkeley. Production Manager: Joseph Boyle. Makeup: Lou Philippi. Wardrobe: Robert Martien. Special Effects: Louis DeWitt and Jack Rabin.

CAST: John Agar (George Hastings), Gloria Talbott (Janet Smith), Arthur Shields (Dr. Lomas), John Dierkes (Jacob), Mollie McCard (Maggie), Martha Wentworth (Mrs. Merchant), Marjorie Stapp (Undressing Woman), Rita Greene (Lucy), Marel Page (Lucy's Beau).

Producer-writer Jack Pollexfen and director Edgar G. Ulmer first worked together on *The Man from Planet X* in 1950. In 1954 Pollexfen produced and directed *Indestructible Man* (q.v.) for Allied Artists and two years later he and Ulmer re-teamed for *Daughter of Dr. Jekyll*, the writer's second foray into the adventures of offspring of the Robert Louis Stevenson characters (he co-wrote 1951's *The Son of Dr. Jekyll*). The movie not only had Miss Jekyll, nee Janet Smith, nicely enacted by the beautiful Gloria Talbott, but it also featured a werewolf. In fact, the script had the Hyde character, Jekyll's horrid alter ego, turning into a lycanthrope before being dispatched with a stake through the heart. The script blurred the folklore of vampires and werewolves and in one scene hero John Agar reads a book about lyncathropy which gives the hairy, murderous beast the blood-drinking traits of a vampire. The feature was made by Film Ventures Productions and issued theatrically in July 1957 on a double-bill with *The Cyclops* (q.v.), also headlining Talbott.

On a foggy night, Janet Smith (Talbott) and her fiancé George Hastings (Agar) arrive at the English country manor of Dr. Lomas (Arthur Shields). The next day is her twenty-first birthday. She is greeted by Mrs. Merchant (Martha Wentworth), the housekeeper, and also meets taciturn Jacob (John Dierkes), the groundskeeper, and Maggie (Mollie McCard), a maid. Maggie expresses fear of the rising moon and says she will not sleep in the manor house; Mrs. Merchant tells Janet the villagers are superstitious. Lomas informs Janet that the house and grounds are hers and she will inherit the estate and a sizable fortune, although her late father's will states that he can live in the house for the rest of his life. The doctor says the young woman was never told of her wealth in order to thwart suitors who might only want her for her money. He also announces that he will have more to tell her the next day. Morning finds Janet and George exploring the house and coming upon a secret room filled with scientific paraphernalia. Lomas finds them there and says the room was used by Janet's father as his laboratory. The doctor asks to talk to Janet alone. Later, the distraught woman informs George that she cannot marry him and asks him to leave the estate. He demands an explanation and she asks Lomas to tell him the truth. The doctor takes them to the family tomb and shows them the grave of Dr. Henry Jekyll, Janet's father. Lomas says that he and Jekyll were medical students together and Henry did great scientific work but a strange experiment caused him to withdraw from the world. Jekyll's theory, Lomas said, was that all men are part good and part evil and he tried to develop drugs to separate them and used himself as a guinea pig, inadvertently turning himself into a murderous fiend. The villagers hunted down the evil Mr. Hyde and drove a stake through his heart — but now they believe he still prowls as a werewolf when there is a full moon. George rebuffs the notion that what her father did will affect Janet and demands they leave the next day to get married. In order to help Janet sleep, Lomas uses hypnosis. As the fearful Maggie walks home under a full moon, Janet dreams that she chases Maggie and kills her. When Janet wakes up screaming, she is comforted by George. Lomas gives her a sedative but she finds blood on her hands and gown, mud on her shoes and sees a hideous visage when she looks in a mirror. The next morning Jacob carries in the body of Maggie, whose throat has been horribly torn. He refers to Janet as Miss Jekyll and later tells Mrs. Merchant the villagers will take care of the young woman like they did her father by driving a stake through her heart. Before going to sleep that night, Janet is given a strong sedative by the doctor as George makes sure that her bedroom windows are tightly sealed. Still she dreams of running through the woods, attacking and murdering a young woman (Rita Greene) who has left her lover (Marel Page) after a spat. She again wakes with blood on her hands and clothes. George explains that the blood came from her cutting herself during the dream. Jacob soon arrives with the news that another girl has been found murdered and says Janet is a werewolf. Lomas fires Jacob; Mrs. Merchant gives her notice. Leaving George to look after Janet, the doctor goes into town for new servants and the young woman begs her fiancé to kill her. Later, when Janet cannot be found, George and Lomas search the grounds and locate her in the family burial vault. Nearby is Jacob fashioning a stake; Lomas orders him off the property. Janet learns from the doctor that she cannot leave the area because she is scheduled to testify at a coroner's inquest regarding the two murders. That night Janet is again given a sedative and Lomas says he will sit with her. After she is asleep, he puts her under hypnosis and has her follow him through a secret passage to the vault. George wakes up and trails them and in the tomb he overhears Lomas tell the hypnotized Janet to hang herself. He then sees the doctor turn into a werewolf. George and Lomas fight, and George is knocked out. The werewolf goes to the village where he spies a young woman (Marjorie Stapp) undressing and attacks her; her screams alert the villagers. They follow the wolfman back to the tomb where he is wounded by Jacob. George wakes up in time to save Janet from hanging herself and tells her Lomas is a murderer who wants her money for himself. Seeing the werewolf return, he tells her to pretend to be asleep. As the beast starts to caress the girl, George jumps him and they fight. The villagers swarm in the crypt and Jacob plunges a stake into the werewolf's heart, killing him.

The film opens and closes with shots of a man in werewolf makeup; at the end of the picture, the monster suggests to the audience he may return. His lyncanthrope makeup was pretty perfunctory, albeit with fangs.

Ulmer has developed a cult following although one is hard pressed to see much reason for it in *Daughter of Dr. Jekyll*. Actor Brian Aherne, in his book *A Dreadful Man* (1979), talked about working on Ulmer's final production, *The Cavern* (1965). He called him "a rather florid, temperamental character who had much experience and some talent but so far not much success." Ulmer's other genre outings include *The Black Cat* (1934), *Bluebeard* (1944), *The Amazing Transparent Man* and *Beyond the Time Barrier* (both 1960) and *Journey Beneath the Desert* (1961).

In *Classic Movie Monsters* (1978), Donald F. Glut said *Daughter of Dr. Jekyll* was "incredibly low budgeted.... Allied Artists' dubious contribution to the mythos[, it] was directed without style by Edgar G. Ulmer, and was the most unorthodox treatment of the Stevenson theme yet." He also noted that the feature was padded for its TV release and "some of the frames were double-printed to stretch out the action, while Janet's nightmare sequence was augmented by stock footage from Allied Artists' *Frankenstein 1970*, made in 1958. Strangely, the Frankenstein Monster of the one film became the Mr. Hyde of the other."

The Day of the Triffids (1962; 94 minutes; Color)

Producer: George Pitcher. Executive Producer: Philip Yordan. Directors: Steve Sekely and (uncredited) Freddie Francis. Screenplay: Philip Yordan (for uncredited Bernard Gordon), from the novel by John Wyndham. Photography: Ted Moore. Editor: Spencer Reeve. Music: Ron Goodwin and Johnny Douglas. Art Director: Cedric Dawe. Sound: Bert Ross and Maurice Askew. Production Manager: George Fowler. Special Effects Photography: Wally Veevers. Wardrobe: Bridget Sellers. Continuity: Pamela Davies. Assistant Director: Douglas Hermes.

CAST: Howard Keel (Bill Masen), Nicole Maurey (Christine Durrant), Janette Scott (Karen Goodwin), Kieron Moore (Tom Goodwin), Mervyn Johns (Mr. Coker), Janina Faye (Susan), Ewan Roberts (Dr. Soames), Alison Leggatt (Miss Coker), Geoffrey Matthews (Luis de la Vega), Gilgi Hauser (Teresa de la Vega), John Tate (SS Midland Captain), Carol Ann Ford (Bettina), Arthur Gross (Flight Radioman), Collette Wilde (Nurse Jamieson), Ian Watson (Royal Botanic Gardens Night Watchman), Victor Brooks (Poiret), Katya Douglas (Mary), Gary Hope (Pilot), Thomas Gallagher (Heavyset Man), Sidney Vivian (Blind Ticket Agent), John Simpson (Blind Man).

Based on John Wyndham's 1951 novel, *The Day of the Triffids* was put together by Philip Yordan, who took screenplay credit for blacklisted Bernard Gordon. Onetime Hollywood

Lobby card for *The Day of the Triffids* (1963)

musical star Howard Keel headlined the production but was not happy with the final product as noted by a career article on him by Michael B. Druxman in *Films in Review* (November 1970) in which he commented, "[T]he screenplay had no story-line and I wrote a lot of my own dialogue. The picture was under-financed and the special effects were very poor. When I left England I told the producer he didn't have a finished film, that he hadn't shot enough footage. I was right. A year later they shot the lighthouse sequences, with Kieron Moore and Janette Scott, which were needed to tie the story together." The additional material was directed by Freddie Francis over a five-week period and interpolated into the footage done by director Steve Sekely. Its working titles were *Invasion of the Triffids* and *Revolt of the Triffids*.

On a night when the world is bombarded by meteors, at the Royal Botanic Gardens a night watchman (Ian Wilson) is devoured by a huge "walking" plant. Bill Masen (Keel), an American seaman, is resting in a nearby English hospital where he underwent eye surgery ten days before. He begs Dr. Soames (Ewan Roberts) to remove his bandages a day early so he can see the meteor show but the physician refuses. When Bill wakes up the next morning, he is unable to rouse anyone. Taking off the bandages, he finds out his sight is normal but the hospital is a wreck and deserted except for Soames, who is blind due to the glare of the meteors. The doctor commits suicide by jumping from a window. At a remote lighthouse, Tom Goodwin (Moore) and his wife Karen (Scott) are carrying out marine biology work. Tom is a heavy drinker and their marriage is on the rocks. When their supply boat does not arrive, they hear on the radio that the meteor shower has blinded most people, and that a new plant that can uproot itself and move around has a fatal sting. Bill leaves the hospital and walks through a mostly deserted London. At a train station he rescues a sighted young girl, Susan (Janina Faye), from the crowd after a wreck. She tells him she ran away from school and had hidden in the train's luggage van and did not see the meteors. As they walk through the city they see a dog killed by a huge plant. After going to Bill's ship they take a deserted car. Getting stuck along the road they search for rocks to put under the wheels for traction. Seeing a giant plant coming toward them, the two barely escape. The next day they arrive at a dock area where they hear a mayday from a ship and see an aircraft crash. Bill and Susan take a speedboat and head to France because they heard a meeting of sighted survivors was to take place in Paris. At the lighthouse, Karen sees a large plant growing; when it tries to attack her and her husband, Tom manages to destroy it. Arriving in Paris, Bill and Susan find the meeting has been cancelled. On the road out of the city they meet sighted Christine Durrant (Nicole Maurey) who takes them to her chateau where Mr. Coker (Mervyn Johns) and his sister (Alison Leggatt) are caring for her blind neighbors. Susan makes friends with a blind young woman, Bettina (Carol Ann Ford). At the lighthouse, Tom and Karen examine the plant in an attempt to determine its makeup; while they rest, it breaks out of the building. Bill decides to find help and he and Coker go for supplies. They see a number of the carnivorous plants growing; Coker calls them Triffids, since their scientific name is Triffidus Celestus, and says they were brought to Earth by the meteors and propagate by emitting millions of spores. The two men see a light plane crash and go to the site but are surrounded by Triffids. As they try to escape, Coker is killed. When Bill returns to the chateau he finds it has been taken over by a band of drunken escaped prisoners. He manages to rescue Susan and Christine but the encroaching Triffids kill Bettina and break into the chateau. Bill, Christine and Susan take the prison van to Toulon, which is in flames, and decide to travel to the U.S. naval base near Cadiz in Spain. Finding a circus truck, they drive it to a villa where they find a couple, the de la Vegas (Geoffrey Matthews, Gilgi Hauser), who are expecting their first child. As Bill places electric wiring around the house, Christine helps the blind woman deliver a baby boy. Hundreds of Triffids converge on the villa and the electric current holds them off as Bill uses fire to burn the vanguard of the invaders. Susan suggests that sound attracts the plants so Bill shuts down the generator, proving her to be correct. To lure the Triffids away from the villa, Bill drives the circus truck and plays music. As the Triffids follow him, Christine and Susan drive away with the trio planning to meet at Alaconte, where a naval rescue is planned. Later Bill abandons the circus truck and after an overland trek he is rescued by a lifeboat and reunited with Christine and Susan. At the light house, the Triffids invade the building, forcing Tom and Karen to climb to its top. In a final desperate act, Tom sprays the invaders with sea water and they dissolve.

Despite its production problems, *The Day of the Triffids* turned out to be a fairly entertaining sci-fi effort with an especially strong performance by Howard Keel as the seaman, along with Janette Scott and Kieron Moore in the claustrophobic lighthouse sequences. Janina Faye was also very good as the orphan; she had earlier been impressive as the little girl who accused a local stalwart of being a child molester in Hammer Films' *Never Take Sweets from a Stranger* (1961). The different sequences directed by Steve Sekely and Freddie Francis mesh well together and the title monsters are quite scary, being tall, mobile, repulsive plants with a taste for human flesh.

Variety opined, "Although riddled with script inconsistencies and irregularities, it is a more-than-adequate film of its genre." The *New York Times* felt the movie was "pretty good, considering the modest budget." *Video Watchdog* (Jan.-Feb. 1991) said it was a "semi-successful filming of John Wyndham's classic novel." In *The Science Fictionary* (1980), Ed Naha stated, "The special effects nearly steal the show in this colorful adaptation of John Wyndham's excellent novel of the same name. Much of the book's tension has been lost in the cinematic narrative, but what remains is riveting."

Apparently footage was cut from the film before its U.S. theatrical release. *Castle of Frankenstein* #3 (1963) has a two-page spread on the production showing a Triffid aboard an airplane, panicking the passengers and attacking the crew. In 1964 the French publication Star-Cine Cosmos issued a photo story magazine of the film entitled *Les Monstres Verts* (The Green Monsters). *The Day of the Triffids* was remade twice, first in 1981 by BBC-TV and again in 2009 as a television mini-series.

Deborah (1974; 110 minutes; Color)

Producer: Paolo Prestano. Director: Marcello Andrei. Screenplay: Marcello Andrei, Piero Regnoli and Giuseppe Pulieri. Story: Giuseppe Puilieri. Photography: Claudio Racca. Editor: Gianni Oppedisano. Music: Alberto Verrecchia. Sound: Roberto Albertini. Makeup: Lamberto Martini. Production Design–Sets: Elena Ricci Poccetto. Production Manager: Diego Spataro. Assistant Director: Alfredo Varelli.

CAST: Bradford Dillman (Professor Michael Lagrange), Marina Malfatti (Deborah "Debbie" Lagrange), Gig Young (Herman Ofenbauer), Delia Boccardo (Mira Wener), Micaela Esdra (Elena), Lucretia Love (Mrs. Ofenbauer), Gigi Casellato (Psychiatrist), Vittorio Mangano (Dr. M. Vajda), Adriano Amidel Migliano (Albert Wener), Mario Garriba (Hospital Doctor).

Attending a carnival with her husband, Professor Michael Lagrange (Bradford Dillman), Deborah (Marina Malfatti) witnesses a trapeze performer fall, something the young woman predicts in her own mind just before it happens. At home Deborah pays more attention to her German shepherd dog Igor than to her husband. When she goes to see Michael at the university research center where he works, she overhears him talk about her to his pretty assistant Elena (Micaela Esdra). When Michael tries to celebrate their anniversary and wants to make love to his wife, Deborah rejects him and he tells her they cannot go on this way. He says she is upset because she cannot become pregnant, something she wants very much. After her doctor (Vittorio Mangano) tells Deborah she cannot have children, she and Michael attend a party given by their friend, parapsychologist Herman Ofenbauer (Gig Young), and his wife (Lucretia Love). Herman conducts an experiment in which he has Deborah pick a book and show it to the other guests. He then sends them to another room and tells them to use their thought processes to tell him its title. While Herman is blindfolded, Deborah sees wine glasses start to tingle and is nearly blinded by a bright yellow light before the glasses shatter; she faints. As Michael is taking her home, they witness a car accident in which a young woman, Mira Wener (Delia Boccardo), is thrown from the vehicle. At home Igor becomes hostile to Deborah. That night she dreams of the crash and the woman and becomes ill. Michael tells Herman about the accident and is told that Deborah is a very powerful medium and that kinetic energy flowing from her caused the glasses to break. Michael says his wife is obsessed with having a baby. After Michael and Deborah read the news reports of the auto accident, Herman takes Deborah to a children's home where she plays with the little ones. Herman tells Michael he and Deborah should adopt a child. As Michael and Deborah dance that night, she informs him she is pregnant. Her doctor later tells him she has a false pregnancy, but it may be dangerous to tell her the truth. As she begins wearing maternity clothes, Deborah meets Mira who says she has been told her baby has died but she does not believe it. The two women become friends and Deborah does a sculpture of her. Going to a zoo, Deborah sees an image of Mira and hears loud, piercing animal sounds. When her friend arrives, she leaves quickly when she sees Michael. Herman informs Michael that since he pretends to accept Deborah's pregnancy, it has heightened her isolation because she does not believe he is telling her the truth. He also tells Michael to go away with his wife. When he tries to make love to her that night, Deborah rejects Michael, saying sex is bad for the child. He informs her she is not pregnant and that she is a lunatic but that he wants to help her. Michael goes to a bar where he is found by Elena, who is in love with him; she tells him he only cares for himself. When Michael returns home he finds his wife in a frantic state, smashing her artwork. Failing to calm her down, he calls in a doctor and blames Herman for her condition. Michael has Deborah placed in a clinic where she has dreams of him having an affair with Elena. Deborah tells Michael she needs for him to believe she is pregnant and asks to be taken home. When Deborah escapes from the clinic, the psychiatrist (Gigi Casellato) calls the police. Michael returns home and finds Igor dead and the house ransacked. Desperate, Michael asks to see Albert Wener (Adriano Amidel Migliano), who survived the car crash, and when he goes to his house he finds a pool party going on. He tells Wener he thinks Deborah is with his wife Mira but the man informs him that Mira died shortly after the wreck. Deborah is inside the Wener home where she finds Mira in a dark room. Mira claims Deborah stole the baby from her after the crash and it belongs to her. When Mira dissolves away, Deborah, who is suffering birth pangs, tries to drive to a hospital but ends up wrecking her car. While waiting with Herman and Elena for information about his wife, Michael gets a telephone call saying she has been taken to a hospital. When the trio arrive there, Michael is informed by the doctor (Mario Garriba) that Deborah has died but they were able to save the baby.

Allied Artists released this Italian import in the U.S.; it was made by Paola Film as *Un Fiocco Nero per Deborah* (A Black Ribbon for Deborah). Its only stateside box office pull came from Hollywood stars Bradford Dillman and Gig Young, who were not dubbed as was the rest of the cast, and that proved to be very slight. Young appears wan and dissipated. When it was shown in Great Britain on video in 1984 it was re-titled *The Torment* and was cut by nine minutes. Luca M. Palmerini and Gaetano Mistretta in *Spaghetti Nightmares* (1996) termed it a "[m]ediocre copy of *Rosemary's Baby.*" For the most part, *Deborah* is a pointless excursion into psychological horror and is padded with long, drawn-out sequences involving dreams, dancing and hallucinations.

Destination 60,000 (1957; 65 minutes)

Producers: Philip N. Krasne and Jack J. Gross. Director-Screenplay: George Waggner. Photography: Hal McAlpin. Editor: Kenneth G. Crane. Music: Albert Glasser. Art Director: Nicolai Remisoff. Sound: Herman Lewis. Sets: Arthur Friedrich. Costumes: Byron Munson. Assistant Directors: Hal Klein and Ira Stewart.

CAST: Preston Foster (Colonel Ed Buckley), Pat Conway (Jeff Connors), Jeff Donnell (Ruth Buckley), Coleen Gray (Mary Ellen), Bobby Clark (Skip Buckley), Denver Pyle (Mickey Hill), Russell Thorson (Dan Maddox), Anne Barton (Grace Hill).

Destination 60,000 is a film with a science fiction plot that has long been outdated. In fact, even before its release, it was already passé story-wise. The feature's highpoint of an aircraft reaching 60,000 feet happened in real life more than two weeks before Allied Artists released the film to theatres in May 1957. On April 26, the Jupiter rocket was launched at Cape Canaveral. The flight was to test the design version of the craft's airframe and rocket engine and lasted 93 seconds, reaching a 60,000 foot altitude. Although terminated, the flight was considered partially successful. On the other hand, Concorde was the first commercial jet to reach the 60,000 feet altitude on March 2, 1969, a dozen years after *Destination 60,000*.

Pilot Jeff Connors (Pat Conway) wants to test-fly *The Dream*, an experimental craft designed and constructed by Colonel Ed Buckley (Preston Foster) and Dan Maddox (Russell Thorson), the owners of Buckley Aircraft Corporation. During World War II, Jeff saved Ed's life and he is a close friend of his wife Ruth (Jeff Donnell) and the godfather of their son Skip (Bobby Clark). He is also attracted to the company's secretary, Mary Ellen (Coleen Gray). After passing a physical examination, Jeff studies with another pilot, Mickey Hill (Denver Pyle), to get back into the regimen of flying jet planes. Hill volunteers to test a new fuel by flying to an altitude of 60,000 feet but since his wife Grace (Anne Barton) is going to have a baby, Ed asks Jeff to carry out the assignment. During the flight, Jeff follows orders and turns off the plane's rockets for ten seconds and then tries starting them again but the latter function fails and Ed radios him to eject from the craft. Jeff tries to fly *The Dream* back to the airfield but it blows up and he is ejected, making a safe landing when his automatic parachute opens. Ed speculates that gases may have accumulated when the rockets were switched off. Jeff cannot remember if he tried to turn on the ignition switch a second time before blacking out. Since he did not carry out orders, Jeff is put on a thirty-day suspension by Ed but he resigns. Ed and Maddox design a new aircraft and when it is completed, Hill is assigned to fly it to the 60,000 foot altitude. Again the rockets fail to restart and the pilot blacks out as the plane dives to the ground. Hill's arm accidentally bumps the seat ejector switch but he is badly hurt upon landing. After talking with Mickey and Grace in the hospital, Jeff realizes that Hill will heal and he makes up with Ed, completes his suspension and starts seeing Mary Ellen again. Maddox concludes that the two planes crashed because of ignition switch failures and he and Ed begin work on a third model but have trouble getting financial support from lending institutions. Although it might be dangerous, Ed decides to conduct a power dive before a second ignition with the new aircraft. The recovered Hill, who has just become the father of a baby boy, wants to fly the mission. Hill's doctor nixes the idea and Jeff, who has become engaged to Mary Ellen, wants to carry out the assignment but Ed declares he will complete the mission. Jeff asks his friend to think of his wife and son but he refuses to listen so Jeff gets permission to trail him in a second craft. Ed flies the new model to 60,000 feet and is able to re-ignite the rockets but passes out. Jeff has Mary Ellen send a radio message to Ed's plane with code words they used during the war. Ed regains consciousness and is able to safely land the new *Dream*.

Only a passable programmer with a paltry sci-fi angle, *Destination 60,000* was the final big-screen outing for director George Waggner, who in the early to mid–1940s made some of Universal Pictures' classic horror films. He directed *Man Made Monster*, *Horror Island* and *The Wolf Man* (all 1941) and *The Climax* (1944). He was also the producer of *The Wolf Man* and *The Climax* and served in the same capacity for *Invisible Agent* and *The Ghost of Frankenstein* (both 1942), *Frankenstein Meets the Wolf Man* and *Phantom of the Opera* (both 1943).

Dig That Uranium (1955; 61 minutes)

Producer: Ben Schwalb. Director: Edward Bernds. Screenplay: Elwood Ullman and Bert Lawrence. Photography: Harry Neumann. Editor: William Austin. Music: Marlin Skiles. Art Director: David Milton. Sound: Ralph Butler. Sets: Joseph Kish. Production Manager: Allen K. Wood. Makeup: Emile LaVigne. Special Effects: Ray Mercer. Wardrobe: Bert Henrikson. Continuity: Richard Chaffee. Assistant Director: Austen Jewell.

CAST: Leo Gorcey (Terence Aloysius "Slip" Mahoney/Lone Disarranger #1), Huntz Hall

(Horace Debussy "Sach" Jones/Lone Disarranger #2), Bernard Gorcey (Louie Dumbrowski/Bartender), Mary Beth Hughes (Jeanette/Saloon Girl), Raymond Hatton (Hank "Mac" McKenzie), Harry Lauter (Ron Haskell), Myron Healey (Joe Hody/Pecos Pete), Richard Powers (Frank Loomis/Idaho Ike), Paul Fierro (Indian), David [Gorcey] Condon (Chuck/Saloon Customer), Bennie Bartlett (Butch/Saloon Customer), Francis McDonald (Indian Chief), Frank Jenks (Mechanic Olaf), Carl "Alfalfa" Switzer (Shifty Robertson), Don C. Harvey (Tex).

When Sach Jones' (Huntz Hall) old pal Shifty Robertson (Carl "Alfalfa" Switzer) arrives in town he takes him to Louie Dumbrowski's (Bernard Gorcey) sweet shop to see their buddies Slip Mahoney (Leo Gorcey), Chuck (David Condon) and Butch (Bennie Bartlett). Shifty brags about owning a uranium mine that has made him rich. When he offers to sell the deed to Louie, Slip talks the old man into buying it. Shifty then makes a quick escape from the Bowery. The group drives their old jalopy to Panther Pass, Nevada, and are shot at by Joe Hody (Myron Healey) and Frank Loomis (Richard Powers), henchmen of hotel owner Ron Haskell (Harry Lauter), who does not want anyone prospecting in the area. While the boys eat at a restaurant, waitress Jeanette (Mary Beth Hughes) hears Sach brag about their uranium mine and she informs Haskell. When Sach accidentally upsets Loomis' drink, the henchman forces him to consume powerful "Old Vesuvius," causing a fight to ensue. Haskell stops the brawl and offers the boys rooms since he wants to find the location of their uranium strike. Jeanette learns from Sach that Louie has the deed to the mine. Haskell gets Louie into a card game along with Hody and Loomis. They plan to fleece him and force him to give up the deed, but the more they try to cheat the more he wins. After getting their car repaired, with the mechanic (Frank Jenks) installing a new reverse gear, the boys drive to Bearclaw Canyon to find their Little Daisy mine. When Slip and Sach argue over the latter's use of a Geiger counter, the two henchmen watch them from a distance through binoculars and think they have found uranium. They two leave to tell their boss as the boys meet old-time prospector Hank "Mac" McKenzie (Raymond Hatton) who says the Little Daisy is a played-out silver mine. When the discouraged New Yorkers return to their hotel, a rock with an attached note telling them to stay out of the area in thrown through their window. That night McKenzie tells them a story about old-time outlaw Pecos Pete. As he talks, Sach goes to sleep and dreams that he and Slip are Rangers who stop Pete (Healey) and his pal Idaho (Powers) from bothering a saloon girl (Hughes) and wrecking Louie's (Bernard Gorcey) saloon. During a showdown, Sach shoots Idaho and Slip eliminates Pecos Pete. Sach wakes up and the boys agree to continue their prospecting the next day. After Hody and Loomis tell him the Little Daisy mine has no uranium, Haskell and his men observe Sach and McKenzie find the ore and attack them. The old prospector makes a getaway on his mule Josephine while Sach is knocked over a cliff. Hank gets to the boys' camp and tells them what happened to Sach and they take their jalopy and try to locate him. Finding Sach on a ledge, they bring him up with a rope but Haskell and his men arrive and promise to shoot them. Much to Slip's chagrin, Sach suggests to the hotel owner that driving them over a cliff in their own car would be easier. Haskell tells Sach to drive the boy's jalopy and he and his men follow him in another car. Sach uses the new powerful reverse gear on the jalopy to outsmart the crooks whose car careens over a cliff. The wreck uncovers uranium at their mine but an Indian chief (Francis McDonald) and his tribe show up, claiming ownership since the area is on their reservation. When the chief offers Slip flowers, he refuses but Sach accepts and the gift proves to be lovely maiden Spring Wildflowers.

The fortieth of forty-eight "Bowery Boys" adventures, *Dig That Uranium* was filmed as *Operation Uranium* and was released to theaters in late December 1955. It was the final series film for both Bernard Gorcey, who was killed in an automobile accident, and Bennie Bartlett. The comedy western fits into the realm of film fantasy due to its dream sequence which David Hayes and Brent Walker in *The Films of the Bowery Boys* (1984) called "one of the best in the series." *Variety* termed it "filler fare" but added that Gorcey and Hall "cavort again in the same manner which seemingly has pleased followers of this series for years, pair having long ago mastered their respective roles." The feature's location shooting was done at the Iverson Ranch in the San Fernando Valley. Western film stalwarts Richard Powers, Harry Lauter and Myron Healey add authenticity to the proceedings as does Mary Beth Hughes as their cohort.

The Disembodied (1957; 68 minutes)

Producer: Ben Schwalb. Director: Walter Grauman. Screenplay: Jack Townley. Photography: Harry Neumann. Editor: William Austin. Music: Marlin Skiles. Art Director: David Milton. Sound: Ralph Butler. Production Manager: Allen K. Wood. Sets: Joseph Kish. Makeup: Emile LaVigne. Continuity: Richard Michaels. Assistant Director: Austen Jewell.

CAST: Paul Burke (Tom Maxwell), Allison Hayes (Tonda Metz), John Wengraf (Dr. Karl Metz), Eugenia Paul (Lara), Joel Marston (Norman "Norm" Adams), Robert Christopher (Joe Lawson), Norman Frederic [Dean Fredericks] (Suba), A.E. Okonu (Voodoo Drummer), Paul Thompson (Gogi), Otis Greene (Kabar), Samadu Jackson (Witch Doctor), Gloria Jean Reynolds, Donna Jean Jones (Dancers), Cecil Penrice, Julius Chabata, Alex Koffi Ametowo (Musicians).

Filmed as *Voodoo Girl* and *Voodoo Queen*, *The Disembodied* was released in the late summer of 1957 on a dual bill with another jungle horror thriller, *From Hell It Came* (q.v.). Since the latter deals with a vengeful, walking tree, it is hard to believe it could be the better of the two offerings but *The Disembodied*, thanks to its vapidity and overall stagebound cheapness, takes second place to its theatrical mate. Phil Hardy in *The Encyclopedia of Horror Movies* (1986) called it a "silly jungle saga" echoing Ed Naha's earlier evaluation in *Horrors: From Screen to Scream* (1975): "Silly tale of voodoo and jealousy.... A real snore fest." Even more critical was Donald C. Willis in *Horror and Science Fiction Films* (1972) who termed the programmer "[c]rude, unpleasant. Grade Triple-Z."

In the African jungle, beautiful Tonda Metz (Allison Hayes) tries to kill her husband, Dr. Karl Metz (John Wengraf), by strangling his effigy, a voodoo doll, but a servant, Suba (Norman Frederic), comes to his rescue. Suba informs his employer that the jungle drums announce the coming of three white men, one of them injured, and Metz tells him to dissuade them. When he fires at the intruders, Tonda stops Suba and meets moviemakers Tom Maxwell (Paul Burke) and Norm Adams (Joel Marston), who are carrying their nearly dead partner, Joe Lawson (Robert Christopher), on a stretcher because he was attacked by a lion. Dr. Metz agrees to treat him but tells the other men they must sleep in a nearby hut and not in his house. The two men find a vulture feather in the hut and their bearer, Gogi (Paul Thompson), calls it black magic and burns it. Tonda meets Suba and they kiss but are seen by his wife Lara (Eugenia Paul). Placing charms on Joe, Tonda dances at a voodoo ceremony. Awakened by the drums, Tom and Norm watch the dance with Gogi, who says the white woman is a voodoo queen and warns them that the act of seeing the dancing is punishable by death. The three men return to the hut. Tonda stabs a voodoo doll, causing Joe to react in pain. The next day Tom and Norm find Joe completely healed but in a state of shock. Dr. Metz refuses to say how his patient was cured so quickly. Suba's dead body is brought to the house and Lara accuses the medical man of killing her husband. Finding Suba's heart has been removed, Tom, Norm and Gogi go to the ceremonial site, find blood on an altar and conclude this was where the servant was murdered. Norm and Gogi go back for their disabled Jeep. Tonda shows up and Tom tells her he saw the ceremony but she denies having been at the place before although she says it seems familiar. Tom later joins Tonda and her husband for coffee and Metz informs him he is a doctor of psychology. Since he did research on voodoo in Haiti, Tom asks Dr. Metz about the subject. After Tonda leaves, her husband tells Tom not to become too curious about voodoo. Tom and Dr. Metz observe a native ceremony of mourning for Suba as Joe rises from his bed and joins the ritual, taking a knife and then going into the jungle. That night Tonda comes to Tom's hut and tells him she is afraid of her husband because he has a strange influence on her and the natives. They kiss. Joe attacks Tom with the knife but Tom knocks him out and carries him into the hut. When Tom cannot revive Joe, he confronts Dr. Metz but is disarmed by his houseboy, Kabar (Otis Greene). Metz asks his wife if she has fallen in love with Tom. Lara goes to Joe, knowing he possesses her husband's soul. Metz tells Kabar to return Tom's gun and they learn that Joe has disappeared from the hut. The doctor urges Tom to leave the area as quickly as possible or remain at his own peril. Norm and Gogi return with the Jeep and Tom tells them they will leave the next morning. That night Metz accuses his wife of having been with Tom. Finding out that the visitors are leaving the next day, Tonda goes to Tom and tells him she fears her husband and he says he will take her with him. When the woman tries to convince Tom to kill Metz, he refuses, slaps her and tells her to return to her husband. The next morning Tom and Norm find their guns are missing and Gogi has been murdered. After they bury him, the two men go to the house in search of guns. Tonda holds them at bay with a pistol which Tom takes away from her as her husband returns with Kabar. Metz asks Tom if he plans to leave with his wife and Tom informs him he does not love her. The doctor gives Tom his prize rifle and asks to go back to Kendar with the two men, leaving Tonda behind permanently. The angry woman stabs her husband and later uses a voodoo doll to eliminate Kabar, who was a witness to the stabbing, since she plans to blame Tom and Norm for her husband's death. To fool Tonda, Tom sets up Kabar's body in the Jeep, making it look like he is alive, and he also stops the woman from trying to smother her unconscious mate. Seeing Norm and Kabar going in the Jeep to Kendar for a doctor, Tonda thinks her voodoo magic has failed so she has the natives capture Tom and plans to use him to save her husband so she will not hang. During the voodoo ceremony, Joe tries to kill Tom with a knife but Lara stabs Tonda, breaking her spell. Joe then frees Tom as the natives flee. When Dr. Metz begins to recover, Tom, Norm and Joe return to Kendar.

The Disembodied was produced by Ben Schwalb, using the same crew that made most of his "Bowery Boys" programmers for Allied Artists. The film's main asset was sexy Allison Hayes as the evil Tonda; the actress headlined *Attack of the 50 Foot Woman* (1958) and *The Hypnotic Eye* (1959) [qq.v.]. She was also in *The Undead, The Unearthly* and *Zombies of Mora Tau* (all 1957) and *The Crawling Hand* (1963), as well as the TV episode "Deep Freeze" (1956), in which she was an alien invader. Norman Frederic, who played Suba, later starred in *The Phantom Planet* (1961), while Robert Christopher, who was Joe, had the ignominious misfortune of being in Jerry Warren's infamous *Frankenstein Island* (1981). John Wengraf seemed somewhat physically feeble in the role of Dr. Metz, a part better suited for Tom Conway or Paul Cavanagh; he appeared in several genre TV outings as well as the features *Paris Playboys* [q.v.] and *Gog* (both 1954), *The Return of Dracula* (1958) and *12 to the Moon* (1960). *The Disembodied* marked Walter Grauman's directorial debut and he went on to helm *Lady in a Cage* (1964) and several genre TV movies like *Daughter of the Mind* (1969), *Crowhaven Farm* (1970) and *The Golden Gate Murders* (1979).

Eugenie (1970; 91 minutes; Color)

Producer-Screenplay: Peter Welbeck [Harry Alan Towers]. Director: Jess Franco. From the novel by the Marquis de Sade. Photography: Manuel Merino. Music: Bruno Nicolai.

CAST: Marie Liljedahl (Eugenie), Maria Rohm (Madame Marianne Saint Ange), Jack Taylor (Mirvel), Christopher Lee (Dolmance), Paul Muller (Monsieur Mistival), Nino Korda (Roches), Herbert Fux (Hardin), Kaplan [Anney Kablan] (Augustin), Ingrid Swenson [Maria Luisa Ponte] (Madame Mistival), Uta Dahlberg (Therese), Colette Giacobine (Colette), Kathy Lagarde (Maid), Jess Franco (Ritual Participant).

Both Allied Artists and Distinction Films released *Eugenie* in the United States although the latter company used a longer title, *Eugenie... The Story of Her Journey into Perversion*. In Great Britain it was issued by Video-International as *Philosophy in the Boudoir*, a general translation of the title of the 1795 Marquis de Sade novel on which it was based. In France it was shown as *Les Brulantes* (The Scorchers) and in West Germany it was called *Die Jungfrau und die Peitsche* (The Young Woman and the Whip). In 1971 Allied distributed a French production based on the same work, *Beyond Love and Evil* (q.v.). Both features received X ratings and did poorly at the box office. Howard Thompson in the *New York Times* called *Eugenie* an "atrociously written, directed and performed waste of perfectly good raw film." *Castle of Frankenstein* #16 (1971) noted, "Jess Franco strikes again with this inept, pretentious and mostly out of focus sex fantasy.... Pseudo-arty romanticism gets repulsive at times with amateur photography no help. Recommended only to drooling masochists and fans of Miss Liljedahl's body." In *The Psychotronic Encyclopedia of Film* (1983), Michael J. Weldon referred to it as an "inept sex sickie.... An X-rated relic, which would probably get an R now." "Twenty years down the pike, *Eugenie* still packs a punch," reported Cathal Tohill and Pete Tombs in *Immoral Tales: European Sex and Horror Movies 1956–1984* (1994).

A satanic cult, lead by Dolmance (Christopher Lee), adheres to the writings of the Marquis de Sade and conducts a ceremony that culminates in the murder of a naked girl. Beautiful teenager Eugenie (Marie Liljedahl), who is constantly being suppressed by her domineering mother (Ingrid Swenson), is unaware her father (Paul Muller) has designs on her friend Marianne (Maria Rohm), who is really Madame Saint Ange. Marianne has sex with him in return for his daughter spending the weekend on her island where she and her stepbrother, Mirvel (Jack Taylor), with whom she is involved in an incestuous relationship, plan to sexually exploit the teenager. She is brought to the island by Augustin (Kaplan), the island gardener and boatman. Once she arrives, the women sunbathe and Marianne initiates Eugenie in lesbian sex. During dinner she and Mirvel drug the girl. As Mirvel carries Eugenie to bed, Kaplan, also Marianne's lover, objects to the way the girl is being abused but she reminds him he had nothing before she rescued him from poverty and gave him his position. Mirvel tells his stepsister he loves Eugenie and he does want to see her sacrificed. Marianne and Mirvel have sex and both of them make love to Eugenie while Therese (Uta Dahlberg), their lovely deaf and dumb servant, watches. The young girl awakes and tells her friend she had a dream so strange it seemed real. After dinner, the trio agree to play a game and Marianne suggests charades. Mirvel gives Eugene a drugged cigarette as a group of libertines, led by Dolmance, arrive dressed in 18th-century costumes and physically abuse the young woman. The following morning the frightened Eugenie tells Marianne about the torture but her friend says it was another dream since she has no marks of physical abuse. After a pleasant day that includes a group sing and boating, Eugenie sleeps as Mirvel enters Therese's room, strangles her with a chain, stabs her and hangs her body from the ceiling. Eugene awakens and finds her favorite doll with its head cut off. Roaming the house, she discovers Therese's body. Mirvel confronts the girl and tells her that Marianne is not only his stepsister but also his mistress. When he tries to rape her, Eugenie stabs Mirvel as Marianne watches. After Eugenie locates Marianne, her friend tells her she is glad Mirvel is dead. The cultists return as Marianne orders them to torture and kill Eugenie but Dolmance decides to sacrifice her instead. Eugenie joins the group in beating Marianne and then stabs her benefactor. Dolmance tells Eugenie that Marianne hated her for winning Mirvel's love and that she will be found with their corpses and condemned as a murderess. A naked Eugenie runs along the beach and finds a graveyard as a rescue boat arrives. Later she is invited by Marianne to partake in a weekend jaunt on her private island.

Christopher Lee apparently did not realize he was filming scenes for a sex movie when he replaced George Sanders in the role of Dolmance, working for only two days on the project. In the editing process, he is made to appear as part of the erotic activities, the director of Eugenie's undoing. Swedish actress Marie Liljedahl, who is quite convincing as the innocent teen turned into a sex slave and killer, earlier headlined the erotic dramas *Inga* (1968) and *Ann and Eve* (1970), and would also appear in *Dorian Gray* (1970) and *The Seduction of Inga* (1971). Maria Rohm, who played Madame Saint Ange, was married to the film's producer-writer Harry Alan Towers, who used the nom de screen Peter Walbeck. Cast members Jack Taylor and Paul Muller often worked with director Jess Franco. The film was made in four weeks at Mercia in Spain and interiors done at the Alcazar Studio in Barcelona.

Franco had an affinity for the works of the Marquis de Sade; he had made *Justine* (1968) and would later film a second *Eugenie* in 1970 with Soledad Miranda, billed as Susan Korda, in the title role (it was never finished due to her death in a traffic accident). Franco went on to film *Plaisir a Trio* (Pleasure for Three) (1974), *Sinfonia Erotica* (Erotic Symphony) and *Erotismo* (*Eugenie, Historia de un Perversion*) [Eugenie, History of a Perversion] (both 1980), *Gemidos de Placer* (Cries of Pleasure) (1983) and *Helter Skelter* (2000), all based on de Sade's writings. *Video Watchdog* #2 (1990) reported that some of composer Bruno Nicolai's score for *Eugenie* appeared earlier in Paul Naschy's first starring horror movie *La Marca del Hombre Lobo* (The Mark of the Wolfman), a 1967 release issued in the U.S. by Independent International as *Frankenstein's Bloody Terror* in 1970.

Face of Fire (1959; 79 minutes)

Producers-Screenplay: Albert Band and Louis Garfinkle. Associate Producer: Gustaf Unger. Director: Albert Band. From the story "The Monster" by Stephen Crane. Photography–Art Director: Edward Vorkapich. Editor: Ingemar Ejve. Supervising Editor: Frank Sullivan. Music: Erik Nordgren. Sound: Per-Olof Pettersson. Sets: Rolf Boman. Production Manager: Gustav Roger. Makeup: Borje Lundh. Wardrobe: Britta Sylwander. Production Coordinator: Albert Jaeger. Assistant Director: Carl-Henry Cagarp.

CAST: Cameron Mitchell (Dr. Ned Trescott), James Whitmore (Monk Johnson), Bettye Ackerman (Grace Trescott), Royal Dano (Jake Winter), Miko Oscard (Jimmie Trescott), Robert F. Simon (Judge Hagenthorpe), Richard Erdman (Al Williams), Howard Smith (Sheriff Nolan), Lois Maxwell (Ethel Winter), Jill Donohue (Bella Kovac), Hjordis Petterson (Mrs. Kovac), Charles Fawcett (Dr. John Moser), Doreen Denning (Frightened Girl), Harold Kasket, Althea Orr, Vernon Young (Townspeople).

Set in 19th century rural America with Hollywood stars, *Face of Fire* was filmed in Stockholm, Sweden, as *Face of the Fire* and *The Monster*, and was produced by Allied Artists in association with Svensk Filmindustries and Mardi Gras Productions. It was based on the 1898 Stephen Crane short story "The Monster." When Allied Artists released it in the U.S. in August 1959, sometimes in tandem with *The Bat* (q.v.), it was played as a horror movie although it is more of a melodrama. During the filming of its house-burning sequence, the fire got out of hand and nearly destroyed the Svenska Films studio. It was publicized that star Cameron Mitchell's eyebrows were burned off during the conflagration. While Ed Naha in *Horrors: From Screen to Scream* (1975) felt it was "[w]ell done," *Face of Fire* garnered little attention at the time of its release. It was very popular in Sweden. It's become one of the more obscure genre releases of the late 1950s. It marked the feature film debut of Bettye Ackerman, who later became popular on the ABC-TV series *Ben Casey* (1961–66), in which she appeared with her husband Sam Jaffe, who played Dr. Zorba, with Vincent Edwards in the title role.

In a small rural community at the end of the 19th century, Monk Johnson (James Whitmore) works as a handyman and groom for Dr. Ned Trescott (Mitchell) and his wife Grace (Ackerman). He is especially close to their young son Jimmie (Miko Oscard), whom he nicknames Pollywog. The well-groomed Monk calls on Bella Kovac (Jill Donohue) and asks her to marry him and gets approval from her widowed mother (Hjordis Petterson). On his way home, Monk hears a fire bell and joins the rest of the community in following it to Trescott's home, which is ablaze. The doctor and his wife try to go into the house to save their son and are restrained by their neighbors but Monk goes inside and, finding the boy, wraps him in a blanket. Seeking a way out of the flames, Monk carries Jimmie to Trescott's basement lab but he falls on the steps and is knocked out. Chemicals blow up due to the heat and splash on Monk's face, horribly burning him. Trescott manages to get into the house and save Jimmie and then goes back with others to bring out Monk. Trescott and his wife stay with their friend Judge Hagenthorpe (Robert F. Simon). Dr. Moser (Charles Fawcett) says Monk's face has been damaged beyond recognition. Trescott has his wife and son stay with his in-laws as their home is rebuilt and he tries to help Monk, whose mind has been affected by the tragedy. When Trescott and other doctors are unable to aid Monk, Judge Hagenthorpe thinks the man may want to die, but Trescott will not hear of it and has Monk wear a black hood. When the new house is completed, the burned man is brought to live again with the Trescotts but all the townspeople who once liked Monk now refuse to associate with him, including Bella. When the sight of him frightens a young girl (Doreen Denning), she runs into the street and is hit by a horse and wagon. The locals chase Monk out of town. Farmer Jake Winter (Royal Dano) shows up armed at Trescott's house and wants to have Monk placed in an asylum. In order to look out for Monk, the doctor joins Winter and his followers at a local game preserve where Monk is thought to be hiding. When a dead body with a mangled face is found near railroad tracks, the people think Monk has been killed and decide to have a memorial for him. Jimmie, whose speech has been impaired by the ordeal, runs to tell his father he has seen a faceless man. Dr. Trescott and Judge Hagenthorpe find Monk and bring him home. Again the townspeople turn against Monk and one day while he is sitting in the backyard of the Trescott property the local children dare each other to get close to him. When the fire bell rings, Monk recoils at the sound but recognizes Jimmie and calls him Pollywog. The boy takes his friend by the hand and they go into the house, giving the Trescotts the strength they need to keep Monk with them.

About the only horrific aspect of *Face of Fire* was the very scary makeup of Monk's horribly burned face done by Borje Lundh. The same year the film was released, associate producer Gustaf Unger also made the science fiction feature *Terror in the Midnight Sun*, which did not see U.S. release until 1962 when Jerry Warren issued a butchered version of it called *Invasion of the Animal People*.

Frankenstein Meets the Space Monster (1965; 76 minutes)

Producer: Robert McCarty. Executive Producer: Alan V. Iselin. Associate Producer: Stanley P. Darer. Director: Robert Gaffney. Screenplay: George Garrett, R.H.W. Dillard and John Rodenbeck. Photography: Saul Midwell. Editor: Lawrence C. Keating. Music: Rose Gaffney. Sound: Maurice Rosenblum. Sets: Charles Bailey. Costumes: Anna Hill Johnstone. Makeup: John D. Alese. Production Manager–Assistant Director: Ben Berk.

CAST: Marilyn Hanold (Princess Marcuzan), Jim [James] Karen (Dr. Adam Steele), Nancy Marshall (Karen Grant), David Kerman (General Bowers), Lou Cutell (Dr. Nadir), Robert Reilly (Colonel Frank Saunders), Bruce Glover (Alien Soldier), Robert Fields (Reporter), Robert Alan Browne (Alien Crewman), Susan Stephens (Blonde Captive).

For those who swallow the Kool-aid that *Plan 9 from Outer Space* (1958) is the worst film of all-time, a look at *Frankenstein Meets the Space Monster* should alleviate such thoughts. At that, the latter production is still a rung above fare like *The Beast of Yucca Flats* (1961) and *The Creeping Terror* (1964). With exterior shooting in Puerto Rico and interiors done in Seneca, New York, *Frankenstein Meets the Space Monster* was originally called *Operation San Juan* and *Frankenstein Meets the Space Men* and was released in Great Britain as *Duel of the Space Monsters*. Produced by Futurama Entertainment Corporation and Vernon-Seneca Films, it was billed as being filmed in "Futurama." Its soundtrack included songs by the Distant Cousins, singing "To Have and Hold," and the Poets performing "That's the Way It's Got to Be." It is chock full of grainy NASA and military stock footage. Anthony Petkovich noted in his career study of Bruce Glover, who played one of the space aliens, in *Psychotronic Video* #20 (1995), "The prop control panel was from *Fail-Safe* and the spaceship was the roof of a hot dog stand. The weapons were Wham-O toy air pistols.... A soundtrack 45 (by Bob Crewe of Four Seasons fame) was released."

Aboard an alien spaceship, Princess Marcuzan (Marilyn Hanold) orders her cohort Dr. Nadir (Lou Cutell) to destroy a just-launched NASA probe. Dr. Adam Steele (James Karen) and his lovely assistant Karen Grant (Nancy Marshall) have developed an astro-robot they call Frank (Robert Reilly). With General Bowers (David Kerman) they take the mechanical man to the NASA Space Center where he is introduced to the press as Colonel Frank Saunders, an astronaut who will fly solo on the first Mars mission. As he is answering questions, Frank's face freezes and Adam and Karen whisk him off to the laboratory where Steele determines that an electrode in his head malfunctioned due to humidity. The general questions them on what might happen to the Mars mission if something goes wrong with the robot's "brain." The next day the Mars probe, with Frank aboard, is launched. Nadir tells the princess it is a weapon sent to attack their ship and she orders it destroyed. Saunders parachutes to safety. When the princess learns of this, she tells Nadir to eliminate the astronaut. After Frank sets down safely in Puerto Rico and begins looking for help, the alien ship lands and he is spotted by a space soldier who shoots at him with a ray gun. The ray destroys the left side of Frank's face and head and short-circuits his memory functions causing him to throttle the attacker and run away. When his comrades take him back to the ship, the injured alien is given over to Moll, a huge monstrous creature, by the vengeful princess and Nadir. That night Frank stops a car and strangles a man but is driven off by the hysterics of his young female companion. The princess begins phase two of their mission on Earth by telling her crewmen their home planet is unfit for habitation due to a recent atomic war and they need good breeding stock to repopulate it. She orders them to kidnap Earth women for that purpose. In their laboratory, Adam and Karen try to pick up signals from Frank, who comes upon a native and murders him with his own machete. General Bowers gets word that the empty Mars capsule has been found in Puerto Rico and there has been violence in the area caused by a man in a spacesuit. Adam, Karen and Bowers fly to the island. The aliens abduct a beautiful blonde woman (Susan Stephens) and incinerate her male companion with a ray gun. Adam and Karen make plans to find Frank but Bowers says the military will capture him. The two lovers, Adam and Karen, take off on a motor bike and leave San Juan and head into the countryside. The signal they have been following leads them to a cave where they find Frank. While Adam remains behind to repair the robot, Karen goes back for help. The aliens raid a pool party and carry off eight pretty girls. On their way back to the spaceship they also abduct Karen. Taken to the princess and Nadir, Karen refuses to talk and she is placed in a cage next to Moll. General Bowers orders troop deployment as Adam repairs Frank and leads him out of the cave. After finding Karen's abandoned motor bike, the two follow her signal and locate the alien craft. Adam tells Frank to watch the ship as he takes the bike and rides for help. The aliens capture Frank and take him to the ship and leave him unconscious on a table next to Karen's cell. She calls to him and he wakes up. Bowers orders a rocket barrage on the UFO. Nadir tells the princess they must leave immediately in case the Earthlings should attack them with atomic weapons. Frank grabs a ray gun and gets the drop on the aliens. The captive women are set free and they flee from the craft. Upon the urging of Adam, Bowers stops the attack when he finds out that Karen is a prisoner of the invaders. One of the aliens opens Moll's cage and, after Karen is out of the ship, the robot fights with the monster. Karen is picked up on the road by Bowers and his crew and she is reunited with Adam. The princess orders Nadir to ignite their ship's rockets but as he does so, Frank uses the ray gun to blast the control panel and the UFO explodes.

Frankenstein Meets the Space Monster was unleashed on theaters in September 1965 as the top half of a double bill with the leaden *Curse of the Voodoo* (q.v.). The script was originally written as a comedy by three University of Virginia graduate students; one of them, George Garrett, wrote an amusing and informative essay on the film that was included as a booklet with the DVD (Dark Sky Films, 2006). Besides relating how the script came about, Garrett provides information on the near loony circumstances surrounding its filming and distribution as well as tidbits like how it was called *Mars Attacks Puerto Rico* in Latin America.

Frankenstein Meets the Space Monster does offer quite a contrast between the beautiful and the grotesque. The bitchy space queen, Princess Marcuzan (Hanold), and Karen (Marshall), the scientist's assistant, are both lovely as are the bevy of abducted girls, especially a blonde bikini wearer (Stephens). Hanold was one of the Venusian vampire women in the Three Stooges short *Space Ship Sappy* (Columbia, 1957). In contrast, the hideous blasted face of Frank (short for Frankenstein?) was nicely designed by John D. Alese. The monster Moll is a fearsome creature: ugly and tall with shaggy hair, huge eyes, fangs and a pointed head with horns. Moll is constantly in motion and always on the attack with his huge swinging arms and clawed hands. Far more on the comedic side is the sadistic Dr. Nadir (Cutell), a short, pudgy troll with large pointed ears, bug eyes and an egg-shaped bald head. His mannerisms and speech were decidedly effeminate in contrast to the cold, calculating princess.

As one would expect, *Frankenstein Meets the Space Monster* did not garner much in the way of plaudits. Donald F. Glut in *The Frankenstein Legend* (1973) thought it was "a travesty of the name of Frankenstein," and C.J. Henderson in *The Encyclopedia of Science Fiction Movies* (2001) noted, "There is no true Frankenstein monster in this picture. There is no Dr. Frankenstein. There is no reason to watch." Michael J. Weldon in *The Psychotronic*

Encyclopedia of Film (1983) said, "Don't miss. It's the worst.... Lots of rock music, stock footage, and laughs." *Video Hound's Complete Guide to Cult Flicks and Trash Pics* (1996) concurred: "A classic grade-Z epic.... It's cheap and stupid, and the makeup and costumes are wonderfully way-out. A must see."

Frankenstein 1970 (1958; 83 minutes)

Producer: Aubrey Schenck. Director: Howard W. Koch. Screenplay: Richard Landau and George Worthington Yates. Story: Aubrey Schenck and Charles A. Moses. Photography: Carl E. Guthrie. Editor: John A. Bushelman. Music: Paul Dunlap. Sound: Francis E. Stahl. Production Design: Jack T. Collis. Sets: Jerry Welch. Makeup: George Bau. Assistant Director: George Vieira.

CAST: Boris Karloff (Baron Victor von Frankenstein), Tom Duggan (Mike Shaw), Jana Lund (Carolyn Hayes), Donald "Red" Barry (Douglas Row), Charlotte Austin (Judy Stevens Row), Norbert Schiller (Shuter), Rudolph Anders (Wilhelm Gottfried), Irwin Berke (Inspector Raab), John Dennis (Morgan Haley), Frank Roehn (Cab Driver), Joe Piloski (Station Master), Otto Reichow (Reactor Expert), Mike Lane (Hans), Jack Kenny (Assistant Cameraman).

Boris Karloff signed a three-picture contract with the production team of Aubrey Schenck and Howard W. Koch in 1957 and that year he headlined their mundane horror effort *Voodoo Island*, released by United Artists. Next the producers landed a deal with Allied Artists to make *Frankenstein 1970*, filmed as *Frankenstein 1960*, giving Karloff in the role of a descendant of the scientist who created the monster. Filmed on the Warner Bros. lot in CinemaScope, the feature was nicely done production-wise but its overall horror content was mediocre following a terrific opening sequence. Professional wrestler Mike Lane, who was billed in the ring as Big Mike Lane, portrays the monster, both at the beginning as a movie actor and later covered with bandages as the creature revived by Frankenstein. Best noted as the tragic boxer in *The Harder They Fall* (1956), Lane later played a kindly Frankenstein Monster, called Frank N. Stein, in the television series *The Monster Squad* (NBC-TV, 1976–77). The third film Karloff was to do with Schenck-Koch, *King of the Monsters*, was never filmed.

A young blonde woman (Jana Lund) runs screaming through a foggy night, pursued by a hulking monster (Lane) with clawed hands. He chases her into a lake and begins strangling her when a voice yells "cut" and TV director Douglas Row (Donald Barry) stops the scene. The soaked actress, Carolyn Hayes, tells publicity man Mike Shaw (Tom Duggan) she deserves plenty of copy for her suffering. The television people are filming at the ancient castle of Baron Victor von Frankenstein (Karloff) commemorating the 230th anniversary of his ancestor, Richard von Frankenstein, creating his murderous monster.

The scientist, who is bent and scarred from World War II torture, has agreed to let his friend Wilhelm Gottfried (Rudolph Anders) lease the castle to the TV crew in order to get money to buy an atomic reactor unit that he, Frankenstein, needs for his experiments. Wilhelm questions him about spending so much money and tells him all of his art treasures have been sold. Frankenstein says he needs the reactor for electricity for the castle and that he only has his work since his captors let him keep his surgeon hands so he could perform the unholy operations they demanded. Frankenstein films an introduction to the television program in the burial vault of his castle, explaining that his ancestor spent seventeen years creating a living man only to find out it was a monster, and how he removed its vital organs and buried it deep in the bowels of the structure for all time. Carolyn becomes uneasy over the fact that Frankenstein pays special attention to her and she also has to ward off the advances of Row, who employs his jealous fourth ex-wife, Judy (Charlotte Austin), as the script girl. Carolyn is quite fond of Frankenstein's family retainer, the loyal Shuter (Norbert

Schiller), and gives him a scarf and a kiss, much to the scientist's chagrin. After the atomic reactor is delivered, Frankenstein works in his hidden laboratory where he has installed listening devices so he can hear what is going on in other parts of the castle. Frankenstein has dug up the body of the monster and plans to re-animate it by replacing its vital organs and using the reactor to return the creature to life — and eventually having his own brain placed in its head to continue the family line. While closing up the castle for the night, Shuter sees a light in the vault and finds the secret entrance to the laboratory. Frankenstein kills his loyal butler and puts his heart and brain in the monster. When Carolyn inquires about Shuter the next day, Frankenstein tells her he has gone to visit relatives. As Frankenstein goes to place Shuter's eyes in the creature, he drops them on the floor and ruins them. That night a drunken Shaw tries to seduce Judy but she locks him out of her room. The monster abducts and accidentally kills Judy as Frankenstein laments that her eyes cannot be used for the creature since he wanted Shaw's orbs. Row tells his cameraman, Morgan Haley (John Dennis), to make some tests with Carolyn in the vault and while they are there the monster nearly grabs the young woman. When she leaves, the creature murders Haley whose blood does not match that of the monster as Frankenstein had hoped. With Judy, Haley and Shuter missing, Row calls in Police Inspector Raab (Irwin Berke) but Frankenstein gives him logical explanations for their leaving. Gottfried asks Frankenstein to disclose the nature of his experiments and he is taken to the laboratory where he meets the monster who murders him so his eyes can be used to make him see. Row and Shaw search the vault and the director finds Haley's viewfinder and goes back to see Raab, telling Shaw to take care of Carolyn. Frankenstein hypnotizes Shaw and tells him to have the actress come downstairs at a certain time. When she does, she is carried to the vault by the monster. Row convinces the inspector to return to the castle with him and when they cannot find Carolyn, Shaw joins them in searching for her. As Frankenstein calls to the monster to bring the actress to the laboratory, the young woman regains consciousness and realizes that Shuter the butler is part of her abductor and tells him to take her back upstairs. The three men hear her calling for help and descend into the vault as the monster confronts Frankenstein and begins destroying the laboratory. The scientist turns on the atomic reactor and its steam kills both him and the creature. After the laboratory is cleared of radiation, Row, Mike and Rabb remove bandages from the head of the monster and the visage of a pre-war Victor von Frankenstein is revealed.

As noted, the best part of *Frankenstein 1970* comes at the beginning with the girl being chased through the fog by the monster. This eerie and scary sequence is particularly well staged and sets the tone for what could have been a top-notch horror film but the rest of the script is a letdown with Karloff's over-the-top performance as Victor von Frankenstein providing very little compensation. The best acting work in the film is done by Donald Barry, best remembered as cowboy star Don "Red" Barry. He dominates every scene in which he appears as the abrasive, self-centered, bombastic and lecherous director. He is ably helped by two beautiful actresses, Jana Lund and Charlotte Austin. Austin starred in *The Bride and the Beast* (q.v.) the same year for Allied Artists.

Variety called the film a "[w]ell-made entry in the horror class.... Camera work is fluid and perceptive [and sets] are a major asset to believability." The British *Kinematograph Weekly* noted, "It follows the pattern of previous Frankenstein films.... [T]he introduction of the television unit gives the shenanigans zip.... Cast iron star and title thriller." Donald F. Glut in *The Frankenstein Legend* (1973) called it "a shoddy production," adding, "There was hardly anything futuristic about the film even when seen in 1958. With the exception of the atomic reactor, the story could have been set earlier in time." Regarding the star he said, "Karloff himself seemed to express a contempt for the role he was playing ... and in one of the only instances of his career, overacted."

Frankenstein 1970 was often dual billed with *Queen of Outer Space* (q.v.) when released by Allied in July 1958. Part of its opening chase scene was later incorporated into the TV version of *Daughter of Dr. Jekyll* (1957) [q.v.] to beef up the running time.

Fright (1956; 68 minutes)

Producer-Director: W. Lee Wilder. Screenplay: Myles Wilder. Photography: J. Burgi Contner. Editor: L. Robert Harris. Music: Lew Davies. Sound: Walter Wood. Makeup: Josephine Cianelli. Wardrobe: Bernard Shaw.

CAST: Nancy Malone (Ann Summers), Eric Fleming (Dr. Jim Hamilton), Dean L. Almquist (Cullen), Frank Marth (George Morley), Humphrey Davies (Dr. Charles Gore), Elizabeth Watts (Lady Olive Fitzmaurice), Walter Klavun (Warden), Amelia Conley (Miss Ames), Tom Reynolds (City Editor Bill), Robert Gardett (Managing Editor), Norman MacKaye (Inspector Blackburn), Ned Glass (Taxi Driver), Don Douglas (Lieutenant White), Sid Raymond (Taxi Driver), Philip Kenealy (Policeman), Chris Bohn (TV Announcer), Norman Burton (Thompkins), Alney Alba (Butler Philip), Mae Clarke (Woman in Restaurant), Jimmy Little (Bartender Joe).

After eluding the New York City police by hiding in a bakery truck, double murderer George Morley (Frank Marth) ends up cornered on the Queens Borough Bridge. When Inspector Blackburn (Norman MacKaye) is unable to talk him down, passing Park Avenue psychiatrist Dr. Jim Hamilton (Eric Fleming) asks permission to try. Believing Morley is obsessive with a highly suggestible mentality, Jim uses the sound of his voice and the bridge lights to put the murderer in a trance, thus permitting the police officers to take him into custody. Among the many spectators is Ann Summers (Nancy Malone). The next day the newspapers are filled with stories about Jim who is called the "Park Avenue Svengali" although he tells the press he used simple suggestion technique on Morley who he feels is an unrepentant killer. As he gets into his car to leave work, the psychiatrist finds he has a passenger, Ann, who says she too may have a criminal mind. Although he denies her request to become his patient, Jim becomes intrigued with the woman after finding she left a German-language book in his car. His friend, history professor Charles Gore (Humphrey Davies), suggests that Jim may be attracted to her; Jim says he was married once and that was enough. Ann calls his office and asks for an appointment and Jim consents but when he meets with her she does not remember the novel and says she speaks no German although she gets notes in that language. She also relates she is a constant traveler and has never married or been in love. Jim goes to the local jail to complete his report on Morley, as requested by Blackburn, and he puts the killer under hypnosis. At his next session with Ann, he hypnotizes her and she starts to talk in German but is told by Jim to use English. She says she is eighteen years old and is with her lover Rudy at his Viennese hunting lodge—and that they both must die. When she comes to, Anne says she has never been in Vienna. She consents to meet the psychiatrist for dinner that night; she does not show up but does send Jim a message written in German (it simply says she will not keep the dinner date). At their next appointment, Anne tells Jim she does remember sending the note and that she often has memory loss. Under hypnosis the woman announces she is Baroness Maria Vetsera, whom Anne is trying to kill, and she is living in January 1889. Late that night Jim meets with Gore who informs him of the Mayerling affair, in which a married Austrian prince, Archduke Rudolf von Hapsburg, the son of Emperor Franz Joseph I, killed Maria Vetsera at their love nest, his hunting lodge Mayerling. When the doctor puts the woman under hypnosis again, she, as Maria, tells him about dying with Rudolf at Mayerling. The next day Jim and Ann have a date in the park and he tells her he is falling in love with her. At the same time, a newsman named Cullen (Dean L. Almquist) comes to the psychiatrist's office and, while waiting for him to return, steps on a foot button that turns on a tape recorder containing Ann's Mayerling story. The reporter takes it to his managing editor (Robert Gardett) and city editor (Tom Reynolds) and they agree to run it despite the probability of a libel suit. When Jim sees the story he demands a retraction. Ann, who feels she has been betrayed, phones the psychiatrist and tells him she never wants to see him again. Determined to win her back, Jim goes to her Sutton Place home and meets with her old family friend, Lady Olive Fitzmorris (Elizabeth Watts). At first the old lady is hostile, but when he tells her he wants to help Ann she informs him about the young woman's past, including the fact that her widowed father had an affair with Ann's Austrian nurse. Jim comes to believe that Ann got her Mayerling story from the nurse as well as a smattering of German and a subconscious guilt complex because of the affair. Ann is considered missing, and police Lieutenant White (Don Douglas) informs Jim that a note in German has been received accusing the psychiatrist of murdering her. In the doctor's office, White finds Ann's purse containing signed travelers checks worth $2,000 and a handkerchief with blood on it. Although he is not arrested, Jim is followed by the law. When he has lunch with Gore, he tells him he has fallen in love with Ann. When asked about Morley, Jim says he is asocial and that he, Jim, has a few more tests to run before the man is sent to the electric chair. Since Gore thinks Ann as Maria is trying to find her lover, Jim comes up with a plan to substitute him with Morley. He gets Cullen to write a story saying the reincarnation of Archduke Rudolf has been found. That night Ann shows up at Jim's apartment. With the warden's (Walter Klavun) permission, Jim hypnotizes Morley into thinking he is Rudolf and then takes Ann to see him. Having left a gun loaded with blanks in the room, Jim puts Ann under hypnosis and as he, Cullen and the warden watch, Morley re-enacts the shooting of his lady love. Jim brings Morley out of his trance and then reawakens Ann, who is now free of Maria and can look forward to the future with her psychiatrist.

Reincarnation became a vogue in Hollywood after the release of *The Search for Bridey Murphy*, a novel by Morey Bernstein. A film version with Louis Hayward, Teresa Wright, Nancy Gates and Kenneth Tobey was beaten to theaters by three months when Allied Artists issued *Fright*. Filmed mostly on location in New York City, *Fright* not only deals with a past life experience, it also interpolates hypnosis, history and split personality into its plotline. The result is a tepid, tacky, poorly acted melodrama done partially in a semi-documentary style. Wilder produced and directed *Fright* and it was penned by his son, Myles Wilder. Filmed as *Cast No Shadow*, it was later reissued by Exploitation Films as *Spell of the Hypnotist*. In *Movies on TV 1975–76 Edition* (1974), Steven H. Scheuer termed it a "[m]eandering psycho-drama."

Second-billed Eric Fleming, who played the stolid psychiatrist, also appeared in *Conquest of Space* (1955), *Queen of Outer Space* (1958) [q.v.] and *Curse of the Undead* (1959). He is best remembered as trail boss Gil Favor in the CBS-TV series *Rawhide*.

Fright (1971; 87 minutes; Color)

Producers: Harry Fine and Michael Style. Director: Peter Collinson. Screenplay: Tudor Gates. Photography: Ian Wilson. Editor: Raymond Poulton. Music: Harry Robinson. Song: Bob Barrett, sung by Nanette. Sound: Spencer Reeves. Sets: Peter Young. Production Design: Disley Jones.

Production Manager: Tom Sachs. Makeup: George Blackler. Costumes: Jean Fairlie. Continuity: Joy Mercer.

CAST: Susan George (Amanda), Honor Blackman (Helen Helston), Ian Bannen (Brian Helston), John Gregson (Dr. Derek Cordell), George Cole (Jim Lloyd), Dennis Waterman (Chris), Tara Collinson (Tara Helston), Maurice Kaufmann (Inspector), Roger Lloyd-Pack (Constable), Michael Brennan (Sergeant).

The precursor of babysitter-in-peril thrillers like *Halloween* (1978) and *When a Stranger Calls* (1979), *Fright* was made at Shepperton Studios in London by Fantale Films in cooperation with British Lion. It got a Certificate X when released in its homeland but was PG when Allied Artists issued it stateside in late May 1971. This was the second time the studio handled a feature with that title, the first being a 1956 W. Lee Wilder feature (q.v.). The British production was also called *Night Legs* and *Wake Up in Fright* and was re-issued in the U.S. as *I'm Alone and I'm Scared*. Susan George, who is quite fetching in a light blue top and mini-skirt, holds the film together with her well-modulated portrayal of the harried babysitter but the film itself seems like a lot of puzzle pieces that barely fit. The British accents are sometimes so heavy as to be almost unintelligible. One amusing scene has the teenager trying to calm her jitters by watching *The Plague of the Zombies* (1966) on television.

Blonde college student Amanda (George) gets off a bus at night and walks on a deserted road to the home of a couple who call themselves the Lloyds. She is met by Helen (Honor Blackman), who seems nervous, and is introduced to her husband Jim (George Cole) and their three-year-old son Tara (Tara Collinson), for whom Amanda is to babysit while they go out to celebrate at a fancy restaurant. Helen berates Jim for letting Spooky, their cat, in the child's bed and Helen becomes unnerved when he jokes that their old house may have an occasional ghost or poltergeist. Anxious about going out, Helen says she does not often leave her little boy and gives the babysitter the telephone number of the restaurant. After they leave, a man watches Amanda as she makes tea. After she puts the boy back to bed, someone taps on a window and the doorbell rings. It is Chris (Dennis Waterman), one of her school chums, who has followed her to the Lloyd house. Helen and Jim arrive at the restaurant to celebrate a divorce and are joined by her psychiatrist, Dr. Derek Cordell (John Gregson). After Amanda lets Chris in the house, he makes sexual advances which she rejects. He tries to scare her with the plot of a horror movie he saw but denies watching her through the window. He also informs her that Helen is not Jim's wife and that her real husband tried to kill her and is now in a mental institution. At the restaurant, Helen asks Derek if her husband could be traumatized by the divorce and he answers in the affirmative. As Amanda and Chris make out, Helen calls to check on her son. Following the phone call, the sexually frustrated Amanda throws Chris out of the house. As he watches Amanda, who is near a second floor window, Chris is attacked and beaten unconscious by a stranger. Amanda turns on the television and watches a horror movie as Helen tells Jim and Derek she thinks something is wrong at home. When the doorbell rings again, the babysitter thinks it's Chris but she sees a strange man at the window and calls the restaurant. Just as Helen is about to take her call, the phone line is cut. Derek calls the Lloyd house but gets no answer. A neighbor (Ian Bannen) brings in Chris, begins massaging his heart and announces the young man has died. Helen and Jim speed home in their car and go off the road with the vehicle getting stuck in mud. The neighbor tries to comfort the now hysterical Amanda as Derek goes to the police and tells them to get to the Lloyd home. As a report is being filled out, a call comes in to the police station that a woman has been murdered near a bus stop. The neighbor, who is really Brian Helston, Helen's estranged husband and

Tara's father, begins calling the young woman "Helen" and she starts to become suspicious of him. After he begins kissing her, Amanda submits to him sexually. As Brian sleeps, Amanda takes Tara and tries to escape. Chris revives as Brian takes his son by the hand and tells the babysitter not to leave. Picking up a heavy statue, Chris tries to hit Brian but is knocked down and beaten senseless. When the police arrive and call to Brian to give himself up, he locks Amanda and his son in the house. As Helen and Jim show up, Brian breaks a mirror and threatens Amanda with a shard of glass. Derek talks to Brian over the police loudspeaker and asks to meet with him but the madman refuses. The psychiatrist tells the police not to provoke Brian who threatens to slit the throats of his captives. Brian says he wants to talk to Helen. Amanda torments him with harangues about his wife not wanting him. The madman again thinks the babysitter is his wife, who comes to the house with a hidden gas canister. Brian welcomes Helen but locks the door, breaking his promise to release Amanda and Tara. Helen drops the canister and when it goes off, Amanda comes up behind Brian and cuts him with the glass before running out of the house. The bleeding Brian grabs the boy and holds the glass to his throat but Helen talks him into giving up their son. As she backs away, holding the little boy, Amanda shoots Brian.

In *The Essential Monster Movie Guide* (1999), Stephen Jones called *Fright* an "[u]npleasant slasher film.... The team of screenwriter Tudor Gates and producers Harry Fine and Michael Style fail to recreate the look of their Hammer productions (*The Vampire Lovers* [1970], etc.) and a cast of fine British character actors look justifiably embarrassed." Phil Hardy in *The Encyclopedia of Horror Movies* (1986) said it was an "openly exploitative film....

Lobby card for *Fright* (1971)

[it] manages to mobilize both mental illness and the notion of woman as automatic victim, sexual and otherwise, for the generation of shock and suspense, while suggesting some sympathy for the male maniac. ... [Peter] Collinson's direction is full of inserted close-ups and over-familiar shots of a telephone looming in the foreground.... [Tudor] Gates's awkward script and the demand for instant shocks leave the solid cast little room for [maneuver]." "Laughably transparent 'maximum suspense' calculations," is how Donald C. Willis summed up the proceedings in *Horror and Science Fiction Films II* (1982).

For a film with such a plethora of talent, both behind and in front of the camera, *Fright* turned out to be a mundane thriller, partially saved, as already noted, by the presence of beautiful Susan George. She was also in *The Sorcerers* (1967) [q.v.], *Dracula* (1970), *Die Screaming, Marianne* and *Dr. Jekyll and Mr. Hyde* (both 1973), *Computercide, The House Where Evil Dwells* and *Venom* (all 1982). Honor Blackman was in such genre efforts as *Daughter of Darkness* (1947), *Breakaway* (1955), *Jason and the Argonauts* (1963), *Goldfinger* (1964), in which she had her most famous role as Pussy Galore, *To the Devil a Daughter* (1976) and *The Cat and the Canary* (1978). Ian Bannen appeared in *Doomwatch* (1972), *From Beyond the Grave* (1973), *The Watcher in the Woods* (1980) and a 1981 TV adaptation of *Dr. Jekyll and Mr. Hyde*. George Cole was featured in *A Christmas Carol* (1951), *The Anatomist* (1961), *Dr. Syn, Alias the Scarecrow (The Scarecrow of Romney Marsh)* (1964), *The Vampire Lovers* (1970) and *The Blue Bird* (1976). Tara Collinson, who played the three-year-old with the same given name, was the son of the film's director, Peter Collinson, who also helmed *Straight on Till Morning* (1972), *Ten Little Indians* and *The Spiral Staircase* (both 1976). Screenwriter Tudor Gates also penned *Barbarella* (1967), *The Vampire Lovers* (1970), *Lust for a Vampire* (1971) and *Twins of Evil* (1972), the last three for *Fright*'s producers, Harry Fine and Michael Style.

From Hell It Came (1957; 72 minutes)

Associate Producers: Richard Bernstein and Byron Roberts. Director: Dan Milner. Screenplay: Richard Bernstein. Story: Richard Bernstein and Jack Milner. Photography: Brydon Baker. Editor: Jack Milner. Music: Darrell Calker. Art Director: Rudi Feld. Sound: Frank Webster, Sr. Sets: Morris Hoffman. Costumes: Frank Delmar. Makeup: Harry Thomas. Production Supervisor: Byron Roberts. Special Effects: James H. Donnelly. Assistant Director: John Greenwald.

CAST: Tod Andrews (Dr. Bill Arnold), Tina Carver (Dr. Terry Mason), Linda Watkins (Mae Kilgore), John McNamara (Professor Clark), Gregg Palmer (Kimo), Robert Swan (Witch Doctor Tano), Baynes Barron (Chief Maranka), Suzanne Ridgeway (Kory), Mark Sheeler (Eddie), Lee Rhodes (Norgu), Grace Mathews (Orchid), Tani Marsh (Naomi), Chester Hayes (Maku/The Tabanga), Lenmana Guerin (Dori).

Natives on Kalai, a small island in the Pacific Ocean, conduct a ceremony in which Kimo (Gregg Palmer) is condemned to die because the tribe's witch doctor, Tano (Robert Swan), said he caused the death of his own father, their former chief, by associating with the American scientists conducting experiments there. Kimo claims his father died from the black plague and begs his wife Kory (Suzanne Ridgeway) to tell the tribe the medicine the white men gave his father did not kill him. She wants to become the bride of the new chief, Maranka (Baynes Barron), and rebuffs her husband who promises to come back from Hell and puts a curse on Tano, Maranka and Kory. Kimo is stabbed in the heart with a dagger. The killing is witnessed by trading post owner Mae Kilgore (Linda Watkins), a Cockney widow. At the scientific compound, Dr. Bill Arnold (Tod Andrews) complains to plant expert Professor Clark (John McNamara) about the island's malaria, jungle rot, insects, heat and the ignorance of the natives. Clark tells Bill he misses his girlfriend, Dr. Terry

Mason (Tina Carver), who rejected his marriage proposal to work on the island of Baku. The two men discuss their study of radioactivity on the island; it was brought there by a typhoon after an atomic blast 1,700 miles away. Clark says there is no more radioactivity on the atoll than in a typical dental x-ray. The natives blame local deaths on atomic fallout although both men agree it is caused by plague. Mae is attacked by a native whom Bill, Clark and their assistant Eddie (Mark Sheeler) scare away. After being revived, Mae tells the Americans she saw the natives murder Kimo. Clark decides to ask Washington D.C. for more help and on the next helicopter flight Terry is brought to assist them. Bill is overjoyed to see Terry but he tells her the island is dangerous and he wants her to return to Baku. She says she must obey orders and remain. Mae gets a pretty local outcast, Orchid (Grace Mathews), to be Terry's servant. Kory confronts Maranka because he has rejected her for another woman, Naomi (Tani Marsh), who brings him poison for darts he plans to use to kill the Americans. Native Norgu (Lee Rhodes) takes his wife Dori (Lenmana Guerin) to the compound to be checked for minor burns and he tells the scientists that Tano poisoned Kimo's father. When Bill and Terry go for a walk in the jungle, he announces he wants them to get married but she prefers to continue her career. Terry notices something odd in the native cemetery and when they investigate they find a tree growing from Kimo's grave. They have Clark look at the site and he speculates that since Kimo was buried standing up in a coffin made from a tree trunk, the roots have somehow come from it. When Norgu returns with Dori the next day, he says the natives believe that Kimo has come back as a Tabanga, a vengeful human tree. He tells of a native chief who was murdered and returned as a Tabanga to get revenge on his killers. Orchid arrives and says the Tabanga has a dagger sticking out of it and a green liquid is dripping from its bark. Bill, Clark and Terry test the Tabanga and find it has a pulse and is radioactive. Clark sends their findings to Washington and is ordered to take the thing to the laboratory and examine it more closely. When Tano and the chief hear of the Tabanga, they make plans to use it to kill Norgu and the Americans. Maranka also wants Kory dead. She hears them talking and goes to the compound, tells the Americans the natives plan to kill them and asks for help. The scientists dig up the Tabanga, which is now taller than a human, and take it to their laboratory where it begins to die. In an effort to save it, Terry injects the tree with an experimental serum which takes at least eight hours to take effect. The next morning the team finds the lab has been destroyed along with their radio, cutting off communications with the outside world, and the Tabanga is gone. While Bill thinks the tree may have come back to life, Clark says the natives took it and destroyed their property. When Kory sees Naomi bathing in a lagoon, she tries to kill her. As the two women fight, the Tabanga shows up and carries off Kory, dropping her in quicksand. The Tabanga comes into the village and crushes the chief against a tree and throws his body into a ravine. Tano lures the Tabanga to a pit his men have dug and when the walking tree falls into it they throw in torches and depart, convinced the monster has burned. During the night the scorched Tabanga comes out of the pit and murders Tano. Mae arrives at the compound with news that the monster is again on the loose and she joins Bill, Terry, Clark and Eddie in looking for the creature. Terry stops to get some rocks out of her shoe and is captured by the monster. The others hear her screams and see the walking tree carry the young woman to the edge of the quicksand. Bill and Eddie shoot at the Tabanga and one of the bullets pushes the dagger into its heart, causing the monster to fall back into the quicksand and disappear. Maku (Chester Hayes) and some of the other natives ask the Americans to stay and help their people. As Bill and Terry kiss, Mae asks Clark if he is married.

From Hell It Came was a Milner Bros. Production; the siblings previously made *The Phantom from 10,000 Leagues* (1955). Allied Artists issued it on a dual bill with *The Disembodied* (q.v.) in the late summer of 1957. The Tabanga, which looked somewhat like a mobile grandfather's clock with arms and eyes, was based on designs by Paul Blaisdell. In his biography *Paul Blaisdell: Monster Maker* (1997), Randy Palmer wrote, "The Tabanga monster was effective, although it was shown a little too often to seem properly intimidating. Still, it looked like what it was supposed to look like: an ambulatory tree sporting the famous 'Blaisdell scowl.'" The Tabanga costume was constructed at Don Post Studios and later showed up as a prop in a warehouse scene in the melodrama *Arson for Hire*, which Allied Artists released as the lower half of a double bill with *The Giant Behemoth* (q.v.) in March 1959.

In *Sleaze Creatures* (1995), D. Earl Worth said *From Hell It Came* was "decently photographed, energetically scored, weird with a cracked sense of conviction and, in its title monster, had a Blaisdell beast the Billiken company should have made a model of." "Very, very bad," is how Donald C. Willis described the feature in *Horror and Science Fiction Films: A Checklist* (1972).

Top-billed Tod Andrews used the name Michael Ames when he earlier appeared in the Warner Bros. sci-fi comedy *The Body Disappears* (1941) and two Bela Lugosi Monogram thrillers, *Voodoo Man* and *Return of the Ape Man* (both 1944). Leading lady Tina Carver was a victim of *The Man Who Turned to Stone* (1957). *From Hell It Came* gave "Introducing" billing to Linda Watkins, but the actress' career of more than four decades also included a leading role in the 1932 mystery *Charlie Chan's Chance*.

The Ghost of Crossbones Hollow (1952; 56 minutes)

Producer: Wesley Barry. Executive Producer: William F. Broidy. Director: Frank McDonald. Screenplay: Maurice Tombragel. Photography: William Sickner. Editor: Ace Herman. Music: Lee Zahler. Art Director: Dave Milton. Sound: John Carter. Sets: Vin Taylor. Makeup: Charles Huber. Set Continuity: Eleanor Donahoe. Assistant Director: William Beaudine, Jr.

CAST: Guy Madison (Marshal Wild Bill Hickok), Andy Devine (Deputy Marshal Jingles P. Jones). "The Tax Collecting Story": Gordon Jones (Curly Wolf), Sam Flint (Judge), Marjorie Bennett (Widow), Mike Ragan [Holly Bane] (Gus), Ray Bennett (Sheriff), Joe Greene (Rancher), James Guifoyle (Old Rancher), Billy Bletcher (Waiter). "Ghost Town Story": Russell Simpson (Sam Overman/Stanton), John Doucette (Stopes), Bart Davidson (Manager).

The Adventures of Wild Bill Hickok was telecast from 1951 to 1958 for 113 half-hour episodes starring Guy Madison in the title role and Andy Devine as his sidekick Jingles P. Jones. The series was so popular that between 1952 and 1955 sixteen feature films were released theatrically, each made up of two segments of the TV show. One of these, *The Ghost of Crossbones Canyon*, came to theaters in November 1952 on the cusp of Monogram being absorbed into Allied Artists. Thus the film played in various locales under the auspices of both with its 1953 showings coming from Allied. "Ghost Town Story" had a pseudo-supernatural plot, giving the feature its title. It was first telecast June 17, 1951.

Stopes (John Doucette) and his gang hold up the Central City Express Office and knock out Deputy Marshal Jingles P. Jones (Devine). Marshal Wild Bill Hickok (Madison) and Jingles track the outlaws for two days before coming to Crossbones City, a ghost town near the Mexican border. Jingles claims the place is haunted by the ghost of outlaw Stanton, whose gang used the town as its headquarters. They are surprised by the appearance of prospector Sam Overman (Russell Simpson), who tells them that there are spirits in the old town. That night the two lawmen ride into Crossbones City and Sam tries to scare them away. They decide to sleep in a hotel. As Jingles stands guard, he is frightened by various noises caused by the old man. Bill tells Jingles to get some sleep as he does guard duty. The next morning Bill sees Sam go into the saloon and follows him. There the old man meets with Stopes and his men as they count the loot from the express office holdup. Sam orders the gang to capture the lawmen as Jingles wakes up and sees Hickok go into the saloon. Stopes gets the drop on the marshal and they fight while Jingles shoots one of the outlaws and holds the other at gunpoint. Sam stops the fight and informs the lawmen he is really Stanton and had faked his death. As Sam is about to shoot Bill and Jingles, he has a falling-out with Stopes over the robbery proceeds and the lawmen go for cover. The distraught Sam falls over a balcony railing and is killed as Stopes tries to escape and has a shootout with Jingles. Bill comes around behind Stopes and subdues him. The outlaw confesses that Sam used the ghost story to scare people away from his hideout.

Guy Madison, the star of *The Ghost of Crossbones Canyon* (1952) and *Phantom Trails* (1955), feature films culled from the television series *The Adventures of Wild Bill Hickok* (1951–58).

Some of the advertising for the film called it *The Ghost of Crossbone Canyon*. In 1955 Allied Artists released *Phantom Trails* (q.v.), another theatrical feature made up of episodes of *The Adventures of Wild Bill Hickok* television series.

The Giant Behemoth (1959; 80 minutes)

Producers: David Diamond and Edward (Ted) Lloyd. Director–Production Design: Eugene Lourie. Screenplay: Eugene Lourie and Daniel James. Story: Robert Abel and Allen Adler. Photography: Desmond Davis and Ken Hodges. Editor: Lee Doig. Music: Edwin Ashley. Art Director: Harry White. Sound: Sid Wiles. Production Manager: Jacques de Lane Lea. Makeup: Jimmy Evans. Special Effects: Willis H. O'Brien, Irving Block, Louis DeWitt, Jack Rabin and Pete Peterson. Assistant Director: Kim Mills.

CAST: Gene Evans (Steve Karnes), André Morell (Professor James Bickford), John Turner (John), Leigh Madison (Jeanie Trevethan), Jack McGowran (Dr. Sampson), Maurice Kaufman (Mini-Submarine Commander), Henri Vidon (Tom Trevethan), Leonard Sachs (Scientist), Lloyd Lamble (Admiral Summers), Howard Lang (Naval Commander), Neil Hallett (Helicopter Pilot), Patrick Jordan, Georgina Ward (Photo Lab Assistants), Arthur Gomez (Quayside Fisherman), Max

Lobby card for *Behemoth the Sea Monster*, the British title of *The Giant Behemoth* (1959)

Faulkner (PLA Radio Operator), Andre Maranne (French Radio Officer), Derren Nesbitt (Radio Officer), Neal Arden (TV Newsman), David McAvoy (Street Broadcaster).

At a meeting of the Atomic Energy Commission in London, American marine biologist Steve Karnes (Gene Evans) warns that the careless disposal of radioactive material will become a threat to the planet. He is scoffed at by several members, but gains the partial support of Professor James Bickford (André Morell), a British physicist. In Cornwall, fisherman Tom Trevethan (Henri Vidon) is hit by a blinding, burning light. His daughter Jeanie (Leigh Madison) later walks to the village pub in search of her dad; another fisherman, John (John Turner), joins her to look for him and they find Tom, his face badly burned, in a dying condition. He tells them something came out of the sea and calls it Behemoth. Following the fisherman's funeral, Jeanie and John walk along the beach and see scores of dead fish. When the young man spies a pulsing white substance between some rocks, he touches it and his hand is burned. Steve is about to leave London as he hears a TV news report that fishing has come to a complete standstill in Cornwall and there have been reports of a sea monster. He visits Bickford who supplies the details of Trevethan's death and the two go to the site. They find the dead fish have been taken out by the tides or destroyed by the locals. One fisherman describes seeing a light under the water. John takes them to see the village doctor who examined the body of the dead fisherman and he also shows them his burned hand. Steve is surprised not to find radiation contamination on the beach. At the lab, Steve notes that one of the fish has a white spot inside it that glows and is radioactive.

Although the specimen came from a beach nowhere near the tragedy, Steve goes to Plymouth for further exploration and hires a boat, the *Molly T*. He eventually spots a huge object rise out of the sea but it moves too quickly to be chased. When a steamship is wrecked on a nearby beach, Steve and Bickford examine it and find no survivors with the craft badly damaged and containing high levels of radiation. Going back to London, the two men inform Royal Navy Admiral Summers (Lloyd Lamble) that they believe a marine animal of tremendous size and strength attacked the ship. Steve also says the white substance found in the radioactive fish was from the stomach lining of a marine creature. As Summers sends out an order to alert naval forces around the world about the monster, the Behemoth attacks a remote farm and incinerates a farmer and his son. Looking at photos taken at the scene of the attack, Steve and Bickford see a huge footprint. They meet with Dr. Sampson (Jack MacGowran), a noted paleontologist, who declares it belongs to a plesiosaurus, a type of dinosaur with the properties of an electric eel. He theorizes that the creature is returning to the shallows that gave it birth and asks to join the two men in trying to find the beast. When Steve tells him the dinosaur is radioactive, Sampson sadly notes it will have to be destroyed. Steve and Bickford meet again with the admiral and recommend that the Thames River be blocked off and London evacuated. Sampson and a helicopter crew try to find the Behemoth but when the pilot (Neil Hallett) drops too near the water, the creature rises up and its radiation incinerates the craft. The monster then emerges from the Thames and overturns a ferry, killing nearly all its passengers. The military plans to blow it up but Steve warns that the radioactive pieces could cause massive health problems. He says that the creature is burning itself up and that shooting pure radium into it will safely bring about its immediate demise. As a warhead is being loaded with the radium, the Behemoth returns to London and goes on a spree of destruction throughout the city, destroying buildings and power lines and starting large fires. After the Behemoth falls through London Bridge and back into the river, Steve and a commander (Maurice Kaufman) take a mini-submarine armed with the warhead and go after the creature. The craft begins leaking after being hit by the monster, but the commander is able to fire the warhead which hits and destroys the Behemoth. When Steve returns to the dock to meet Bickford, they hear a radio report about masses of dead fish being found on the shores of the United States from Maine to Florida.

Filmed in England as a co-production of Allied Artists and Eros Films as *The Behemoth*, the movie was released in Great Britain by Eros as *Behemoth the Sea Monster* with an X Certificate. In its day it was a fairly popular monster outing with its reputation being further enhanced by the fact that legendary stop-motion animator Willis H. O'Brien worked on the project. His classics in the field of special effects include *The Lost World* (1925), *King Kong* and *The Son of Kong* (both 1933), *Mighty Joe Young* (1949) and *The Black Scorpion* (1957). *The Giant Behemoth*, however, was not one of his career highlights. While the title monster was fairly realistic, the production was plagued by the use of obvious miniatures. Fortunately the plot leading up to the scenes with the monster is interesting. The film was not helped by the taciturn hero played by Gene Evans. Jack MacGowran overplayed the part of the seedy paleontologist. André Morell, as always, is sound as the British physicist.

The Giant Behemoth was directed and designed by Eugene Lourie and is similar in plot and execution to his earlier *The Beast from 20,000 Fathoms* (1953). In *Science Fiction Film Directors, 1895–1998* (2000), Dennis Fischer noted that the film "benefit[s] from superior performances by its leads, Gene Evans and André Morell.... Lourie shot the film on location documentary style, which adds a feeling of realism to the proceedings.... Lourie's direction is both atmospheric and inventive, but the inadequate budget prevents *The Giant Behemoth* from eclipsing *The Beast from 20,000 Fathoms*." Among the director's other genre credits are *The Colossus of New York* (1958), *Gorgo* (1961) and second unit work on *Crack in the World* (1965). He was art director for two other Allied releases, *Confessions of an Opium Eater* (1962) and *Shock Corridor* (1963) [qq.v.].

The Golden Idol (1954; 71 minutes)

Producer-Director-Story-Screenplay: Ford Beebe. Photography: Harry Neumann. Editor: John Fuller. Music: Marlin Skiles. Art Director: Dave Milton. Sound: Charles Cooper. Sets: Robert Priestley. Production Supervisor: Allen K. Wood. Makeup: Norman Pringle. Special Effects: Ray Mercer. Assistant Director: Edward Morey, Jr.

CAST: Johnny Sheffield (Bomba), Anne Kimbell (Karen Marsh), Paul Guilfoyle (Prince Ali Ben Mamoud), Leonard Mudie (Commissioner Andy Barnes), Smoki Whitfield (Eli), Rick Vallin (Abdullah), Lane Bradford (Joe Hawkins), Roy Glenn (Gomo), James Adamson (Ezekial), William Tannen (Sergeant Reed), Don C. Harvey (Officer Graves), Bill Walker (Nadji), Robert Bice (Guard), Nakimba (Chimp).

Following his appearance as Boy, the adopted son of Tarzan and Jane, in eight "Tarzan" films (from *Tarzan Finds a Son!* in 1939 through *Tarzan and the Huntress* in 1947), Johnny Sheffield took on the role of Bomba, the Jungle Boy, in a dozen features released between 1949 and 1955. The Monogram series entries *The Lost Volcano* (1950) and *The Hidden City* (1953) dealt with lost civilizations and *The Golden Idol*, issued by Allied Artists early in 1954, revolved around a priceless native idol. The character originated in a popular series of books published by the Stratemeyer Syndicate. Between 1926 and 1938 twenty novels about Bomba by Roy Rockwood (a pseudonym) were published, the first ten with South American settings and the rest in Africa. Thanks to the popularity of the Bomba films, the initial ten volumes were reissued by Grosset and Dunlap and later by Clover Books.

Bomba (Sheffield) retrieves the Lost Idol of Watusi from the emir, Prince Ali Ben Mamoud (Paul Guilfoyle), who stole it from a Tanganyikan witch doctor. The emir pays dishonest hunter Joe Hawkins (Lane Bradford) to get the priceless treasure back for him because he wants to collect a huge reward for it from the British government. Since Commissioner Andy Barnes (Leonard Mudie) is set to arrive to get the idol, Mamoud tells Hawkins to abduct Bomba and torture the young man in order to find its whereabouts. As Mamoud, Hawkins and Gomo (Roy Glenn), a tracker, set out to find Bomba, the jungle boy sees Barnes traveling in a motorboat and beckons him to shore. With the commissioner and his underlings Eli (Smoki Whitfield) and Ezekiel (James Adamson) is archaeologist Karen Marsh (Anne Kimball) who wants the Idol of the Watusi for a museum. Karen thinks she will get the idol from Mamoud but Bomba informs her he has it and will give it to her for the reward which he will distribute among the tribe of the witch doctor murdered by the emir. Mamoud and Hawkins see Bomba talking to Karen and the commissioner so Hawkins decides to pretend to be a big game hunter in order to join their party and let the jungle boy lead him to the idol. A lion tries to kill Karen but she is saved by Bomba. Hawkins comes to their camp and finds out that the young man is going for the idol. When he leaves, Bomba is captured by the emir's henchmen and soon finds out that Hawkins is in cahoots with Mamoud. When he is threatened with torture, Bomba tells his captors that if they kill him, they will never find the idol. Hawkins returns to camp with the emir's men and captures Barnes and his party. When Mamoud shows up with Bomba, he threatens to torture Karen. Bomba then agrees to return the idol by the end of the next day and he leaves but is guarded by two of the emir's henchmen (Bill Walker, Robert Bice). During the night, Bomba's pet chimp Nakimba knocks out guard Gomo with a rock and unties Eli, who

Roy Glenn, Leonard Mudie, Paul Guilfoyle, Rick Vallin, and Anne Kimball in *The Golden Idol* (1954)

releases Karen and Barnes, and they run into the jungle. Gomo revives and tells Mamoud and Hawkins, who set out after the escapees. Bomba has knocked out his guards and is using jungle drums to send a message for help to district policemen Sergeant Reed (William Tannen) and Officer Graves (Don C. Harvey). When morning comes, Bomba arrives at the Pangola Basin where he has hidden the golden idol underwater. After he dives for it, the commissioner, Eli and Karen show up but they are followed by Mamoud and Hawkins. Bomba brings up the idol and gives it to Karen. As she and the commissioner leave with it, he swims to overturn Mamoud's boat. Bomba and Hawkins fight in the water while the emir is killed by a huge serpent. The policemen arrive and place Gomo and the other henchmen under arrest as Bomba gives them a badly beaten Hawkins.

Filmed at Gene Autry's Melody Ranch in Newhall, California, as *Bomba and the Golden Idol*, the film was the tenth entry in the series. The *Motion Picture Exhibitor* said, it "should find the usual clientele awaiting it. The story is interesting and the cast, direction, and production are also in the usual category." The feature was produced, directed and written by Ford Beebe whose career went back to the silent days. During the sound era he helmed a plethora of genre serials as well as producing and directing *Night Monster* (1942) and *The Invisible Man's Revenge* (1944) and producing *Son of Dracula* (1943), all for Universal.

When the Bomba series ended in 1955, Sheffield teamed with his producer-director-actor father, Reginald Sheffield, in the TV pilot *Bantu, the Zebra Boy*. When it failed to sell, he retired from acting and pursued a successful career in real estate. In 1967 DC Comics published seven issues of the *Bomba, Jungle Boy* comic book. In 2010, veteran jungle-movie tree climber Sheffield died after a fall from a ladder.

Hands of a Stranger (1962; 85 minutes)

Producers: Newton Arnold and Michael du Pont. Director-Screenplay: Newton Arnold. From the novel *Les Mains d'Orlac* (The Hands of Orlac) by Maurice Renard. Photography: Henry Cronjager. Editor: Bert Honey. Music: Richard LaSalle. Song: John Mosher. Art Director: Ted Holsopple. Sound: Victor B. Appel and Glen Glenn Co. Production Manager: Vernon Keays. Sets: John Sturtevant. Makeup: Charles Gemora. Technical Advisor: Dr. Richard Gans. Assistant Director: Jack C. May.

CAST: Paul Lukather (Dr. Gil Harding), Joan Harvey (Dina Paris), James Stapleton (Vernon Paris), Irish McCalla (Holly), Barry Gordon (Skeet Wilder), Ted Otis (Dr. Ross Compton), Michael Rye (George Britton), Larry Haddon (Lieutenant Syms), Elaine Martone (Eileen Hunter), George Sawaya (Tony Wilder), Michael du Pont (Dr. Ken Fry), Sally Kellerman (Sue), David Kramer (Carnival Barker), Carl Carlsson (Juggler), The Red Norvo Quintette [Red Norvo, Red Wootten, Jimmy Wyble, Jerry Dodgion, John Markham].

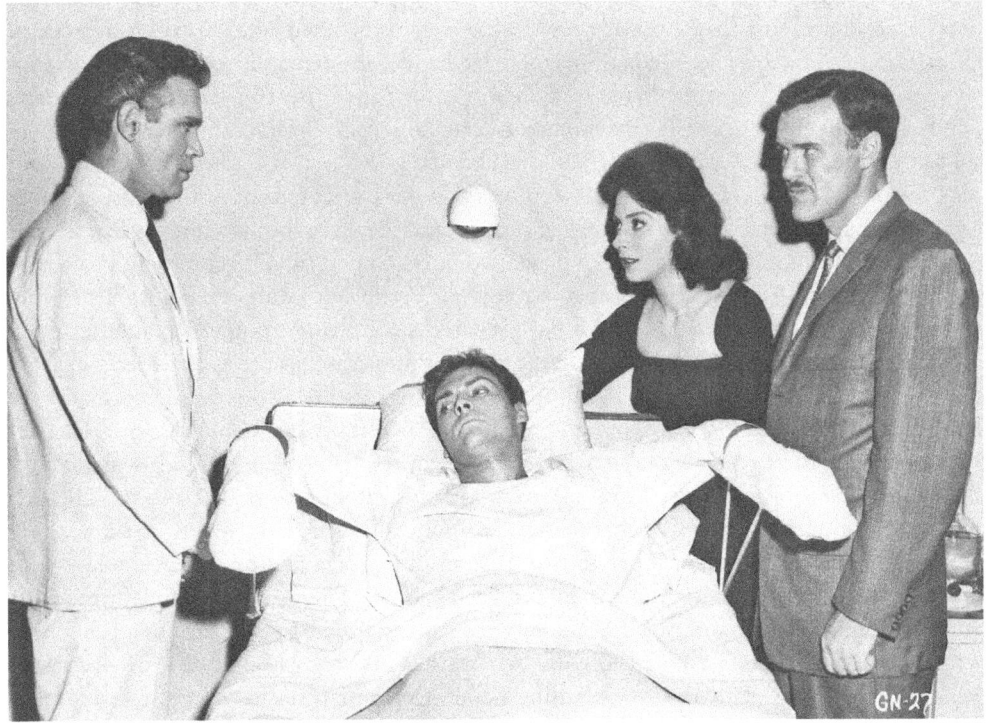

Paul Lukather, James Stapleton, Joan Harvey and Michael Rye in *Hands of a Stranger* (1962)

Maurice Renard's novel *Les Mains d'Orlac* (The Hands of Orlac) was first filmed in Austria in 1924 as *Orlacs Haende* (The Hands of Orlac), directed by Robert Wiene and starring Conrad Veidt as the pianist whose new transplanted hands turn him into a murderer. The first sound version of the book came in 1935 with MGM's *Mad Love* starring Peter Lorre, Frances Drake and Colin Clive, with the emphasis on the crazed Dr. Gogol, portrayed by Lorre. In 1959 the British production *The Hands of Orlac* was done by Britannia–British Lion starring Mel Ferrer as Stephen Orlac with Christopher Lee as the evil magician Neron. It was shown in the U.S. in 1964 as *Hands of a Strangler*. Two years before that, Allied Artists released a screen version of Renard's work, *Hands of a Stranger*, in April 1962.

While walking down a street, a man is shot and robbed and left for dead, his powerful hands clinging to a lamp post. He is taken by ambulance to a hospital where Dr. Gil Harding (Paul Lukather), the chief of surgery, tries in vain to save his life. The doctor is questioned by Police Lieutenant Syms (Larry Haddon) in an attempt to find some clue to the murdered man's identity. That night, pianist Vernon Paris (James Stapleton) gives a triumphant concert before a capacity crowd and afterward is greeted by his sister Dina (Joan Harvey), his girlfriend Ellen Hunter (Elaine Martone) and his manager George Britton (Michael Rye). He sends the trio on to a party and later takes a cab driven by Tony Wilder (George Sawaya) who tells Paris that his young son also plays the piano. When Wilder attempts to show Vernon a picture of the boy, he loses control of the vehicle, causing a head-on crash. At the hospital, Harding gets Britton's permission to replace Vernon's hands, which have been destroyed in the accident, with those of the murdered man, although the manager says the pianist would be better off dead. Harding and his associates, Dr. Ross Compton (Ted Otis), Dr. Ken Fry (Michael du Pont) and nurse Holly (Irish McCalla), perform the first-time procedure of grafting a dead man's hands onto a living body. After the operation, Harding tells a distraught Dina that surgically everything went as planned and she calls him a crazed monster. After he shows her the pianist's mangled hands, she demands to know whose hands were grafted onto her brother. Syms asks the surgeon what happened to the murdered man's hands and the doctor requests two months to carry out an experiment. When Paris comes to, he demands to know what happened to his hands. Dina assures her brother he will again play the piano. After x-rays show that Vernon's body has accepted the new hands, Harding and his associates remove the bandages and the pianist realizes they are not his hands. The doctor informs his patient he has been given two normal hands and it is up to him to accept them or give up. When he tries to play the piano, Vernon can only remember his former triumphs. He goes to see Eileen, who has prepared a candlelight dinner for another man, and the two argue. She backs into the table and her dress catches fire as Paris refrains from helping her. After Syms informs Harding that the fingerprints of the murdered man have not revealed his identity, Dina tells the doctor that Vernon has become depressed over Eileen's death. Paris goes to the home of the cab driver, Tony Wilder, and is met by his ten-year-old son Skeet (Barry Gordon), who says his father will be back soon. The boy notices the stranger's interest in his piano and invites him to play. When he cannot, the boy makes a caustic comment that throws Vernon into a rage and he shoves the boy with his powerful hands, causing him to fall and hit his head. The blind Wilder returns home with his seeing eye dog and calls for his son, not realizing the boy is dead. Dina has dinner with Harding and talks about life with her brother and asks him about the origins of Vernon's new hands. The next day Harding examines the pianist's hands and tells him that full dexterity will return, especially with exercise. That night Vernon goes with his sister and the doctor to a carnival but when he cannot hit targets at a carnival booth he assaults the barker (David Kramer). After Dina tells her brother she has fallen in love with Harding, he goes to see Fry, who is with his girlfriend Sue (Sally Kellerman), and he murders them. When Syms shows Harding the bodies of Fry and Sue, and also tells him about the Wilder boy, he theorizes that the surgeon gave Vernon new hands and the pianist is taking revenge on those involved in his tragedy. At his apartment, Vernon tells his sister he will play for her but he wants her to listen from another room. After Compton assures his colleague they must continue his work, Harding goes to see Dina and they find the music they are hearing is from a recording. At the same time, Vernon murders Compton and takes his body to the theater where he had his greatest triumph. Harding and Dina drive to the empty concert hall and confront Vernon who shows them Compton's corpse. Vernon demonstrates that he cannot play the piano and grabs Dina as Harding tells him his body accepted the new hands but his mind did not. The pianist tries to strangle Harding and during the struggle he is shot and killed by Syms.

Hands of a Stranger is a low-budget, talky melodrama which emphasizes the use of hands in everyday activities. Filmed as *The Answer* by Glenwood-Neve Productions, it apparently was cut before its theatrical release since the Red Norvo Quinette gets special billing but is only heard briefly on a phonograph record playing the song "How's Your Mother." When it was released in Great Britain in August 1962 by Warner-Pathé it ran 73 minutes, twelve minutes shy of its stateside running time. The acting is uniformly good, especially Paul Lukather as the dedicated surgeon and Joan Harvey as the tragic pianist's loving sister. Lukather also starred in *Dinosaurus!* (1960) [q.v.] but is probably best remembered for starring in the daytime serial *Bright Promise* (NBC-TV, 1969–72). The film's director-scripter, Newton Arnold, also helmed *Blood Thirst* (1971) and was assistant director for *Blade Runner* (1982). The makeup was done by Charles Gemora, best known for appearing in his custom-made gorilla outfit in many horror films including *Seven Footprints to Satan* (1929), *Murders in the Rue Morgue* (1932), and *The Monster and the Girl* (1941). Gemora died in 1961, making *Hands of a Stranger* one of his last films. Production manager Vernon Keays co-directed the serial *The Mysterious Mr. M* (1946).

Perhaps the most memorable scene in the film occurred at the carnival, when the pianist suddenly looks in a distorted mirror and sees his hands, which appear to be monstrous talons. *Castle of Frankenstein #3* (1963) called *Hands of a Stranger* "[g]ood, but not outstanding," and Steven H. Scheuer's *Movies on TV 1975–76 Edition* (1974) proclaimed, "Wildly implausible — some good moments." Phil Hardy in *The Encyclopedia of Horror Movies* (1986) termed it "worthy but dull" while *John Stanley's Creature Features Movie Guide Strikes Again* (1994) thought it an "[i]nteresting variation" on Renard's work, adding, "Writer-director Newton Arnold creates good characters and dialogue but there are times when he goes off the Freudian end." In *Horror and Science Films: A Checklist* (1972), Donald C. Willis stated, "None of the *Hands of Orlac* adaptations is better than mediocre, and this may be the worst."

Hell's Five Hours (1958; 73 minutes)

Producer-Director-Screenplay: Jack L. Copeland. Associate Producer–Editor: Walter A. Hannemann. Photography: Ernest Haller. Music: Nicholas Carras. Art Director: David Milton. Sound: Jim Mobley and Harold E. McGhan. Sets: Herman Schoenbrun. Production Manager–Assistant Director: Stanley Goldsmith. Costumes: Bert Henrikson. Makeup: Emile LaVigne. Special Effects: Milton Rice.

CAST: Stephen McNally (Mike Brand), Coleen Gray (Nancy Brand), Vic Morrow (Burt Nash), Maurice Manson (Dr. Howard Culver), Robert Foulk (Jack Fife), Dan Sheridan (Ken

Archer), Will J. White (Al Parker), Robert Christopher (Bill), Charles J. Conrad (George Knight), Ray Ferrell (Eric Brand), Richard Warren (Mack), Artie Lewis (Reporter), James Parnell (Pete), Joe Devlin (Cook), John Mitchum (Roadblock Officer), Bru Danger (Squad Car Policeman), Joey Ray, Robert Colbert, John Damler, Louis Hart, Jim Cathey, Bill Gallant (Policemen), Norman Nazarr, Leo Needham (Photographers), Tony Lockridge (Helper), Bill Hughes, Frank Hagney (Guards), Ann Staunton (Customer), Cappy Carey, Hart Wayne (Evacuees), Ed Richard (Man).

Allied Artists' *Port of Hell* (1954) [q.v.] and *Kiss Me Deadly* (1955) from United Artists fit nicely into the *film noir* category but both touched on sci-fi as they edged into the realm of nuclear apocalypse. Another Allied feature, *Hell's Five Hours*, produced by the Muriel Corporation and issued on a double bill with *Macabre* (q.v.) in April 1958, is more insular in that it deals with a psychopathic terrorist who sets himself up as a human bomb in order to take out a military-industrial manufacturer of rocket fuel as his means of revenge for perceived ill treatment at the hands of the system. The feature was produced, directed and written by Jack L. Copeland, a maker of documentaries, and it was his only theatrical outing. The exteriors were shot at a steam plant in the San Fernando Valley and its initial reel contains no dialogue. The *New York Times* reported, "The first ten minutes of *Hell's Five Hours* move swiftly. It's a simple — sometimes too simple — clockwatching chore thereafter."

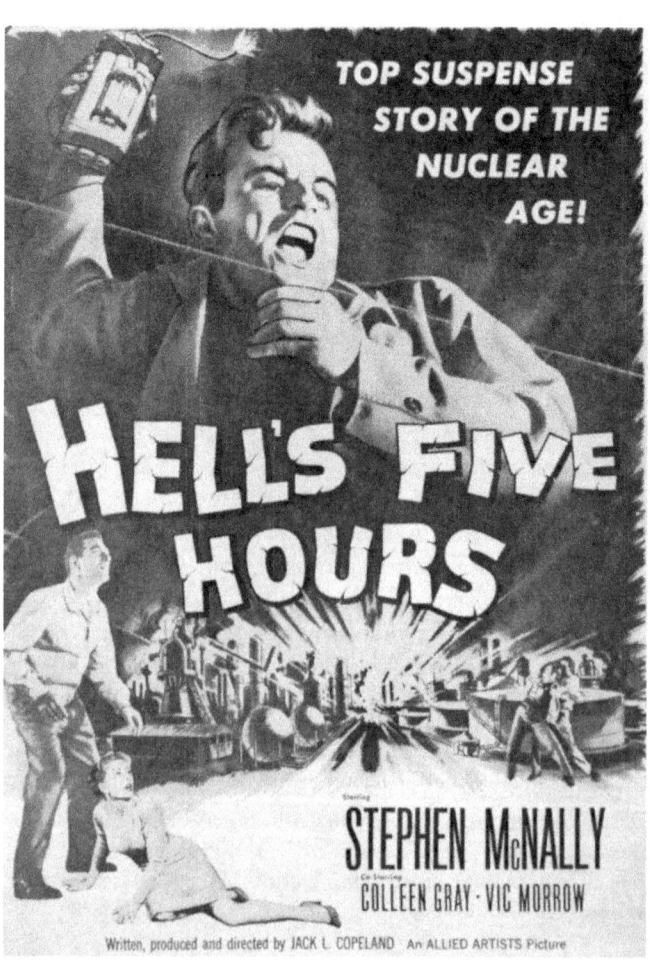

Poster for *Hell's Five Hours* (1958)

Mike Brand (Stephen McNally), the manager of the Exiter Fuel Corporation which makes rocket fuel for the government, is told there has been a robbery resulting in the shooting of a security guard and a tank set on fire and that dynamite has been stolen. As he meets with the local police and FBI men, he receives a telephone call from a man who says he will blow up the plant. An order is issued to evacuate everyone within three miles of the complex and Mike mandates that the gasoline at the site be pumped to another location one hundred miles away, a process taking five hours to complete. Mike calls his wife Nancy (Coleen Gray) and tells her to take their young son Eric (Ray Ferrell) to his mother's home in a nearby city. Jack Fife (Robert Foulk), a plant foreman, informs his boss that he fired worker Burt Nash (Vic Morrow) earlier in the day for smoking and the man promised retaliation. As the gas is being pumped, Nash hovers around the area with dynamite cinched to his body; he later telephones Mike with another promise to blow up the complex. The police notify Mike that Nash has a history of suicidal talk and they believe his being fired caused him to seek revenge. They arrange for psychiatrist Dr. Howard Culver (Maurice Manson) to assess Nash's actions, not knowing the psychopath has gone to Mike's home where he makes Nancy call her husband demanding to go inside the plant. After Nancy drives Nash and Eric to the plant, the police do not try to capture the suspect as the three enter one of the buildings. The FBI men find evidence in Nash's abode of his constructing a device to set off a bomb by employing liquid mercury. As Culver tells the police not to make any sudden moves toward the suspect, Mike meets with him in the plant. When Eric tries to get away, a policeman comes to his aid, saving the boy but getting shot by Nash. Burt tells Mike that Fife beat him up, compounding all the other mistreatment he has received over the years. As Nash forces Nancy to get into one of the tankers, Mike and the police learn from Fife that Nash told the truth about being beaten. Nancy tries to humor her captor while the psychiatrist says he believes Nash is not suicidal and suggests he may be open to an offer of money. After Mike says he will give Nash $5,000, the man agrees to consider it but informs Nancy it will never happen since he has committed two murders. While Mike and the police wait for a bank vault to open so they can get the money, Nash moves Nancy deeper into the plant, shows her how his bomb trigger works and tells her he wants her to leave with him. When one of the steam lines buckles, the explosion frightens Fife and he runs into Nash, who shoots him. Nash takes Nancy to a rooftop, unaware they are being followed by Mike. The police inform Nash they have the promised money but he becomes agitated by the sound of a siren announcing that the gas transfer has been completed. Nancy attempts to escape and Nash shoots at her. Mike fights with him and when they hit the ground the bomb does not go off. Moving back to a rail, Nash wires the trigger but falls and is blown up.

Hold That Hypnotist (1957; 61 minutes)

Producer: Ben Schwalb. Director: Austen Jewell. Screenplay: Dan Pepper. Photography: Harry Neumann. Editor: George White. Music: Marlin Skiles. Art Director: Dave Milton. Sound: Ralph Butler. Sets: Joseph Kish. Production Manager: Allen K. Wood. Makeup: Emile LaVigne. Wardrobe: Bert Henrikson. Continuity: Richard M. Chaffee. Assistant Director: Edward Morey, Jr.

CAST: Huntz Hall (Horace Debussy "Sach" Jones/Algy Winkle/Marc Antony), Stanley Clements (Stanislaus "Duke" Coveleskie/Bartender), Jane Nigh (Cleo Daniels/Inn Girl), Robert Foulk (Dr. Simon Noble), James Flavin (Jake Morgan), Queenie Smith (Kate Kelly), David [Gorcey] Condon (Chuck/Inn Customer), Jimmy Murphy (Myron/Inn Customer), Murray Alper (Gail), Dick Elliott (Hotel Clerk), Mel Welles (Blackbeard), Edward Stepner (Bruno), Frank Orth (Beedle), Mary Treen (Maid), Irving Mitchell (Agnew), Lee Roberts, Robert Bice, Bob Roark (Reporters), John Close (Sergeant Benton), George Barrows (Pirate).

Kate Kelly (Queenie Smith) is the landlady of the Bowery Boys: Sach Jones (Huntz Hall), Duke Coveleskie (Stanley Clements), Chuck (David Condon) and Myron (Jimmy Murphy). When she becomes interested in reincarnation, she decides to pay Dr. Simon Noble (Robert Foulk), a best-selling author, to hypnotize her so she can be regressed into former lives. The boys want to prove the man is a fake. As Noble and Jake Morgan (James Flavin), his partner, host a press conference, the Bowery Boys show up and Duke demands to be hypnotized. When this fails, Sach is put into a trance after staring at an earring worn by Noble's feather-headed secretary, Cleo Daniels (Jane Nigh). He is taken back to the 17th century as Algy Winkle, a tax collector in Charleston, South Carolina. There he tells the pirate Blackbeard (Mel Welles) to pay his taxes and is suckered into a game in which he ends up with a map showing the whereabouts of a treasure hidden by the buccaneer. Sach comes back to the present before he can relate the location of the treasure. Going to the library, the boys learn about Winkle and find out he was killed in a storm at sea on his way to get the riches. Duke offers Noble and Morgan part of the loot if the doctor will hypnotize Sach again so he can reveal its location. Noble realizes he cannot put Sach in a trance without Cleo's earring but he and Morgan got rid of her because she knew the regression subject of his book was paid to talk about phony previous lives. The boys find Cleo modeling swimsuits in Jersey City but she too demands a cut of the treasure before she will cooperate. Noble hypnotizes Sach again but this time he goes back to ancient Rome where he is Marc Antony. Coming forward, Algy Winkle says the treasure is in a cave at Hudson's Cove and the two crooks tell Sach to hold off his pals at gunpoint as they go to find the grotto. Cleo brings Sach around by kissing him and the Bowery Boys drive to the cave. In their jalopy, Sach finds a magazine with the story of Blackbeard and they realize this is where he got the idea of the hidden treasure. Sach runs into a cave to get away from his upset pals and finds a case full of jewelry. When the two crooks try to steal it, the Bowery Boys overpower them and head home where they celebrate with Cleo and Mrs. Kelly. Police Sergeant Benson (John Close) shows up to tell them they found the proceeds of a jewel robbery but Sach is placated when Cleo kisses him.

The year before *Hold That Hypnotist* was released by Allied Artists, the studio issued a more melodramatic outing dealing with hypnotic regression *Fright* (q.v.). Made as *Out of This World* and *Roving Eyes*, *Hold That Hypnotist* came to theaters in March 1957 and was the forty-fourth of forty-eight "Bowery Boys" films. The whimsical plot satirized the then current fad of delving into previous lives by hypnosis, popularized by Dr. Morey Bernstein's book *The Search for Bridey Murphy*, which Paramount filmed under that title in 1956. The Bowery Boys outing, however, is all levity and gives top-billed Huntz Hall a chance to enact three roles. Not only does he play the goofy series character Sach, but he also is tax collector Algy Winkle and Rome's Marc Antony. Austen Jewell, who had served as assistant director on several of the series' previous entries, made his directorial debut in *Hold That Hypnotist* and it proved to be one of better outings in the Bowery Boys' post–Leo Gorcey films with Stanley Clements.

House on Haunted Hill (1959; 75 minutes)

Producer-Director: William Castle. Associate Producer–Screenplay: Robb White. Photography: Carl E. Guthrie. Editor: Roy Livingston. Music: Von Dexter. Song: Richard Kayne and Richard Loring. Art Director: David Milton. Sound: Ralph Butler. Sets: Morris Hoffman. Production Manager: Edward Morey, Jr. Makeup: Jack Dusick. Special Effects: Herman Townsley. Continuity: Virginia Mazzuca. Assistant Director: Jack R. Berne.

CAST: Vincent Price (Frederick Loren), Carol Ohmart (Annabelle Loren), Richard Long (Lance Schroeder), Alan Marshal (Dr. David Trent), Carolyn Craig (Nora Manning), Elisha Cook, Jr. (Watson Pritchard), Julie Mitchum (Ruth Bridgers), Leona Anderson (Mrs. Slydes), Howard Hoffman (Jonas Slydes).

For his second "gimmick" horror film, following the success of *Macabre* (1958) [q.v.], producer-director William Castle made *House on Haunted Hill* that featured "Emergo." To further chill an already frightened audience, this gimmick had a prop skeleton swinging through theaters on wires at the same moment that its counterpart emerged from an acid vat on screen. Produced for $150,000, the horror thriller grossed over four million dollars. The feature also solidified Vincent Price as a star of scary movies, the actor having previously done *The Invisible Man Returns* (1940), *Shock* (1946), *House of Wax* (1953), *The Mad Magician* (1954), *The Fly* (1958), et al. Castle and Price would re-team for *The Tingler* the same year at Columbia Pictures. The premise of *House on Haunted Hill* (a group of people locked in a spooky old house for a night) was reminiscent of the 1930 novel (by Gwen Bristow and Bruce Manning) and play (by Owen Davis) *The Invisible Host* which Columbia filmed in 1934 as *The Ninth Guest* and later partially remade as *The Man They Could Not Hang* (1939) and *The Missing Juror* (1944).

Variety said, "*Haunted Hill* is expertly put together. There is some good humor in the dialog which not only pays off well against the ghostly elements, but provides a release for laughter so it does not explode in the suspense sequences. The characters are interesting and not outlandish, so there is some basis of reality. Director William Castle keeps things moving at a healthy clip." The *Los Angeles Examiner* reported, "If you want the living daylights scared out of you, go visit *House on Haunted Hill*," and the *Motion Picture Herald* called it "[a] very commercial piece of nerve-wracking horror entertainment." Phil Hardy wrote in *The Encyclopedia of Horror Movies* (1986), "Efficient, considerably boosted by [Vincent] Price's sinisterly genial performance, and quite enjoyable in its old-fashioned horror-comedy way.... [It] has a plot which seems like one of his [Castle's] own promotional gimmicks." "Ghostly gimmickry abounds.... Hokey but entertaining murder mystery," is how Ed Naha described *House on Haunted Hill* in *Horrors: From Screen to Scream* (1975). *Harrison's Reports* noted, "There long has been an absence of ghost stories from the screen and this one should be welcomed by exhibitors who can use such fare because it is a very good picture of its kind." In Hollywood's typical fashion of not leaving well enough alone, the film was redone in 1999 as a horror-comedy that *Leonard Maltin's 2004 Movie and Video Guide* (2003) termed "[a] dreary remake.... Heavy-handed, and no fun at all."

Opening to the sounds of groans, chains rattling and

Poster for *House on Haunted Hill* (1959)

screams, *House on Haunted Hill* has Watson Pritchard (Elisha Cook, Jr.), the owner of the century-old mansion, saying he only spent one night there and the next day he was almost dead. Pritchard has rented the house to rich Frederick Loren (Price) who claims his fourth wife Annabelle (Carol Ohmart) wants to give a haunted house party. Loren is paying each of the invited guests $10,000 if they can spend a night in the abode and he arranges for them to arrive in funeral cars. Those invited all need the money. They are Lance Schroeder (Richard Long), a test pilot; Dr. David Trent (Alan Marshal), who is doing a study on hysteria; typist Nora Manning (Carolyn Craig), who works for one of Loren's companies and is the sole support of her family; newspaper columnist Ruth Bridgers (Julie Mitchum), who wants to do a feature on ghosts but needs the money to pay off gambling debts; and the alcoholic Pritchard. After they show up, Lance saves Nora from being killed when a chandelier falls near her. Frederick informs Annabelle that their guests have arrived but she tells him she does not want to attend the party and they argue with him accusing her of trying to poison him for his money. Pritchard tells the others there have been seven murders in the house, including that of his brother who was killed by his wife (who also did in her sister at the same time). He said their heads were never found and the ghosts in the place will come for all of them soon. Frederick appears before the invited guests and informs them they will be locked in at midnight with no electricity or telephones. He asks Pritchard to give the others a tour of the house. In one room, dark drops fall from the ceiling onto Ruth's hand with Pritchard announcing she has been marked by the ghosts. In the cellar he tells how a man murdered his wife over jealousy and he shows them the acid pit into which her body was thrown. When the others leave, Lance and Nora remain. After Lance disappears into another room, Nora sees a white-haired crone in a floor-length black outfit. Lance is later found in the room with a head wound, claiming someone knocked him out. Lance and Nora go back to the basement where she again sees the old woman float across the room but becomes incensed when the test pilot does not believe her story. Going upstairs, Nora meets Annabelle, who tells her that Frederick is planning something. She also informs Nora that she is afraid of her husband due to his jealousy and that he would kill her if he could. In her room, Nora opens a traveling case and finds the bloody, severed head of a woman and runs screaming into the hallway where she is grabbed by a man who tells her to get out of the house before she is killed. Finding the others in the living room, the hysterical Nora announces she wants to leave but calms down when she sees the caretakers (Leona Anderson, Howard Hoffman) whom she recognizes as the old woman and the man who warned her. She still demands to leave but the elderly couple quickly depart and everyone is locked inside the house. Annabelle makes an appearance and Frederick gives the guests toy caskets, each containing a revolver, but Pritchard warns they are no good against the dead, only the living. Nora takes the others to her room but finds her traveling case empty and refuses a sedative offered to her by Trent. Going to see Nora in her room, Lance finds it deserted but does locate the fake head in a closet and confronts Pritchard with it. As they argue they hear a scream and they find a woman hanging from a rope in the hallway. Trent takes her down and carries her to a bedroom. Lance fears that it is Nora but it turns out to be Annabelle. Nora grabs Lance in the hallway and informs him she thinks Frederick tried to choke her. Lance gives her his gun and tells her to lock herself in her room. In the living room, Frederick asks Trent if his wife committed suicide or was murdered while Lance declares that one of them is a killer and suggests they all stay in their rooms until morning. Going back to Nora, Lance says he thinks Frederick murdered his wife and he plans to try and get help. Lance finds a secret panel as a thunderstorm breaks loose and Nora sees a rope climb into the house snake-like through her window where stands the specter of Annabelle. The young woman runs from the room and sees Annabelle's body again hanging in the hallway. Hearing Nora's screams, Trent goes to Frederick's room and the two men agree to search the house with Frederick taking the downstairs. Trent goes to Annabelle's room and tells her their plan is working: The hysterical Nora will soon kill Frederick and then they will have his fortune. Trying to find Lance, Nora goes to the basement. When Frederick shows up she shoots him and runs upstairs. Trent emerges from the darkness and begins moving the body, intending to drop it into the acid vat, as the lights go out. Annabelle comes to the basement and sees a skeleton rise from the acid as Frederick's voice admonishes her for killing him. Backing away from the skeleton, Annabelle falls into the vat and is consumed as Frederick emerges holding a puppeteering mechanism that controls the actions of the skeleton. With the help of Pritchard and Ruth, Nora locates Lance in a secret passage and the quartet go to the basement where Frederick tells them it will be up to the law to decide if he is guilty or innocent in the deaths of his wife and her lover. Pritchard announces that the ghosts have taken nine people and will soon be coming for him and *you*.

The Human Duplicators (1965; 80 minutes; Color)

Producers: Hugo Grimaldi and Arthur C. Pierce. Executive Producer: Lawrence H. Woolner. Director: Hugo Grimaldi. Screenplay: Arthur C. Pierce. Photography: Monroe P. Askins. Editor: Donald Wolfe. Music Director: Gordon Zahler. Art Director: Paul Sylos. Sound: Robert Reeve and Jean G. Valentino. Sets: Raymond Boltz, Jr. Production Manager-Assistant Director: Jesse Coralles. Makeup: Bob Mark. Special Effects: Roger George. Special Effects Makeup: John Chambers. Wardrobe: Carol Brooks and Mickey Meyers.

CAST: George Nader (Glenn Martin), Barbara Nichols (Gale Wilson), George Macready (Professor Vaughn Dornheimer), Dolores Faith (Lisa Dornheimer), Hugh Beaumont (Austin Welles), Richard Arlen (Lieutenant Shaw), Richard Kiel (Dr. Kolos), Tommy Leonetti (Android Spy), Lonnie Sattin (Dr. Lin Yung), John Indrisano (Thor), Margot Teele, Alean "Bambi" Hamilton (Laboratory Assistants), Ted Durant (The Galaxy Master), Mel Ruick (Dr. Munson), Larry Barton (Android), Andrew Johnson (Guard), Bill Hampton, Walter Maslow, Richard Schuyler, John Dasten, Lori Lyons, Benito Prezia.

Released in March 1965 as the top half of a double bill with *Mutiny in Outer Space* (q.v.), *The Human Duplicators* is more interesting for its cast and settings than its convoluted plot. Cheaply made by Woolner Bros. and distributed by Allied Artists, the production was top-billed George Nader's last Hollywood outing; in the interim he went to Europe and headlined a series of popular Jerry Cotton spy melodramas. Here Nader appears jaded and a bit long in the tooth to be playing an action-romantic leading man. Even more offbeat is the casting of shrill-voiced, hard-boiled blonde Barbara Nichols as his lady love and agent partner. In the scene where Nader's android tries to kill Nichols, her piercing screams are so loud they could burst glass. Outside of the two leads, the rest of the cast is quite good, especially George Macready as the kindly scientist and his evil android counterpart, Hugh Beaumont as Nader's boss, veteran film star Richard Arlen as a police lieutenant, and beautiful Dolores Faith as the scientist's blind niece. Faith also starred in *Mutiny in Outer Space*. Although he is not billed in the film's advertising, Richard Kiel has a large role as the invading alien, Dr. Kolos. After he gained fame in as the gigantic Jaws in the James Bond outings *The Spy Who Loved Me* (1977) and *Moonraker* (1979), *The Human Duplicators* was issued on video in the mid–1980s as *Jaws of the Alien*. Given "introducing" billing, but little to do, in the sci-fier are pop singer and composer Tommy Leonetti and Lonnie Sattin, sister of the equally exotic Tura Satana. Much of the film's action takes place in a huge old

Hollywood mansion that looks like something out of *Sunset Blvd.* (1950) with Paul Sylos' art direction and set decoration by Raymond Boltz, Jr., giving the proceedings a much richer look than most of its ilk. Unfortunately the spaceship shown at the start of the movie looks like a Christmas tree decoration and the interior of Kolos' craft is short on futurist gadgetry.

Giant alien Kolos (Kiel) is assigned by his superiors, led by the Galaxy Master (Ted Durant), to establish a colony on Earth in order to expand their domination. Kolos is told that if he fails, he will be destroyed. Kolos is tele-transported to the mansion of eccentric scientist Professor Vaughn Dornheimer (Macready) who is working to create a perfect android in hopes of bettering human life. The alien meets the scientist's blind niece Lisa (Faith), whom Dornheimer hopes to some day give the power of sight, and he tells the old man he can assist him in his experiments by being able to create an android in a few days. Kolos places Dornheimer and his two female assistants (Margot Teele, Alean "Bambi" Hamilton) under his spell and soon replaces them with lookalike androids. Dr. Munson (Mel Ruick), a colleague of Dornheimer's, robs the Space Research Corporation's laboratory and bullets do not faze him as he escapes. National Intelligence Agency master spy Glenn Martin (Nader) is called into the case and consults with Police Lieutenant Shaw (Arlen) and later they find Munson's body near the Dornheimer estate. Glenn reports to his boss, Austin Welles (Beaumont), and is told by another agent, Gale Wilson (Nichols), that Munson died from electrocution. She also says that Munson and two other scientists who died after committing robberies of highly classified materials were friends of Dornheimer. Glenn decides to talk with the scientist and, claiming to be a writer for *View* magazine, he goes to the estate where he meets Lisa, who warns him not to remain there. Dornheimer informs Glenn that he wants to rectify physical and mental illnesses and give Lisa sight. When the scientist leaves briefly to consult with Dr. Kolos, Glenn rummages through his papers and finds a photograph of physicist Dr. Lin Yung (Lonnie Sattin) but is spied upon by Dornheimer's butler Thor (John Indrisano), who is also an android. When Glenn and Gale go to dinner that night, they are trailed by another android (Tommy Leonetti). After reading some of the professor's books on cybernetics, Glenn tells his girlfriend he has to get into Dornheimer's laboratory. The next day he locates a cave that leads him to a room filled with dummies, several face masks (including that of Munson), and coffins containing duplicates of members of the scientist's staff. Locating the laboratory, Glenn observes Dornheimer creating an android of Dr. Yung by draining off her life forces into a synthetic body. Lisa tells Glenn to leave because her uncle is locked in a cell and the Dornheimer he sees is really an android created by Kolos. Glenn is captured by the alien and duplicated. Welles gets a telephone call saying another robbery has been committed and the suspect is Dr. Yung. Glenn's android goes to see Welles and says he wants to go to Washington, D.C., to further investigate the case, but Gale senses something strange about her boyfriend. At the estate, Lisa overhears Kolos telling the Galaxy Master about the creation of Glenn's android and is told to duplicate her because humans cannot be trusted. Dornheimer's android then confronts Kolos about Lisa but the alien, who has fallen in love with the blind girl, tells him that if he interferes he will be destroyed. Lisa visits Glenn in a cell that also houses her uncle, who needs medical attention. Gale follows Glenn's android to an electronics warehouse where she finds him committing a robbery. The Glenn android tries to kill her; Gale is rescued by Welles and his men who corner the android, whose arm breaks off after being caught between two closing doors. The android manages to drive away. At the mansion, Kolos informs Lisa that his superiors will destroy him if he does not carry out his orders. The

Hugh Beaumont (left) and George Nader and Barbara Nichols (on stairs) in *The Human Duplicators* (1965). Actors on the floor are unidentified.

androids, led by Dornheimer's duplicate, turn on Kolos. Lisa is also captured after she makes a return visit to Glenn's cell, bringing him a coin he dropped. Glenn opens the coin and uses its concealed coils to saw through the bars on his cell as the professor tells him the androids can be disabled by using an electrical beam aimed at their brains. Going to the laboratory, Glenn finds Kolos chained to a wall and the androids about to duplicate Lisa. He uses the electronic beam on the androids while Kolos breaks free and begins fighting them. Dornheimer's android is confronted by Glenn's android. When the scientist's android tells Glenn's double to kill the secret agent, the one-armed mechanical man says he will only take orders from Kolos. The two androids fight and destroy each other. Kolos rescues Lisa and takes her upstairs as Gale arrives with Welles and his men. The alien tells them he must leave knowing he will be destroyed but he says he no longer cares since he has learned that he too is an android. Kolos gives Lisa her eyesight before returning to his spaceship.

Co-financed by the Italian company Independenti Regionali, *The Human Duplicators* was released in that country as *Agente Spaziale K1* (Space Agent K1) and in France as *Les Creatures de Kolos* (The Creatures of Kolos). Its director, Hugo Grimaldi, earlier handled the U.S. version of the second "Godzilla" feature, *Gigantis, the Fire Monster* (1959), and he also helmed and produced *Duplicators*' co-feature, *Mutiny in Outer Space* (q.v.).

The Human Vapor (1964; 81 minutes)

Producers: Edward L. Alperson and Stanley D. Meyer. Executive Producer: Tomoyuki Tanaka. Director: Ishiro Honda. Screenplay: Takeshi Kimura. Photography: Hajime Koizumi. Editors: Kenneth Wannberg and Kazuji Taira. Music: Kunio Miyauchi. Production Design: Kiyoshi Shimizu. Sound: Masao Fujiyoshi. Production Executive: Sanezumi Fujimoto. Production Manager: Yasuaki Sakamoto. Special Effects: Eiji Tsuburaya. Assistant Director: Koji Kajita.

CAST: Keiko Sata (Kyoko), Tatsuya Mihashi (Detective Okamoto), Kaoru Yachigusa (Fujichiyo Kasuga), Yoshio Tsuchiya (Mizuno), Fuyuki Murakami (Dr. Sano), Bokuzen Hidari (Jiya), Takamaru Sasaki (Police Chief), Tatsuo Matsumura (Editor Ikeda), Ko Mishima (Detective Fujita), Hisaya Ito (Police Scientist), Yoshifumi Tajima (Sergeant), Yoshio Kosugi (Detective), Minosuke Yamada (Official), Kozo Nomura, Tetsu Nakamura (Reporters), Ren Yamamoto (Nomura), Sensho Matsumoto (Dance Teacher), Toki Shiozawa (Dance Teacher's Wife), Kamayuki Tsubono (Officer Ozaki), Yashushima Tsutsumi (Bank Manager), Wataru Omae, Hideo Shibuya (Rowdy Theater Patrons), Akio Kusama, Yutaka Olca (Policemen), Yukihiko Gondo, Shoichi Hirose (Murdered Guards), Takuzo Kumara (Kajimoto), Mitsuo Matsumoto (Crime Lab Assistant), Junpel Netsuke (Bystander), Haruo Nakajima (Vapor Man), James Hong (Voice of Mizuno).

Brenco Pictures distributed *The Human Vapor* in the United States in the spring of 1964 although some of its play dates in the southwest were under the auspices of Allied Artists. This sci-fi outing was made by the Toho Company in Japan as *Gasu Ningen Dai Ichigo* (The First Gas Man) and released there in 1960. Ten minutes were sliced from the original for its stateside showings. *The Human Vapor* was similar in plot to another 1960 Toho release, *Denso Ningen*, which was shown on U.S. TV as *Secret of the Telegian*. Both films had the same producer (Tomoyuki Tanaka) and special effects director (Eiji Tsuburaya). Yoshio Tsuchiya, who had the title role in *The Human Vapor*, played a police detective in *Secret of the Telegian*.

The Human Vapor was directed by Ishiro Honda, who is most famous for his "Godzilla" and other monster movies for Toho. In 1958 he directed *Bijo to Ekitai Ningen*, shown stateside as *The H-Man*; dealing with the theme of human transformation in the milieu of the gangster film, it was one of Honda's most entertaining sci-fiers. *The Human Vapor* is "not as visually impressive as the previous movie, probably because invisibility and gaseous substances are not notably photogenic material" (Phil Hardy, *The Encyclopedia of Horror Movies* [1986]). Instead of involving the underworld, this outing was basically a love story that interpolated traditional Japanese dance into its plotline with the heroes being a policeman and a female reporter. The title character is not often seen in vaporous form, and when he is the Vapor Man he's hardly frightening. Overall, *The Human Vapor* is a lesser Toho production and one that usually gets lost in the shuffle with the company's other science fiction efforts.

Mizuno (Tsuchiya) meets with newspaper editor Ikeda (Tatsuo Matsumura) and some reporters and tells them he is the Vapor Man who has been terrorizing Tokyo. He says he was working as a librarian when he was visited by the eminent scientist Dr. Sano (Fuyuki Murakami) of the Japanese Space Association. Mizuno, once a top test pilot, was grounded due to illness and Sano offers him a chance to fly in space. He goes to the scientist's laboratory where he signs a contract and is given a shot before being placed in a chamber where he sleeps for ten days. During that time he is turned into vapor by the scientist's rays. When he returns to normal, Mizuno realizes he has been transformed into something terrifying. Instead of the superman he intended, Sano has created a Vapor Man. After the scientist admits that Mizuno was not his first experiment but the only one that lived, the librarian kills him. Mizuno knows he is a freak but that he also has superhuman power and can

The title character in *The Human Vapor* (1964), given regional release by Allied Artists.

vaporize at any time. He decides to rob a bank to get the money needed by the woman he loves, noted dancer Fujichiyo Kasuga (Kaoru Yachigusa), so she can dance again after being in a sanitarium. During the robbery, Mizuno kills a policeman and steals a bank car, leading the police on a chase around Tokyo, before wrecking the vehicle near Fujichiyo's home. The police go to the house and are told by the dancer's attendant, the elderly Jiya (Bokuzen Hidari), that they cannot see his mistress. Detective Ikamoto (Tatsuya Mihashi) tells his girlfriend, reporter Kyoko (Keiko Sata), that the hunted man disappeared. Mizuno robs another bank. A guard is later found dead behind a locked vault door and an autopsy reveals he died from some kind of gas. Ikamoto asks Kyoko to check on the background of the dancer, who has not worked in a long time. Both of them go to see Fujichiyo but Kyoko gets there first and is told by the dancer that she plans on giving a recital. When the suspect leaves in an expensive car, the detective and the reporter follow her to the public library where Mizuno gives her a book of traditional dance prints. Fujichiyo goes to her dancing instructor (Sensho Matsumoto) and attempts to pay him for lessons but he refuses the money, saying she needs to rest before she resumes dancing. When Ikamoto finds out from Kyoko that it costs thirty million yen to stage a dance recital, he vows to find out who is giving the dancer the money she needs to perform. Mizuno calls the newspaper and announces he plans to rob the Kyoto bank the next day. The police set a trap for him only to bring in Nomura (Ren Yamamoto), who robbed another bank at the same time and claims to be the man they want. When some of the stolen money is found among the payment for Fujichiyo's dancer posters, Okamoto and his men go to her house where she is rehearsing and locate more stolen loot. The dancer is taken into custody. Fujichiyo tells the police the money was given to her so she could dance again but she refuses to reveal the source and is put in jail. Going to the newspaper office, Mizuno announces that he robbed the bank. When Okamoto shows up, he agrees to go back to one of the vaults to prove how it was done. During the demonstration, Mizuno vaporizes and kills two men and demands that his girlfriend be released from jail or more people will die. As the newspapers proclaim that Tokyo is at the mercy of the Vapor Man, Mizuno returns to the police and confronts Okamoto who asks him if Fujichiyo knows about him. The policeman shoots Mizuno who vaporizes, proclaiming that his lady love will be released from jail and will dance again. He goes to her cell and sets all the prisoners free, but the dancer refuses to go as the escapees riot. Kyoko suggests to Ikeda that the newspaper give a forum for Mizuno to tell his story. Later, when he does so, the police break into the newsroom and try to kill him but he vaporizes and rises into the air. The chief of police (Takamaru Sasaki) asks Fujichiyo to help eliminate Mizuno for the good of humanity. After she is released from jail, the dancer is told by her teacher that the musicians will not play for her. Mizuno informs Fujichiyo that he has rented a theater for her recital and asks her to fulfill her destiny because he loves her and that her glory will he his. Kyoko talks to the dancer and tells her many people will be killed if she carries out her plans to perform and asks her to cancel the recital. Fujichiyo replies that she will give her performance for Mizuno, the man she loves. That night she dances, accompanied by Jiya, with only Mizuno in the audience. Unbeknownst to him, the police plan to fill the hall with gas and blow it up in an attempt to kill the Vapor Man. The crowd outside the theater gets out of hand and breaks into the hall and becomes rowdy with Mizuno ordering them to leave. When he is manhandled by some ruffians, Mizuno vaporizes and the crowd stampedes. The detective and Kyoko try to get the dancer and her accompanist to leave but they refuse. When the crowd is gone, Fujichiyo resumes her dance for Mizuno. When the performance is over, the two dance as the police set off the detonator to blow up the hall only to find it has been sabotaged by the Vapor Man. As she embraces her lover, Fujichiyo ignites a lighter which blows up the theater. The crowd watches as the Vapor Man drags the dancer out of the hall but she dies, leaving him to wander through eternity alone.

The Hunchback of Notre-Dame (1957; 110 minutes; Color)

Producers: Robert Hakim and Raymond Hakim. Director: Jean Delannoy. Screenplay: Jean Laurence and Jacques Prevert, from the novel by Victor Hugo. Photography: Michel Kelber. Editor: Henri Taverna. Music: Lavagnino. Music Director: Jacques Metehen. Production Design: Rene Renoux. Sound: Jacques Carriere. Sets: Maurice Barnathan. Costumes: Georges Benda. Production Manager: Ludmilla Goulian. Unit Manager: Paul Laffargue. Makeup: Bonnemaison and Klein. Special Effects: Gerard Cogan. Choreographer: Leonide Massine. Assistant Director: Pierre Tyberghein.

CAST: Gina Lollobrigida (Esmeralda), Anthony Quinn (Quasimodo), Jean Danet (Captain Phoebus de Chateaupers), Alain Cuny (Claude Frollo), Robert Hirsch (Pierre Gringoire), Danielle Dumont (Fleur de Lys), Philippe Clay (Clopin Troulliefou), Maurice Sarfati (Jehan Frollo), Jean Tissier (King Louis XI), Valentine Tessier (Aloyse de Gondelaurier), Jacques Dufilho (Guillaume Rousseau), Roger Blin (Mathias Hungadi), Marianne Oswald (La Faloudel), Roland Bailly (Hangman), Pieral (Dwarf), Camille Guerini (President), Damia (Beggar Woman), Robert Lombard (Jacques Coppenole), Albert Remy (Jupiter), Hubert Lapparent (Guillaume de Harancourt), Boris Vian (Cardinal), Georges Douking (Hoodlum), Paul Bonifas (Lecornu), Madeleine Barbules (Madame Outarde), Albert Michel (Night Watchman), Daniel Emilfork (Andre le Rouge), Germaine Delbat (Parishioner), Jean Martin (Pickpocket), Jean Thielment, Doudou Babet (Beggars), Frank Maurice (Executioner Andre), Paul Bisciglia (Man at Feast of Fools), Dominique Marcas (Woman at Court of Miracles), Nadine Tallier (Girl at Court of Miracles), Pierre Fresnay (Narrator).

Victor Hugo's 1831 novel *The Hunchback of Notre Dame* has been filmed several times, the most noted being the 1923 Universal production starring Lon Chaney and RKO's 1939 version with Charles Laughton. More faithful to the original work was Allied Artists' 1957 release *The Hunchback of Notre-Dame* which was made by Paris Films in France in the spring of 1956 and released in that country as *Notre-Dame de Paris*, the original title of Hugo's book. It was made as *The Hunchback of Paris* because RKO owned the rights to the original title; just before the film's stateside release in November 1957, RKO decided to permit Allied to use it. The U.S. release, at 110 minutes, was five minutes shorter than the French version. The actual Notre Dame Cathedral in Paris was used for the filming, giving it an authentic look. The mass poverty and sordid conditions of the populace was somewhat glossed over.

Besides the film's colorful production values, its main asset is the cast. Gina Lollobrigida is a very beautiful and believable Esmeralda. Anthony Quinn brings out the humanity of the deformed Quasimodo, although in deference to both Chaney and Laughton, his hunchback is not particularly physically repulsive, only a bit misshapen. Alain Cuny is particularly good as the alchemist-priest who is outwardly cold but burns with lust for Esmeralda. Jean Tissier gives a wonderfully underplayed performance as the cunning King Louis XI. While Jean Danet, as Phoebus, and Robert Hirsch, as Pierre, are only adequate, Valentine Tessier is quite good as the king's attorney as is Maurice Sarfati as the priest's libertine brother.

In 1482 Paris, poet-author Pierre Gringoire (Hirsch) watches as an unruly audience makes a mockery of his morality play, *The Quest for Beauty*. At the behest of Clopin Trouillefou (Philippe Clay), the king of beggars, the crowd goes to the Feast of Fools as Pierre attempts to get solace from priest Claude Frollo (Alain Cuny). Gypsy girl Esmeralda (Lollobrigida) dances at the feast and draws the attention of Frollo, who lusts for the beautiful maiden. Calling the feast a blasphemy, the priest has Quasimodo (Quinn), the nearly deaf and deformed bell ringer at the Notre Dame Cathedral, break up the crowd and destroy their altar. Esmeralda and the others go to the crowning of the King of Fools and, after several candidates are rejected, she calls attention to Quasimodo and he is declared the winner. He is paraded through the streets wearing a robe and crown until Frollo disperses the participants and tells his servant to bring him the gypsy girl. Quasimodo carries out his orders but Esmeralda's screams bring soldiers led by Captain Phoebus de Chateaupers (Danet), and the hunchback is arrested. Phoebus takes Esmeralda to a nearby inn where he plans to have sex with her but she holds him off with a knife and laughingly runs away. The broke Pierre wanders through Paris in search of a place to sleep and ends up in the Court of Miracles, the kingdom of thieves and beggars, where he is sentenced to be lynched in retaliation for King Louis XI (Tissier) having ordered the hanging of a thief the previous week. Just as he is about to die, Pierre is saved by Esmeralda, who agrees to marry him. He goes with the gypsy to her home where he finds out his only husbandly duty will be to be the groom for her female goat Charlie. He tells him she is in love with Phoebus. The next day the king and his attorney, Gondelaurier (Tessier), go incognito to see Frollo, who is also an alchemist trying to make gold which the monarch needs for his treasury. Quasimodo is tethered in the cathedral courtyard and whipped for abducting Esmeralda. When he begs for water, the crowd mocks him but the gypsy girl shows mercy and complies with his wishes. During her street act, Esmeralda has the goat spell out Phoebus' name, and the jealous Frollo calls her a witch. Phoebus comes to see his betrothed, Fleur de Lys (Danielle Dumont), whose home is near the courtyard, and she demands he clear the area since she is jealous of Esmeralda. He carries out her orders but makes a date to meet the gypsy girl that night. Frollo gets wind of the rendezvous and goes to the inn where he tells a tipsy Phoebus to leave Esmeralda alone because she belongs to someone else and is a witch. Ignoring the priest, Phoebus goes to an upstairs room and finds Esmeralda waiting. To prove she wants him, the girl throws her knife out a window. Frollo picks up the knife, stabbing Phoebus in the back. The gypsy is placed on trial and the inn's owner (Marianne Oswald) and her dwarf companion (Pieral) tell of seeing a man in black at the scene. Their testimony is ignored and the girl is tortured into confessing that she stabbed her lover. Sentenced to hang, Esmeralda is taken to the front of the cathedral to receive the blessing of the monks before being put to death. Quasimodo carries her inside where she receives sanctuary since Notre Dame is a house of refuge. Upon awakening, the girl screams at the sight of the hunchback who tells her he is sorry for being so ugly. He gives her a whistle, which he can hear, to call him. Frollo finds her wandering one of the cathedral's parapets and tries to rape her after she recalls he was the man in black who stabbed Phoebus. She uses the whistle to bring Quasimodo, who comes to her defense. As Frollo departs, the hunchback tells her it was the priest who ordered him to kidnap her. The girl again screams the next morning when the hunchback awakens her and he runs into the bell tower for solace. The gypsy follows and apologizes. She sings and dances for the hunchback and he gives her a concert of the bells with the sound so deafening she has to run below, although she is glad to see Quasimodo so happy. Later he gives her flowers and wishes she would stay with him forever in the cathedral. She spies Phoebus riding below and calls to him but the captain ignores her. The gypsy tells the hunchback to bring Phoebus to her so she can tell him she does not love him any more but the captain rides away to see his fiancée. To protect her feelings, Quasimodo brings Esmeralda flowers he claims are from Phoebus but she knows better. Fearful there will be a revolt of the peasants if the gypsy girl is taken from the cathedral, King Louis and his attorney go to see scholar Rousseau (Jacques Dufilho), who has been imprisoned in a cage for fourteen years, to get his opinion on the monarch's power to break the rule of sanctuary. The learned man advises there is a precedent for such an action. The next day, Frollo tries to get Quasimodo to leave the cathedral but he refuses and bars the doors. Lead by Trouillefou, an army of thieves and beggars storms Notre Dame to release Esmeralda. Quasimodo throws down heavy stones to deter them. When Esmeralda sees the crowd, she begs the hunchback to desist but he pours a cauldron of boiling wax out of the church's gargoyles' mouths and onto the invaders. As the rabble are about to batter down the cathedral door, the king's foot soldiers and archers arrive. An archer, Frollo's brother (Sarfati), climbs a ladder onto a parapet but Quasimodo throws the man into the street below. The door is knocked down and as Esmeralda is carried out, the king's soldiers attack the crowd and she is killed by an arrow. Following the carnage, Quasimodo sees the gypsy's body being dragged away for hanging and throws Frollo from the parapet. The hunchback later finds Esmeralda's body in a burial vault and lies down beside her. Years later their two skeleton are found entwined.

In *The Films of Anthony Quinn* (1975), Alvin H. Marrill stated, "Quinn played his Quasimodo as a more pitiful and less monstrous figure than did [Chaney and Laughton], while maintaining the actor's privilege of donning bizarre makeup—a twenty-five-pound hump on his back, orthopedic braces to twist his body, false nose and teeth, five-pound lead weights in his shoes, and other 'monster' accouterments. It was Quinn's vigorous performance, together with Gina Lollobrigida's alluring Esmeralda, which provided the production with whatever merits it had. ... "The intertwined stories of Esmeralda and Quasimodo are muddled under [Jean] Delannoy's static direction, reduced to a series of mass scenes and slow-moving vignettes.... Much of the rich atmosphere so vividly described in the Hugo tale ... provides the spectacle filmed at the expense of plot in this French-made recapitulation of the classic." In a similar evaluation, the *New York Times* said, "The intertwined stories of Esmeralda, the strange, wild gypsy girl, and the deformed bell-ringer of the title, are oddly disjoined affairs that only fitfully come half-alive through a series of mass scenes and static vignettes. The cathedral and the citizens of high and low degree of fifteenth-century Paris loom higher than the muddled intrigue and romance of this ponderous adventure. The producers, director and scenarists seem to have been more intent on providing spectacle than a sharply etched story line." *Variety* reported, "[A]lthough beautifully photographed and extravagantly produced, [it] is ponderous, often dull and far over length." The reviewer felt Lollobrigida "appears to be somewhat miscast" but thought Quinn "gives a well-etched impression of the difficult role. His makeup is not as extreme as either of the two previous characterizations."

The Hypnotic Eye (1960; 79 minutes)

Producer: Charles B. Bloch. Executive Producer: Ben Schwalb. Director: George Blair. Screenplay: Gitta Woodfield and William Read Woodfield. Photography: Archie Dalzell. Editor: William Austin. Music: Marlin Skiles. Art Director: Dave Milton. Sound: Ralph Butler. Sets: Frank Wade. Production Manager: Edward Morey, Jr. Makeup: Emile LaVigne. Special Effects: Milt Olsen. Wardrobe: Roger J. Weinberg. Hypnosis Technical Advisor: Gil Boyne. Continuity: Virginia Barth. Assistant Director: Ray Gosnell, Jr.

CAST: Jacques Bergerac (The Great Desmond), Marcia Henderson (Marcia Blaine), Merry Anders (Dodie Wilson), Allison Hayes (Justine), Joe Patridge (Detective Sergeant Steve Kennedy), Fred Demara (Doctor), Lawrence Lipton (Poet), Eric "Big Daddy" Nord (Bongo Player), Guy Prescott (Dr. Philip Hecht), James Lydon (Emergency Doctor), Carol Thurston (Doris Scott), Phyllis Cole (Mrs. McNear), Holly Harris (Mrs. Stevens), Mary Foran (June Mayes), Eva Lynd (Miss Thompson), Evan MacNeil (Victim).

A young woman (Eva Lynd) tries to wash her hair over a lit gas burner and dies. Detective Sergeant Steve Kennedy (Joe Patridge) tells the attending physician (James Lydon) she is the eleventh beautiful girl who has mutilated herself with one woman using a straight razor thinking it was a lipstick brush, another drinking lye and a third cutting her face with a fan's blades because she thought it was a vibrator. Kennedy consults his friend, psychiatrist Dr. Philip Hecht (Guy Prescott), and they agree to meet to discuss the cases. That evening Kennedy accompanies his girlfriend, Marcia Blaine (Marcia Henderson), and secretary Dodie Wilson (Merry Anders) to see Desmond (Jacques Bergerac), a hypnotist, at the Hayes Theatre. During the show, Desmond convinces a man he cannot open his eyes, has another believe he is in the desert, a third man feeling he is alone on a cold night and the fourth that he is a dog. He then asks for three female volunteers and his assistant, Justine (Allison Hayes), nods to him to select Dodie. He places her under hypnosis and convinces her she has turned to stone and then is light as a feather and finally he has her floating in air. Before bringing her back to consciousness, Desmond whispers in her ear. While leaving the theater, Dodie passes a poster of the hypnotist, prompting her to tell Kennedy and Marcia she has to go home right away. Dodie pretends to take a cab but doubles back to the theater. That night she washes her faces with sulfuric acid and is badly burned. When Kennedy and

Marcia go to the hospital to see her, Dodie says she has no recollection of why she used the acid. Marcia later suggests that Dodie having been hypnotized may be involved. When the policeman gets a call about someone jumping off a bridge, Marcia insists on going back to the theater where she plans to be hypnotized by Desmond. At Justine's urging, he chooses Marcia who avoids being hypnotized when he flashes a blinking eye light, concealed in his left hand, at her. Later she tells Kennedy and Hecht about the light, how she pretended to be hypnotized and thinks Desmond may be involved in the mutilations. She also says Desmond told her to meet him at the theater at midnight. The three go to the theater and Marcia meets Desmond in his dressing room, and he uses the hypnotic eye to put her under his spell. They go to a café where they hear a beatnik poet (Lawrence Lipton) accompanied by a bongo drummer (Eric "Big Daddy" Nord). Kennedy and Hecht follow Desmond and Marsha back to her apartment where the two are interrupted by Justine while they kiss. As Desmond leaves, he asks Justine how many more will there be and she replies it will happen as long as there are pretty faces like Marcia's. Justine orders Marcia into a boiling hot shower but is interrupted by Kennedy's arrival. Justine tells him she is an old school roommate of Marcia's and is staying with her for a few days. Justine hides when Marcia greets Kennedy, who questions her about Desmond and his possible connection to Dodie's disfigurement. Justine overhears the conversation and runs away. Hecht agrees that Marcia was put under Desmond's spell and Kennedy asks him to help question the other victims to see if they had been hypnotized and knew Desmond or Justine. Both the facially scarred Mrs. McNear (Phyllis Cole) and the blind Doris Scott (Carol Thurston) say no to the queries but Kennedy finds one of the balloons Desmond uses in his act in Doris' purse. Since they know Dodie was hypnotized, they talk to her but she too denies such an event. When Hecht asks her doctor's (Fred Demara) permission to hypnotize her, he says not for at least a week but he informs the psychiatrist that Dodie repeated the name Justine when she was brought to the hospital. Kennedy and Hecht go to Marcia's apartment in hopes of putting her under hypnosis so she can recall what happened when she was with Desmond in the theater, but they find she is not there. They theorize she has gone back to see the hypnotist and go to the theater where they find her in the audience. When Justine sees Kennedy, she tells Desmond to stop him and the hypnotist uses the flashing light but the detective pulls a gun on him. Justine leads Marcia back stage and onto a high catwalk. Kennedy goes after them as Hecht holds Desmond at gun point and tries to talk Justine into surrendering. When Hecht tells her she is beautiful and has much to live for, she laughs at him and pulls off a skin-tight mask, revealing a terribly scarred face. Desmond knocks the gun out of Hecht's hand and tries to strangle him but is shot by Kennedy. When Justine sees her lover lying dead on the stage floor, she jumps off the catwalk and dies beside him. Marcia nearly falls but comes out of hypnosis and is saved by Kennedy. Hecht tells the audience that hypnosis can be dangerous and to only submit to it when carried out by a doctor.

Made as *The Screaming Sleep* and filmed in "Hypnovision," *The Hypnotic Eye* was released theatrically in February 1960. Ben Schwalb, who produced the studio's "Bowery Boys" outings, served as executive producer for this Bloch-Woodfield Production that used "HypnoMagic." This gimmick had magician the Great Desmond (Bergerac) pretending to place the audience under hypnosis by ordering them to participate in a number of acts, including blowing up and lifting balloons given out during the performance. Unfortunately this audience participation near the film's finale greatly slowed the pace of the picture. In an attempt to appeal to the beatnik audience, the film featured poet Lawrence Lipton reciting his self-composed "Confessions of a Movie Addict or Holy Barbarian Blues." Lipton, who billed himself as King of the Beatniks, appeared at a coffee house and was accompanied by bongo drummer Eric "Big Daddy" Nord. The shooting for this sequence was done at Los Angeles' The Gas House, which was owned by Nord. The two performers were given special billing as was Fred Demara, whose life story as master of pretending to be something he was not in various professions was filmed in 1961 as *The Great Imposter* starring Tony Curtis as Demara.

Jacques Bergerac is adequate as Desmond, the magician, in a role better suited for Bela Lugosi two decades before. Joe Patridge has the bulk of the footage as the police detective hero but he is rather bland in comparison to the film's three lovely leading ladies, Marcia Henderson, Merry Anders and Allison Hayes. While the latter's part was not large, she dominated her scenes as the vengeful Justine. Unfortunately the overall film was not very horrifying, or even entertaining. Donald C. Willis in *Horror and Science Fiction Films: A Checklist* (1972) found it "[s]omething less than hypnotic" while Ed Naha in *Horrors: From Screen to Scream* (1975) declared, "Must be seen at a kiddie matinee for full effect." Regarding the audience hypnosis trick, he opined, "Even if you don't go into a trance, you get to stomp your feet and wrestle with a Hypnotic Eye balloon. The balloon is almost worth watching the movie for."

Almost a decade after its initial outing, Allied re-issued the feature as *The Torturer! Master of "The Hypnotic Eye"* with the come-on this time dubbed "Touch-O-Vision."

Indestructible Man (1956; 70 minutes)

Producer-Director: Jack Pollexfen. Screenplay: Vy Russell and Sue Bradford. Photography: John Russell, Jr. Editor: Fred Feitshans, Jr. Music: Albert Glasser. Art Director: Ted Holsopple. Production Manager: Chris Beute.

Lon Chaney in *Indestructible Man* (1956)

CAST: Lon Chaney (Charles "Butcher' Benton), Marian Carr (Eva Martin), Casey Adams [Max Showalter] (Police Lieutenant Dick Chasen), Ross Elliott (Paul Lowe), Stuart Randall (Police Captain J.L. Lauder), Kenneth Terrell (Joe Marcelli), Marjorie Stapp (Hysterical Woman), Rita Greene (Carny's Girl), Robert Shayne (Professor Bradshaw), Roy Engel (Police Sergeant), Peggy Maley (Francine), Madge Cleveland (Bar Lush), Marvin Ellis (Squeamy Ellis), Joe Flynn (Laboratory Assistant), Eddie Marr (Carny), Dorothy Ford (Tall Dancer).

One of the great pleasures for Baby Boomers watching horror and science fiction movies on television in the early 1960s, *Indestructible Man* is one of those films beloved by fans but shunned by critics. Michael J. Weldon in *The Psychotronic Encyclopedia of Film* (1983) hit the nail on the head when he termed it "*great* junk ... classic trash." More typical is Ed Naha in *Horrors: From Screen to Scream* (1975) who said, "Dreadful gangster story is heightened in sheer futility by a ludicrous 'you are there' type narration..." while Stephen Jones in *The Essential Monster Movie Guide* (2000) termed it "low-budget madness" and *John Stanley's Creature Features Movie Guide Strikes Again* (1994) dubbed the film "[b]ottom-of-the-barrel pulper.... So poorly scripted and directed it's bad enough to be entertaining." Even Richard Bojarski, a devotee of the feature's star Lon Chaney, wrote that it "bears a slight resemblance in plotting to the earlier *Man Made Monster* [1941] but has little else to recommend it" in his article "Son of Chaney" in *Castle of Frankenstein #7* (1963).

Indestructible Man is remindful of *Man Made Monster,* the Universal production that launched Chaney as the studio's top horror star of the 1940s, but lacks its finesse and solid production values. The 1956 release has a semi-documentary feel about it along with a *film noir* façade that appears to be *Dragnet*-influenced, as well as interpolating footage from the 1948 production *He Walked by Night.* Filmed at Jerry Fairbanks Studios late in 1954, the feature also includes quite a bit of footage of downtown Los Angeles with some scenes in the Bradbury Building and around Angels' Flight, the Bunker Hill district cable railway. Chaney, in mostly a mute performance, dominates the proceedings as the revenge-bent "Butcher" Benton and tight close-ups of his face are seen in several scenes. Toward the end of his career, Chaney played a scientist who revives a corpse, the plot ploy of *Indestructible Man,* in the "Spark of Life" segment of the atrocious *Dr. Terror's Gallery of Horror* (1967). Some sources claim the 1956 film is a loose remake of the Boris Karloff starrer *The Walking Dead* (1936), while its finale sequences in the Los Angeles sewers ape *The Third Man* (1949).

Police Lieutenant Dick Chasen (Casey Adams) relates the happenings from the previous seventy-two hours, beginning with the Los Angeles Police Department closing the case of a $600,000 armored car payroll committed robbery by Charles "Butcher" Benton (Chaney). On the eve of his execution, Benton is visited by his lawyer, Paul Lowe (Ross Elliott), who wants to know where he hid the stolen loot. Although he is about to die, Benton vows to kill Lowe and his cohorts, Joe Marcelli (Kenneth Terrell) and Squeamy Ellis (Marvin Ellis), who testified against him. (Lowe set up the heist and Marcelli and Ellis took part in it.) Chasen goes to see Benton's friend, stripper Eva Martin (Marian Carr), hoping she can lead him to the stolen payroll. She claims to know nothing about the matter. After he leaves, Eva is visited by Lowe, who also wants to find out if she knows where the money is hidden. While she performs her act, Lowe finds a letter from Benton in her dressing room. It contains a map of the city sewer system showing the place where he concealed the payroll. Lowe takes the map and replaces it with a fifty dollar bill. News of Benton's San Quentin execution is broadcast and later his body is procured from the morgue by a laboratory assistant (Joe Flynn) who takes it to his employer, Professor Bradshaw (Robert Shayne), who is working on a cancer cure. The biochemist sends nearly 30,000 volts of electricity into the corpse to see the effects on cell structure, and to his surprise Benton returns to life. The experiment has left Benton mute and superhuman, with a maniacal desire to get revenge on the three men who betrayed him. Benton kills Bradshaw and the assistant and begins walking toward Los Angeles. Along the way he meets a carnival barker (Eddie Marr) and his young girlfriend (Rita Greene) and lifts the man's car so he can fix a flat tire. Benton kills the man and takes the car and later murders two policemen who try to stop him at a roadblock. Chasen takes Eva to a drive-in for dinner and she explains she was never romantically involved with Benton, although she felt sorry for him after he was jilted by her roommate. Chasen is assigned by his boss, Captain Lauder (Stuart Randall), to find the mad killer who cannot be stopped by bullets. Once in Los Angeles, Benton sees Eva at the Follies and finds out that Lowe has taken the map he left for her. When he departs, the stripper tries to inform Chasen that Benton is still alive. Unable to reach him, she tells Squeamy. Benton hunts down Marcelli and kills him and then goes to Lowe's office but finds it deserted. Squeamy comes to see Lowe and runs into Benton who tosses him to his death from the building's fifth floor. Eva goes to the police with her story but Chasen and Lauder do not believe her until they learn of Bradshaw's murder and how his assistant bribed a morgue attendant in order to obtain Benton's body. The two policemen then interrogate a young woman (Marjorie Stapp) who describes how her boyfriend's spine was broken by a tall man with superhuman strength. Upon their return to the police station, Chase and Lauder are confronted by Lowe who demands protective custody. When they refuse he strikes a desk sergeant (Roy Engel) and is put in jail. Chasen conceives a plan to make the lawyer admit he was behind the payroll robbery: He and Lauder pretend to drop the charges against Lowe; fearing for his life, the attorney admits his part in the stickup and gives the policemen the map revealing the hiding place of the stolen money. Lawmen begin a thorough search of the city's sewers with plans to stop Benton by using flame throwers. Benton finds the loot but is surrounded by the police and his face is badly burned by the fiery weapons. He manages to escape to a power station and as the police follow him he mounts a huge machine and sets it in motion. It crashes into an electrical unit and Benton is burned to death. With the payroll retrieved and the case definitely closed, Chasen asks Eva to marry him.

In *Keep Watching the Skies! The 21st Century Edition* (2009), Bill Warren states that several scenes shot for *Indestructible Man* do not appear in the final product. Among them is Butcher breaking into the city jail and murdering Lowe. It does seem strange that the attorney, who was the cause of all the mayhem, does not get his comeuppance and is allowed to live. Apparently another subplot had the killer abducting Eva and taking her to Bronson Caverns where she is saved by Chasen who uses tear gas on the Butcher. The young woman is sent to a hospital after suffering a injury during the fray; in the released version she does mention being hospitalized. This, however, could be attributed to her having been confronted by an ex-beau who has returned from the dead and sets about murdering most of her underworld acquaintances, and anyone else who gets in his way!

Allied Artists released *Indestructible Man* in March 1956, usually as the lower half of a double bill with *World Without End* (q.v.).

Invasion of the Body Snatchers (1956; 81 minutes)

Producer: Walter Wanger. Director: Don Siegel. Screenplay: Daniel Mainwaring, from the magazine story and novel by Jack Finney. Photography: Ellsworth Fredricks. Editor: Robert S. Eisen. Music: Carmen Dragon. Production Design: Edward Haworth. Sound: Ralph Butler. Sets: Joseph Kish. Production Manager: Allen K. Wood. Makeup: Emile LaVigne. Special Effects: Milt Rice. Assistant Directors: William Beaudine, Jr. and Richard Maybery.

Lobby card for *Invasion of the Body Snatchers* (1956)

CAST: Kevin McCarthy (Dr. Miles Bennell), Dana Wynter (Becky Driscoll), Larry Gates (Dr. Dan Kaufman), King Donovan (Jack Bilicec), Carolyn Jones (Teddy Bilicec), Jean Willes (Sally Winters), Ralph Dumke (Chief Nick Grivett), Virginia Christine (Wilma Lentz), Tom Fadden (Ira Lentz), Kenneth Patterson (Stanley Driscoll), Guy Way (Officer Sam Janzek), Eileen Stevens (Anne Grimaldi), Beatrice Maude (Mrs. Grimaldi), Jean Andren (Eleda Lentz), Bobby Clark (Jimmy Grimaldi), Everett Glass (Dr. Ed Pursey), Dabbs Greer (Mac Lomax), Pat O'Malley (Baggage Carrier), Guy Rennie (Club Proprietor), Marie Selland (Martha Lomax), Sam Peckinpah (Meter Reader Charlie), Harry Vejar (Mr. Grimaldi), Whit Bissell (Dr. Hill), Richard Deacon (Dr. Harvey Bassett), Robert Osterloh (Ambulance Attendant), Frank Hagney (Night Watchman).

The best of Allied Artists' science fiction releases, and one of the finest films issued by the studio, *Invasion of the Body Snatchers* remains one of the true cinema classics of its genre. Perhaps Bill Warren summed it up best in *Keep Watching the Skies! The 21st Century Edition* (2009): "The picture is so well directed and imaginatively conceived it overrides objections to details." Based on the 1954 *Collier's* magazine serial "The Body Snatchers," the film was released in February 1956 doubled-bill with *The Atomic Man* (q.v.). Made on a $300,000 budget with a nineteen-day shooting schedule and produced by Walter Wanger Pictures, it was lensed early in 1955. Allied executives apparently felt the ending of the picture was too grim and sought to soften it with a semi-happy, or at least hopeful ending. *Variety* opined, "This tense, offbeat piece of science-fiction is occasionally difficult to follow due to the strangeness of its scientific premise. Action nevertheless is increasingly exciting [and] characterizations and situations are sharp. Don Siegel's taut direction is fast-paced generally,

Larry Gates, Kenneth Patterson, King Donovan and Kevin McCarthy in *Invasion of the Body Snatchers* (1956)

although in his efforts to spark the climax he permits [Kevin] McCarthy to overact in several sequences." *The Hollywood Reporter* said it "contains a great deal of solid emotion and suspense."

Dr. Miles Bennell (McCarthy) is brought to a hospital where Dr. Harvey Bassett (Richard Deacon) calls in psychiatrist Dr. Hill (Whit Bissell) to examine him. After being found trying to halt traffic on the freeway, Miles is raving about giant pods taking over people's minds and souls. Hill agrees to listen to his story and Miles relates how he was called back to the small California town of Santa Mira from a medical convention by his nurse Sally Winters (Jean Willes), due to a sudden influx of patients. Driving to his office with Sally, the doctor almost runs over a young boy, Jimmy Grimaldi (Bobby Clark), whose grandmother (Beatrice Maude) says will not go to school. Noticing that the Grimaldis have closed their profitable roadside vegetable business, the doctor and his nurse proceed to his office where he finds only a handful of patients with the usual complaints. As Miles is about go to lunch, his former sweetheart, Becky Driscoll (Dana Wynter), whom he has not seen in five years, arrives. She says her cousin Wilma Lentz (Virginia Christine) claims that her uncle Ira Lentz (Tom Fadden) is an imposter and not the man who raised her. He agrees to see Wilma and, leaving with Becky, the doctor learns she is no longer living in England and has just come back from Reno after getting a divorce. On the street they meet an old classmate, police officer Sam Janzek (Guy Way), who was one of the people who cancelled out on seeing the doctor. That afternoon Jimmy is brought by his grandmother to Miles in a near hysterical state claiming his mother is an imposter. Miles later goes to the Lentz home where he finds Ira mowing the lawn. He talks with Wilma who can give no definite reason for her feelings about her uncle other than he has no emotions, just a pretense of sensitivity. Miles tells Wilma he wants her to see his friend, Dr. Dan Kaufman (Larry Gates), a psychologist, and she asks him to make an appointment for her. Miles takes Becky to dinner and, arriving at a swanky club they meet Kaufman and the town's oldest practitioner, Dr. Ed Pursey (Everett Glass), who both mention the strange phenomenon, which they term a form of mass hypnosis. The restaurant is nearly empty, the owner (Guy Rennie) saying business has fallen off drastically in the last two weeks. Just as they are about to have cocktails, Miles gets an urgent call from writer Jack Belicec (King Donovan). When Miles and Becky arrive at the Belicec home, they find Jack and his wife Teddy (Carolyn Jones) in an agitated state and they are shown what appears to be a corpse lying on a pool table. The body has waxen features and no fingerprints and Teddy notices that it resembles Jack. Before taking Becky home, Miles tells the couple to stay up and watch the body and, if nothing happens by morning, to call the police. At the Driscoll house, Miles and Becky arrive to find her father (Kenneth Patterson) emerging from the cellar where he says he has been working. As Jack sleeps, Teddy sees the body's eyes open and becomes hysterical when she spies a cut on the palm of its right hand, the same place Jack cut his hand when he accidentally broke a liquor bottle earlier in the evening. The Belicecs drive to Miles' house, and he gets Kaufman out of bed with the story. When Jack mentions Becky, Miles quickly drives to her house and breaks in through a basement window. There he discovers a developing body resembling Becky and he runs upstairs and carries the sleeping woman back to his house. After Becky wakes up and Kaufman arrives, the men go back to the Driscoll house but find nothing in the basement. Becky's father shows up with a shotgun, after having called the police, and soon Chief Nick Grivett (Ralph Dumke) arrives and says that a corpse matching the one at the Belicec home is in the morgue after having been found on a burning haystack. Kaufman convinces Miles that his mind was playing tricks on him in the darkened basement and that he did not see Becky's double there. On the way to his office the next morning, Miles runs into Wilma in front of her antique shop and she tells him she woke up without the mistrust of her uncle. That day Jimmy and his grandmother return with the boy now completely calm and the doctor begins to wonder why people's symptoms vanish so suddenly. In his greenhouse, Miles hears popping noises and sees four large pods opening up, spewing liquid and bubbles. He calls to guests Becky, Jack and Teddy and they watch as the pods begin to evolve into human bodies, one for each of them. Miles speculates these new bodies take over the minds of a person as they sleep, thus the recent epidemic of people being called imposters. Becky remembers her father has been acting differently. Miles tries to call both the Federal Bureau of Investigation and the state governor but the telephone operator claims that all the lines are in use. After using a pitchfork on the pods, Miles tells Jack to take the women and go for help but not to call the police since he thinks they too have been changed. Becky refuses to leave Miles. When Miles and Becky stop for gas, the attendant (Dabbs Greer) puts two pods in the trunk of his car. Miles later becomes suspicious and stops the vehicle, finds the pods and sets them on fire. The two drive to Sally's home but when Miles looks through a window he sees her with the Lentz family and Becky's father, who is carrying a pod intended for the nurse's little daughter. They go to Miles' office while the police continue to search for them. Miles and Becky take pills to keep them awake and he tells her they cannot close their eyes and sleep or they will be transformed.

When morning arrives they watch the sheriff distribute pods in the town square, the things having been brought in trucks from area farms. As they are trying to figure out their next move, Kaufman, Jack and the police chief break into the office and Mr. Grimaldi (Harry Vejar) brings in two pods for Miles and Becky's transformation. Kaufman explains to them that seeds drifting through space took root in nearby farm fields and as pods they have the power to take on the physical characteristics of any living thing and absorb its mind and memories. He says this makes for a perfect world without disease or troubles. When Miles asks him if this also rules out love, Kaufman replies there is no room for feelings as Miles notes that their only instinct is to survive. Locked in his office as Jack and Kaufman sit in the waiting room watching the pods develop, Miles fills syringes with a strong sedative and manages to give the shots to the two men as Becky does the same to the police chief. Deciding their only hope is to get to the nearest highway, Miles and Becky walk calmly through the streets but when she sees a dog nearly run over by a truck the woman cries out, alerting Janzek, who finds his drugged comrades. The lawman and the citizens run after Miles and Becky who make their way into a mining tunnel where they hide in a shaft and avoid detection. Later they hear music playing and, admonishing Becky not to doze off, Miles goes to find its origin only to realize it is coming from the radio of a truck loaded with pods. He returns to the tunnel and finds Becky nearly asleep and tries to carry her away but they fall down. Miles kisses Becky and realizes she has been transformed. She begins hollering to the others to get him as the doctor runs to the highway where he is horrified to see a truck filled with pods. When he has finished talking to the doctors at the hospital, Bassett declares him a mental case but just then a traffic accident victim is brought in and the ambulance attendant (Robert Osterloh) is talking about seeing strange-looking pods. This is overheard by Hill who orders the local law enforcers and the FBI be notified. Miles is relieved as he fights to stay awake.

Over the years, much has been made of the plot intonations of *Invasion of the Body Snatcher*. Theories about its underlying motivations, ranging from it being a denunciation of United States Cold War policies, a repudiation of the House of Representatives and the Senate's attempt to ferret out Communists in government and the private sector and its being a proponent of isolationism. On the other hand, there are those who have felt it is a jarring overview of autocratic mind control as exemplified by the rulers behind the Iron Curtain. In this context the film would be an offshoot of George Orwell's 1949 novel *1984*, which Columbia released as a movie the same year *Invasion of the Body Snatchers* opened. The mind-numbing, euphoric consequences of being transformed could also have its origins in the Soma drug prominent in *Brave New World* (1932) by Aldous Huxley. As noted, the film was based on a magazine story that was novelized in 1955 and its author, Jack Finney, always maintained it had no deep meanings and was designed as "popular entertainment."

Invasion of the Body Snatchers was shot in SuperScope as *The Body Snatchers* and *They Came from Another World*. It was filmed in several of the towns surrounding Los Angeles, including Chatsworth, Glendale, Hollywood, Los Feliz, Sierra Madre and Woodlands Hills, along with Bronson Canyon (the location of the mineshaft) and the Hollywood Freeway, where Kevin McCarthy's gave his now famous warning, "They're here already! You're next!."

King Donovan, who plays Jack Belicec, told me in an April 1974 interview that *Invasion of the Body Snatchers* was one of his favorites among the many movies he made, including *The Beast from 20,000 Fathoms*, *The Magnetic Monster* (both 1953) and *Riders to the Stars* (1954). He worked on the production for twelve days and referred to it as a "minor classic" although he claimed "it was not made as it should have been made." He noted that some fifteen to twenty pages of the script were cut before it went into production. Donovan said this was done by the movie's producers and he called the action "a good example of creative persons being put down by money." He said he enjoyed working with the rest of the cast and he felt Siegel was a fine director. According to Donovan, Siegel had a grueling task, having to work all day filming with long evenings spent looking at rushes and planning the next day's shooting.

Invasion of the Body Snatchers spawned several vastly inferior remakes. Using the same title, a big-budget 1978 production starred Donald Sutherland and Brooke Adams; its only highlight was McCarthy doing a cameo repeating his maniac freeway sequence. It was also more graphic than the original in detailing the development of the pods. United Artists released this second version that also had Siegel doing a bit as a cab driver. In 1994 Warner Bros. did a third outing, *Body Snatchers*, with Meg Tilly and Gabrille Anwar, set at a military compound. A fourth version, with the microorganisms instead of pods, came out in 2007 as *The Invasion*.

In 1988 Republic Pictures Home Video issued a colorized VHS tape version of the 1956 film. Surprisingly, the fairly muted colors do not take away from the overall effect of the original.

Island of the Doomed (1967; 86 minutes; Color)

Producer: George Ferrer. Director: Mel Welles. Screenplay: E.V. Theumer. Story: E.V. Theumer and Ira Meltcher [Mel Welles]. Photography: Cecilio Paniagua. Editor: Antonio Canovas. Music: A. Garcia Abril and Jose Munoz Molleda. Art Director: Francisco Canet. Production Manager: Enrique Sagaseta. Makeup: Juana Culell. Assistant Directors: Juan Ignasio Galvan, Fanny Wesling and Joseph Galliar.

CAST: Cameron Mitchell (Baron von Weser), Elisa Montes (Beth Christianson), George [Jorge] Martin (David Moss), Kay [Kai] Fischer (Cora Robinson), Ralph Naukoff [Rolf von Nauckhoff] (Jim Robinson), Hermann Nehlsen (Professor Jules Demerest), Matilde Sampedro (Myrtle Callihan), Ricardo Valle (Alfredo), Mike Brendel (Baldi/Accident Victim).

Filmed in Spain as *La Isla de la Muerte* (The Island of the Dead), this Spanish–West German co-production was made by Orbita Film, Madrid, and Tefi Film, Munich. In West Germany it was released as *Das Geheimnis der Todesinel* and was edited by Siegfried Kramer, with a running time three minutes less than its original 88 minutes. When Allied Artists issued it in the U.S. as *Island of the Doomed* in November 1967 it ran 86 minutes. In Great Britain it was called *Blood Suckers* and in France *Le Baron Vampire* (The Vampire Baron). It was later shown on U.S. television as *Maneater of Hydra*.

Tour guide Alfredo (Ricardo Valle) persuades six people to go with him on a two-day jaunt to a small Italian island owned by reclusive Baron von Weser (Cameron Mitchell). They are architect David Moss (George Martin), beautiful Beth Christianson (Elisa Montes), businessman Jim Robinson (Ralph Haukoff) and his much younger wife Cora (Kay Fischer), matronly Myrtle Callihan (Matilde Sampedro), and University of Michigan botanist Professor Jules Demerest (Hermann Nehlsen). Upon reaching the island by ferry, the visitors drive to the villa. Along the way Cora flirts with Alfredo, who tells them all the inhabitants except the baron and his servants left the island due to a vampire scare. A man (Mike Brendel) with a scarred face jumps in front of the car and is killed. Weser arrives and says the man is his cook and that he was suffering from an incurable disease that drove him mad. Weser shows the group his botanical gardens with imported orchids and then takes them to his villa where he gives them rooms for the night. Robinson argues with his wife over her attentions to the driver and at dinner Weser informs his guests that their food is made up vegetables grown on the island. Myrtle comments that the cucumbers taste like meat. She is frightened when she sees the butler, Baldi (Brendel), the mute twin brother of the dead man. Cora drinks too much and Weser takes her to the kitchen for coffee. Upon returning, Weber warns Robinson not to touch a porcupine plant which he says can cause temporary paralysis. While Weser shows his guests some of his specimens, including a meat-eating plant he developed by combining a Cross a Century plant with a Venus Flytrap, Alfredo is murdered in his car. As the Robinsons and Myrtle retire for the night and Weser confers with fellow botanist Demerest, David and Beth go outside for air and he warns her to lock her doors and windows. During the night, the restless Cora seeks out Alfredo but finds Weser feeding his plants and tries to seduce him but is thwarted. Cora returns to her room and, finding her husband gone, goes to bed and is attacked and murdered. The next morning Weser, David, Beth and Myrtle meet Robinson who has come back to the villa after some early morning fishing. Going to his room, Robinson finds his dead wife with a large puncture mark on her face. At the same time, Myrtle goes to the car, sees Alfredo and collapses. The woman accuses Demerest of the killings since she saw him lurking in the hallway the night before. After David questions Weser about the murders, the baron phones for the police but finds the line is dead and indicates that the ferry will not be back until the next afternoon. Robinson speculates that the killings were done by vampire bats since blood was drained from the victims. David suggests they leave the island and he and Weser go to ready a boat but find it has been sabotaged. Beth and Myrtle explore the woods, with the older woman taking pictures and telling the younger one they will not get off the island alive. This causes Beth to panic and she runs away, eventually falling into the grave Baldi is digging for his brother. He brings the unconscious woman to David as Demerest takes a rabbit from its cage and watches as it is devoured by a huge tree. When Demerest confronts Weser with the anomaly, he regretfully kills the botanist with a knife embedded in a statue of the Indian goddess Kali. He has Baldi remove the body. David finds the phone line cut and observes the servant carrying the corpse. When Weser arrives on the scene, David accuses Baldi of being the killer. The servant knocks down both men and escapes on a bicycle and they follow him in the car. He ends up in an abandoned chapel next to the island's cemetery where he climbs on the roof and tries to kill his pursuers by hurling boulders at them. The wall on which Baldi is standing collapses and he is buried in the rubble. As a thunderstorm approaches, Myrtle goes outside to take pictures and is attacked and killed by a large bloodsucking tree. Weser and Robinson take Baldi's body to the island's mausoleum and return to the villa where the wind blows open a window. When Beth closes it, she sees Myrtle's body in the courtyard and goes there only to be attacked by the tree. Robinson hears her screams as a branch of the tree breaks through the bedroom window and tries to kill him. He runs downstairs saying the tree is the killer as David hears Beth's cries and takes an axe and frees her. As Weser and Robinson fight, the latter is paralyzed by the porcupine plant. Weser kills him with another axe and goes out to stop David from destroying his creation. As the two men fight, Weser accidentally cuts the tree with his weapon and it devours him.

One of the truly ludicrous moments in horror film history has to be the finale scene in *Island of the Doomed* when mad scientist Weser tells the vampire tree that he loves it and wants to give it his blood and die with it. The tree itself is a shaggy thing with its petals unfolding to reveal erotic looking stamen that disgorge red liquid and penetrate flesh to draw off a victim's blood. It is remindful of the scene with the two sex object monsters fighting in *Battle Beyond the Sun* (1963).

While *Island of the Doomed* did quite well at the box office, it was hardly a favorite with critics. In *The Encyclopedia of Horror Movies* (1986), Phil Hardy dubbed it a "cheap shocker" adding, "The direction is token and the movie's only watchable scene is the latterday Eve's reunion with the tree in the baron's obscene garden of Eden followed by the surreal image of the profusely bleeding tree." *John Stanley's Creature Features Movie Guide Strikes Again* (1994) called it "crudely photographed and acted... [It] plays almost like a stereotyped whodunit, yet has a compulsion in the way the decadent characters behave, setting themselves up for the slurping green creepers and wriggling branches." *Movies on TV 1975–76 Edition* (1974), edited by Steven H. Scheuer, gave the film its lowest rating, adding, "Clichés! Forgettable foreign-made entry."

The film's director, Mel Welles, had to use the name Ernst von Theumer, one of *Island of the Doomed*'s producers, since it was a co-production, but his name appeared on prints seen outside Europe. He also directed *Lady Frankenstein* (1971), which von Theumer produced. Welles is best known as an actor in Roger Corman films like *The Undead* (1957), *Attack of the Crab Monsters* (1957) [q.v.] and *The Little Shop of Horrors* (1960) [q.v.]. He also acted in *Abbott and Costello Meet the Mummy* (1955), *The 27th Day* (1957), *She Beast (Revenge of the Blood Beast)* (1965) and *Dr. Heckyl and Mr. Hype* (1980), and provided the voice of ESS in *Wolfen* (1981).

Jalopy (1953; 62 minutes)

Producer: Ben Schwalb. Director: William Beaudine. Story-Screenplay: Tim Ryan and Jack Crutcher. Additional Dialogue: Bert Lawrence. Photography: Harry Neumann. Editor: William Austin. Music: Marlin Skiles. Art Director: David Milton. Sound: Charles Cooper. Sets: Robert Priestley. Production Manager: Allen K. Wood. Special Effects: Ray Mercer. Continuity: Ilona Vas. Assistant Director: Austen Jewell.

CAST: Leo Gorcey (Terence Aloysius "Slip" Mahoney), Huntz Hall (Horace Debussy "Sach" Jones), Bernard Gorcey (Louie Dumbrowski), Robert Lowery (Skid Wilson), Leon Belasco (Professor Bosgood Elrod), Richard Benedict (Tony Lango), Jane Easton (Bobbie Lane), Murray Alper (Red Barker), David [Gorcey] Condon (Chuck), Bennie Bartlett (Butch), Tom Hanlon (Race Announcer), Mona Knox (Dream Girl), Bob Rose, Carey Loftin, George Dockstader, Louis Tomei, George Barrows, Dude Criswell, Fred Lamont, Dick Crockett, Teddy Mangean, Pete Kellett, Bud Wolfe (Drivers), Conrad Brooks (Party Guest).

The twenty-eighth film in the long running "Bowery Boys" series, *Jalopy* was the initial entry under the Allied Artists banner and it was also the first to be produced by Ben Schwalb, who remained with the series until 1957. Regarding his influence on the productions, David Hayes and Brent Walker wrote in *The Films of the Bowery Boys* (1984), "The gangster characters are now played for buffoons, and so are the boys. Schwalb elected to instill into the series a purer form of comedy, as he felt that a policy of piling laughs upon laughs would create comedies that were made as they were supposed to be made. It was a smart move on his part to transform the Bowery Boys into buffoons, as they were obviously getting older, and audiences might tire of grown men who appeared to be retreating into adolescence." *Jalopy*'s slight sci-fi angle dealt with the creation of a superspeed formula that also seems to materialize dream girls. *Variety* dubbed it "an above-average programmer," adding, "[Leo] Gorcey and [Huntz] Hall romp through the roles they've long mastered.... Ben Schwalb, in producing, has stuck to the proven formula for the series to turn film into success. William Beaudine's direction wisely accents the laugh potential...."

Jalopy racer Skid Wilson (Robert Lowery) has been making a killing at the track with his car driven by Tony Lango (Richard Benedict) and serviced by mechanic Red Baker

(Murray Alper). When he finds out that a new entry, "Mahoney's Meteor," owned by Slip Mahoney (Leo Gorcey) and his pals Sach Jones (Huntz Hall), Chuck (David Condon) and Butch (Bennie Bartlett), has entered the next race, he tells his girlfriend Bobbie Lane (Jane Easton) to get details. Slip test drives the jalopy but the noise it makes drives away customers from Louie Dumbrowski's (Bernard Gorcey) sweet shop as the car overheats at a standstill. They placate Louie by promising to take part of their race purse to pay off his rent since they are using the back room his shop for Professor Elrod Bosgood (Leon Belasco) to work on a new fuel formula. Sach mixes up a concoction that explodes when he drops it. After the smoke clears, Bobbie shows up and he thinks he created her. The young woman makes a play for Slip so he gives her a pass to the races but the next day his car is passed by all the others and he ends up running into a wall. Sach tries to aid Slip by running on the track but he instead causes a series of wrecks. The angry drivers unite to pursue Slip and Sach, who jump over a wall and run away. Back at the sweet shop, the angry Slip tells Sach to wax the floor while he tries to get more money out of Louie for the next race. Sach puts the formula he invented in Louie's rented waxer and it flies out a window, shoots up in the air and crashes back to the street. Slip decides to use the formula in his jalopy and it circles the track in eleven seconds. Skid and his cohorts try to find out the secret of Slip's success, and Sach mentions putting something in the gas tank. Sach and the professor stir up a batch of the formula and when Sach drops some of it on the floor, Bobbie returns inviting the gang to a pre-race party at Skid's apartment. Once the boys get to the festivities, Lango and Barker search for the formula but fail to find it, so Skid tries to force the gang and Louie to reveal its whereabouts. Sach throws some of the formula on the floor and he and his pals escape and go back to the sweet shop where they are accosted by Skid, Lango and Barker. During the melee, Louie calls for the cops. The thieves return after the law departs, and find out the new batch is no good. They leave in disgust as Sach realizes that he forgot to put seltzer water in the formula. At race time Skid feels he has nothing to fear from Slip and he is proved correct when the Meteor barely makes it around the track at the start of the big $1,500 race. Sach shows up with a new batch of the formula, runs onto the track and puts it in the jalopy's tank. Slip's car flies around the track in reverse with Sach clinging to its side. Slip wins the race, and a disappointed Skid tells Bobbie to return the fur coat he bought her. During a post-race celebration at Louie's place, Sach again throws some of the formula on the floor and a beautiful girl materializes (Mona Knox) and goes off with Slip. He tries again but this time a girl wearing horn-rimmed glasses arrives for Elrod. Sach follows Slip as Louie decides to try his luck with the formula but ends up in tears when it fails to produce his dream girl.

Jennifer (1953; 73 minutes)

Producer: Berman Swartz. Director: Joel Newton. Story: Virginia Myers. Photography: James Wong Howe. Editor: Everett Douglas. Music: Ernest Gold. Song: Matt Dennis and Earl Brent. Sound: Jean L. Speak. Sets: George Sawley. Production Manager: Lonnie D'Orsa. Makeup: Dan Greenway. Wardrobe: Ruth Matthews. Continuity: John Franco. Assistant Director: Austin Jewell.

CAST: Ida Lupino (Agnes Langley), Howard Duff (Jim Hollis), Robert Nichols (Orin Slade), Mary Shipp (Lorna Gale), Ned Glass (Grocery Clerk), Kitty McHugh (Mrs. Canaway), Russ Conway (Gardener), Lorna Thayer (Molly), Matt Dennis (Singer).

Ida Lupino and Howard Duff were married from 1951 to 1968. They first appeared together on film in 1949's *Woman in Hiding* and after their marriage they teamed for *Jennifer*, followed by *Private Hell 36* (1954), *Women's Prison* (1955) and *While the City Sleeps* (1956). They also co-starred in the CBS-TV comedy series *Mr. Adams and Eve* (1957–58). *Jennifer* borders on horror with its spooky old house location and *noir* atmosphere, along with a ghostly shadow seen at the beginning and end of the film. *Jennifer* is perhaps the least known of the couple's films; it is highlighted by offbeat camerawork, often involving dark shadows, but it is laden with long, drawn-out scenes containing almost no action. Allied Artists released it in the fall of 1953. *Leonard Maltin's 2004 Movie and Video Guide* (2003) termed it a "[t]urgid programmer." In Spanish-language countries it was called *La Sombra* (The Shadow).

Secretary Agnes Langley (Lupino) is hired for $150 a month by Lorna Gale (Mary Shipp) to live at her family's sumptuous estate near the small California town of Montecito. The previous caretaker, Jennifer Brown, Lorna's cousin, left without giving notice. Lorna tells her friend, local businessman Jim Hollis (Duff), to keep an eye on Agnes since she is alone in the old house. Agnes finds Jennifer's diary and starts to read it and becomes unnerved by strange sounds in the dark mansion. Jim decides to introduce himself to Agnes by personally delivering an order she made to his grocery store. After she tells him about hearing strange noises, he searches the grounds but finds nothing out of the ordinary. He tells her he thinks Jennifer got lonely and did not like living in the country. Jim also offers to let Agnes stay at his inn but she declines. When Agnes goes to Jim's store to get more supplies, she overhears gossip regarding Jennifer from the clerks (Ned Glass, Lorna Thayer) and a customer (Kitty McHugh). Back at the house, she continues to read the diary and finds a broken record Jennifer abandoned called "Vortex." An employee of Jim's, 19-year-old Orin Slade (Robert Nichols), arrives to repair the water heater and tells Agnes that Jennifer worked for a local attorney named Sampson, who killed himself after the young woman allegedly

Spanish lobby card for *Jennifer* (1953) picturing Howard Duff and Ida Lupino

took important documents from him. He theorizes that something violent happened to Jennifer. When Jim asks Agnes to dinner, she declines the invitation and drives to a Santa Barbara music store to listen to the record that Jennifer apparently broke. Agnes later finds a bank book with numerous deposits and a $70,000 balance. When she shows it to Jim, he opines that the young woman may have been involved in blackmail although there are no withdrawals from the account. Agnes comes to the conclusion that Jennifer died in the house. She and Jim search a passageway that leads below the cellar but find only a storage area. Jim gets Agnes to talk about her past and she admits she was dumped by her fiancé for another woman. Jim again asks Agnes to stay at his inn but she refuses although accepting his invitation to a dance there that evening. After he tells Orin not to talk to Agnes about Jennifer, Jim receives a telephone call from Lorna who says she needs to see him the next day. During the dance, Orin rummages through his boss' desk and locates the bank book that might belong to Jennifer. After the dance, Jim and Agnes kiss and set a date for the next night. When he is delayed, she looks through some of Jennifer's things and finds a note hidden in a ball of twine stating that the young woman was afraid and planned to hide in the furnace room. Orin shows up and tells Agnes about finding the bank book and that he thinks Jim was involved with Jennifer. He says Jim and Lorna are talking at the inn and he believes they know the truth about Jennifer's disappearance. Agnes goes to the furnace room and sees a woman's face in a pool of water and tries to get away from Jim when he arrives. Jim catches up with her in the garden and she accuses him of murdering Jennifer. According to Jim, Lorna informed him that Jennifer died after having been placed in a sanitarium because the Gale's could not face insanity in the family. The nearly hysterical Agnes tells Jim she saw Jennifer's body in the basement and he takes her back there and shows her that the face she saw in the water was her own reflection. Realizing that her imagination was the cause of her fears, Agnes looks forward to the future with Jim. As they walk away hand in hand, the dark shadow of a woman slithers unto the front steps of the mansion.

Jennifer introduced the popular standard "Angel Eyes," written by Matt Dennis and Earl Brent; Dennis sings the song in the film. It was also recorded by others, including Herb Jeffries, Nat (King) Cole, Ella Fitzgerald and Frank Sinatra.

Jungle Gents (1954; 63 minutes)

Producer: Ben Schwalb. Director: Edward Bernds. Screenplay: Elwood Ullman and Edward Bernds. Photography: Harry Neumann. Editor: Sam Fields. Music: Marlin Skiles. Art Director: David Milton. Sound: Ralph Butler. Sets: Joseph Kish. Production Manager: Allen K. Wood. Makeup: Edward Polo. Wardrobe: Bert Henrikson. Special Effects: Augie Lohman. Continuity: John L. Banse. Assistant Director: Austen Jewell.

CAST: Leo Gorcey (Terence Aloysius "Slip" Mahoney), Huntz Hall (Horace Debussy "Sach" Jones), Bernard Gorcey (Louie Dumbrowski), Laurette Luez (Anatta), Patrick O'Rourke (Alf Grimshaw), Rudolph Anders (Dr. Goebel), Harry Cording (Dan Shanks), David [Gorcey] Condon (Chuck), Bennie Bartlett (Butch), Emory Parnell (Captain Daly), Woody Strode (Malaka), Joel Fluellen (Rangori), Murray Alper (Fats Lomax), John Harmon (Harmes), Roy Glenn (Chief Omotowa), Emil Sitka (Crewman Painter), Pat Flaherty (Officer Cady), Jett Norman [Clint Walker] (Jungle Man), Ned Glass (Laboratory Technician), Eric Snowden (Trader Holmes).

After taking a new antibiotic for a head cold, Sach Jones (Huntz Hall) has a heightened sense of smell and aids the police by literally sniffing out stolen diamonds in Louie Dumbrowski's (Bernard Gorcey) sweet shop, secreted there by Fats Lomax (Murray Alper). Officer Cady (Pat Flaherty) arrests Sach along with Fats. At the police station Captain Daly (Emory Parnell) tries to make Sach confess that he lied about smelling the diamonds. A laboratory technician (Ned Glass) convinces the chief that the antibiotic gave Sach a sharper sense of smell and he is freed. Alf Grimshaw (Patrick O'Rourke), the grateful owner of the gems, tells Sach and his pals Slip Mahoney (Leo Gorcey), Chuck (David Condon) and Butch (Bennie Bartlett) that they can make a fortune searching for a cache of missing diamonds in Africa using Sach's new gift. The Bowery Boys, along with Louie and Alf, sail to Africa, and after traveling inland on the *River King*, they confer with Holmes (Eric Snowden), a trader who is in partnership with Grimshaw. Suffering from jungle fever, Holmes informs them another partner had found diamonds but was murdered before he could reveal the location. The partners had earlier agreed that the gems were hidden in some remote grottos and Holmes gives Sach a map to the area as the ailing man's attendant, Dr. Goebel (Rudolph Anders), arrives to check on him. Holmes tells Sach to guard the map with his life. As Slip, Sach, Louie, Chuck, Butch and Grimshaw head into the jungle, they are followed by Goebel and his cohort Dan Shanks (Harry Cording), who want the diamonds for themselves. Sach accidentally uses the map to start a fire in order to ward off lions. During the night, one of the beasts enters Slip and Sach's tent and they run through the jungle and get caught in a trap. After they are rescued, Sach leads the party on a wild goose chase over the African veldt, with Goebel and Shanks trailing them. At last Sach admits burning the map and Slip finds out he used a girdle advertisement as his pretend chart. Sach says he will kill himself but when his gun misfires the others make him take up the rear of their safari. When a lion tries to attack Sach, he is saved by beautiful jungle girl Anatta (Laurette Luez), who kills the lion and takes a shine to Sach but flees when his friends return. The local natives think Sach killed the lion and declare he is a great white hunter. Goebel and Shanks talk Chief Omotowa (Roy Glenn) of the Nadoros tribe into having his men eliminate all the newcomers except Sach. The safari members are captured by the hostile tribe and are told by Goebel that Sach will help him find diamonds while the rest have their heads shrunk. Slip and the others cause Sach to get a head cold so that he cannot sniff out the precious gems. When he finds out Sach has a cold, Goebel takes him to masked witch doctor Rangori (Joel Fluellen) for a cure. Anatta returns and disables the shaman and Sach puts on his mask and attire and sets his pals free. Now that Sach is over his cold, Slip asks Alf to have Anatta take them to the Nalabarani, caves allegedly containing the tomb of an ancient king and his headless ghost, to find the diamonds. When Slip and Sach run into each other in the caves, the latter's nose is injured and he again loses his sense of smell. Pursued by the specter, Sach accidentally stumbles on the diamonds but Goebel and Shanks get the drop on him and his pals. The ghost, who is really Holmes, shows up and the crooks shoot at him. The boys subdue the baddies. Holmes declares that Goebel and Shanks eliminated his partner. Later, as the boys get ready to go back home, they say farewell to Alf and Holmes. Sach plans to stay in Africa with his newfound love Anatta but quickly changes his mind when her boyfriend, a tall jungle man (Clint Walker), arrives on the scene.

Jungle Gents was the twenty-fifth "Bowery Boys" outing. The film starts out with plenty of humor and does well until the location switch from the Bowery to Africa slows down the affair, with plenty of jungle, animal and native stock footage. It becomes rather plodding from that point until the amusing finale. The second part of the film is also shackled with the plot ploy of Sach contemplating suicide, hardly a good idea considering the juvenile nature of the series' audience. On the plus side, there is beautiful *Life* magazine pin-up Laurette Luez as the jungle girl and a young Clint Walker (billed as Jett Norman) as her Tarzan-like boyfriend. Luez earlier appeared in *Prehistoric Women* (1950) and *Siren of Bagdad* (1952). *Jungle Gents* is a minor "Bowery Boys" effort. *Variety* complained, "Not much of a plot and stock footage doesn't help matters any, neither the narration from Gorcey. Screenplay by Elwood Ullman and director Edward Bernds is below-par for both."

Macabre (1958; 71 minutes)

Producer-Director: William Castle. Screenplay: Robb White, from the novel *The Marble Forest* by Theo Durrant. Photography: Carl E. Guthrie. Editor: John F. Schreyer. Music: Les Baxter. Art Directors: John T. Collis and Robert Kinoshita. Sound: George J. Eppich, Frank Webster and Clem Portman. Makeup: Jack Dusick. Special Effects: Irving Block, Louis De Witt and Jack Rabin. Wardrobe: Irene Caine and Bert Henrikson. Assistant Director: Paul Wurtzel.

CAST: William Prince (Dr. Rod Barrett), Christine White (Nancy Wetherby), Jim Backus (Sheriff Jim Tyloe), Jacqueline Scott (Polly Baron), Susan Morrow (Sylvia Stevenson), Dorothy Morris (Alice Wetherby Barrett), Philip Tonge (Jode Wetherby), Jonathan Kidd (Ed Quigley), Ellen Corby (Miss Kushins), Howard Hoffman (Hummel), Linda Guderman (Marge Barrett), Voltaire Perkins (Minister).

After directing films for fifteen years, William Castle financed his first independent production, *Macabre*, with the assistance of screenwriter Robb White, who adapted the film from the 1951 novel *The Marble Forest* by "Theo Durrant" (a pseudonym for a dozen mystery writers who collaborated on the enterprise). Castle allegedly mortgaged his home in order to pay his part of the nearly $90,000 production that was filmed at the Ziv Studios in Hollywood. Although this was Castle's first horror film he had directed films with genre

Spanish lobby card for *Macabre* (1958) picturing Jacqueline Scott and Philip Tonge

overtones such as *The Whistler*, *Mark of the Whistler* and *When Strangers Marry (Betrayed)* (all 1944), *Voice of the Whistler* and *The Crime Doctor's Warning* (both 1945) and *Just Before Dawn* (1946). To bolster *Macabre*'s box office potential, Castle came up with the gimmick of taking out a $1,000 insurance policy on each theater patron, collectable if they died of fright while watching the movie. Allied Artists released the production in time for Halloween in 1958 and it was a big success with some sources claiming it had a total gross in excess of five million dollars. It launched Castle's career as a horror film director as well as one of the cinema's premier showmen and paved the way for his next blockbuster for Allied, 1959's *House on Haunted Hill* (q.v.).

Filmed in nine days, *Macabre* is a tense thriller that has some spooky cemetery scenes that include a couple hiding in a grave, a hand coming from behind a tombstone and a repulsive corpse. The production opens with a narrator telling audience members to watch out for each other and to contact the management if anyone becomes uncontrollably frightened. At the finale the same voice asks patrons not to reveal the ending. During the proceedings, the film often cuts to a clock showing viewers the progression of the plot. Overall, the film fills its scare quota. Top-billed William Prince makes a most unappealing leading man while Jim Backus nicely plays against type as a vengeful lawman. The picture's four leading ladies, Christine White, Jacqueline Scott, Susan Morrow and Dorothy Morris, are all very good, with White especially fine in the difficult part of a blind free spirit. Ellen Corby makes the most of her brief scenes as the caring nanny, while Philip Tonge nicely captures the character of an old man who appears to be holding on to life by a thread. Jonathan Kidd does a good job as a harried undertaker. The film's credits are not shown until the end; there are cartoon caricatures of Castle and White riding in a car followed by hearses giving the names of the cast members killed in the proceedings as "The Dead" with the survivors listed as "The Living," leading to the production credits. *Castle of Frankenstein* #17 (1971) called the film an "uneven mixture of straight suspense and black humor spoof.... Basically rather unpleasant, not as much fun as later Castle epics."

Undertaker Ed Quigley (Kidd) informs Jim Tyloe (Backus), the sheriff of the small town of Thornton, that a child's coffin has been stolen from his mortuary. The lawman chides him for his gambling debts and intimates he may be trying to collect on insurance. To avoid the subject, Ed questions Tyloe about rich Jode Wetherby (Tonge) having the funeral of his daughter Nancy (White) scheduled for midnight. Jim sees Dr. Rod Barrett (Prince) coming to his office and blames him for Nancy's death as well as that of her sister Alice (Morris), the physician's late wife. He also asks about the doctor's three-year-old daughter Marge (Linda Guderman) and advises the medical man to get out of town. Upset about being blamed for the deaths of his wife and sister-in-law, Rod is consoled by his nurse Polly Baron (Scott), who is in love with him. She says the locals think he was with divorcee Sylvia Stevenson (Morrow) when his wife went into labor and tells him he should leave town with Marge and take her with them. Rod suggests he and Polly take Marge for a picnic in the park since he has no patients but when they go to his home they cannot find the little girl. Her nanny, Miss Kushins (Corby), says the child was brought home by Sylvia and was playing with her teddy bear when last seen. Believing his daughter is with Sylvia, Rod goes to her home but the child is not there. Sylvia questions him about Marge not liking her and expresses jealousy over his relationship with Polly. The nurse answers a phone call and upon hearing the what the caller says, she faints. Rod arrives home to see Miss Kushins tending to Polly, who tells him the man on the phone said to tell Rod that the little girl is in a coffin and has five hours to live. The nanny wants to call the sheriff but Rod stops her, saying the lawman hates him and will not help. He also tells her not to go to his father-in-law, Wetherby, because the news might be fatal as he has a bad heart. When the doctor and his nurse find the child's Teddy bear on his front porch, it is covered with clay and Rod suggests to Polly that Marge may be buried in the town's cemetery. As they go there, Miss Kushins walks to Wetherby's home and tells him what is happening. In the graveyard, Rod and Polly check several recently dug plots but find nothing. When they come across Nancy's open grave, Rod decides to dig deeper for the child. As he and Polly are shoveling out dirt, they hear a noise and hide as someone covers the opening with a tarp. It turns out to be Mr. Hummel (Howard Hoffman), the caretaker; someone hits him and knocks him out. As the doctor is tending to the caretaker, a hand reaches from behind a tombstone and grabs Polly. It turns out to be Wetherby, who said he hit Hummel because he thought the man kidnapped the little girl. The old man then relates (via flashbacks) how his blind daughter returned to town where she meets Jim, an old friend. They make love and he asks her to marry him but she refuses since he loves her sister Alice, who married Rod. Nancy finds out she is pregnant and asks her brother-in-law for an abortion saying she does not want to be a wife or mother. Rod refuses her request and she dies shortly thereafter. The doctor informs his father-in-law that he killed Hummel and tells Polly to take him home. Rod later calls Polly and suggests that Marge may be at the funeral home; she and Wetherby join him there. They search the caskets but find them empty and are confronted by Ed, whom Rod accuses of abducting his daughter. The undertaker denies the charge as Jim arrives. The men take Nancy's coffin to a hearse. Rod and Polly return to the cemetery where she blames him for the tragedy because of his relationship with Sylvia. The nurse remembers (in flashbacks) how Rod's wife Alice, ordered to bed for the duration of her pregnancy, came to his office when he was with Sylvia. That night, while Rod was at Sylvia's home, Alice went into labor and Polly could not locate Rod. When the doctor goes back to his office, he finds Jim waiting for him with the announcement of his daughter's birth and the death of Alice. The lawman beats Rod and promises further revenge. Polly slaps Rod when he accuses her of the kidnapping. Their argument is interrupted by the sheriff; Polly tells him about Marge's disappearance. The trio find one mausoleum unlocked and when Polly goes inside looking for the little girl, she sees Hummel's bloodied corpse. Nancy's funeral takes place during a thunderstorm. After the service, Rod, Jim and Ed begin filling in her grave when the doctor's shovel hits a metal object. It turns out to be a child's coffin. When he opens it, he finds a mutilated corpse. Wetherby sees the body, suffers a fatal heart attack and nearly falls into his daughter's grave. Rod is shot by Ed, who throws money at him and confesses to joining the doctor in a plot to kill Wetherby so he could pay off his gambling debts. He tells Jim that Rod wanted the old man's millions and fabricated the kidnapping and had him (Ed) make the grotesque dummy to scare Wetherby to death. Rod could have saved Nancy's life but she stood in the way of his getting the money. Before going to the hospital, Rod asks to go to his office where he plays a tape recording to Polly of the call he faked about Marge being kidnapped. After he dies, the nurse locates the little girl asleep in her father's office.

The Magic Weaver (1965; 77 minutes; Color)

Producer-Director: Alexander Row [Aleksandr Rou]. Screenplay: Eugene Schwartz [Yevgeni Shvarts]. Photography: David Suren [Dmitri Surensky]. Music: Andrew Wolkon [Andrei Volkonsky]. Conductor: A. Roitman. Songs: A. Kolinsky and V. Lifshiz. Production Design: Yevgeni Galej. Special Effects: L. Askimov. Designers: Arseni Klopotovsky and V. Nititchenko.

CAST: Michael [Mikhail] Kuznetsov (The Old Soldier), Nina Kishkon [Nelli Myshkova] (Mariya), Vito Pereva [Vitya Perevalov] (Ivan), Anatoil Kubatsky (Water Wizard), Georgi Millyar (Prime Minister Croak), Olya Khadhapuridze (Alyonushka), Vera Altayskaya (Ttushka-Nepogodunska), S. Trotsky (Altyn Altynych), Aleksandr Khvyla (Mudrets-Molchanik).

An Old Soldier (Michael Kuznetsov) leaves the service and with his drum walks through a forest. After sharing his lunch with talking squirrels, he meets two bear cubs who inform him that their grandfather has been caught in a trap. He frees the older bear who tells him that a fiend has taken over the forest and turned it into a horrible place. As he walks along, he sees a small boy, Ivan (Vito Pereva), who says he is looking for his mother, Mariya (Nina Kishkon), who has been carried off by the evil Water Wizard (Anatoil Kubatsky), because she is the world's finest weaver. He also informs the Old Soldier that his father was lost in a blizzard years before and the drummer offers to help the boy find his mother. The giant Water Wizard materializes, causing the Old Soldier to bang his drum in a call for his comrades. The Wizard becomes normal size and begs the man to quit banging the drum as he cannot stand loud noise. The boys tells the Wizard he wants his mother and, although the evil one denies having her, he promises to take them to his palace and give the Old Soldier a slave for his drum. After traveling down a long stone stairway into the underwater kingdom, they enter the Wizard's coral palace where they see various aquatic monsters. The drummer is offered a frog man, Prime Minister Croak (Georgi Millyar), for a slave but he refuses. As the mother begs for her son in a prison cell, she is put under a spell by a transparent woman (Vera Altayskaya) who tells her freedom and slavery are one. The Water Wizard displays to the Old Soldier and Ivan the wonders of his palace along with various servants, including a silent walrus, a giant lobster and his human-rooster guardian, three mathematicians, several trained dancing and singing pirates, and miniature mermaids. When the Old Soldier refuses these wonders, he and the boy are taken to a guest room filled with food.

Poster for *The Magic Weaver* (1965), the U.S. release of the Soviet film *Marya-Iskusnitsa* (Maria, the Wonderful Weaver) (1959).

The drummer suspects it is poisoned and he and Ivan dine on the child's provisions. When Croak reports to the Wizard that the guests did not eat the tainted food, the evil one commands his court to think of a way to get rid of the unwanted visitors. Upon the advice of the walrus, the king consults with an underground deity, and when he returns he orders rich gifts for the strangers. He also calls for his little granddaughter, Alyonushka (Olya Khadhapuridze), who distrusts the Wizard, and he informs her that a dangerous swamp cousin and his nephew have come to take away her friend Mariya. She demands to meet the newcomers and he takes her to their chamber but uses magic to distort their images, making them look evil. The Wizard tells her to hide the weaver and say six magic charms over her for protection. After she leaves, he orders Croak to follow the little girl; once she has said the charms, he is to push her into boiling water. As the Wizard takes the Old Soldier and Ivan to this treasures and tells them to take what they want, Alyonushka leads Mariya into a remote water cavern. After she recites the charms, the weaver turns into six transparent likenesses of herself. When Croak tries to push the little girl into the boiling water, he slips and falls in himself. The six beings arrive at the court and the Wizard orders Ivan to identity his mother or she will be his forever. He also takes the drum from the Old Soldier. On the third try, the boy sees his mother but the Wizard refuses to keep his part of the bargain. Alyonushka comes to the defense of the strangers and leads them out of the court as the Old Soldier orders a magic harp to play, making the Wizard and his minions dance. The Old Soldier, Ivan, Mariya and Alyonushka escape from the palace. Eventually the pirates are able to subdue the harp and go after them. The Old Soldier is caught in their net but escapes and beats up the pirates as Croak follows the escapees into the forest. After an encounter with the grandfather bear, Croak reverts to being a frog but the transparent woman brings torrential rain. Back at her home, Mariya cannot come out of the spell placed on her. When Ivan goes to the well for water, the Wizard rises out of it and tries to abduct the boy. Her son's screams rouse the mother and she runs to save him, joined by the Old Soldier and Alyonushka. The weather clears and the transparent woman becomes a bird that is eaten by a cat. On dry land the Water Wizard turns into a mud puddle. Mariya and the Old Soldier find they are attracted to each other as they all plan a feast of celebration for the entire world.

Released stateside in a dubbed version by Allied Artists in late September 1965, *The Magic Weaver* was made in the Soviet Union at Maxim Gorky Studios as *Marya-Iskusnitsa* (Maria, the Wonderful Weaver) and issued there in 1959. Bellucci Productions prepared the English-language version and its running time is nearly twenty minutes less than the original. Based on Russian folk tales, the production is a lavish one, with colorful undersea sets and characters. Most of the film's songs were cut for the American version and what remained were rarely dubbed in English. Although the feature teems with fantasy elements, there is very little overtly horrific about it; even the evil Water Wizard is hardly frightening. In some of the publicity for the film, the villain is dubbed His Royal Wetness, Whirlpool III.

Allied issued advertising material for the fantasy, which gives some background on its making. It states, "*The Magic Weaver* was filmed in Russia using many of the Soviet Union's top stars. Unusual because it does not resort to animation to achieve its magical effects, it is doubly surprising coming from the USSR, which for the last 30 years has been making mostly propaganda films. Much of the credit can be given to Director [Alexander] Row, who convinced the Soviet officials to let him make pictures based on the old legends. According to Row, children, and adults too, are in danger of losing touch with these wonderful old stories, merely because most filmmakers find them too difficult to produce. Willing to make a special effort, he has created a new and exciting kind of picture, combining reality and fantasy in a way that few will be able to resist."

The Magic Wizard was produced and directed by Row, the Americanized name for Soviet helmsman Aleksandr Rou, who made fantasy films for 35 years, including *Po Shchuchjemu Velenyu* [As If By Magic] (1938), *Morozko* [Jack Frost] (1965) and *Zolotye Roga* [Golden Horns] (1972), as well as the dramas *May Night* and *Stars of the Ukraine* (both 1953). According to *Video Watchdog* #9 (Jan-Feb. 1992), Rou "was the most beloved of all Russian film fantasists, an essentially juvenile filmmaker whose popularity eclipsed even that of the more ambitious Aleksandr Ptushko."

The Maze (1953; 80 minutes)

Producer: Richard Heermance. Executive Producer: Walter Mirisch. Director–Production Designer: William Cameron Menzies. Screenplay: Daniel B. Ullman, from the novel by Maurice Sandoz. Photography: Harry Neumann. Editor: John Fuller. Music: Marlin Skiles. Sound: Charles Cooper. Sets: Robert Priestley. Production Manager: Allen K. Wood. Special Effects: Augie Lohman. Technical Advisor: Maurice Davidson. Continuity: Ilona Vas. Assistant Director: Austen Jewell.

CAST: Richard Carlson (Sir Gerald MacTeam), Veronica Hurst (Kitty Murray), Katherine Emery (Edith Murray), Michael Pate (William), John Dodsworth (Dr. Bert Dilling), Hillary Brooke (Peggy Lord), Stanley Fraser (Robert), Lillian Bond (Margaret Dilling), Owen McGiveney (Gardener Simon), Robin Hughes (Richard Robar), Clyde Cook (Cab Driver), The Phelans (Dancers), Jack Chefe (Waiter), Bess Flowers, Harold Miller, Bert Stevens (Night Club Patrons).

At the remote Castle Craven in Scotland, servants William (Michael Pate) and Robert (Stanley Fraser) find their master, Sir Samuel MacTeam, has died so they notify his heir, Gerald MacTeam (Richard Carlson). The ensuing events are then told (in flashbacks) by Edith Murray (Katherine Emery), whose niece Kitty (Veronica Hurst) is engaged to marry Gerald. The three are on vacation in Cannes with Kitty's former suitor Richard Robar (Robin Hughes). Gerald tells them his Uncle Samuel is a recluse who will not be attending his and Kitty's nuptials in two weeks. As Kitty and Richard dance, Gerald relates to Edith that it has been fifteen years since he was at Castle Craven where his uncle locked him in his room at night and forbade him to go into a large maze on the grounds. He also says that the castle is without modern conveniences including telephone, electricity and central heating. Gerald is next in line to inherit the castle and Edith worries because none of the baronets lived long after getting the title. Gerald gets an express letter and he informs Kitty and her aunt that he has been called to Castle Craven but he wants to wait until after the wedding. Kitty tells him to go now. Weeks pass before the two women read that Sir Samuel has died and Gerald is the new baronet. Kitty relates to Edith that all her cables to the castle have been received but none answered and her aunt tells the young woman to forget Gerald. Edith receives a letter from Gerald telling her he cannot leave Castle Craven and that he is releasing Kitty from their marriage bargain. A line in the letter is heavily crossed out and Kitty erases the mark over to find the words "unless there is a death." Feeling that he needs her, Kitty asks her aunt to accompany her to Scotland so she can find out what is the matter. The two arrive at the castle on a foggy night and their cab driver (Clyde Cook) departs hastily. William informs them that Sir Gerald cannot be disturbed but Kitty says they are tired of standing in the fog and goes inside. Gerald, who looks twenty years older, angrily informs the women they must leave immediately but they insist on staying the night. They are taken to adjoining rooms with walled-up windows and Kitty comments on the rubber covering in the hallway and stairs. When the women are locked in their rooms, they complain to no avail. During the night, Kitty is awakened by a dragging sound in the hallway and sees a light move past the bottom of her door. She locates a door to a bat-infested passage that leads to a lookout tower over the maze and again she hears the dragging sound. When she finds that Edith is suffering from a cold, Kitty tells Gerald they will stay until her aunt is well. Kitty notices strange webbed prints on the hall floor which Robert quickly wipes away. Feeling that Gerald is not well, Kitty tells him she wants to help but he refuses to see a doctor. Kitty writes a letter to their mutual friends, Dr. Bert Dilling (John Dodsworth) and his wife Margaret (Lillian Bond), and invites them to the castle, along with Richard and Peggy Lord (Hillary Brooke). Kitty finds the gate to the maze open and she ventures inside where she finds the same strange prints but Gerald makes her go back to the castle. That night Edith hides before her bedroom door is locked and goes into a tower room where she spies something large and black that emits a loud croak before scampering away. She screams and faints. Gerald carries her back to her room, telling her she is a victim of her imagination. Kitty is awakened by the dragging sound in the hall and the light passing by the door. When morning comes, Gerald tells the women to leave and as they are about to do so the quartet of friends Kitty invited show up at the castle. After he reluctantly gives them rooms, Gerald voices his displeasure with Kitty for inviting the four but she tells him she only wants to help him; he tells her that the only way she can help is to leave. As they have drinks that evening, Gerald's demeanor improves until he hears a loud noise from upstairs and he and the servants lock the guests in the dining room. Bert tells the others that he plans to have Gerald taken into custody for observation and he fears the man might be dangerous. When Gerald returns, he tells the group they must be locked in their rooms for the night. The doctor later informs his wife that the men of the MacTeam line suffer from a congenital illness that causes them to die at an early age; the last wife of one of them died after only a few days in the castle, two hundred years ago. He says the family line has been carried on through nephews. Kitty and Edith go back to the tower room where they find seaweed, a bowl of tomatoes and a book on human monstrosities. A loud noise causes them to run back to their rooms and not long after Gerald and the servants soon come down the hall leading something shrouded by a sheet. Kitty and Edith follow them to the maze but eventually get separated. Edith faints after seeing a large, screaming frog. The thing jumps past Kitty and goes into the castle where William and Robert help it to the tower room. Gerald finds Edith and Kitty and takes them back to the castle and all three look up in time to see the thing jump out of the tower window and crash to the pavement below. The servants tell Sir Gerald they tried to calm the creature but it was agitated and afraid after being seen by the two women. As Kitty and Edith are about to leave the next day, William summons them to the dining room where Gerald has convened the others. He explains that the creature they saw was Sir Roger Philip MacTeam, who was born in 1750 and lived in an amphibious state for over two hundred years. He says his ancestor had developed mentally but not physically and his death resulted from his being too proud and too weak to reveal his existence to the outside world. Gerald asks Kitty to forgive him. Narrator Edith reports that the two are now married and living at modernized Castle Craven.

Filmed in Hollywood in 3-D, *The Maze* was issued theatrically in the summer of 1953 (it was Allied Artists' only feature in that format). It was directed and designed by William Cameron Menzies, who had a number of genre credits in both fields. He was art director for *The Thief of Bagdad* (1924) and *The Bat* (1926) in the silent days and had the same chore on *Alice in Wonderland* (1933). He directed *The Spider* (1931) and *Chandu the Magician* (1932), both starring Edmund Lowe, and he was both director and art director of *Things* to Come (1936) and *The Whip Hand* (1951). He produced the 1940 version of *Thief of Bagdad*. His penultimate genre effort was a sci-fi thriller, *Invaders from Mars* (1953), which featured Hillary Brooke, who has only a minor role in *The Maze*, his last directorial outing. Top-billed Richard Carlson was also a genre veteran with numerous credits, including *The Ghost Breakers* and *Beyond Tomorrow* (both 1940), *Hold That Ghost* (1941), *The Magnetic Monster* and *It Came from Outer Space* (both 1953), *The Creature from the Black Lagoon* and the Carlson-directed *Riders to the Stars* (both 1954), *Tormented* (1960) [q.v.], *The Power* (1968) and *The Valley of Gwangi* (1968). Michael Pate, who played the silver-haired servant William, made several other horror films like *The Strange Door* (1951), *The Black Castle* (1952), *Curse of the Undead* (1959), and *Tower of London* (1962). More than two decades before she portrayed the doctor's wife in *The Maze*, Lillian Bond co-starred in another horror thriller, *The Old Dark House* (1932).

Variety noted, "Allied Artists makes its bid in the 3-D market with an exploitation horror feature that can be ballyhooed for sturdy grosses.... It's an old-fashioned thriller that starts slow and builds methodically to a climax that should have chill seekers screeching. William Cameron Menzies designed and directed the melodrama in an upbeat manner that keeps attention going with the subject, even though the plot is implausible and the script inclined towards talkiness. A feeling of expectancy is sustained through to the climax, a horror sequence that virtually puts a hideous, frog-like monstrosity into the laps of the audience." "A highly original, flawed piece," is how Phil Hardy described *The Maze* in *Science Fiction* (1984). He added, "Shot in 3-D (and replete with numerous extraneous 'pelt and burn' effects), this is a very strange, grotesquely fascinating, piece competently directed by Menzies and full of suspense, yet almost ruined by a small budget." Donald C. Willis in *Horror and Science Fiction Films: A Checklist* (1972) felt it "looks suspiciously like a dull, run-of-the-mill horror movie." In *Science Fiction Film Directors, 1895–1998* (2000), Dennis Fischer called it "outrageously oddball." Regarding the not particularly frightening amphibious monster, he said, "Naturally, Menzies' effectiveness is undermined by an unconvincing frog costume, sodden if unusual (to say the least) story, and pathetic explanation for this strange condition.... Still, Menzies is able to muster up some sympathy over this peculiar plight, though most of his genius seems to have been devoted to creating an interesting look to the castle and maze on a minuscule budget."

Castle of Frankenstein #17 (1971) opined, "Weird, occasionally near-excellent 3-D sleeper set in old Scottish castle with terrible secret. Moody quality is result of expert production design.... Very atmospheric, even scary, until the end, which proffers what is probably the most incredible, albeit unusual, denouements in horror — or any other genre of film. Don't tell!"

In 1982 *The Maze* was reissued by StereoVision International as *Creature of the Maze* and advertised as being in "StereoVision 3-D."

Mission Mars (1968; 89 minutes; Color)

Producer: Everett Rosenthal. Executive Producers: Lawrence Appelbaum and Morton Falick. Director: Nick Webster. Screenplay: Mike St. Clair. Story: Aubrey Wisberg. Photography: Cliff Poland. Editor: Paul Jordon. Supervising Editor: Michael Calamas. Music: Berge Kalajian and Gus Pardalis. Song: Gus and Sturg Pardalis; sung by Forum Quorum. Sound: Jack Barry and Sanford Rackow. Production Designer: Hank Aldrich. Makeup: Clay Lambert. Special Photographic Effects: Haberstroh Studios. Costumes: Grover Cole. Assistant Directors: Don Moody and Sal Scoppa, Jr.

CAST: Darren McGavin (Colonel Mike Blaiswick), Nick Adams (Nick Grant), George De

Vries (Duncan), Heather Hewitt (Edith Blaiswick), Shirley Parker (Alice Grant), Michael DeBeausset (Cliff Lawson), Bill Kelly (Soviet Cosmonaut), Chuck Zink (Radio Operator Chuck), Ralph Miller (Simpson), Art Barker (Dr. Everett), Monroe Myers (Lawson's Aide Laird), Jay W. Jensen (Space Center Employee).

Filmed in Miami, Florida, by Sagittarius Productions and Red Ram Productions as *Red Planet Mars*, *Mission Mars* saw theatrical release in February 1968, just before *2001: A Space Odyssey*, which had a much bigger budget and plot substance. The Allied Artists release was not much more than a patchwork of NASA technical and stock footage sewn into a sci-fi story about astronauts leaving their women on Earth to fly to Mars and encounter a hostile alien life form. Along the way they run into the traditional meteor shower. In the finale, an American and a Russian unite to make a triumphant voyage home. Tacky production values and trite special effects did not help matters, with the lead performers being hamstrung by a mundane script. Phil Hardy in *Science Fiction* (1984) called it "absurd, yet appealing" while *John Stanley's Revenge of the Creature Features Movie Guide* (1988) best summed it up by saying, "Laughable kiddie stuff with Darren McGavin and Nick Adams as hysterically incompetent astronauts.... Their ship looks like an inverted Campbell Soup can, the alien life form (called a Polarite) resembles Gumby and an E.T. sphere is a golf ball magnified. Incompetently directed.... So abort it!"

Edith Blaiswick (Heather Hewitt) wakes up screaming from a dream in which her astronaut husband Mike (McGavin) is killed when a rocket explodes. He consoles her and they go for an early morning swim. Astronaut Nick Grant (Adams) similarly assures his wife Alice (Shirley Parker) and says the upcoming mission will be his last; she is skeptical. The two astronauts, along with navigator Duncan (George De Vries), take their final physicals and are briefed by NASA's chief of operations Cliff Lawson (Michael DeBeausset) about their eighteen-month round trip journey to Mars. The trio blast off and after orbit is achieved they switch the ship over to manual control. The booster rockets are jettisoned and the craft connects with its supply ship and they begin the 35 million mile flight to the Red Planet. Lawson meets with Edith and Alice and informs them all is going well on their husbands' voyage. The astronauts spy the bodies of two Soviet cosmonauts floating in space, apparently victims of a failed mission a few months earlier. After the ship survives a meteor storm, they close in on Mars and descend to the planet. They land successfully and the three men suit up and set out to explore. As they search for the supply ship, the men leave balloon markers along the way. Nick comes across the body of a frozen Soviet cosmonaut and takes him back to the ship. Mike and Duncan are bombarded by a blinding light from a metallic, robot-like thing which they destroy with a ray gun. Back on board the ship, the two astronauts inform Earth of the attack and Lawson dubs the thing a Polarite. He tells them NASA is scrapping the mission because the Polarites are possibly being used by a hostile alien host. As they talk, a huge round sphere appears near the ship and they lose contact with Earth. When Mike tries to blast off, nothing happens and he says some force is stopping them. He orders Nick and Duncan to check out the sphere. When they do so, it opens, blinding Duncan and dragging him inside. The two survivors try to get the booster unit from the supply ship and use it to increase the rocket's power so it can return home. Mike notices that the Polarite is immobile when in a shadow so he goes for the power unit. As Mike returns to the ship, the Polarite revives and Nick puts it out of commission with his ray gun. The booster unit is installed but communications are again cut off as a second attempt to blast off fails. When Mike goes to the sphere and tries to communicate with it, the object repeats his words and tries to pull him inside, but he makes it back to the rocket. The Rus-

Darren McGavin and Nick Adams in *Mission Mars* (1968)

sian, now revived, informs Mike and Nick that if a disk inside the sphere is destroyed, they will be able to leave Mars. Against Mike's orders, Nick goes to the sphere and fires at it but is engulfed in a burning light. He is pulled into the object and causes it to explode. Mike and the Russian blast off and begin their return voyage to Earth as Nick's sacrifice is related to Lawson. Edith, who is with Lawson, informs her husband that he is to be a father.

Although they both had successful film careers, Darren McGavin and Nick Adams were best known as television stars. McGavin headlined *Mickey Spillane's Mike Hammer* (Syndicated, 1957–59), *Riverboat* (NBC-TV, 1959–61) and *Kolchak: The Night Stalker* (ABC-TV, 1974–75). Adams' greatest fame came as Johnny Yuma in ABC-TV's *The Rebel* from 1959 to 1961 and he also starred in *Saints and Sinners* (NBC-TV, 1962–63). He was nominated for a Best Supporting Actor Oscar in *Twilight of Honor* in 1963. Two years later Allied Artists headlined him in *Young Dillinger* but its puny box office returns failed to give the studio a much needed financial boost. Adams' career quickly descended to the point where he starred in a trio of Japan's Toho Studios outings, *Frankenstein Conquers the World*, *Invasion of the Astro-Monster (Monster Zero)* (both 1966) and *The Killing Bottle* (1967).

Mission Mars is sometimes mistakenly called *Murder in the Fourth Dimension* which was an Italian film that was to co-star Aldo Ray and Nick Adams but never went into production.

Moonwolf (1966; 74 minutes)

Producers: Wolf Brauner and Martin Nosseck. Directors: George Freedland [Georges Friedland] and Martin Nosseck. Screenplay: George Freedland [Georges Friedland] and Johannes

Hendrich. Photography: Herbert Korner and Antun Markic. Editor: Rudolph Cusumano [Ralph Cushman]. Music: Henri Price and Albert Sendry. Art Directors: Max A. Bienek and Aaree Koivisto. Sound: Erwin Schanzle and Kurt Vilja. Sound Effects Supervisor: Jack Cornall. Unit Managers: Bolko Marcard and Tuukka Soitso. Assistant Director: Jochen Wiedermann.

CAST: Carl Moehner (Dr. Peter Holmes), Ann Savo (Ara), Helmut Schmidt (Johann), Paul Dahlke (Ara's Father), Richard Häussler (Professor Albert Robert), Ingrid Lutz (Ilona), Horst Jentzen (Jimmy), Ake Lindman, J. Kovacs (Lumberjacks), Inken Deter (Pilot), Paavo Jannes (Doctor), Wolf (Himself).

Martin Nosseck Productions copyrighted *Moonwolf* in 1964 but Allied did not release it theatrically in the U.S. until the spring of 1966. It is a dubbed version of the 1959 West German film *Und Immer Ruft Das Herz*, also called *Zuruck aus dem Weltall*, that ran 14 minutes longer than the stateside release. Made by CCC Productions in Berlin with location shooting in Lapland, its sci-fi angle deals with a dog sent into space in order to test the effects of weightlessness. *Moonwolf*, which contained quite a bit of space launch footage, is mainly a boy and a girl and a dog love plot sewn into the fabric of a travelogue. Phil Hardy in *Science Fiction* (1984) noted, "A story no doubt partly inspired by the Sputnik II flight with the dog Laika (1957). The plot is similar to that of countless Disney features...." *Movies on TV 1969–70 Edition*, edited by Steven H. Scheuer, called it a "[m]ildly interesting tale" but listed it as an Italian production set in Alaska.

At the International Space Conference in Geneva, Professor Albert Robert (Richard Haussler) gives a report on a possible Moon landing but expresses doubts about man being able to cope with weightlessness in outer space. He goes to see his friend, Dr. Peter Holmes (Carl Moehner), a zoologist and veterinarian who has promised to let the space program use his dog Wolf to test endurance in space. Peter balks at his promise when he learns the animal will have tiny electronic probes placed in his brain and body. Peter recounts to Robert how some years before, as a college senior working on a thesis in zoology, he was in the north country of Lapland where he saw a mother wolf killed by a wildcat as she tried to protect her young. A violent summer storm arose and the next day he saw a young wolf pup foraging for food before falling into a river. Returning to the present, Robert informs Peter that the space probe *Moonwolf* is scheduled to take place in four weeks and the doctor reluctantly agrees to train Wolf for the flight. A month later the rocket takes off. After contact with it is lost twice, Robert projects it will return to Earth in Lapland. The two men fly to the locale and along the way Peter resumes his story about how Wolf came to be his pet. Two years before he had returned to Lapland at the time of a reindeer roundup. After going further north he saw a wolf-dog that led him to a young woman, Ara (Ann Savo), who had fallen into a snow pit. He took her to a cabin where she told Peter she was chasing snowbirds and fell and that Wolf is her dog. Ara said she pulled him out of a stream when he was a pup and Peter realized it was the same animal he thought drowned two years before. The woman's fiancé, lumberjack Johann (Helmut Schmidt), came for her and Peter returned with them to her father's (Paul Dahlke) home which also housed the area's weather station. That night during a fierce blizzard, Ara became delirious and Peter used the station's radio to request that penicillin be dropped by parachute in order to save her. Disregarding Peter's warning that he cannot survive the storm, Johann headed out on skis to bring back a doctor for Ara. When her father found out about Peter calling for help, he radioed the flight to bypass the station due to the terrible storm although it may cost his daughter her life. Peter tended to Ara and the next morning the parachute landed and he and Wolf picked up the medicine which Peter gave to Ara. Wolf got his paw caught in a trap and some Laplanders, who thought it was a dangerous wolf, started to shoot him but he was saved by

Peter. After Ara recovered, she asked Peter to accompany her to a festival in a nearby village, making Johann jealous. When they returned home, Ara informed Peter that she loved him and not her fiancé, but he said he must go and she told him to take Wolf with him so he would remember her. He chained up the dog and left but was confronted by Johann and the two men fought. Wolf broke his chains, leapt through a window and stopped Johann from stabbing Peter. As they are about to land in Lapland, Peter informs Robert the reason he did not want to risk Wolf's life was because of Ara. The capsule containing the dog ejects and lands near Ara's father's weather station, a forest area that cannot be reached by helicopter. Peter goes there on skis and meets Ara again. She tells Johann to use his sled and go with Peter to find Wolf. As they trudge through deep snows, the two men are surrounded by hungry wolves. The sled overturns and Johann hits his head on a rock as Peter holds off the animals with a rifle. Johann dies from his injury. The next morning, Peter locates the capsule and frees Wolf, and they return to Ara.

Credited with co-writing the music score for the U.S. version of *Moonwolf* is Albert Sendry, longtime conductor for singer Tony Martin.

Mutiny in Outer Space (1965; 82 minutes)

Producers-Story: Hugo Grimaldi and Arthur C. Pierce. Executive Producers: Bernard Woolner, Lawrence Woolner and David Woolner. Screenplay: Arthur C. Pierce. Photography: Archie Dalzell. Editor: George White. Music Supervisor–Sound Effects Supervisor: Gordon Zahler. Production Designer: Paul Sylos. Sound: John Doye, Jr. Sound Effects: Josef von Stroheim. Sets: Raymond Boltz, Jr. Production Supervisor: Jack Voglin. Makeup: Ted Coodley. Special Effects: Roger George. Assistant Director: Flip Cook.

CAST: William Leslie (Major Gordon Towers), Dolores Faith (Faith Montaine), Pamela Curran (Lieutenant Connie Engstrom), Richard Garland (Colonel Frank Cromwell), Harold Lloyd, Jr. (Sergeant Andrews), Glenn Langan (General Knowland), James Dobson (Dr. Hoffman), Ron Stokes (Sergeant Sloan), Robert Palmer (Major Olsen), Francine York (Captain Stevens), Gabriel Curtiz (Dr. Stoddard), Carl Crow (Captain Don Webber), H. Kay Stephens (Sergeant Engstrom), Robert Nash (Colonel Howard), Joel Smith (General).

Space Station X-7 is in the path of an out-of-orbit thirty-year-old communications satellite. To avoid a collision, X-7 commander Frank Cromwell (Richard Garland) orders an evasive maneuver. Cromwell is informed that a spaceship (carrying geological specimens found in a lunar ice cave) is about to blast off from Luna Base II on the Moon and will dock with X-7 in a few hours. Major Gordon Towers (William Leslie) and Captain Don Webber (Carl Crow) are bringing the cargo; Towers tells his co-pilot he is looking forward to the layover so he can see his girlfriend, civilian biochemist Faith Montaine (Dolores Faith), who has been assigned to X-7. During the flight, Don complains about an irritation on his right leg. On the station, communications officer Lieutenant Connie Engstrom (Pamela Curran) informs Cromwell of their impending arrival while the ship's physician, Dr. Hoffman (James Dobson), says the commander needs to get more rest. Connie, who is in love with Cromwell, thinks the commander is headed for a mental collapse and needs to be transferred. Gordon and Don float from their craft to the space station where they undergo cleansing before greeting the crew. As they are being shown to their quarters, Don passes out and is taken to the infirmary where he registers a high temperature. Tests run by Faith show that his body has been invaded by some type of spores that appear to be a fungus. She immediately goes to check the Moon samples to see if they are the source of the fungus. The ship is clipped by a meteor that damages the laboratory, upsetting the crate holding the geological specimens. Gordon and Faith are called to the infirmary by Hoffman who informs them that Don has died from fungus infection and that all their lives are in jeopardy. Cromwell demands to see the dead man, who is covered by the fungus, and sends information to Earth command that he died from space weightlessness complications, despite Gordon's objections. General Knowland (Glenn Langan), the chief of the satellite program, is given the coded message from Cromwell by his assistant, Captain Stevens (Francine York). It also states that Gordon's behavior is not in the best interest of the space agency. Connie later informs Cromwell that the general wants clarification on his message, especially in regards to Gordon. When Gordon tells Connie the commander is a sick man, she says she will not be a part of any conspiracy against him. Faith and Hoffman find the lab a mess following the meteor hit with some of the lunar specimens ruined. She goes to work studying the remaining samples, not realizing the fungus has multiplied and started to spread around the lab. Gordon prepares a report about Cromwell to send to General Knowland. When he calls Faith, he gets no answer. He and Hoffman run to the lab where they find her surrounded by the expanding fungus. Gordon grabs hold of a pipe near the ceiling and gets to Faith and has her climb on his back and is able to get her to safety. Hoffman speculates that the fungus thrives on light so Gordon orders computer operator Sergeant Andrews (Harold Lloyd, Jr.) to seal the lab and cut off its electric power. When Gordon informs Cromwell about the fungus, he refuses to act. After Gordon objects he is ordered arrested along with Faith and Hoffman, who back Gordon. Cromwell orders Connie to send Knowland a full account of the mutiny, including Gordon's threatening him with a gun. Realizing the commander is not lucid, she sends a tape recording of their conversation. After receiving the recording, the general consults with Dr. Stoddard (Gabriel Curtiz) and sends orders to Major Olsen (Robert Palmer) on X-7 to release the prisoners and relieve Cromwell of his command. He also orders all craft to stay away from the space station due to the growing fungus. Cromwell eludes Gordon, Faith and Sergeant Sloan (Ron Stokes) as they search the craft for him. Andrews reports that the commander has sabotaged the ship's communications system. While Andrews fixes the radio, Hoffman alerts Faith that he has been infected by the fungus and she takes him to the infirmary. Gordon radios Knowland not to send a supply ship to the station because of the growing fungus that destroys all living cells on contact. The general quarantines X-7 and initiates a plan to destroy it if it shows signs of falling to Earth. After Faith confirms that Hoffman is infected, he tells her the fungus thrives on heat, not light, and asks to be placed in a refrigeration chamber to destroy the microorganisms. Cromwell shows up in the control room with a vat of acid and holds the crew at bay as he activates the ship's gravitational control, causing the airlock to the lab to open with the fungus starting to spread to the outside of the craft. Gordon and the others manage to subdue Cromwell and place him in restraints. The fungus also spreads inside the station. With food running out, Gordon orders the crew to put on survival suits so he can lower the temperature in the craft to zero in hopes of destroying the invaders. He goes to the control room, killing the fungus there with a spray, and shuts down the heating system. Knowland gets a message from the X-7 crew that they are running out of oxygen and the fungus on the outside of the ship must be destroyed. His assistant, Colonel Howard (Robert Nash), suggests cutting off the sun's heat to the craft and the general orders a rocket to take off and spray an ice crystal cloud around the space station. When this occurs, the fungus is eradicated and Gordon is able to restart the ship's heating system. With the crew saved, Knowland announces that a relief ship will reach them in three hours. Gordon hugs Faith.

Mutiny in Outer Space was made by Hugo Grimaldi Productions and Woolner Bros. Pictures and released on a double bill with the same outfits' *The Human Duplicators* (q.v.)

by Allied Artists in March 1965. The film's working titles were *Invasion from the Moon*, *Space Station X* and *Space Station X-14*. It is a surprisingly entertaining and fast-paced affair with many plot elements and highlighted by a fine cast. It is padded with some NASA stock footage. One amusing aspect of the plot has the fungus holler (sounding like a creaking door) when destroyed. Low-key lighting and a claustrophobic setting add much to the low-budget film's overall suspense. It also manages to predict finding ice on the Moon.

Cast-wise, stoic hero William Leslie is the weakest link; he earlier had the same effect on *The Night the World Exploded* (1957). Just the opposite is beautiful and talented Dolores Faith, whose too-short film career also includes the genre efforts *The Phantom Planet* (1961) and *House of the Black Death* (1965), as well as *Mutiny*'s co-feature, *The Human Duplicators*. Richard Garland was in *The Undead* (1957), *Attack of the Crab Monsters* (1957) [q.v.] and *Panic in Year Zero!* (1962), while Harold Lloyd, Jr., appeared in *Frankenstein's Daughter* (1958). Had *Mutiny in Outer Space* been made a decade before, Glenn Langan would have been perfect for the leading role; here he is well cast as General Knowland. He had the title role in *The Amazing Colossal Man* (1957) and was also in *The Return of Doctor X* (1939), *Hangover Square* (1945) and *The Andromeda Strain* (1971). Cast in the small role of the general's associate, pretty Francine York had the misfortune of being the leading lady in *Space Monster* (1965) and *Curse of the Swamp Creature* (1967), two films American International Pictures made for television.

Nightmare Castle (1966; 80 minutes)

Producer-Director: Allen Grunewald [Mario Caiano]. Screenplay: Mario Caiano and Fabio De Agostini. Photography: Enzo Barboni. Editor: Renato Cinquini. Music: Ennio Morricone. Production Designer–Sets: Massimo Tavazzi. Sound: Bernardino Fronzetti. Production Manager: Pietro Nofri. Makeup: Duilio Giustini. Costumes: Mario Giorsi. Assistant Director: Angelo Sangermano.

CAST: Barbara Steele (Muriel Hampton Arrowsmith/Jenny Hampton Arrowsmith), Paul [Muller] Miller (Dr. Stephen Arrowsmith), Helga Line (Solange), Lawrence Clift (Dr. Dereck Joyce), Rik Battaglia (David), John MacDouglas [Giuseppe Addobbati] (Jonathan).

During the 1960s, Barbara Steele established herself as one of the most popular players in horror films and has since had a cult following. Although she appeared in many mainstream features like Federico Fellini's *8½* (1963) and *Der Juge Torless* (*The Young Torless*) (1966), her reputation remains in macabre cinema. She later branched out into the production side of movies with the ABC-TV telefilms *The Winds of War* (1983) and *War and Remembrance* (1988). One of her best genre outings is the Italian production *Amanti d'Oltretomba* (Love Beyond the Tomb), released in that country in 1965 and in the U.S. in the summer of 1966 by Allied Artists as *Nightmare Castle*, running 80 minutes. It originally ran 104 minutes; when it was issued in Great Britain as both *The Faceless Monster* and *Night of the Doomed* it clocked in at 100 minutes. The footage missing from the stateside showings is mostly extended scenes and the lesser running time does not hurt the flow of the film or its horror impact. *Nightmare Castle* gives Steele dual roles, that of half-sisters, one brunette and the other blonde.

At Hampton Castle, heiress Muriel Hampton Arrowsmith (Steele) taunts her scientist husband, Dr. Stephen Arrowsmith (Paul Muller), about his experiments involving frogs and electricity. He says he is going to a medical conference in Edinburgh and as she gives him a kiss they are observed by their aged housekeeper, Solange (Helga Line). As Stephen leaves, he entrusts his wife's safety to his gardener David (Rik Battaglia). Muriel and David later run to the greenhouse where they make love but are caught by Stephen, who hits

Rik Battaglia and Barbara Steele in *Nightmare Castle* (1966)

David with a cane. He chains his wife and her lover and promises to make them suffer before they die. Muriel informs him that she has made a new will, leaving all her money and property to her half-sister Jenny (Steele). Stephen offers to let the two go free in exchange for the will, but David tells Muriel not to give it to him because he will kill them anyway. Solange scolds Stephen and tells him he will have to let the pair live but he replies that since Jenny is in an asylum, he will get control of the estate. Taking the lovers to his bedroom, Stephen drops acid on Muriel before throwing David over her and electrocuting them. He drains Muriel's blood, places the lovers' hearts in a container below a statue and burns their bodies. He puts their ashes in an urn in which he grows a fleshy plant. Later, after Stephen has used Muriel's blood to restore Solange's beauty, he returns to Hampton Castle with a new bride, Jenny. Solange demands to know why he married the young woman and he tells her that Jenny's sanity hangs by a thread and he plans to use drugs to put her back in an asylum so he can get her money. On her wedding night, Jenny awakes to hear a pulsing sound and sees blood pouring from the plant. As the room spins, she dreams of David helping her out of a crypt. When they go to the greenhouse to have sex, a faceless man strikes the gardener. She wakes up calling David's name and trying to choke her husband. The next night, Stephen and Solange hear Jenny scream and they find her in the castle's vault with blood on her hands. She tells them she is not mad and begs not to be sent back to the asylum. Stephen informs his wife that he plans to write to her physician, Dr. Dereck Joyce (Lawrence Clift), and ask him to come to the castle to tend to her. When he arrives, Jenny tells Dereck about her dream and begins laughing when her husband mentions his experiments. She takes the doctor to the greenhouse where they find an earring she claims to remember losing there in her dream. Solange tells Dereck that Jenny has a habit of hiding things and then forgetting their location and she secretly places the earring's mate in the young woman jewelry box. When Dereck asks to examine the box, the earring is found there, and Jenny begins to doubt her sanity. At dinner that evening, Solange cuts her hand and Stephen takes her to his laboratory where he gives her an injection of Muriel's blood. Jenny hears a voice telling her to go to the lab as Dereck inspects the vault and finds Muriel's tomb empty. Jenny comes into the lab and slashes Stephen's face with a scalpel. After Dereck takes her back to her bedroom, Solange tells her lover that the young woman had Muriel's face. Muriel takes over Jenny's mind, causing her to try and seduce Dereck, but a window blows open and the young woman comes to her senses. In the greenhouse, Jenny asks Dereck why Muriel torments her and she begs him not to leave her. He says they must get away from the castle. The physician informs Stephen that the castle has ghosts and he wants to get Jenny away before they destroy her mind. Stephen attaches an electric wire to the bathtub next to Dereck's room and when he hears someone enter he turns on the power, but ends up electrocuting a servant (John MacDouglas). When Jenny tells her husband she is leaving with Dereck, he accuses the physician of trying to seduce her. Stephen tells his wife he loves her and promises to take her on a long trip the next day. Dereck agrees to leave but tells Jenny he will always try to help her. Solange becomes very cold and informs Stephen she needs Jenny's blood. Dereck finds the young wife having a dream: She speaks to him as Muriel and says her heart is below a statue and that Stephen killed her. The physician pretends to leave the castle as a storm arises and Jenny begins to pack. She goes to see Stephen, who carries her to the laboratory where he tells his wife he will free her from nightmares forever and gives her chloroform. He begins the two-hour process of putting Jenny's blood into Solange's veins and goes to prepare for the next day's trip with his lover. Dereck returns to the castle, opening a hiding place under the statue and finding the hearts of Muriel and David. When he pulls out a dagger and separates them, their spirits become visible. Stephen knocks Dereck out with a candle holder and then sees his first wife. As David's bloody corpse removes the needle from Solange's arm, Muriel promises Stephen eternal ecstasy and takes him to his bedroom where she straps him in the chair and sets him on fire. As Solange turns into a skeleton, Dereck recovers and carries Jenny into the living room, but they are trapped there by the ghosts of Muriel and David. When Dereck throws their hearts into the fireplace, the spirits disappear. Jenny and Dereck flee Hampton Castle by running outside into the storm.

Steele's horror film career was launched in 1960 when she starred in Mario Bava's *La Maschera del Demonio (The Mask of the Demon)* which was released in the U.S. as *Black Sunday*. She followed it with *Pit and the Pendulum* (1961), *The Horrible Dr. Hitchcock* (1962), *The Ghost* (1963), *Castle of Blood* [q.v.] and *The Long Hair of Death* (both 1964), *Terror Creatures from the Grave* (1965), *An Angel for Satan* and *She Beast* (both 1966) and *Curse of the Crimson Altar* (1968), shown stateside as *The Crimson Cult*. The actress went on to appear in *The Space Watch Murders* (1975), *Shivers (They Came from Within)* (1975), *Piranha* (1978), *The Silent Scream* (1980) and the TV film *Dark Shadows* (1990) and its 1991 spin-off TV series.

Co-stars Paul Muller (billed in the U.S. version as Paul Miller) and Helga Line also had extensive genre careers. Muller was in *Mystery of the Black Jungle* and *Black Devils of Kali* (both 1954), *I Vampiri* (1956), released in the U.S. as *The Devil's Commandment*;

Minotaur, the Wild Beast of Crete (1960), *Kali Jug, Goddess of Vengeance* (1963), *Malenka (Fangs of the Living Dead)* and *Venus in Furs* (both 1969), *Eugenie* [q.v.] and *Count Dracula* (both 1970), *Vampyros Lesbos* (1971), *Lady Frankenstein* (1971), *A Virgin Among the Living Dead* (1973), a second version of *Eugenie* (1974) and *Bloody Psycho* (1989). Line appeared in *The Blancheville Monster* (1963), *Mission Bloody Mary* (1965), *Exorcism's Daughter* (1971), *Horror Express* (1972), *The Mummy's Revenge, The Dracula Saga, The Vampire's Night Orgy, Santo contra Dr. Muerte (Santo vs. Dr. Death)* and *Horror Rises from the Tomb* (all 1973), *When the Screaming Stops (The Lorelei's Grasp)* (1974), *Killing of the Dolls* (1975), *Curse of the Black Cat* (1977), *Stigma* (1980) and *The Devil's Breath* (1993). Rik Battaglia, who played the ill-fated David, was best known for European Westerns and adventure films but he was also in *Minotaur, the Wild Beast of Crete* (1960), *Sandokan the Great* (1963), *The Treasure of the Aztecs* and *Pyramid of the Sun God* (both 1965), *Mysterious Island* (1973) and *Ten Little Indians* (1974).

Nightmare Castle's director, Mario Caiano, helmed nearly 50 features, including *Vampire in Venice* (1988).

Phil Hardy in *The Encyclopedia of Horror Movies* (1986) was critical of *Nightmare Castle*: "Less a horror film than a well intentioned, but bad, love poem addressed to Steele, this picture's complicated plot is simply strung together to allow us to see her being lustful, tortured, disfigured, sleeping, walking, fainting, loving, afraid, and so on…. [It is] completely structured around her presence…. The film seems frozen in its fetishistic contemplation of Steele, an impression underlined by Ennio Morricone's repetitive score." More on the mark was James O'Neill in *Terror on Tape* (1994): "Robust Steele vehicle…. Barbara excels in a typical dual role, while the pale gray photography and Ennio Morricone's richly romantic music create a marvelous mood." *The Phantom's Ultimate Video Guide* (1989) noted, "This Italo horror has truly eerie photography and the sepulchral beauty of Barbara Steele…" while Luca M. Palmerini and Gaetano Mistretta in *Spaghetti Nightmares* (1996) called it an "[e]legantly executed story of love after death." Donald C. Willis in *Horror and Science Fiction Films: A Checklist* (1972) opined, "Notable mainly for Morricone's wildly romantic renditions of 'Sweet Genevieve.' (He uses the melody much as Victor Young used it in *The Sun Shines Bright* [1953]. Coincidence?)."

While some sources claim Steele did not dub her voice in the English-language versions of her horror movies, *Video Watchdog* #7 (September-October 1991) states, "In her dual role in [*Nightmare Castle*], Barbara Steele dubs the voice of Jenny Hampton, but not Muriel."

Not of This Earth (1957; 69 minutes)

Producer-Director: Roger Corman. Screenplay: Charles Griffith and Mark Hanna. Photography: John Mescall. Editor: Charles Gross, Jr. Music: Ronald Stein. Sound: Philip Mitchell. Production Manager-Assistant Director: Lou Place. Makeup: Curly Batson. Special Effects: Paul Blaisdell. Titles: Paul Julian.

CAST: Paul Birch (Paul Johnson), Beverly Garland (Nadine Storey), Morgan Jones (Officer Harry Sherbourne), William Roerick (Dr. F.W. Rochelle), Jonathan Haze (Jerry "Pittsburgh" Perrin), Dick Miller (Joe Piper), Anne Carroll (Alien Woman), Pat Flynn (Officer Simmons), Barbara Bohrer (Waitress), Roy Engel (Police Sergeant Walton), Tamar Cooper (Joanne Oxford), Harold Fong (Chinese Victim), Gail Ganley, Ralph Reed (Teenagers), Hank Mann (Drunk), Tom Graeff (Parking Attendant), Jan Boleslavsky (Alien Contact), Lyle Latell (Second Paul Johnson).

One of the best low-budget science fiction films of the 1950s, *Not of This Earth* was produced and directed by Roger Corman and double-billed with his *Attack of the Crab Monsters* (q.v.) early in 1957. Although cheaply, and somewhat carelessly made (a microphone

Lobby card for *Not of This Earth* (1957) picturing Beverly Garland and Paul Birch

is visible in a scene where the nurse serves her policeman boyfriend coffee), the film is good entertainment in its mixture of horror, science fiction and underplayed comedy. Paul Birch dominates the proceedings as the alien vampire who eschews fangs in favor of blood transfusions, and Beverly Garland is just as good as his self-reliant nurse. Jonathan Haze is amusing as the alien's seedy houseboy and Dick Miller contributes a memorable cameo as a vacuum cleaner salesman who fast talks his way into oblivion. Made for under $100,000 by Corman's Los Altos Productions, *Not of This Earth* brought in over one million dollars at the box office.

Two teenagers (Gail Ganley, Ralph Reed) make out in a car parked on a suburban street and when the girl says goodnight and walks home she meets a mysterious man who uses his eyes to kill her and then draws off her blood. The man is an alien from the wartorn planet Davanna who has come to Earth in search of blood for his people. He takes on the guise of Earthman Paul Johnson (Birch) but always wears dark glasses to conceal he has no pupils. He uses the power of his own eyes to destroy those of his victims and burn out their brains but he cannot tolerate loud noise. He goes to a hospital for a blood transfusion and meets nurse Nadine Storey (Garland) and gets an appointment with Dr. Rochelle (William Roerick) who refuses to give him help without first finding out his blood type. Johnson places the doctor under his spell and orders him never to discuss his case. After receiving the transfusion, Johnson offers Nadine $200 a week to live at this home and tend to his daily need of new blood. She agrees to do so as the doctor confirms his patient is dying from the destruction of the cellular structures of his blood. When Johnson's houseboy and chauffeur, Jeremy Perrin (Haze), spies his boss putting containers of blood in a refrigerator, the alien threatens to eliminate him if he does not mind his own business. Arriving at Johnson's rented house, Nadine meets Jeremy who makes overtures to her, which she rejects. Johnson shows her to her room and then locks her in but Nadine objects. He tells her that no person sleeps in insecure quarters where he comes from but when Nadine asks him about his origins, the foreign-accented Johnson does not reply. That night the alien uses a teleporter to communicate with his contact (Jan Boleslavsky) on Davanna, who details his assignments on Earth. Since Johnson has already taken human form, he is next to increase the amount of blood teleported to Davanna and send a sub-human specimen. If these phases are successful he is then to conquer the Earth, and if they are not he is to obliterate the planet before he dies. The next morning Nadine questions Jeremy about his job with Johnson and he tells her he is being paid $300 a week, mainly to drive his boss various places and keep everyone out of the basement. Johnson answers the door for a vacuum cleaner salesman (Dick Miller) who wants to demonstrate his product. The alien allows the man to go to his basement to use his product to unplug a pipe and while there he burns out the man's brain, drains his blood and puts his body in the furnace. When Johnson notices a trio of winos in a park, he orders his servant to invite them to his house that night for dinner. Nadine decides to explore the basement and finds empty flasks but accidentally leaves her bathing cap behind. Dr. Rochelle shows up with her boyfriend, police motor patrolman Harry Sherbourne (Morgan Jones). When Johnson and Jeremy get back home, Harry recognizes the chauffeur as Pittsburgh Perrin, an ex-convict. That night Jeremy brings the three derelicts who are promptly done away with by the alien, who teleports their blood to his planet. The local police find a thirteenth victim with her eyes and brain burned out and Sergeant Walton (Roy Engel) worries about vampire killer headlines. While walking that night, the alien meets a Chinaman (Harold Fong) who he puts under a spell and takes back home. He is transported to Davanna via the teleporter. The next day Jeremy tells Nadine about the winos and the Chinaman and she takes a sample of liquid from a glass Johnson drank from for analysis. Rochelle informs her it is a compound made up of every known vitamin, the perfect food. In town, the alien meets a woman (Anne Carroll) who has come from Davanna. She informs him the war there is finished, all the blood on the planet is gone, and his contact has been murdered. The woman also tells Johnson they will not be able to return home. Since she is badly in need of blood, he breaks into Rochelle's hospital office and gives her a transfusion, not knowing it is the blood of a rabid dog. Johnson tells the woman to go to a hotel but after he leaves she becomes nauseous and goes back to the hospital where she collapses. Johnson tries to abduct a parking lot attendant (Tom Graeff) but when someone honks a horn the young man manages to escape. The alien hunts him down and kills him. Rochelle gets a call to come to the hospital to tend to the dying woman and Harry goes with him. After finding the woman has died, the two men sees she has no pupils and was wearing dark glasses like Johnson. Harry calls Nadine and tells her to get out of the Johnson house since he thinks her boss may not be human, but she decides to stay and look for evidence. She and Jeremy find the teleporter, and Jeremy sees a skull in the furnace and throws it at Johnson. Johnson fries Jeremy's brain and then attempts to kill Nadine, but is put off by her screams and she runs away. The alien materializes a bat-like creature that he sends to kill Rochelle. Johnson is able to catch up with Nadine and place her under his telepathic control. Johnson kills motorcycle cop officer Simmons (Pat Flynn) with his eyes and tries to do the same to Harry but he loses control of his car, wrecks it and is consumed when it explodes. The entranced Nadine, who has walked to the house, is about to teleport herself to Davanna when the alien's death breaks his spell over her. Nadine and Harry later stand at Johnson's tombstone which reads "Here Lies a Man Who Is Not of This Earth." They do not see another alien coming toward them.

Many consider *Not of This Earth* to be one of Roger Corman's more noteworthy early films. *Variety* touted it as a "[g]ood science fiction thriller" while the British *Monthly Film Bulletin* stated, "This grisly little tale, falling into a division between horror and science fiction, introduces one or two relatively original variations on the macabre." In a detailed article on the film in *Castle of Frankenstein* #23 (1974), Abbie Herrick wrote, "The dialogue is snappy and realistic.... Every element blends in effectively to progress the film to its culmination.... The film is exciting in its Einensteinian ending ... terrifying in that its evil is 'something' that could pass as one of us, and universal in its anti-war message." Randy Palmer in *Paul Blaisdell: Monster Maker* (1997) stated, "It was made with the same brevity as most of his other productions, but the ... screenplay contained enough off-the-wall elements to make it seem fresh and exciting."

Paul Blaisdell created the briefly seen bat-like monster and the teleporter. The former was a silly looking thing that resembled a flying lamp shade with an insect-like creature atop it. The scene where the thing drops on Dr. Rochelle's head and apparently sucks out his brain is scary, especially when blood begins oozing out from under the creature.

To show the pupil-less eyes of the alien, Birch wore white contact lenses that proved to quite painful if left in too long. Near the end of filming he got frustrated with production delays and refused to finish the picture. Veteran actor Lyle Latell, who had the physical build of Birch, was called in to complete the movie.

Parts of the music score for the film are included in the compact disc *Not of This Earth!: The Film Music of Ronald Stein* (Varese Sarabande VSD-5634), released in 1995.

Roger Corman later produced three remakes. The first (1988) starred Traci Lords and Arthur Roberts and was directed by Jim Wynorski. While not as good as the original, it was a worthy follow-up. As a sign of the times, Beverly Garland's bathing suit scene from the original was replaced by Lord's nude shower. Terence H. Winkless directed the third version, a 1995 teleflick starring Michael York, Elizabeth Bardondes and Mason Adams. In 1998 the property was done again as *Star Portal*, starring Athena Massey as a female alien and Steven Bauer as the doctor; it was directed by Jon Purdy.

Oh! Those Most Secret Agents! (1965; 83 minutes; Color)

Executive Producer: Antonio Colantuoni. Director: Lucio Fulci. Screenplay: Vittorio Vighi, Mario Guerra, Amedeo Sollazzo, Lucio Fulci and Vittorio Metz. Photography: Bitto [Adalberto] Albertini. Editor: Ornella Micheli. Music: Piero Umiliani. Sound: Franco Groppioni. Sets–Special Effects: Sergio Canevari. Production Managers: Albino Morandini and Orlando Orsini. Makeup: Telemaco Tilli. Assistant Directors: Nino Zanchin and Giorgio Galizia.

CAST: Franco Franchi (Franco), Ciccio Ingrassia (Ciccio), Ingrid Schoeller, Aroldo Tieri (Married Couple), Carla Calo, Nino Terzo, Enzo Andronico (Soviet Agents), Annie Gorassini (Maid), Poldo Bendandi (Soviet Chief), Nando Angelini, Piero Morgia (American Agents), Puccio Ceccarelli (Chinese Torturer), Alessandro Tedeschi (Soviet Assassin), Seyna Seyn (Chinese Agent), Nicola di Gioia (Goat Torturer), John Bartha (Electronic Treatment Doctor).

The Italian comedy team of Franco Franchi and Ciccio Ingrassia began working together in the 1950s; during the 1960s and 1970s they starred in over one hundred feature films, mainly satirizing popular movie genres. Despite their hefty cinematic output, the duo's movies rarely made it stateside and those that did were mostly incomprehensible to viewers thanks to the team's silly "comedy" antics that did not translate well this side of the

Atlantic. Their only film to get wide distribution in the U.S. was *War, Italian Style* (1967) and that was due to having Buster Keaton, Martha Hyer and Fred Clark in its cast. Produced by Mega Film in Italy as *002 Agenti Segretissimi* (The 002 Secret Agents), *Oh! Those Most Secret Agents!* poked fun at the popular James Bond craze but it failed to attract an audience when Allied Artists released it in late March 1965, a year after its Italian premiere. Later in 1965 Sherpix Pictures reissued the feature as *00-2 Most Secret Agents*. The film's original running time of 90 minutes was cut by seven minutes for U.S. bookings.

At a Mediterranean resort filled with beautiful girls, vagabonds Franco (Franchi) and Ciccio (Ingrasia) read a newspaper advertisement that convinces them to rob what they think is a vacant palatial villa. They are unaware that the ad was placed by an espionage ring working for a voyeuristic robot wanting patsies for an experiment. The two bunglers are captured by the spies and a microchip containing a supposedly bogus formula for a powerful new secret weapon is implanted in Franco's tooth. The spies hope to use the duo to fool agents from other countries while they work to perfect the real formula, which they put in Franco's head by mistake. Operatives from the United States, the Soviet Union and Red China converge on Franco and Ciccio in hopes of getting the microchip while the two chase scantily clad young women on the beach. When the spies realize that Franco has the real formula, they try to communicate with him and Ciccio by sending messages written on women's panties but the duo prefer the wearers. Mostly through ignorance and accidents, Franco and Ciccio manage to avoid being captured until the Americans finally pull all their teeth and obtain the formula. No longer of use to the secret agents of the world, the vagrants return to their lives of petty thievery.

While *Oh! Those Most Secret Agents!* contains a modicum of spy film ingredients, like futuristic gadgetry and semi-naked girls, plus a subplot of a jealous husband (Aroldo Tieri) suspecting Franco and Ciccio of compromising his beautiful wife (Ingrid Schoeller), it mainly concentrates on the woes of Franco in trying to get rid of the unwanted tooth and the boys' avoidance of being captured by foreign operatives. Matt Blake and David Deal in *The Eurospy Guide* (2004) stated, "If the mere prospect of a Franco and Ciccio film doesn't break you out in a cold sweat ... [this] is a neatly made, hugely enjoyable film. It's not, perhaps, as well constructed as some of their other vehicles ... but it certainly speeds along at a rate of knots and has a few good gags. There's plenty of mileage made of general clichés...." For the majority of viewers, Paul Mavis summed it up best in *The Espionage Filmography* (2001) when he commented, "Unwatchable."

Oh! Those Most Secret Agents! was directed by Lucio Fulci who helmed Franco and Ciccio the next year in the sci-fi spoof *002 Operazione Luna* (002 Operation Moon), which had no stateside showings. Fulci, later dubbed the "Godfather of Gore," is best remembered for such stomach-turning horrors as *Zombie* (1979), *The Beyond* (*Seven Doors to Death*), *The Gates of Hell*, *The House By the Cemetery* and *The Black Cat* (all 1981) and *Zombie 3* (1988).

Paris Playboys (1954; 62 minutes)

Producer: Ben Schwalb. Director: William Beaudine. Screenplay: Elwood Ullman and Edward Bernds. Photography: Harry Neumann. Editor: John C. Fuller. Music: Marlin Skiles. Art Director: David Milton. Sound: Charles Cooper. Production Manager: Allen K. Wood. Sets: Robert Priestley. Wardrobe: Smoke Kring. Special Effects: Ray Mercer. Continuity: John Franco. Assistant Director: Edward Morey, Jr.

CAST: Leo Gorcey (Terence Aloysius "Slip" Mahoney), Huntz Hall (Horace Debussy "Sach" Jones/Professor Maurice Gaston Le Beau), Bernard Gorcey (Louie Dumbrowski), Veola Vonn

(Mimi Du Bois), Steven Geray (Dr. Gaspard), John Wengraf (Vidal), Marianna [Mari] Lynn (Celeste Gambon), David [Gorcey] Condon (Chuck), Bennie Bartlett (Butch), Fritz Feld (Maitre d' Marcel), Gordon Clark (Jacques Gambon), Alphonse Martell (Butler Pierre), Robin Hughes, Roy Gordon (Henchmen).

Sach Jones (Huntz Hall) is a look-a-like for noted French physicist Professor Maurice Gaston Le Beau (Hall); when the scientist goes missing, he is reported to be a denizen of Louie Dumbrowski's (Bernard Gorcey) sweet shop in the Bowery. Le Beau's rocket fuel is coveted by foreign powers and he has been the target of several assassination attempts. Members of the Scientific Section of the United Nations' Intelligence Agency seek out Le Beau at Louie's place only to meet the simple-minded Sach. After they show Slip Mahoney (Leo Gorcey) pictures of the scientist, they come up with the idea of having Sach impersonate Le Beau, hoping his kidnappers will set him free. Leaving their pals Chuck (David Condon) and Butch (Bennie Bartlett) behind, Slip, Sach and Louie fly to Paris with the scientists. Slip tells Sach that Le Beau, who has been reported by the media as being an amnesiac, has a beautiful fiancée, Mimi Du Bois (Veola Vonn). When Mimi learns that Le Beau has been found, she consults with his physician, Dr. Gaspard (Steven Geray), who tells her he can be cured of his amnesia. The doctor is secretly working with Vidal (John Wengraf), an underworld figure representing spies who are after the rocket fuel formula. In Paris, Sach, despite his usual loony antics, is able to convince both Mimi and Dr. Gaspard that he is Le Beau but when it is suggested by the doctor that he renew his research, the young woman says he must have his memory restored. Mimi informs Sach they will be married the next week and go on a prolonged honeymoon. When secret agents try to murder Sach, he decides to go back to the Bowery but Slip tells him they must stay in Paris and uphold the honor of their country. Le Beau, who is incognito on a tropical isle and has been romancing several young women, sees a picture of Sach with Mimi in a newspaper, becomes jealous and goes home. Once in Paris, Le Beau finds Louie in his house and tells him to get out. When Sach asks Louie why he is packing, the old man becomes bewildered at his friend's quixotic behavior. Le Beau then proposes to Mimi as Slip becomes confused over what he thinks is Sach's strange actions but he soon realizes what has happened when the two look-a-likes come face to face. Le Beau goes after Sach with a sword, ends up fighting with Slip and is then secreted in a closet. Vidal, Dr. Gaspard and their henchmen (Robin Hughes, Roy Gordon) demand that Sach, who they now think is the real Le Beau, prove that the rocket fuel formula works and he puts together a recipe that he pours into a miniature missile. Le Beau is set free by Mimi but the henchmen bring them to the lab as the small rocket zooms around the room. It crashes and the explosion knocks out the spies, who are taken into custody. For his heroism, Sach is awarded the Legion of Honor by French officials while the disappointed Le Beau is comforted by Mimi.

The thirty-third "Bowery Boys" production, *Paris Playboys* has only a faint sci-fi angle, the development of a futuristic rocket fuel. Made as *Paris Bombshells*, it is a below-average entry. *Variety* stated, "The laughs don't come frequently nor with ease in the script.... Main springboards, per usual, are the malaprops of Leo Gorcey and Huntz Hall's crazy antics...." *The Hollywood Reporter* labeled it "typical Bowery Boys filmfare, wild and noisy slapstick." David Hayes and Brent Walker in *The Films of the Bowery Boys* (1984) called it "a labored non-comedy. Shot on a set that looks like the one used for *Loose in London* [1953], and resembling that picture in some other ways, it is no more than a dull procession of misunderstandings." The authors note that a scene where Sach is nearly murdered while reading in bed is a reworking of a similar one in *Loose in London*.

Phantom Trails (1955; 52 minutes)

Producer: William F. Broidy. Photography: John J. Martin. Editor: Carl L. Pierson. Music: Lee Zahler. Art Director: David Milton. Sound: Frank Webster. Sets: Mowbray Berkeley and Vin Taylor. Production Supervisor: A.R. Milton. Makeup: Charles Huber. Special Effects: Ray Mercer. Assistant Director: William Beaudine, Jr.

CAST: Guy Madison (Marshal Wild Bill Hickok), Andy Devine (Deputy Marshal Jingles P. Jones). Episodes: "Ghost Rider": Director: Wesley Barry. Screenplay: Bill Raynor. CAST: Paul Bryar (Ed Grannis), Steve Pendleton (Gurt Lesley), Hank Patterson (Jess Morgan), William Vedder (Pops Garroway), Ethan Laidlaw (Ben Lesley). "A Close Shave for the Marshal": Director: Frank McDonald. Screenplay: Maurice Tombragel. CAST: Steve Brodie (Matt), Byron Foulger (Henry Hopper), Harry Harvey, Sr. (Sheriff), Robert Filmer (Banker Wade), Burt Wenland (Jake).

Like the earlier *The Ghost of Crossbones Canyon* (1952) [q.v.], *Phantom Trails* was made up of two episodes of the popular *The Adventures of Wild Bill Hickok* television series that ran from 1951 to 1958 for a total of 118 episodes. Its popularity spawned a 217-episode radio show of the same title, also starring Guy Madison and Andy Devine, that was broadcast from 1951 to 1954.

The TV entries "Ghost Rider" (originally telecast in 1952) and "A Close Shave for the Marshal" made up *Phantom Trails*. While the latter had nothing to do with the supernatural, "Ghost Rider" told of U.S. Marshal Wild Bill Hickok (Madison) having his deputy, Jingles P. Jones (Devine), dress like a ghost and ride through Banshee City's cemetery in order for them to capture an outlaw gang plaguing area ranchers.

Allied Artists released this pastiche to theaters in May 1955 without advertising that it was made up of television shows.

Port of Hell (1954; 80 minutes)

Producer: William F. Broidy. Associate Producer: A. Robert Nunes. Director: Harold D. Schuster. Screenplay: Gil Doud, Tom Hubbard and Fred Eggers. Story: D.D. Beauchamp and Gil Doud. Photography: John J. Martin. Editor: Ace Herman. Music Director: Edward J. Kay. Art Director: George Troast. Sound: Al Overton. Production Supervisor: A.R. Milton. Makeup: Philip Scheer. Special Effects: Ray Mercer. Continuity: Joyce Webb. Assistant Director: William Beaudine, Jr.

CAST: Dane Clark (Gibson "Gib" Pardee), Wayne Morris (Stanley Povich), Carole Mathews (Julie Povich), Marshall Thompson (Marshall "Marsh" Walker), Marjorie Lord (Kay Walker), Otto Waldis (Captain Snyder), Harold Peary (Leo), Tom Hubbard (Nick), Gene Roth (Enemy Ship Captain), Victor Sen Yung (Enemy Radio Operator), Jim Alexander (Chief Parker), Charles E. Fredericks (John Reynolds), Dee Ann Johnston (Walker Child).

Kiss Me Deadly (1955) is considered the landmark feature film to deal with an atomic weapon brought into the country for the purpose of detonating a nuclear holocaust, but it was preceded by *Port of Hell*, which Allied Artists put in theaters late in 1954. Four years later, the studio's release *Hell's Five Hours* (q.v.) covered some of the same ground although it was more narrow in that it involved the possible destruction of a government defense facility. Made as *Dynamite Anchorage*, *Port of Hell* was dubbed an "exciting, suspenseful drama" by *Film Daily*. *Variety* declared it "a notch above average supporting fare." On the other hand, the *New York Times* thought it was a "mild, shipshod little drama" but liked the work of Dane Clark: "It has a good, forthright performance by [Clark] and some picturesque glimpses of an active waterfront, both of which are wasted…. [I]t's admirable to find Mr. Clark trouping instead of merely ambling."

Former Navy commander Gib Pardee (Clark) takes over the position of Los Angeles harbor port warden and, strictly adhering to rules, he arrests Stanley Povich (Wayne Morris),

Lobby card for *Port of Hell* (1954) picturing Carole Mathews, Wayne Morris and Dane Clark

a tugboat operator, for smoking in an off-limits locale. Later Povich's sister Julie (Carole Mathews) chews Gib out for his actions and warns him that his stiff-necked attitude could lead to his demise. That evening Kay Walker (Marjorie Lord) shows up to take her wheelchair-bound husband Marsh (Marshall Thompson) to their anniversary dinner at the White Swan Café. Gib declines an invitation although he and Marsh, who is his harbor assistant, were in the Navy together. He tells them he is a loner without friends. Gib and Parker (Jim Alexander), the harbor police chief, check the area and find fishing boat moorings are packed; since this presents a fire hazard, Gib says he plans to put new rules in place. While Marsh and his wife are having dinner, he learns that ship captain Snyder (Otto Waldis) has been sending coded messages. The freighter *Beneva* is supposed to have a cargo of Mexican firecrackers but is really concealing an atomic bomb. Nearby is an enemy ship set to detonate the bomb in 24 hours in a plan dubbed "Operation Thunderbolt," which is designed to wipe out Los Angeles. When Gib's orders about the moorings are put into effect, several fishing boat owners become upset; Leo (Harold Peary) refuses to obey them and is jailed. Gib also has problems with a security guard who has not been keeping track of trucks carrying cargo as they arrive and leave the docks and he gets into a fight with one of the truckers, Nick (Tom Hubbard). Snyder receives a message from the captain (Gene Roth) and radio operator (Victor Sen Yung) of the detonator ship saying that Operation Thunderbolt is on schedule. Gib and Julie are attracted to each other but Stan warns his sister

Lobby card for *Port of Hell* (1954) picturing Otto Waldis, Dane Clark and Marshall Thompson

to stay away from the port warden. When Marsh is radioed that the *Beneva* and its cargo of firecrackers is nearing Los Angeles, he tells Gib who boards the freighter along with Chief Parker as it anchors outside the harbor. When Snyder tells Gib the ship was last at a port with cholera and there may be rats on board, the port warden implements new regulations and tells the captain he and his crew must remain on board the vessel for 24 hours. The port warden later finds Snyder on shore in violation of his ship's quarantine. The agitated Snyder is arrested after he confesses about the atomic bomb and its planned detonation. Gib decides to try and tow the *Beneva* out to sea. Marsh wants to call in the authorities but Gib fears this will cause mass panic and he goes to seek Stan's help but finds he is not at home.

Gib does see Julie and he tells her he loves her. When Gib finds Stan in a café, he gets hit but when he explains about the bomb, the tugboat owner agrees to help and enlists Nick and Leo as his crew. It will take about ten hours to get the freighter safely out of the range of the city. Gib, Marsh and the three tug boaters go to the now deserted *Beneva* and Gib gets on board as Marsh, Stan and his crew begin to tow the ship out to sea. When they get thirty miles from the harbor, Stan tells Nick and Leo to drop the tow lines. Picking up Gib, they head back to Los Angeles harbor. The atomic bomb is detonated but causes no damage and the government announces the explosion was only a test. Julie is waiting for Gib when he returns to port.

Private Eyes (1953; 64 minutes)

Producer: Ben Schwalb. Director: Edward Bernds. Screenplay: Elwood Ullman and Edward Bernds. Photography: Carl Guthrie. Editor: John C. Fuller. Music: Marlin Skiles. Art Director: David Milton. Sound: Charles Cooper. Sets: Clarence Steensen. Production Manager: Allen K. Wood. Wardrobe: Smoke Kring. Makeup: Norman Pringle. Continuity: Ted Schilz. Assistant Director: Austen Jewell.

CAST: Leo Gorcey (Terence Aloysius "Slip" Mahoney), Huntz Hall (Horace Debussy "Sach" Jones), Bernard Gorcey (Louie Dumbrowski), Joyce Holden (Myra Hagen), Robert Osterloh (Professor Damon), William Phillips (Soapy), Rudy Lee (Herbie), William Forrest (John Graham), Chick Chandler (Eddie), David [Gorcey] Condon (Chuck), Bennie Bartlett (Butch), Lou Lubin (Oskar), Tim Ryan (Policeman Andy), Peter Mamakos (Chico), Edith Leslie (Nurse Aggie), Myron Healey (Karl), Gil Perkins (Al), Emil Sitka (Wheelchair Patient), Steve Stevens (Boy), Carl Saxe (Attendant).

Bowery denizens Slip Mahoney (Leo Gorcey) and Sach Jones (Huntz Hall) are in charge of a youth athletic club at the back of Louie Dumbrowski's (Bernard Gorcey) sweet shop; Louie complains the noise is keeping customers away. Young Herbie (Rudy Lee) clips Sach on the chin during a sparring match and the latter finds he is now a mind reader. When Eddie (Chick Chandler) offers to sell Slip his Eagle Eye Detective Agency for $400, the profit-minded Slip buys it for $200 borrowed from Louie, figuring Sach's new powers (Slip says Sach is "wired for mental telegraphy") will bring in business. Once the boys are in business, beautiful blonde Myra Hagen (Joyce Holden) shows up wanting protection from an assassin. Giving Slip a manila envelope containing the names of those she suspects if she is murdered, the young woman flees and leaves behind a fur coat. Sach, who wears a deerstalker and sports a pipe, puts the envelope in the office safe and, needing a place to hide its combination, he also puts that inside and locks the door. Myra is abducted by an armed man, Chico (Peter Mamakos). Officer Andy (Tim Ryan) inspects the fur coat and identifies it as part of a heist. Professor Damon (Robert Osterloh) operates a sanitarium as a front for a theft ring that steals fur coats nationwide and alters them for re-sale. Myra worked for Damon but wants out of the racket and tells him about the letter she left with the detectives. Slip and Sach receive a visit from Apex Insurance Company investigator John Graham (William Forrest) who is looking into the stolen fur coat racket. He offers the boys a $10,000 reward to help catch the gang and he also wants Myra's letter. As Slip, Chuck (David Condon) and Butch (Bennie Bartlett) look for Myra, Sach decides to use a shotgun to open the safe and when that fails he makes a bomb out of gunpowder. He blows the safe apart but the blast knocks him out and he loses his mind-reading abilities. Damon forces Myra to telephone the detectives and ask for the return of her envelope. When two of the professor's henchmen, Chico and Soapy (William Phillips), show up to get it, the missive cannot be found. Herbie, who has been brought in to hit Sach again so he will regain his powers, is abducted by the thugs and taken to the sanitarium. Slip calls Graham, the head of the fur theft gang, and tells him Herbie has been kidnapped. Damon later phones Slip and tells him the boy will be returned when he gets the letter. Karl (Myron Healey), one of Damon's men, loves Myra and warns her that his boss plans to do away with her and the boy. She finds Herbie, who calls Slip and Sach and tells them what is happening. Slip locates the envelope and, disguised as the noted Viennese Dr. Hockenlopper, goes to the sanitarium with Sach, who pretends to be his wealthy patient, Mrs. Abernathy. Slip and Sach look for Herbie with the latter encountering Graham. Telling Graham who he really is, Sach hands him the envelope so he can get the promised reward. Graham sends his henchmen after the detectives. Slip locates Myra and Herbie but the boy slugs Sach, thinking he is one of the crooks. The punch brings back Sach's mind-reading abilities. When Graham promises to help Slip, Sach, Myra and Herbie escape, Sach reads his mind. Graham holds them at gunpoint but is stopped by Karl. Slip takes the envelope and is chased by the thugs. He lures them into the water therapy bath area where Herbie knocks them out with a barbell and they fall into the vat. After receiving their reward, Slip and Sach open the Bowery Boys' Club, with Karl as the athletic director. During the ceremonies, in which Myra serves as hostess, the kids start a food fight with Slip, Sach and Louie getting pies in the face.

Private Eyes, the thirty-third "Bowery Boys" entry, was released at the end of 1953. Made as *Bowery Bloodhounds,* it was one of several that used a genre hook to exploit otherwise low-grade comedy. In this case it was Sach's ability to read minds. *Variety* noted, "There are some funny moments in pic.... Gorcey with his malaprops and Hall's craziness make film enjoyable." David Hayes and Brent Walker wrote in *The Films of the Bowery Boys* (1984), "*Private Eyes* is the fastest-paced entry in the Bowery Boys series and one of the funniest. Transcending its meager budget, the film is consistently brisk and does not let up for a moment, allowing Gorcey and Hall to romp freely. Much of the credit must be given to director Edward Bernds, who lets the boys perform without too much plot interference." The authors noted that one scene in the film involving a man (Emil Sitka) in a wheelchair was reworked from the 1946 Three Stooges short *Monkey Businessmen,* also directed by Bernds. A major asset to the film was beautiful leading lady Joyce Holden.

Queen of Outer Space (1958; 80 minutes; Color)

Producer: Ben Schwalb. Director: Edward Bernds. Screenplay: Charles Beaumont. Story: Ben Hecht. Photography: William P. Whitley. Editor: William Austin. Music: Marlin Skiles. Art Director: Dave Milton. Sound: Charles G. Schelling and Joe Lapis. Sets: Joseph Kish. Production Manager: Edward Morey, Jr. Makeup: Emile LaVigne. Special Effects: Milt Rice and Jack Cosgrove. Wardrobe: Irene Caine, Sid Mintz, Sophia Scott Stutz, Thomas Pierce and Neva Bourne. Assistant to Producer: Lester A. Sansom. Assistant Director: William Beaudine, Jr.

CAST: Zsa Zsa Gabor (Talleah), Eric Fleming (Captain Neal Patterson), Dave Willock (Lieutenant Mike Cruze), Laurie Mitchell (Queen Yllana), Lisa Davis (Motiya), Paul Birch (Professor Konrad), Patrick Waltz (Lieutenant Larry Taylor), Barbara Darrow (Kaeel), Marilyn Buferd (Odeena), Guy Prescott (Colonel Ramsey), Joi Lansing (Blonde Girlfriend), Mary Ford, Marya Stevens, Laura Mason, Lynn Cartwright, Kathy Marlowe, Coleen Drake, Tania Velia, Norma Young, Marjorie Durant (Venusians), Gerry Gaylor, Brandy Bryan (Venusian Guards), June McCall, Ruth Lewis (Amazons).

Queen of Outer Space was made by Ben Schwalb, the producer of the "Bowery Boys" series, and directed by Edward Bernds, who often worked on the same programmers. It was written by Charles Beaumont from a story, "Queen of the Universe," by Ben Hecht; that was also the film's working title. Filmed in CinemaScope with color by De Luxe, the production was released in the fall of 1958, sometimes co-featured with *Frankenstein 1970* (q.v.). A cheap, light-hearted space romp, it was noteworthy at the time because its credits did not roll until nearly fifteen minutes had elapsed. Reused from Bernds' *World Without End* (1956) were sets, special effects and a tatty-looking giant spider. Some of the costumes in *Queen of Outer Space* came from MGM's *Forbidden Planet* (1956). Although the script is written as a spoof, Bernds directed it as a straightforward space melodrama, which is surprising considering his lengthy background in comedy writing and directing.

The film's chief asset, as well as box office pull, is Zsa Zsa Gabor, who handles her role with finesse and is stunning as a Venusian scientist with perfect hair and wearing a series of lovely gowns designed by Thomas Pierce. While considered far more of a personality than an actress, Gabor had several legitimate film credits including *Moulin Rouge* (1952), *The Story of Three Loves* and *Lili* (both 1953), *Death of a Scoundrel* (1956), in which she appeared with her third husband George Sanders and his brother Tom Conway; *Touch of Evil* (1958), *Picture Mommy Dead* (1966), *Every Girl Should Have One* (1979), and *Johann Strauss—Der Konig ohne Krone* (1986). Although the film is filled with pretty Venusian maidens, the rest of the cast is bland when compared to glamour queen Zsa Zsa. Eric Fleming, who earlier starred in Allied's *Fright* (1956) [q.v.], is a stilted hero and Dave Willock and Patrick Waltz are blah as his wisecracking sidekicks. Only Paul Birch manages to instill some dignity in the role of a seasoned scientist, and it is his character who ends up with a bevy of beauties at the film's finale; Birch starred in Allied's *Not of This Earth* (1957) [q.v.]. The title role in the film is played by Laurie Mitchell as the radiation-scarred Queen Yllana. Concealed behind a mask in most scenes, she can do little with the role other than act bitchy.

In 1985, astronauts Captain Neil Patterson (Fleming), Lieutenant Mike Cruze (Willock) and Lieutenant Larry Turner (Waltz) are assigned by Colonel Ramsey (Guy Prescott) to take scientist Professor Konrad (Birch) to a way station in space. As they get close to it, the four men see a series of beams shoot through space and one of them obliterates the space port. When the beams start coming at their rocket, Patterson orders a maneuvering technique but they end up traveling at such a terrific speed that all the men pass out. When they awake, the ship is in a snow-covered area thanks to its automatic landing controls. They decide to explore the planet after finding it has an Earth-like atmosphere. Once they get below the snow line and into a jungle-like area, Konrad announces he believes they have landed on Venus. The only sound they hear is an electronic signal. The next day they are captured by six beautiful women in short skirts and high heels who take them to a palace. There they meet the masked Queen Yllana (Mitchell) who tells them the Earth has been monitored for years and she believes they have come to Venus to make war. Motiya (Lisa Davis), one of the lovely Venusians, reports to her boss, scientist Talleah (Gabor), about the men's arrival and she vows to see them. Mike and Larry note the absence of men on Venus. The prisoners are sent to a cell as Yllana declares they will be put to death. Konrad tells the others he believes the Venusians destroyed the space station. Talleah brings them food and says she is the leader of a group of rebels fed up with the queen's cruelty. She tells them that several years before, Venus nearly lost a war with the planet Mordo and that Yllana led a women's revolt against the men who started the conflict. Only the males who were needed survived, and they are housed on Tyrus, a prison colony. As Talleah hides, the queen returns and offers to meet with Neil. After she leaves, his friends declare that Yllana is attracted to the captain and suggest he use romance to change her mind about them. In Yllana's quarters, the woman continues her tirade against the astronauts, saying their space outpost was to be used to attack Venus. After she confesses to being lonely, Neil tries to get her to take off the mask she wears but she refuses. When he pulls it off, her he finds her face is horribly disfigured and she tells him it was caused from the radiation that resulted because of the war the men of Venus started. She orders Neil back to confinement. Later he and his comrades are taken to Talleah's laboratory where she says the queen has ordered the destruction of Earth with a beta-disintegrator ray. When guards come looking for the men, Talleah, Motiya and Kaeel (Barbara Darrow) lead them through a secret door and out of the palace. They hide in the jungle but are hunted by the guards. The group takes refuge in a cave. Larry is attacked by a giant spider but Neil kills it. As they wait in the cave the captain finds he is falling for Talleah, while Mike becomes attracted to Kaeel and Larry to

Motiya. Realizing they cannot survive without provisions, Konrad suggests that Talleah and the other women pretend to take them prisoners so they can try and destroy the ray machine, which is housed deep in the jungle. At the palace, Talleah and her aides turn on the queen. Neil removes Yllana's mask and gives it to the scientist so she can pretend to be the monarch and stop the attack on Earth. The queen finds a ray gun and calls in her guards who capture the astronauts and Talleah. As Yllana makes the captives watch, she begins the procedure to aim the nuclear energy projector at Earth but it malfunctions and explodes. Talleah gives a signal to Motiya and her allies to storm the palace. Yllana is incinerated by her own weapon and her guards are overpowered. Talleah is made the new queen of Venus. After several weeks the astronauts' ship is repaired and the women tell them goodbye. Just before they depart, the men receive a message from Colonel Ramsey telling them to stay on Venus until a relief expedition arrives, although it may take up to one year. The three astronauts prepare for romance with their beautiful Venusian lovers. Even Dr. Konrad finds himself surrounded by a flock of admiring beauties.

As to be expected, *Queen of Outer Space* was not taken seriously by either viewers or critics. *Castle of Frankenstein* #24 (1974) noted, "Seems to have been intended as a spoof, but it's funny in exactly the opposite way...." In *Horror and Science Fictions Films: A Checklist* (1972), Donald C. Willis felt the film was "Drab s-f" and Welch Everman in *Cult Science Fiction Films* (1995) opined, "If you are really a student of bad cinema, you really couldn't ask for much more in a sci-fi film." A "Standout 'Best Worst' movie" is how *Time Out Film Guide, 9th Edition 2001* (2000) termed it, adding, "The Place may be Venus, but the Time looks more like cocktail hour than the future; everyone's wearing vintage Swanky Modes and ice-staking skirts. There's also a fine display of '50s sublimated sexuality in

Poster for *Queen of Outer Space* (1958)

the endless kissing scenes...." Most critics took potshots at the tacky special effects and sets, the most ludicrous being the cardboard beta-disintegrator which looks like it was designed for a junior high school play.

Queen of Outer Space was turned into photoplay magazines in Brazil and France several years after its theatrical release. In 1963 Cosmos Aventuras published it in Brazil as *A Raggia de Venus* (The Queen of Venus) and the next year Star-Cine Cosmos did the same in France where it was titled *La Reine de Venus* (The Queen of Venus).

Sabu and the Magic Ring (1957; 61 minutes; Color)

Producer: Maurice Duke. Director: George Blair. Screenplay: Samuel Roeca, Benedict Freedman and John Fenton Murray. Photography: Harry Neumann. Editor: William Austin. Music: Harry Sukman. Art Director: Dave Milton. Sound: Ralph Butler. Production Manager: Allen K. Wood. Sets: Hal Gossman. Makeup: John Holden. Special Effects: Augie Lohman. Costumes: Eileen Younger. Continuity: James West. Assistant Director: Grayson Rogers.

CAST: Sabu (Himself), Daria Massey (Zumila), William Marshall (Ubal), Peter Mamakos (Mazufar), Vladimir Sokoloff (Old Fakir), John Doucette (Kimal), Robert Shafto (Caliph of Samukan), Bernard Rich (Ali), Robin Morse (Yunan), George Khoury (Phransigar), Cyril Delevanti (Abdul), Kenneth Terrell (Guard), John Lomma (Soldier).

Sabu (1924–63) was discovered by documentary film legend Robert Flaherty in India, where he (Sabu) was the stable boy for a maharajah. He starred in Flaherty's British production *Elephant Boy* in 1937 and came to Hollywood where he appeared in *The Jungle Book* and *Arabian Nights* (both 1942), *Cobra Woman* (1944), *Song of India* (1949), *Savage Drums* (1951) and *Jaguar* (1956). He returned to England to make *Black Narcissus* and *The End of the River* (both 1958). *Sabu and the Magic Ring*, which ironically cast its star as a stable boy, was originally filmed as two episodes for a proposed television series that did not sell. Allied Artists issued it in November 1957. The *Arabian Nights*–themed fantasy was released on the lower half of a twin bill and then became kiddie matinee fare before going full circle, ending up on television in the late 1960s. Although shown theatrically in color, its TV prints were black and white. Sabu's final films were *Rampage* (1963) and *A Tiger Walks* (1964).

In the kingdom of Samukan, Sabu happily tends the caliph's (Robert Shaffto) elephants until he is charged with stealing a priceless diamond. He tries to find the gem but ends up with a ring that he wants to give to his lady love, fruit seller Zumila (Daria Massey). They take it to storyteller Abdul (Cyril Delevanti) who recites a tale of King Solomon, who finds a silver ring and rubs it with a genie materializing and giving him his every wish. Sabu rubs his ring and Ubal (William Marshall), a giant genie, emerges and performs several chores at his new master's behest. The diamond had been stolen by stable master Kimal (John Doucette) for prime minister Mazufar (Peter Mamakos), who sells it to get money to get rid of the caliph and take his place. The prime minister attempts to steal the magic ring from Sabu but is thwarted by the genie. Sabu is whipped by the prime minister's henchmen but he will not reveal where he hid the ring. Yunan (Robin Morse), a magician banished from his kingdom for practicing the black arts, offers to help the prime minister obtain it. Sabu is set free and goes to Zumila but she is abducted and put under a spell by Mazufar and Yunan. Having hidden the magic ring on his best elephant, Sabu tries to find it without success. Ubal appears and gives the ring to his master. When the genie locates Zumila, he is frozen by Yunan. Sabu finds the ring cannot help him rescue the girl. Mazufar and Yunan have a falling out over the ring. The imprisoned genie frees himself and helps Sabu rescue Zumila. Ubal sends Yunan to the South Pole. The lovers find out that Mazufar is slowly poisoning the caliph. A goose swallows the magic ring; after Sabu picks it out of a flock of geese, he and Zumila take refuge in a grotto at the behest of an old fakir (Vladimir Sokoloff). Mazufar learns from the caliph that he plans to unite Samukan with Damascus when he dies and will hold a feast for its ruler, Prince Achmed. The prime minister hires Phransigar (George Khoury) and his men to murder the prince. The old fakir tries to keep Sabu and Zumila in the grotto so he can collect a reward posted for them. After laying an egg, the goose runs away but the egg falls from a ledge and lands on the young man's head and breaks, revealing the magic ring. After Sabu and Ubal successfully battle forty thieves, the old fakir gets his reward. Zumila orders the genie to set her and Sabu free. The genie makes his master a prince who rides an elephant to the caliph's palace, causing the prime minister to believe he is Achmed. Mazufar finds out he has been made a fool when the assassin returns to say he killed the prince but by now the genie has cured the caliph of food poisoning. Mazufar and his henchmen kidnap the caliph but he is saved by Sabu who uses a magic carpet given to him by the genie. Sabu, Ubal and Ali (Bernard Rich), another stable boy, fight Mazufar's men until Zumila tells the genie to end all hostilities. Giving the magic ring to the genie so he can find eternal rest, Sabu and Zumila return to their former happy existence.

Steven H. Scheuer's *Movies on TV 1969–70 Edition* (1969) called *Sabu and the Magic Ring* an "OK fantasy for the kiddies; it's played for laughs, but could have used more." *Leonard Maltin's 2004 Movie and Video Guide* (2003) says it is "[l]ow-budget backlot Arabian Nights nonsense...."

Sex Kittens Go to College (1960; 94 minutes)

Producer-Director-Story: Albert Zugsmith. Associate Producers: Robert Hill and Martin Milner. Screenplay: Robert Hill. Photography: Ellis W. Carter. Editor: William Austin. Music: Dean Elliott. Songs: Conway Twitty. Sets: John Sturtevant. Sound: Robert Post and Charles Schelling. Production Manager-Assistant Director: Ralph Black. Makeup: Monte Westmore. Special Effects: Augie Lohman. Wardrobe: Claire Cramer and Rudy Harrington. Dialogue Director: Jackie Coogan. Continuity: Frank Kowalski.

CAST: Mamie Van Doren (Dr. Mathilda Gabrielle West), Tuesday Weld (Jody), Mijanou Bardot (Suzanne de la Cour), Mickey Shaughnessy (Boomie), Louis Nye (Dr. Ernst Zorch), Pamela Mason (Dr. Myrtle Carter), Martin Milner (George Barton), Conway Twitty (Himself), Jackie Coogan (Admiral "Wildcat" MacPherson), John Carradine (Dr. Harvey Watts), Vampira [Maila Nurmi] (Etta Toodle), Norman "Woo Woo" Grabowski (Himself), Irwin Berke (Professor Towers), Allan Drake (Legs Raffertino), Jody Fair (Bartender), Arline Hunter (Nurse), Buni Bacon (Hostess), Babe London (Amanda Cadwallader), Charles Chaplin, Jr. (Fire Chief), John Van Dreelen (Bullets), Barbara Pepper (Woman in Torn Dress), Harold Lloyd, Jr., Jack Carr (Policemen), Jose Gonzalez Gonzalez (Mexican Bookie), Noel de Souza (Arab Bookie), Cherrio Meredith (Miss Everleigh), Beverly Englander (Shoeshine Girl), Buddy Douglas (Midget), Edwin Randolph (Railroad Conductor), Chim the Chimpanzee (Abraham Q. Voltaire).

Filmed as *Sexpot Goes to College*, *Teacher vs. Sexpot* and *Teacher Was a Sexpot*, this so-called comedy from Photoplay Associates, Inc. (Albert Zugsmith Productions), has a slim sci-fi connection in that it features a talking robot called Thinko and star Mamie Van Doren's character registers an IQ of 298, 40 points above genius.

The robot was actually Elektro, which was made by Westinghouse and first displayed in 1939; for the film its appearance was somewhat altered. When *Sex Kittens Go to College* was released to TV it was called *Beauty and the Robot*. Under any name it is a clunker. The *New York Herald Tribune* called it "[p]uerile and precious.... It is a very sorry venture into slapstick that never manages to get within halooing distance of merit." The *Hollywood*

Reporter felt it was a "harmless little farce.... There isn't really any plot, just [a] series of blackout gags and situations." *Movies on TV 1969–70 Edition* (1969), edited by Steven H. Scheuer, stated, "Computer that picked the plot for this one has a screw loose somewhere; ghastly attempt at farce has nothing." C.J. Henderson in *The Encyclopedia of Science Fiction Movies* (2001) noted, "The title tells one all there is to know."

The main asset of *Sex Kittens Goes to College* is an admixture of talent headed by gorgeous blonde Mamie Van Doren, who handles her thankless role of a genius ex-stripper college professor with exuberance. She gets to look and act sexy and rattle off all kinds of intellectual jargon, and also sings the song "Baby" and does a lengthy, sexy dance alongside Jackie Coogan, John Carradine, Irwin Berke and Louis Nye. Conway Twitty back ups Mamie musically on her vocal and he also sings the title song "Sexpot Goes to College" as well as "Miss Mamie." Tuesday Weld has her usual coy co-ed part and Brigitte Bardot's little sister, Mijanou, plays a love-crazed journalism major; while very beautiful, she has no screen presence. Martin Milner, who was also an associate producer, is the stiff leading man, while Mickey Shaughnessy and Allan Drake mug their way through comic gangster roles. Jackie Coogan, also the film's dialogue director, imitates W.C. Fields in the part of a philandering benefactor, and Carradine and Berke ham it up as professors hot for Van Doren. Pamela Mason appears far too old to be playing Milner's girlfriend. Norman "Woo Woo" Grabowski tries to be amusing, but fails on all fronts. Wasted in passing bits are Vampira, Jody Fair, Arline Hunter, Babe London, Barbara Pepper, Charles Chaplin, Jr., Harold Lloyd, Jr., and Jose Gonzalez Gonzalez. Only Chim the Chimpanzee and Thinko manage to escape unscathed.

At Collins College, a computer dubbed Sequential Auxiliary Modulator, or Thinko, spews out information on the new head of the science department, Dr. Mathilda West (Van Doren), for its inventor Dr. Ernst Zorch (Nye) and his bookish brunette assistant Etta Toodle (Vampira). It not only reveals she has an IQ of 298 and holds thirteen degrees, but it gives her perfect measurements and reveals that she is very beautiful and sexy. Zorch runs to the train station to tell Dr. Myrtle Carter (Mason) that the newcomer is not what the school expected as she waits for Mathilda's arrival with her boyfriend, George Barton (Milner), the school's head of public relations, and an all-girl band. A member of the band is blonde Jody (Weld) who is smitten with dimwitted "Woo Woo" Grabowski (himself), president of the student body and captain of the football team, who is to give a welcoming speech. After the train stops, the group mistake a dowdy brassiere salesperson (Babe London) for the new professor but finally meet beautiful Mathilda, who is so stunning she causes Grabowski to faint. Also getting off the train are Chicago hoodlums Legs Raffertino (Allan Drake) and Boomie (Shaughnessy), who are looking for Sam Thinko, a bookie who has been winning all bets and bankrupting their boss. Legs attracts French exchange student Suzanne (Bardot) who is writing a book on American men as lovers and she tells them to go to the college to find Thinko. Suzanne warns Jody to beware of Mathilda because of her effect on Grabowski, so on her way to class the coed breaks her bra strap and gets the footballer to give her his fraternity pin to hold it together. Myrtle is jealous of the beautiful Mathilda and to disrupt her first lecture on applied psychology, she releases Abraham Q. Voltaire, a chimp, who is mistakenly introduced by the addled Zorch. Mathilda wins over the students by shooting off two pistols to demonstrate the psychology of fear and then talks with Grabowski about his dread of the opposite sex only to find he is attracted to her. Professors Watts (Carradine) and Towers (Berke) invite Mathilda for barbequed ribs at a club called the Passion Pit that evening. Dressed as college students, the gangsters go to Zorch's

Martin Milner, Louis Nye and Mamie Van Doren in *Sex Kittens Go to College* (1960)

lab to find Sam Thinko and, believing the professor is the bettor who has been causing all their troubles, they knock him out and leave him hanging on a clothes hook. When Mathilda watches football practice, Grabowski faints. George tells her to stay away from the field due to her effect on the players. He also warns her that Watts and Towers are married men before going to Zorch's lab where he gets a phone call from "Wildcat" MacPherson (Coogan), an admiral in the Nevada navy and the school's wealthy benefactor. "Wildcat" announces he is coming to the Passion Pit that night. Legs and Boomie spy Mathilda getting ready for her date and the latter recognizes her as Tassles Monclair, "The Tallahassee Tassle Tosser," a noted striptease dancer. As she is leaving to go to dinner with the two professors, Mathilda is confronted by Jody who says she is a menace for taking away Grabowski's affections. As Mathilda is dining with Watts and Towers, the jealous Myrtle shows up and gets Suzanne, who moonlights as the club photographer, to change clothes with her so she can take pictures of the new professor with "Wildcat" and George. Legs and Boomie also show up. As Suzanne romances Legs, Boomie and Myrtle get tangled when the strap of her camera becomes entwined around the gangster and his violin case which houses a sub-machine gun. Zorch informs George that Thinko has not only given him the names of the last 75 winners of the Kentucky Derby, but also has predicted the next three winners. The two men meet "Wildcat" and at the club he thinks Mathilda is Watts' wife. George gets a call from Etta who tells him Thinko has dug up the fact that Mathilda worked as a stripper. When he asks the new professor about it, she demands to know why her past should affect her ability to teach. After singing a song and dancing, Mathilda hypnotizes "Wildcat," Watts, Towers and Zorch into doing a wild dance with her. When it is finished, she drops a drum on George's head and pours water in it. The still entangled Boomie and Myrtle cause a panic when she accidentally sets off his sub-machine gun. The police show up and arrest "Wildcat" for public misconduct. George goes to the science lab and finds Mathilda, who says she is sorry for the way she treated him, and the two begin to realize they are in love. The gangsters shows up and Legs accuses Mathilda of running the bookie racket and offers her $100,000 to quit. Recalling that he fed Thinko gambling statistics, Zorch is unable to explain how the robot placed the bets. Just as Thinko names more winners, bookies from around the world show up in the lab and a melee takes place. Sleepwalking Grabowski arrives and tampers with Thinko, who begins to go haywire. Mathilda and George use fire extinguishers to run off the crowd so the robot will not be destroyed. When he comes to, Grabowski realizes he has been placing the bets predicted by Thinko in his sleep. After she makes sure the robot will be all right, Mathilda decides to give up teaching and return to being a striptease dancer. The next day, a trim and blonde Myrtle dumps George in favor of "Wildcat," who has asked her to marry him, and Grabowski, using the $100,000 offered by the gangsters, drives away with Jody in a new convertible. George borrows a fire engine and, with Zorch steering, speeds to the train station to find Mathilda before she can leave town. At the station, George proposes but Mathilda says he must accept her for herself and he agrees. Suzanne informs Legs that she must give him up in order to research and write her book, and a now blonde and sexy Etta consoles Zorch, who had also fallen for Mathilda.

An alternate version of *Sex Kittens Go to College*, running ten minutes longer than the one shown to the general public, was made for exhibition in art and "adult only" theatres. It added a sequence near the end in which the ailing Thinko dreams of watching four strippers do their acts. The quartet appear topless with only minimal attire for their performances.

About the same time *Sex Kittens Go to College* was issued by Allied Artists in August 1960, Universal released *College Confidential*, also produced and directed by Albert Zugsmith. Its cast included several of *Sex Kittens*' players, including Van Doren, Shaughnessy, Grabowski, Mason, Arline Hunter and Conway Twitty.

Shinbone Alley (1971; 86 minutes; Color)

Producer: Preston M. Fleet. Executive Producer–Director: John David Wilson. Associate Producer: David Detiege. Screenplay-Lyrics: Joe Darion. Story Continuity: John David Wilson, David Detiege, Dick Kinney and Marty Murphy, from the play by Mel Brooks and Joe Darion and the "Archy and Mehitabel" stories by Don Marquis. Photography: Wally Bullock, Gene Borghi and Ted Bemiller. Editor: Warner Leighton. Music: George Kleinsinger. Sound: James L. Alcholtz. Production Design: John David Wilson, David Detiege, James Bernardi, Cornelius Cole, Sam Cornell, Jules Engel and Gary Lund. Production Coordinator: Christine Decker. Animators: Frank Andrina, Bob Bemille, Bob Bransford, Brad Case, Rudy Cataldi, Selby Daley, Fred Grable, Frank Gonzales, Jil Hiltz, Barrie Nelson, Frank Onaitis, Amby Paliwoda, Spencer Peel, Gil Rugg, John Sparey, Ken Southworth, Russ Von Neida and George Waiss.

VOICE CAST: Carol Channing (Mehitabel), Eddie Bracken (Archy), Alan Reed (Big Bill), John Carradine (Tyrone T. Tattersall), Byron Kane (Narrator), Hal Smith (Freddie the Rat/Prissy Cat), Joan Gerber (Penelope the Fat Cat/Ladybugs of the Evening), Ken Sanson (Rosie the Cat), Sal Delano (Beatnik Spider), The Jackie Ward Singers.

Don Marquis created the characters of Archy, the lovesick cockroach, and Mehitabel, the promiscuous feline fatale, in his "Sun Dial" column in the *New York Sun* in 1916. In 1954 Columbia Records did a long-playing album based on the characters, "Archy and Mehitabel" (ML/OL-4963), with music and lyrics by George Kleinsinger, who also conducted, and Joe Darion, with Carol Channing providing the voice of Mehitabel, Eddie Bracken as Archy and David Wayne as the narrator. Mel Brooks and Darion wrote a play based on the LP and as *Shinbone Alley* it opened on Broadway in the spring of 1957 with Bracken repeating the role of Archy, Eartha Kitt as Mehitabel and Erik Rhodes as bombastic theatrical producer Tyrone T. Tattersall. The supporting cast included George S. Irving and Ross Martin. Tom Poston and Chita Rivera were the standbys for the lead players. The production lasted for only 49 performances. Bracken was Archie for the third time in the May 16, 1960, *Play of the Week* TV telecast "Archy and Mehitabel." This version was based on Marquis' book *The Life and Times of Archy and Mehitabel* and in it Tammy Grimes was Mehitabel and Jules Munshin was Tattersall. Bracken, Kitt and Grimes appeared on the 1960 record album "Shinbone Alley" (Sound of Broadway 300/1), with music from both the 1957 Broadway show and the 1960 TV production. Channing and Bracken were back as the voices of Archy and Mehitabel in the animated screen version *Shinbone Alley*, produced by Fine Arts Film in 1969 but not issued theatrically by Allied Artists until the spring of 1971.

After he commits suicide, depressed poet Archy (Bracken) is reincarnated as a cockroach and has to live among the denizens of shabby Shinbone Alley. He decides to become the greatest cockroach poet of the ages and jumps on the keys of his old typewriter at the newspaper where he once worked but soon comes to realize he is only a humble insect. He falls in love with exotic dancer Mehitabel (Channing) but is soon out of her life when an old boyfriend, gangster cat Big Bill (Alan Reed), returns to town with two pals. Archy tries to convince Mehitabel to get a job as a housecat but she says she loves Bill. When the cockroach objects, Bill flicks him away. Archy buries his disappointment by writing about philosophy, politics, ethics, nature studies and adventures in song. When Bill rejects Mehitabel again, Archy goes to see her at her home in a trash can. When he preaches to her about her morals, the cat becomes angry and Archy decides to try and commit suicide again but fails. Mehitabel takes up with theatrical impresario Tyrone T. Tattersall (John Carradine). After three days, Tattersall becomes frustrated in trying to make an actress of the no-talent cat, and the final straw comes when she bowdlerizes Shakespeare and they split after a bitter fight. Bill and Archy watch the fray. The tomcat later tells Mehitabel he liked her acting and she takes him back with her to Shinbone Alley. The angry Archy plunges into a work that is an indictment of mankind. He plans to organize all the insects of the world against humans until he finds out that Bill has again ditched Mehitabel after denying he is the father of her five kittens. During a storm, she is tempted to let her offspring drown but saves them at Archy's behest. With winter coming on, Mehitabel takes Archy's advice and becomes a high society housecat but quickly becomes bored with her new owners and always chasing after her mischievous kittens. When Archy comes to visit, Mehitabel says he cannot stay because people hate cockroaches. He gets drunk and dreams of pretty ladybugs of the evening who steal his love poems about Mehitabel. When he comes to, he challenges Bill to a fight. Archy then admits he ruined Mehitabel, and Bill realizes the cockroach loves the cat. As he wanders through a snowstorm, Archy hears Mehitabel singing and he follows her to Shinbone Alley where he says he loves her for what she is, his best friend. Archy then sees his bylined story in the newspaper.

Shinbone Alley is an overlong and not particularly entertaining animated fantasy that is too mature for children and too juvenile for adults. In *The Family Guide to Movies on Video* (1988), Henry Herx and Tony Zaza called it "[disappointing] ... [T]he result simply lacks the elemental zest and witty irony of the Marquis original." In *Theatre: Stage to Screen to Television* (1981), William Torbert Leonard noted, "The cartoon feature had little of the Disney studio's expertise and, being poorly distributed, passed quickly into oblivion." *Leonard Maltin's 2004 Movie and Video Guide* (2003) declared, "Genuinely odd.... Episodic, to say the least, with some witty and tuneful moments, and great vocal performances by Bracken and Channing. Not really for kids."

John Stanley's Creature Features Movie Guide Strikes Again (1994) thought it was a "[d]elightful cartoon.... Quaint and entertaining."

The film version of *Shinbone Alley* contained more than a dozen songs, the highlight being Carradine and Channing's rousing rendition of "Ah, the Theatre, the Theatre." Carradine and Alan Reed add zest to the proceedings as the voices of the ham actor and hoodlum tomcat Big Bill.

Shock Corridor (1963; 100 minutes)

Producer-Director-Screenplay: Samuel Fuller. Executive Producer: Leon Fromkess and Sam Firks. Photography: Stanley Cortez and (uncredited) Samuel Fuller. Editor: Jerome Thoms. Music: Paul Dunlap. Music Supervisor–Sound Effects Supervisor: Gordon Zahler. Art Director: Eugene Lourie. Sets: Charles Thompson. Costumes: Einar H. Bourman. Makeup: Dan Greenway. Production Manager: Rudolph Flothow. Special Effects: Charles Duncan and Linwood G. Dunn. Choreographer: Jon Gregory. Assistant Director: Floyd Joyer.

CAST: Peter Breck (Johnny Barrett), Constance Towers (Cathy), Gene Evans (Dr. Boden), James Best ("Jeb" Stuart), Hari Rhodes (Trent), Larry Tucker (Pagliacci), Paul Dubov (Dr. J.L. Menkin), Chuck Roberson (Wilkes), Neyle Morrow (Psycho), John Matthews (Dr. L.G. Cristo), Bill Zuckert ("Swanee" Swanson), John Craig (Lloyd), Philip Ahn (Dr. Fong), Frank Gerstle (Police Lieutenant Kane), Rachel Roman (Singing Nympho), Linda Randolph (Therapy Dance Teacher), Wally Campo (Inmate with Hand Over Right Eye), Marie Devereux, Barbara Perry, Marlene Manners, Lucille Curtis, Jeanette Dana, Karen Conrad, Allison Daniell, Ray Baxter, Linda Barrett, Harry Fleer (Inmates), Chuck Hicks (Attendant).

Filmed as *Straitjacket* and given the pre-release title *Long Corridor*, *Shock Corridor* was released in the fall of 1963. The black-and-white feature contained color hallucination sequences that were interpolated into the plot by producer-director-writer Samuel Fuller, who filmed them for his previous projects *House of Bamboo* (1955) and the uncompleted *Tigrero*, lensed in the Matto Grosso area of Brazil. Made in ten days without exteriors, *Shock Corridor* was considered somewhat controversial and it was denied a release in the United Kingdom, where it did not debut until 1990. The film is a psychological horror affair that provides a chilling look at the terrors of a mental hospital ward, its denizens and the mental deterioration it causes the movie's chief protagonist.

Overlong and talky, it is held together by Peter Breck's performance as the grasping newsman who loses his sanity over greed for a Pulitzer Prize. Sexy Constance Towers is just as memorable as his caring, but long-suffering, stripper girlfriend. Gene Evans, James Best and Hari Rhodes are quite good as the mental patient witnesses to a murder who are mostly delusional with short periods of lucidity. Chuck Roberson is impressive as the hospital's seemingly humane but firm attendant.

Wanting to win a Pulitzer Prize, news reporter Johnny Barrett (Breck) devises a plan with his *Daily Globe* managing editor, "Swanee" Swanson (Bill Zuckert), to solve the murder of Sloane, an inmate at the State Mental Hospital. He tries to enlist the aid of his exotic dancer lover Cathy (Towers) in a scheme that will place him in the facility so he can talk to the three men who witnessed the crime. (Johnny wants her to pretend to be his sister and file a complaint stating he has incestuous desires toward her.) A reluctant Cathy goes to the police, and Lieutenant Kane (Frank Gerstle) has Johnny arrested as she files a formal complaint saying he is insane. Johnny is questioned by Dr. Menkin (Paul Dubov), whom he attacks; this pretense of violence lands him in the mental facility where he is met by attendants Wilkes (Roberson) and surly Lloyd (John Craig). He becomes acquainted with inmate Pagliacci (Larry Tucker), a rotund opera fancier who murdered his wife, and he ingratiates himself with one of the murder witnesses, Stuart (Best), who believes he is Civil War general Jeb Stuart. Johnny meets with psychiatrist Dr. Cristo (John Matthews), who asks him if he hears voices, and he is later given hydrotherapy. Johnny is brutally attacked by a group of nymphomaniacs before being rescued by the attendants. When he again talks to Stuart, the young man recalls being in Korea and going over to the Communist side but eventually changing his mind; after being part of a prisoner exchange, he was given a dishonorable discharge. After saying he was rejected by his family and friends in Arkansas, he tells Johnny he did not see the face of the killer but he did see his white hands. On visiting day, Johnny informs Cathy of Stuart's story. She goes to Swanson and tells him to get Johnny out of the hospital because the experience is making him sick. Johnny meets the second crime witness, Trent (Rhodes), a black man who suffered a mental collapse from the hostility he met as the first person of his race to enroll in a Southern college. He now is a flaming racist who leads the other inmates in trying to kill another black man; as a result of the melee, he and Johnny end up in straightjackets. During moments of sanity, Trent informs Johnny that the killer was an attendant but he will not reveal the name. The next visiting day, Johnny tells Cathy he is getting close to learning the killer's identity but when she kisses him he becomes upset, thinking she is his sister. Johnny is given shock treatments and now has trouble talking. He becomes acquainted with the third crime witness, Dr. Boden (Evans), a renowned physicist who went insane working on nuclear fission. With the mind of a six year old he draws a picture of Johnny. Boden is eventually reveals that the killer was Wilkens, whom Sloane had accused of taking sexual advantage of female patients. Johnny attacks Boden over the drawing and later tells Cristo he knows who killed Sloane, but he keeps getting the identity mixed up with others. After he hallucinates about being caught in a torrent of rain in the hospital corridor and being struck by lightning, Johnny recalls the name of the killer. When Cristo refuses to believe him, Johnny goes to the hydrotherapy unit to confront Wilkes. The two men have a violent fight with Johnny forcing the attendant to admit his guilt. Johnny then informs Cristo he is a plant and asks permission to call Swanson so he can write his story. Months later, after Johnny wins the Pulitzer Prize, Cathy talks with Cristo, who informs her the man she loves is not a catatonic schizophrenic. When she embraces Johnny he does not respond.

 A.H. Weiler wrote in the *New York Times* that the movie "certainly succeeds in shocking, if not particularly convincing.... Mr. Fuller's melodrama does describe — without probably too deeply into complex psyches — schizophrenia, dementia praecox, nymphomania and other aspects of alternating worlds of fantasy and reality in which the patients live.... [The film is] vividly shocking, if not a scientist's dream." *Variety* felt that "the film is dominated by sex and shock superficialities.... The dialog is unreal and pretentious, and the direction is heavyhanded, often mistaking sordidness for realism. The performers labor valiantly, but in vain." Danny Peary opined in *Guide for the Film Fanatic* (1986), "More than any other film, Sam Fuller's cult favorite treads a fine line between art and trash. The dialogue is stilted, yet every few minutes one of the characters says something more honest and brave and moving than we are used to in American cinema. The film thrives on sensationalism; all the sexual content seems solely intended to make the picture lurid. Beneath the sleaze is a mature, sad-eyed view of America, where people are encouraged to strive beyond their capacities for accomplishment and to do their country proud even if they can't accept responsibility or fame.... Shadowy cinematography by Stanley Cortez, who photographed midgets at the end of the corridor set so that it would appear to be longer than it was."

Fuller's *Shock Corridor* screenplay was novelized by Michael Avallone and published by Belmont Books in 1963 to coincide with the film's release. It was reissued by Texas Bookman in 1990, the same year it was first published in Great Britain (along with the film's first issuance there) by Xanadu Books as part of its "Blue Murder" series.

The Sorcerers (1967; 87 minutes; Color)

Producers: Tony Tenser and Patrick Curtis. Executive Producer: Arnold L. Miller. Director: Michael Reeves. Screenplay: Michael Reeves and Tom Baker, from the novel by John Burke. Photography: Stanley A. Long. Editors: Susan Michie and David Woodward. Music: Paul Ferris. Songs Sung by Toni Daily with Lee Grant and the Capitols. Art Director: Tony Curtis. Makeup: Geoff Rodway. Continuity: Doreen Soan. Assistant Director: Keith Wilkinson.

Lobby card for *The Sorcerers* (1967)

CAST: Boris Karloff (Professor Marcus Monserrat), Ian Ogilvy (Mike Roscoe), Elizabeth Ercy (Nicole), Victor Henry (Alan), Dani Sheridan (Laura Ladd), Catherine Lacey (Estelle Monserrat), Susan George (Audrey Woods), Alf Joint (Ron), Meier Teenier (Snack Bar Owner), Gerald Campion (China Shop Customer), Ivor Dean (Inspector Matalon), Peter Fraser (Detective), Martin Terry (Tobacco Shop Owner), Bill Barnsley (Fur Store Constable), Maureen Booth (Disco Girl), Arnold L. Miller (Taxi Driver), Toni Daly (Singing Voice of Laura Ladd).

Director Michael Reeves (1944–1969) completed a trio of horror movies before his death from a drug overdose but he displayed such promise he has become a cult figure to genre fans. At age 20 he was hired to be assistant director on *Il Castello dei Morti Vivi* (Castle of the Living Dead) (1964) and ended up shooting some footage used in its final release. As a result he helmed the Italian-Yugoslav production *La Sorella di Santana* (The Sister of Satan) (1965), released in the U.S. as *She Beast* and in Great Britain as *Revenge of the Blood Beast*. This low-budget but well received outing starred Barbara Steele, with Ian Ogilvy in the supporting cast. Due to its success, Reeves was assigned to direct *The Sorcerers*, headlining Boris Karloff with Ogilvy co-starred. Tony Tenser co-produced *The Sorcerers* and his Tigon Productions next hired Reeves to do *Witchfinder General* (1968), released in the U.S. by American International Pictures as *Conqueror Worm*; it starred Vincent Price and Ogilvy. This well-made 17th century witch hunt drama proved to be Reeves' final cinema outing.

The Sorcerers was filmed on location in London and at West London Studios, giving the production a gritty look, especially in its street and disco scenes. The latter feature the Paul Ferris songs "Sweet Nothin'" and "Your Love," sung by Toni Daly with accompaniment by Lee Grant and the Capitols. Daly dubbed the singing voice of Dani Sheridan, who portrays a tragic disco slut singer. Top-billed Boris Karloff, who appears rather feeble, was the film's box office bait and he played the role of a practitioner of medical hypnosis in fine fashion but it is Catherine Lacey who takes the acting honors as his wife, a woman who descends into madness as her powers to control a young subject increase. Ogilvy nicely handles the part of the guinea pig, with good support from beautiful Elizabeth Ercy as his French girlfriend and Victor Henry as his pal. A young, brunette Susan George has a small but memorable role as one of the victims of a mental telepathy experiment that goes badly awry.

Professor Marcus Monserrat (Karloff) has spent most of his adult life trying to perfect a machine that will transfer thoughts, assisted by his loyal wife Estelle (Lacey). Barely making a living from his practice of medical hypnosis, Monserrat finally perfects his invention and sets out to find a young person to be the first experimental subject. At a disco, Mike Roscoe (Ogilvy) becomes bored with his girlfriend Nicole (Ercy) and leaves her to his friend, mechanic Alan (Henry), and ends up in a diner where he meets Monserrat, who offers him ultimate excitement. Going with the inventor to his small flat, Mike is placed in a chair with electrodes attached to his head. As Monserrat operates his invention, the young man experiences mind alteration and comes under control of the old couple who can rule him telepathically. Telling Mike he will remember nothing of their encounter, the Monserrats send him away to see if they can control him at a distance. Going back to the disco, Mike picks up Nicole and the two sneak into a hotel where they enjoy its swimming pool with Monserrat and Estelle experiencing the same physical sensations as the young couple. Finding the activity tiring, the scientist and his wife relax their concentration. Monserrat tells his wife he wants to get financing for the invention and put it to good use. Estelle complains that after thirty years of poverty due to medical science scoffing at his ideas, the two of them deserve to use the young man to bring themselves pleasures they have missed. The next day Estelle sees a coat at a fur store and her husband agrees to help her use Mike to get it. That night Mike is telepathically told by the Monserrats to get the coat. During the robbery he is almost caught by a constable (Bill Barnsley) and in escaping he cuts his hand. Both Monserrat and Estelle now have identical cuts on their hands as she tells him she enjoyed the danger and they now can do things without fear of the consequences. Nicole calls Alan and asks him to take her out; they go to the disco. Later that night Mike shows up at Nicole's flat and tells her he cannot remember what he did that evening and they end up in bed. Estelle wants to experience speed so she and Monserrat command Mike to steal Alan's motorcycle and take Nicole on a wild ride in the country. When they return, Alan reprimands Mike for taking his bike and scaring Nicole. Upon Estelle's command, Mike beats up Alan and hits his boss (Alf Joint) with a tire iron. Although Estelle is jubilant over the fight, her husband says he will no longer help her. She announces that her will is stronger than his. When Monserrat threatens to bring Mike back to his senses, Estelle knocks him down and destroys the mind machine so he cannot carry out his threat. Nicole tells Alan she wants nothing more to do with Mike, who goes to see an old girlfriend, Audrey (Susan George). Estelle makes Mike stab Audrey to death with a pair of scissors. Monserrat tells the crazed Estelle he will stop her but she laughs at him. Nicole and Alan spot Mike at the disco where he picks up singer Laura Ladd (Sheridan) and takes her away. She follows him to an alley where he strangles her upon Estelle's command. The next day Alan shows Nicole newspaper stories about the two murdered young women. Since they saw Mike with the singer, Alan wants to call the police but Nicole insists they go to his flat, which they find empty. At his business, a china shop called the Glory Hole, Mike refuses to talk to them. When Alan accuses him of the murders, Estelle orders Mike to kill him. The two fight as Nicole goes for the police. A taxi driver (Arnold L. Miller) recalls seeing the murdered singer with a young man and goes to the police, who after visiting Mike's flat are on the way to his shop. As Inspector Matalon (Ivor Dean) and his men approach the china shop, Mike stabs Alan in the arm and steals a car. Alan joins Nicole in the police car and they chase Mike as Monserrat and Estelle vie to mentally control him. After a lengthy car chase, Monserrat gets the upper hand and causes Mike to crash the car, which explodes and catches fire. Monserrat and Estelle's bodies are charred as they die with him.

Variety called *The Sorcerers* "[a] straightforward thriller slanted to 'horror' addicts.... Eastman Color lensing by Stanley Logan makes good use of several London locations.... Karloff handles his role with noble professionalism...." When Allied Artists issued the movie in the U.S. in November 1967 it had running times of between 82 and 87 minutes while its British releases ran between 79 and 85 minutes. When it was issued in the latter country in May 1967 by LMG, it was given an X Certificate and *Kinematograph Weekly* commented, "The plot is quite ingenious and obviously well suited to the particular talents of Boris Karloff, but the really exciting part of the acceptably incredible story takes a long time working up." David Pirie wrote in *A Heritage of Horror: The English Gothic Cinema 1946–1972* (1974), "In some ways *The Sorcerers* is the ultimate portrayal of the tabloid society and it is only a pity the young people in it, including Mike and his girlfriend, are not strong enough to provide much more than a token presence against the old couple. For this and other reasons, the film certainly stops short of being a masterpiece. However, Reeves succeeded marvelously well in communicating the essential components of this theme and the result is constructed like a series of Chinese boxes, which open into one another."

When Allied Artists released *The Sorcerers* on video in the late 1970s, all the violence was cut out.

Spook Chasers (1957; 62 minutes)

Producer: Ben Schwalb. Director: George Blair. Screenplay: Elwood Ullman. Photography: Harry Neumann. Editor: Neil Brunnenkant. Music: Marlin Skiles. Art Director: David Milton. Sound: Ralph Butler and Charles Schelling. Sets: Robert J. Mills. Production Manager: Allen K. Wood. Wardrobe: Bert Henrikson. Special Effects: Augie Lohman. Makeup: Emile LaVigne. Continuity: Richard Michaels. Assistant Director: Austen Jewell.

CAST: Huntz Hall (Horace Debussy "Sach" Jones), Stanley Clements (Stanislaus "Duke" Coveleskie), Darlene Fields (Dolly Owens), David Gorcey (Chuck), Jimmy Murphy (Myron), Eddie LeRoy (Blinky), Percy Helton (Mike Clancy), Peter Mamakos (Snap Sizzolo), Ben Welden (Ziggie), Robert Shayne (Lieutenant Harris), Bill Henry (Harry Shelby), Pierre Watkin (Dr. Moss), Robert Christopher (Ernie), Bill Cassidy (Photographer), Anne Fleming, Audrey Conti (Beautiful Escorts).

The Bowery Boys' final escapade with the supernatural, *Spook Chasers* was issued in June 1957. The fourth from the last film in the series, it is a fast-paced, cheap-looking affair that uses a bevy of retread spook bits, some of them dating from the silent days. Although passable for its ilk, it sorely needed Bela Lugosi and Bernard Gorcey, both of whom had gone to their rewards by the time the film was made. An amusing plot ploy had the chief gangster, Snap Sizzolo (Peter Mamakos), giving orders to his underlings by constantly snapping his fingers. Regarding its early summer playdates, *Variety* noted it "might have done well at the box office if released later in the year, say October."

The owner of Clancy's Café in the Bowery, Mike Clancy (Percy Helton), is on the verge of a nervous breakdown, due to overwork and having to deal with local freeloaders Sach (Huntz Hall), Duke (Stanley Clements), Chuck (David Gorcey), Myron (Jimmy Murphy) and nearsighted Blinky (Eddie LeRoy). Mike's physician, Dr. Moss (Pierre Watkin), pays him a visit and orders rest and lots of fresh air. Two of his customers, slick realtor Harry Shelby (Bill Henry) and his beautiful secretary-girlfriend Dolly (Darlene Fields), overhear the conversation and offer to sell Mike a palatial place in the country called Cedarcrest, near the village of Thornton. They convince him to make a down payment on the house but they do not tell him it last belonged to murdered gangster Wee Willie Dolan, whose ghost is supposed to haunt the place. Arriving at the abode with the boys in their old jalopy, Mike finds his purchase to be falling apart. While his cohorts offer to help him fix it up, he phones Shelby demanding his money back only to be informed by Dolly that he is in Florida. The boys set out to repair the house and its contents; Sach tries to fix a faucet and crosses some electric wires, causing considerable damage. Duke takes after him and Sach falls on a tea wagon that runs into a wall, dislodging a sack of paper money. Duke convinces Mike to use some of the money to pay off the house so they will be free to search it. The boys go to Shelby's office with the money and he pretends to have just returned from Florida. He accepts the payment, saying he will send Mike the deed to the property. Shelby is visited by gangster Snap Sizzolo (Mamakos) and his thugs, Ziggie (Ben Welden) and Ernie (Robert Christopher). When Snap sees the cash Mike gave Shelby, he thinks it may be part of the robbery loot Dolan hid in the house and he orders the realtor to buy the place back. When Mike declines Shelby's offer, he is told the house may contain ghosts and to watch out for his health. This causes Duke to suspect that the realtor may know about the money they found. Shelby tells Dolly to use her charms on Sach to find out what he knows regarding the loot. She invites Sach to her apartment, gets him drunk on champagne and feigns an interest in him, and he admits finding the money. Mike and the boys arrive back at Cedarcrest during a thunderstorm and find there is no electricity. They pair up in three different rooms for the night. Chuck and Myron are tied up by two ghosts while Blinky's bed disappears with him in it, causing a frightened Sach to seek out Duke and Mike. They see what they think is Blinky in the bed but it is one of the ghosts, with a hairy arm, that later causes Sach to go running out of the room. Snap and his thugs show up looking for the money. Sach runs into a revolving wall, which has bags of money on its other side. Blinky finds Sach and they return to their room and see one of the beds occupied. They hit the sleeper, who turns out to be Duke. Duke goes back in his own room with Mike and the two see a gloved hand with a trumpet and a skull. Mike runs into Sach's room and is chased by a ghost who then goes after Sach but is knocked out by Blinky. Sach runs back into the living room's revolving wall, knocks down more money and is heard by the gangsters. The hoodlums try to get the money from Sach and in the struggle Snap's gun fires, bringing Duke, Mike and Blinky. A melee ensues with the boys battling the thugs. The two ghosts show up and hold off both sides at gunpoint. Police Lieutenant Harris (Robert Shayne) and his men, who had been trailing Snap, arrive and arrest the gangsters and unmask the ghosts, who turn out to be Shelby and Dolly.

Spy in the Sky! (1958; 75 minutes)

Producer-Director: W. Lee Wilder. Screenplay: Myles Wilder, from the novel *Counterspy Express* by A.S. Fleischman. Photography: Jimmy Harvey. Editors: Lien d'Oliveyra and Loet Roozekrans. Music: Hugo de Groot, performed by The Netherlands Philharmonic Orchestra. Art Director: Nico Van Baarle. Sound: Wim Huender. Production Supervisor: Bobby Rosenbloom. Costumes: Max Heymans. Makeup: Fa. Michels. Assistant Directors: Piet Van Mook and Joseph Van Weeren.

CAST: Steve Brodie (Vic Cabot), Andrea Domburg (Alexandrine Duvivier), George Coulouris (Colonel Benedict), Sandra Francis (Eva Brandisi), Herbert Curiel (Pepi Vidor), Bob De Lange (Sidney Jardine), Hans Tiemeyer (Dr. Fritz Keller), W.R. Melchers (Ridolfo), Leon Dorian (Max Maxwell), Harold Holsten (Pawn Shop Clerk), Antonie Zoet (Jeorgi), Monica Witkowna (Gypsy Singer), E.F. Beavis, Alex Zweers, Robert H. MacDowell (Radio Newscasters), Dity Oorthuis (Fritzi), Albert E. Gollin (Consul Representative Martin), Roland Wagter, Jr. (Soldier), R. Borello (Milkman), H.J. Hagemeyer (Policeman), Johann Schmitz (Headwaiter), J.K. Krees (Croupier).

The Soviet Union launched the first satellite, *Sputnik*, on October 4, 1957. Not only did it spur a U.S. initiative to duplicate the feat, it also was the beginning of Hollywood movies dealing with the space race. Allied Artists had *War of the Satellites* (q.v.) in theaters in May 1958, and followed it two months later with *Spy in the Sky!*, made by W. Lee Wilder Productions and Domino Pictures Corporation. Filmed at Cinestone Studios in Amsterdam, it was scripted by Wilder's son Myles from the 1954 novel *Counterspy Express* by A.S. Fleischman. *Spy in the Sky!* contains only a tinge of sci-fi in its storyline of a satellite sending coded information to the Soviets, a portent of the near future. The film's trailer, however, declared it dealt with a Secret code "that could start a space war" and its poster highlighted "Secret Agents of the Satellite Era!" Basically the film is an anemic spy thriller with a decided tacky look. Location shooting in The Netherlands gives it some visual interest, although most of its scenes are either interiors or at night. The Wilders previously did *Fright* (1956) [q.v.] for Allied and would go on to make the bigger budgeted *Bluebeard's Ten Honeymoons* (1959) [q.v.] for the company.

Nations around the world are made aware that the Soviet satellite *Sputnik* is sending coded signals. Dr. Fritz Keller (Hans Tiemeyer), a German scientist captured by the Russians and made to work on their space program, escapes, disguised as farmer Hans Krauss. He carries with him the secret code used to decipher the satellite's signals. Arriving in Vienna, Keller pawns a guitar and its case and sends the ticket to the American consulate. He is rec-

Spanish lobby card for *Spy in the Sky!* (1958) picturing Herbert Curiel and Hans Tiemeyer

ognized by gambler Pepi Vidor (Herbert Curiel) who pulls a gun on the scientist and kidnaps him, planning to use Keller for ransom. Vic Cabot (Steve Brodie), an American agent, arrives in Vienna and at the airport he is approached by a mysterious woman who wants him to take a package through customs for her; he refuses. That night Vic meets another agent, Max Maxwell (Leon Dorian), in an alley and is told he is to locate Keller. Max suggests that Vic meet Pepi, who has been trying to date his girlfriend, singer Eve Brandisi (Sandra Francis). As they are talking, a car drives by and Max is shot and killed. Vic goes to Club Caprice, where Eve sings, and is told it is her night off, but he meets the owner, Colonel Benedict (George Coulouris), who wears a neck brace. As they converse, the woman Vic saw at the airport arrives but leaves quickly. Benedict tells Vic that Eve lives at the Park Apartments and he goes there and reveals Max's murder to her. When Vic spots Benedict and his henchman Jeorgi (Antonie Zoet), he and Eve leave by the back entrance and he takes her to his hotel. She tells Vic that Pepi can usually be found gambling at a casino in the town of Belton and they agree to go there the next day. While Eve sleeps the next morning, Vic goes out and is met by Sidney Jardine (Bob De Lange), who claims Max worked for him and that he will give him Keller if the money is right. Vic declines the offer and runs into Benedict, who later informs Jardine that he is treading on dangerous ground. Back at the hotel, Vic finds Eve is gone so he goes to the U.S. consulate where government man Martin (Albert E. Gollin) gives him the pawn ticket. Vic tries to redeem the item, an old guitar and its case, but finds it has been sold to a man with a neck brace. He returns to Club Caprice, searches Benedict's office and finds the instrument but is nearly caught by the arrival of the mysterious woman. Back at his hotel, Vic has the guitar sent to the consulate and returns to his room and finds Eve. At his remote farmhouse, Pepi tells his girlfriend Fritzi (Dity Oorthuis) he plans to make Keller talk. The scientist is kept in the attic and has not eaten for six days. When Pepi cannot break the old man's silence, he beats him. Fritzi screams at him to leave Keller alone. Not finding Pepi at the casino, Vic and Eve return to the hotel. The gambler sees them, telephones Vic and sets up a meeting to trade for the scientist. Benedict overhears Pepi's conversation with the American. As Vic and Eve drive to meet with Pepi, Vic stops at a service station and calls Benedict, finding out he is not at the club. Driving on, they are stopped by a motorcycle cop (H.J. Hagemeyer) and then by a drawbridge before finding Pepi, who has been murdered in his car. Soon Vic and Eve see Benedict in his vehicle along with Jeorgi and another henchman, Ridolfo (W.R. Melchers), who is fixing a flat tire. Leaving Eve in their car and telling her to go for the police, Vic sneaks up behind Ridolfo, slugs him and takes his place in the back seat of Benedict's car as Jeorgi drives on. Vic conceals his face with the lapel of his coat and finds he is sitting next to the mysterious woman. He keeps her quiet at gunpoint. When they stop to get directions to Casa Milano, the house where Keller is supposed to be held, she translates when talking to an Italian milkman (R. Borello). Upon arrival at the house, Vic walks up to it with the woman and Jeorgi, whom he knocks out. Once inside, the woman identifies herself as Duvivier (Andrea Domburg), a counterspy who pretends to be Benedict's confidant, but has been investigating him until assigned to find Keller. Vic fires his gun, causing Benedict to come to the house as he and Duvivier take the car and go to Pepi's abode to find Keller. Vic tells Fritzi about Pepi's murder but they are too late to rescue Keller, who has hanged himself. In the scientist's shoe Vic finds a scrap of paper containing the numbers 1344. Returning to Belton, Vic has Duvivier drop him off and he goes to his hotel where he locates Eve. They board a train for Vienna but Jardine shows up and Vic learns that he and Eve are in cahoots in trying to get the code. Taking Vic's gun, Jardine promises him a split in the profits but the agent manages to get the weapon and holds the conspirators for the police. Duvivier meets Vic at the train when it arrives in Vienna and as they drive away in Benedict's car he gets the drop on them. He makes Duvivier drive him to the club but once in his office Vic gets the best of him and he is arrested. Going to the American consulate, Vic works with Martin to decipher the code that Keller had hidden on one of the strings of his guitar. When the code is finally broken, Vic and Duvivier realize they are in love.

Regarding *Spy in the Sky!*, *Variety* complained, "[It] is the kind of story that will confirm European pessimism about the capabilities of American agents to best their Russian opposites. [Steve] Brodie is represented as a chuckle-headed bungler and incompetent…. The continuity is confusing and finally annoying." The British *Monthly Film Bulletin* concurred, "This story is full of complications which scarcely compensate for the lengths which the basically simple plot is stretched."

The Strangler (1964; 89 minutes)

Producers: Samuel Bischoff and David Diamond. Director: Burt Topper. Screenplay: Bill S. Ballinger. Photography: Jacques Marquette. Editor: Robert S. Eisen. Music: Marlin Skiles. Art Directors: Eugene Lourie and Hal Pereira. Sound: Hugo Grenzbach. Production Manager: Edward Morey, Jr. Sets: Sam Comer and James W. Payne. Makeup: Wally Westmore. Assistant Director: Clark Paylow.

CAST: Victor Buono (Leo Kroll), David McLean (Lieutenant Frank Benson), Diane Sayer (Barbara Wells), Davey Davison (Tally Raymond), Baynes Barron (Sergeant Mack Clyde), Ellen

Victor Buono, Diane Sayer and Davey Davison in *The Strangler* (1964)

Corby (Mrs. Kroll), Michael Ryan (Detective Mel Posner), Russ Bender (Dr. Clarence Sanford), Jeanne Bates (Clara Thomas), Wally Campo (Eggerton), Mimi Dillard (Thelma), Byron Morrow (Dr. Morton), John Yates (Intern), James Sikking (Sketch Artist), Robert Cranford (Jack Rosten), Selette Cole (Helen Lawson), Victor Masi (Carnival Attendant).

In his official screen debut as effete pianist Edwin Flag in *What Ever Happened to Baby Jane?* (1962), Victor Buono received an Academy Award nomination. The hefty actor's work in that horror melodrama launched his successful screen career and he followed it with his first starring role in *The Strangler*, released in the spring of 1964. It was based on then-current serial killings that traumatized the city of Boston, where the film debuted; the case was officially brought to the screen in *The Boston Strangler* (1968) starring Tony Curtis. Although a low-budget programmer from producer Samuel Bischoff, *The Strangler* was well directed by Burt Topper and dominated by Buono as the deceptive woman hater who takes out his mother domination frustrations by murdering comely young women. In homage to *Baby Jane*, a doll broken by the killer after he murders a nurse closely resembles the one featured in that movie. Davey Davison and Diane Sayer manage to corral some attention as two young carnival workers who become involved with the demented killer and Ellen Corby is good as his self-centered, bossy mother. Buono later portrayed another serial killer in the Italian macabre comedy *Il Strangolatore di Vienna* (The Strangler of Vienna) (1972), issued in the U.S. as *The Mad Butcher* in 1974.

As nurse Helen Lawson (Selette Cole) undresses, she is watched by Leo Kroll (Buono), a thirty-year-old, 300-pound hospital laboratory technician, who strangles her and leaves behind a small doll. Police Lieutenant Frank Benson (David McLean) and Sergeant Mack

Spanish lobby card for *The Strangler* (1964)

Clyde (Baynes Barron) arrive to investigate after the murder is reported by the victim's fiancé, Jack Rosten (Robert Cranford), who discovered the body. Since this is the eighth strangling in a row, the homicide division detectives question all the employees of the hospital where Helen worked, including Leo, who says he knows nothing of the crime. Leo's invalid mother (Ellen Corby), a patient at Park Sanatorium, calls to see if he is going to visit her but he says he is tired and instead goes to the Odeon Fun Palace where he plans to give an engagement ring to Tally Raymond (Davey Davison), who operates the carnival's toss-a-ring game where he wins the dolls he leaves with his victims. He drums up the courage to see Tally but she is with a relief girl, Barbara Wells (Diane Sayer), so he wins the game, gets a doll and leaves. Leo takes flowers to his mother but she berates him for not visiting her for two nights and tells him she nearly died of heart trouble the night before but she was saved by her nurse, Clara Thomas (Jeanne Bates). That night Leo goes to Clara's apartment and strangles her for saving his hated mother's life. Benson and Clyde investigate the homicide and question people at the sanatorium. Psychiatrist Dr. Sanford (Russ Bender) tells Benson the last killing did not match the pattern of the previous ones. Benson goes to Leo's house and asks him to come to police headquarters to answer some questions and there Leo demands a lie detector test. Eggerton (Wally Campo), who conducts the test, tells Benson that Leo shows no evidence of lying and he is released. Sanford theorizes that the killer is a schizophrenic who can lie around a test and has a deep hatred of women. At the sanatorium, Leo is told by an intern (John Yates) that his mother's heart condition is so delicate she has not been told of Clara's murder. Mrs. Kroll is upset because Leo has not seen her for another two nights and she accuses him of having a girlfriend and warns him against women, saying they will ruin his life. She tells him no girl would want him because he is fat, not rich nor good-looking, and that no one but her has ever liked him. When she says she misses Clara, Leo informs her the nurse has been murdered, and his mother has a heart attack. When Leo gets home he receives a telephone calling saying she has died and he celebrates by smashing her photographs. Clyde goes to the Fun Palace and questions Barbara. Leo sees them and, after the detective leaves, he asks her what the lawman wanted; she tells him he asked about dolls. When Barbara goes home that night, Leo watches her undress, breaks into her apartment and strangles her, leaving behind a doll she gave him. Benson learns of the killing and, when Clyde tells him he interviewed the latest victim, they agree to stake out the toss-a-ring booth. That night Leo goes back to the booth and presents Tally with the engagement ring. When he tells her he loves her and wants to get married, she rejects him. Leo becomes angry and agrees to Tally's request to leave, but he promises to see her again. Clyde arrives and talks to the young woman who tells him about Leo and the dolls he wins. She goes with him to police headquarters, giving a sketch artist (James Sikking) a description that turns out to be a likeness of Leo. Benson orders Clyde and Detective Posner (Michael Ryan) to arrest Leo but he is not home. Clyde finds a drawer full of dolls and informs his boss. Tally refuses to be a decoy to catch the killer and demands to go home so she can pack and leave town. Clyde goes with Tally to her apartment and plants a radio microphone. He and Benson remain outside the apartment building in hopes of catching Leo. As Tally packs, she covers up the microphone; hearing no sound the worried policemen run into the building. Leo comes out of a closet and begins strangling the young woman. The detectives break down the door and shoot Leo, who falls out of a six-story window onto the pavement below. He dies with a doll lying beside him.

Variety wrote, "Dramatically skillful direction by Burt Topper and a firm level of histrionic performances help *The Strangler* over some rough spots and keep the picture from succumbing to inconsistencies of character and contrivances of story scattered through the picture.... Bueno for Buono, a convincing menace all the way. There's always a place on the screen for a fat man who can act, and Buono has the avoirdupois field virtually to himself." *The Phantom's Ultimate Video Guide* (1989) said Buono "is quite impressive" and James O'Neill in *Terror on Tape* (1994) agreed: "Buono is ideally cast.... [T]his suffers from an abrupt ending ... but is worth seeing for Vic's intense acting in one of his few starring roles." *Time Out Film Guide, 9th Edition 2001* (2000) noted, "Victor Buono brought a certain class to this compelling tawdry exploiter...."

Target Earth (1954; 75 minutes)

Producer: Herman Cohen. Director-Editor: Sherman A. Rose. Screenplay: Bill [William] Raynor, Wyott Ordung and James H. Nicholson, from the story "Deadly City" by Ivor Jorgensen [Paul W. Fairman]. Photography: Guy Roe. Music: Paul Dunlap. Production Designer: James W. Sullivan. Sets: Morris Hoffman. Production Manager: Clarence Eurist. Sound: Earl Synder. Makeup: Stanley Orr. Special Effects: Dave Koehler. Special Optical Effects: Howard Anderson Company. Wardrobe: Robert Olivas. Assistant Director: Jack Murphy.

CAST: Richard Denning (Frank Brooks), Kathleen Crowley (Nora King), Virginia Grey (Vicki Harris), Richard Reeves (Jim Wilson), Robert Roark (Davis), Mort Marshall (Charles Otis), Arthur Space (Lieutenant General Wood), Whit Bissell (Scientist Tom), Jim Drake (Lieutenant), Steve Pendleton (Colonel), House Peters, Jr. (Technician), Herman Cohen (Lab Technician Barton), Jeffrey Sayre (Army Staff Officer), Steve Calvert (Robot).

Target Earth was filmed in the summer of 1954 at Kling Studios by Abtcon Pictures in collaboration with Allied Artists, which released it in November of that year. It was based on the story "Deadly City" by Paul W. Fairman, writing under the pseudonym Ivor Jorgensen, published in the March 1953 issue of *If: Worlds of Science Fiction*. The hero of the film, in theorizing that the invading aliens came from Venus, admits to being a reader of science fiction magazines. For the most part, *Target Earth* is a pretty entertaining sci-fi production whose use of sound waves to thwart alien invaders predates *Earth vs. the Flying Saucers* (1956) by two years. Its chief deficits are an obviously low budget, lots of military stock footage and an "army" of invaders made up of exactly one robot who looks like a walking pile of tin cans. James H. Nicholson, who would soon form American Releasing Corporation, which evolved into American International Pictures, worked on the script, as did Wyott Ordung, who the same year directed producer Roger Corman's first genre outing, *Monster from the Ocean Floor* (1954).

Poster for *Target Earth* (1953)

Waking up after trying to commit suicide with sleeping pills, Nora King (Kathleen Crowley) fails to find anyone in her apartment house. She walks outside and goes for many blocks until she comes upon the body of a dead woman and is frightened when a man (Richard Denning) walks up behind her. She runs from him and he pursues her, eventually cornering her in a dead end alley. The man slaps Nora to calm her down and tells her he is not going to harm her. He says his name is Frank

Brooks and that he woke up at noon after having been mugged and robbed the night before. The two cannot figure why a city of 500,000 people is deserted but Frank suggests some type of evacuation has taken place. After hearing music, they go to a restaurant where they meet Jim Wilson (Richard Reeves) and his long-time girlfriend Vicki Harris (Virginia Grey), who are enjoying free food and drink. They tell Frank and Nora they missed the evacuation because they were celebrating Jim's winning the daily double. After having dinner, the quartet leave the restaurant and find a car with a dead man inside. When Frank and Jim try to start the vehicle, they find it is disabled. A stranger, Charles Otis (Mort Marshall), appears and says that all the cars he has seen will not run and that he came from an area where houses and stores were wrecked and dozens of people killed. After they see a giant shadow, Frank suggests they take refuge in Hotel Bateman, where they find a newspaper detailing the evacuation caused by unidentified invaders. Afraid to stay at the hotel, Charles runs into the street and is confronted by a large robot that kills him with a ray emanating from its head. At a military command center, Lieutenant General Wood (Arthur Space) is informed that the 387th Airborne Division has been wiped out by the invaders, whom he speculates may be from Venus. He says the robots in the city are probably a vanguard for a much larger invasion force and orders two dozen bombers to attack the enemy but they too are destroyed. The four people in the hotel witness the massacre. Nora tells Frank about her suicide attempt and how six months before her husband Jerry was killed in an automobile accident. At the time of the wreck she was driving and they were arguing. She also says she now wants to live and they realize they are attracted to each other. As Wood orders atomic weapons and missiles prepared to destroy the city, he learns that an inactive robot has been located and taken to a laboratory for study. Tom (Whit Bissell), the head scientist, tells Wood the robot is made of surgical steel and guided by electro-magnetic impulses and it is apparently invincible. That night, Nora is awakened by someone trying to break into her bedroom. It turns out to be gun-toting Davis (Robert Roark), who holds them all hostage for the rest of the night. The next morning he tells Nora he wants her to go with him in an escape route through the city sewers. She slaps him when he kisses her. He takes Frank, Nora, Jim and Vicki to the hotel lobby where Vicki recognizes him as the killer of a woman on Skid Row. He admits to the crime as well as killing a guard during the evacuation and tells the group he plans to use them as decoys so he can escape the robots. When Vicki tells him he does not have the courage to pull the trigger, he shoots her and wounds Frank. Jim fights with Davis and strangles him just as a robot breaks into the hotel. The three survivors run for the roof, followed by the mechanical invader. When Jim tries to climb a ladder, he is killed by the robot's ray. It takes aim at Frank and Nora but collapses when a military convoy arrives with a high-frequency sound transmitter. Joining the military men, Frank and Nora are informed that the robot's cathode ray tubes were destroyed by the high-pitched sound. Our planet will be safe from the alien invaders.

Donald C. Willis in *Horror and Science Fiction Films: A Checklist* (1972) called *Target Earth* "[m]ediocre at best" and Phil Hardy reported in *Science Fiction* (1984), "The robots are disappointing, poorly designed and lumbering, but the initial scenes of the characters alone in the deserted city are surprisingly compelling." C.J. Henderson opined in *The Encyclopedia of Science Fiction Movies* (2001), "*Target Earth* is an unfortunate movie. It opens impressively enough for a black-and-white '50s sci-fi film. The credits and music are strong, and the plot has a nicely moody kickoff. The story starts off wonderfully dark and cynical, striking the right mood for a perfect sci-fi/noir motion picture, but after about 20 minutes, the film falls apart. The dialogue grows more and more inept. The story loses all its drive, wandering in circles to kill time." *The Phantom of the Movies' Videoscope* (2000) declared, "[A] mixed bag, it boasts its share of low-budget pluses.... [Producer Herman] Cohen and crew make their obvious lack of funds work to their atmospheric advantage, creating a mood of overwhelming gloom and doom by plunging us into a big city stripped of its noise, clutter, and very pulse." In *Keep Watching the Skies! The 21st Century Edition* (2009), Bill Warren termed it "a tidy, efficient film that overcomes its budget and the awkwardly designed robots."

Top-billed Richard Denning was one of the quintessential monster fighters of the 1950s. After starring in *Unknown Island* in 1948 he headlined *Creature from the Black Lagoon* (1954), *Creature with the Atom Brain* (1955), *Day the World Ended* (1956) and *The Black Scorpion* (1957). He was married to 1940s horror favorite Evelyn Ankers.

Tormented (1960; 75 minutes)

Producers: Bert I. Gordon and Joe Steinberg. Director-Story: Bert I. Gordon. Screenplay: George Worthing Yates. Photography: Ernest Laszlo. Editor: John Bushelman. Music: Albert Glasser. Additional Jazz Sequences: Calvin Jackson. Song: Lewis Melzer and Albert Glasser; sung by Margie Rayburn. Art Director: Gabriel Scognamillo. Sound: John Kean. Sets: Gene Redd. Makeup: Bill Cooley. Wardrobe: Marge Corso. Special Effects: Herman Townsley. Special Visual Effects: Bert I. Gordon and Flora M. Gordon. Assistant Directors: Joe Boyle and Bill Forsyth.

CAST: Richard Carlson (Tom Stewart), Susan Gordon (Sandy Hubbard), Lugene Sanders (Meg Hubbard), Judi Reding (Vi Mason), Joe Turkel (Nick Lewis), Lillian Adams (Mrs. Ellis), Gene Roth (Mr. Nelson), Vera Marsh (Mrs. Hubbard), Harry Fleer (Frank Hubbard), Merritt Stone (Minister), George Stanley (Photographer), Dick Walsh (Doctor), Leslie Thomas (Guest).

After six years of making films dealing mainly with giant insects and monsters, producer-director Bert I. Gordon turned to a ghost story with *Tormented*, scripted by George Worthing Yates, who also wrote *Earth vs the Spider, Attack of the Puppet People* and *War of the Colossal Beast* (all 1958) for him. In addition, Yates did the story for *Them!* (1953) and the scripts for *It Came from Beneath the Sea* and *Conquest of Space* (both 1955), *Earth vs. the Flying Saucers* (1956), *The Flame Barrier, Frankenstein 1970* and *Space Master X-7* (all 1958). Relying more on emoting than tacky special effects, *Tormented* (released in the fall of 1960) is a fairly scary spook show that moves along quickly, easily carrying out its duty as a double bill item, usually paired with *Caltiki the Immortal Monster* (q.v.). While he is best known for his cinema outings dealing with giantism, Gordon's greatest contribution to the entertainment field was his daughter Susan, who debuted in his *Attack of the Puppet People* and appeared in his *The Boy and the Pirates* (1960). A sweet, unassuming child, Susan took all the acting honors in *Tormented*. She went on to appear in her father's second supernatural melodrama, *Picture Mommy Dead* (1966).

Tom Stewart (Richard Carlson) has rented a beach house on an island where his young fiancée Meg Hubbard (Lugene Sanders) lives with her wealthy parents (Vera Marsh, Harry Fleer) and eight-year-old sister Sandy (Susan Gordon). Tom and Meg are to be married in two weeks and he is then to give a piano jazz concert at Carnegie Hall. He is visited by his old girlfriend, singer Vi Mason (Judi Reding), who demands he give up Meg and return to her. They meet at an old lighthouse and when Tom refuses to knuckle under, Vi threatens to blackmail him with letters he wrote to her. The two climb to the top of the lighthouse and as they argue, Vi leans against a railing that gives way and she falls, barely hanging onto the rail. She begs Tom to help her but he watches as she falls to her death in the sea. The following morning Tom goes to the beach in search of Vi's body and sees it floating near the shore. He carries the corpse and places it on the sand only to have it turn into a mass of seaweed. Sandy, who is very attached to Tom, arrives and finds Vi's watch, which the pianist later throws into the sea. As he broods in the lighthouse over Vi's death, Meg arrives and tries to cheer him up. Tom begs her to marry him immediately so they can get off the island. When she refuses, they leave as a shadow envelops the place and they smell perfume. Walking along the beach with Meg, Tom spies a third set of footprints in the sand but before he can show them to her the waves wipe them away. As Tom works at his beach house, Vi's record of the song "Tormented" begins playing on the phonograph. He takes it off the turntable but a few minutes later it plays again and he smashes the recording. When Mrs. Ellis (Lillian Adams), a blind real estate agent, brings Tom flowers, he inquires if she believes in ghosts. She tells him about a family named Samuels who rented a house from her. Their young son and his dog went missing and after that tenants would not remain in the house due a scratching sound at the door, along with coldness and seaweed in the boy's room. Tom dreams of Vi that night. When he wakes up, he goes to the lighthouse where he calls to her and says that he will no longer pay attention to her and that he will marry Meg. The next day Sandy comes to see Tom and she tells him that Meg wants to reconcile with him. She asks to see her sister's engagement ring but when Tom takes it out of the box it disappears—and he then sees it on Meg's crawling hand. Telling Sandy to leave, Tom implores Vi to not torment him. He runs to the beach where she sees Meg and they embrace. They go back to her house where the young woman is horrified to see her wedding dress covered in seaweed. Sandy later tells Mrs. Ellis about Tom going to the lighthouse and the blind woman goes there and confronts Vi's ghost and almost falls off the railing but stops herself in time and calls the spirit a fiend. Meg's father returns from a business trip to attend her wedding but expresses displeasure with her marrying a jazz musician. Sandy goes to the lighthouse to see Tom and finds a medallion belonging to Vi. Boat operator Nick Lewis (Joe Turkel) goes to Tom's beach house wanting him to pay the five dollar cost of the return boat ticket Vi promised him. To get rid of the intruder, Tom gives him the money. At a beachfront café, Nick overhears the proprietor (Gene Roth) talking with Mrs. Ellis about Tom and Meg's upcoming wedding. Later he goes to their wedding rehearsal and tells Tom he wants to see him again. That evening at a pre-wedding party, a picture of Tom and Meg is taken but when Tom sees it, Vi's face is also visible. The next morning Vi's head appears at Tom's house and says she plans to tell the world he killed her. He wraps it in a towel and takes it outside where it rolls down a flight of wooden steps. Nick picks up the bundle, which turns out to be a bunch of wilted flowers. He tells Tom he wants $5,000 to keep quiet about Vi, since he has possession of the medallion found by Sandy. Tom agrees to talk with him at the lighthouse. When they get there Vi's ghost urges him to kill the blackmailer, which he does with a lead pipe. Sandy comes down the lighthouse stairs, having witnessed the murder. During the wedding, the minister (Merritt Stone) asks if anyone knows any reason for the marriage not to take place and just as Sandy is about to speak up, a chilling breeze blows through the church, wilting all the flowers. When her bridal bouquet also wilts, Meg screams and runs from the church. The defeated Tom goes to the lighthouse and informs Vi's ghost that he will leave the island without getting married. The Hubbards realize that Sandy has not returned home, unaware that she has gone to the lighthouse to find out why Tom killed the boat man. Knowing he has to silence the little girl, Tom takes her to the top of the building. As he starts to push her through the railing, Vi's ghost lunges at him and he plunges to his death in the water. When the Hubbards and other residents go to the beach, Vi's body is brought to the shore, followed by that of Tom. Vi's arm falls over Tom in an embrace, revealing the wedding ring on her left hand.

Tormented did not see British release until 1964; thirteen minutes were trimmed from the proceedings in that territory. There the *Monthly Film Bulletin* declared it a "[f]aintly idiotic ghost story redeemed by a few of its hallucinatory effects ... mainly routine." Donald C. Willis commented in *Horror and Science Fiction Films: A Checklist* (1972), "Though one of Gordon's better pictures, it's still no great shakes." "[Richard] Carlson and [Judi] Reding are good in this more 'adult' than usual Gordon flick, which mixes creepy atmosphere with blatant special effects," wrote James O'Neill in *Terror on Tape* (1994). Joe Kane in *The Phantom of the Movies' Videoscope* (2000) opined, "Gordon's ghost story relies on cheap FX and a moody lighthouse setting to nudge it along but stacks up as agreeably tacky '50s fun." Charles Kilgore wrote in *Ecco the World of Bizarre Video* #14 (1990), "To be sure, *Tormented* bears the mark of a Bert I. Gordon production. It suffers from laughably bad special effects (courtesy of Bert and wife Flora), occasionally painful stabs at acting from a seemingly bewildered cast, and Gordon's nonchalant shrug towards establishing story credibility. What makes *Tormented* memorable is Gordon's subversive reworkings of ghost story conventions and his cheap shock tactics — which occasionally backfire — to relate its seamy account of a scorned floozy whose ghost returns from the grave to claim her killer.... [A]lthough Gordon's skill at directing motion pictures has been justifiably lambasted by critics, *Tormented* — along with his best work — reveals the touch of a director who understood how to entertain audiences by coyly toying with their expectations."

Twilight's Last Gleaming (1977; 144 minutes; Color)

Producer: Merv Adelson. Executive Producer: Helmut Jedele. Director: Robert Aldrich. Screenplay: Ronald M. Cohen and Edward Huebsch, from the novel *Viper Three* by Walter Wager. Photography: Robert Hauser. Editors: Michael Luciano, William Martin and Maury Winetrobe. Music: Jerry Goldsmith. Title Song Sung by Billy Preston. Art Director: Werner Achmann. Sound: James Willis, Gordon Daniel, Gordon Davidson and Gilbert Marchant. Production Designer: Rolf Zehelbauer. Production Manager: Harry Sherman. Production Supervisor: Harry Sokal. Special Effects: Henry Millar and Willi Neuner. Makeup: Georg Jauss and Hans-Peter Knoepfle. Costumes: Tom Dawson. Assistant Directors: Rolf M. Degener and Wolfgang Glattes.

CAST: Burt Lancaster (General Lawrence Dell), Richard Widmark (General Martin MacKenzie), Roscoe Lee Browne (Professor James Forrest), Joseph Cotten (Secretary of State Arthur Renfrew), Melvyn Douglas (Secretary of Defense Zachariah Guthrie), Charles Durning (President David T. Stevens), Richard Jaeckel (Captain Sanford Towne), William Marshall (Attorney General William Klinger), Gerald S. O'Loughlin (Brigadier General Michael O'Rourke), Paul Winfield (Willis Powell), Burt Young (Augie Garvas), Charles Aidman (Bernstein), Leif Erickson (CIA Director Ralph Whittaker), Charles McGraw (Air Force General Peter Crane), Morgan Paull (First Lieutenant Louis Cannellis), Simon Scott (Chairman of the Joint Chiefs Phil Spencer), William Smith (Hoxey), Bill Walker (Willard), David Baxt (Sergeant Willard), Glenn Beck (Lieutenant), Ed Bishop (Major Jack Fox), Phil Brown (Rev. Cartwright), Gary Cockrell (Captain Jackson), Don Fellows (General Stonesifer), Weston Gavin (Lieutenant Wilson), Garrick Hagon (Driver Alfie), Elizabeth Halliday (General Stonesifer's Secretary), David Healy (Major Winters), Thomasine Heiner (Nurse Edith), Bill Hootkins (Sergeant Fitzpatrick), Ray Jewers (Sergeant Domino), Ron Lee (Sergeant Rappaport), Robert Sherman (Major LeBeau), John Ratzenberger (Sergeant Kopecki), Robert MacLeod (State Trooper Chambers), Lionel Murton (Colonel Horne), Robert O'Neil (Briefing Officer), Shane Rimmer (Colonel Alexander B. Franklin), Pamela Roland (Sergeant Kelly), Mark Russell (Airman Mendez), Rich Steber (Captain Roger F. Kincaid), Drew W. Wesche (Lieutenant Witkin), Kent O. Doering (Barker), Allan Moore, M. Phil Senini, Rich Demarest (Sharpshooters).

Set in the near future, *Twilight's Last Gleaming* was filmed in West Germany by Gerie Productions as *Silo III* and *Viper Three*. Slow-paced and overlong, it was one of the last films made by director Robert Aldrich, who had done the earlier genre outings *Kiss Me Deadly* (1955), another movie dealing with atomic weapons, *What Ever Happened to Baby Jane?* (1962) and *Hush... Hush, Sweet Charlotte* (1964). The film's protagonists' desire to have the U.S. government come clean on the real reasons for the Vietnam War were nullified since the release of the Pentagon Papers in 1971 and various other sources had basically revealed this long before the film came to theaters in February 1977. Vincent Canby wrote in the *New York Times*, "[T]he film has the appearance of a rather classy television show.... Mr. Aldrich obtains a good deal of suspense from idiotic material, though his use of the split-screen doesn't double suspense as often as it cuts it in half." *Variety* termed it an "intricate, intriguing and intelligent drama." Marc Sigoloff said in *The Films of the Seventies* (1984), "Well-done thriller.... [It] may be a message movie, but its never overly preachy or boring...." Joe Kane in *The Phantom of the Movies' Videoscope* (2000) termed it a "far-fetched but watchable pulp thriller." In *Movie Guide for Puzzled Parents* (1984), Lynn Minton warned, "The moviemakers exploit the current cynicism about our military and intelligence establishments by telling us — chillingly — how the joint chief would answer. There's raw language and some shooting and killing, but it's the movie's message that would upset many children, and I'd want to be around to talk about it with them. Not for under 14 or 15."

On November 16, 1981, Professor James Forrest (Roscoe Lee Browne) comes to the president of the United States, David T. Stevens (Charles Durning), to plead for the life of his daughter's lover, a man who murdered a foreign potentate. Stevens refuses his request. Former Air Force General Lawrence Dell (Burt Lancaster) breaks out of a Montana prison with three other death row inmates, Willis Powell (Paul Winfield), Augie Garvas (Burt Young) and Hoxey (William Smith). They waylay a military Jeep with Hoxey killing the driver. The four men gain entrance to an Air Force security base as Hoxey shoots a guard before he is killed by Dell. Getting control of the base's missile launch control center, they secure it and knock out Captain Towne (Richard Jaeckel) and First Lieutenant Cannellis (Morgan Paull). Now controlling nine Titan missiles equipped with atomic warheads, Dell informs Duty Control that Silo 3 is in hostile hands and asks to speak with General MacKenzie (Richard Widmark). He tells his old adversary he has full launch control of the missiles but MacKenzie thinks he is bluffing. Dell tries to get Towne, an old friend, to give him the combination to the safe housing the keys needed to launch the missiles, saying he wants to expose the government's true intentions. When Towne refuses, Garvas uses a ruse to make Cannellis think he has put out one of his commander's eyes and will do the same with the other if he does not get the information. Cannellis gives him the combination, which is imprinted on his dog tags. MacKenzie orders the situation labeled top secret and contacts the president, who is meeting with Secretary of Defense Guthrie (Melvyn Douglas), who has been bickering with Secretary of State Arthur Renfrew (Joseph Cotten). MacKenzie informs the president about the situation, saying the warheads are probably aimed at the Soviet Union, but he feels Dell does not have the capacity to launch them. Bypassing the National Security Council, Stevens calls a meeting with Renfrew, Guthrie, Attorney General William Klinger (William Marshall), Air Force General Pete Crane (Charles McGraw), CIA Director Ralph Whittaker (Leif Erickson) and Phil Spencer (Simon Scott), chairman of the Joint Chiefs, along with a presidential attaché, Brigadier General O'Rourke (Gerald S. O'Loughlin). Scott informs the group that Dell was demobilized after five years in a Viet Cong prison camp and came home to find his wife had left him. Renfrew claims Dell was revolutionized by the enemy and it is brought out he was sent to death row in Montana on a murder charge. Stevens calls Dell who tells him he and his partners want ten million

Burt Lancaster, Paul Winfield and Charles Durning in *Twilight's Last Gleaming* (1977)

dollars in cash and transportation out of the country to a safe haven. He also demands the president be his hostage and that he disclose to the American people the true reasons for the Vietnam War. Stevens asks for time to consider the proposals and he and Dell agree on 90 minutes. MacKenzie sets up a camp outside camera range of the base and waits for presidential authority to launch Operation Gold, a small nuclear device that will take out the intruders. Guthrie suggests Stevens call Dell a second time and he is offered twenty million dollars, a full pardon and safe transit. Much to the chagrin of Powell and Garvas, Dell refuses the offer, demanding the president expose the Vietnam War documents. Stevens orders MacKenzie to carry out Operation Gold but when Dell sees tanks approaching the base he calls the general and demands the attack be stopped. Clandestinely a chopper delivers infantrymen and the bomb to the site. As they are setting up the device, an alarm is set off and Dell keys one of the missiles to launch. Towne and Cannellis manage to get free and attack the invaders. Cannellis shoots Garvas before he is killed by Powell. Towne is knocked out and tied up as MacKenzie asks the president for permission to set off the nuclear bomb but is told to hold back. Dell halts the missile launch. The president and his advisors go over the government's Vietnam policy which called for limited wars in order to avoid an nuclear conflict. Guthrie tells the upset Stevens that an open government is needed but most of the others disagree. Klinger suggests such action might take place slowly over a period of years. All the advisors agree that the president should go to Montana to meet with Dell so that protective measures can be taken after Dell and his cohorts evacuate Silo 3. Stevens angrily refuses but, after consulting O'Rourke, he changes his mind, admitting he is scared. Stevens tells Guthrie that if he is killed, the new president must release the secret documents after two weeks. As Air Force One flies to Montana, Dell learns that MacKenzie is in command near the silo. When he calls him, the general says the president is about to land. Powell suggests to Dell that the chief executive may be a double and they all will be killed before the documents are exposed. Dell wants to launch the missiles but Powell refuses to help him. After getting word that Air Force One has landed, Dell and Powell watch the president enter the silo. He takes the elevator to the control center; the three men leave the compound and head for the plane but as they near it they are shot by sharpshooters. Before dying, Stevens tells Guthrie to keep his word.

While lacking in plot plausibility, *Twilight's Last Gleaming* is a delight for fans of veteran Hollywood actors as its cast is filled with famous names, all of whom give well-modulated performances. Burt Lancaster is quite good as the chief protagonist, wavering between self-sacrificing patriotism and obvious mental imbalance. Paul Winfield and Burt Young handle their roles as hardened criminals in good fashion and William Smith is outstanding in his cameo as the trigger-happy Hoxey. Joseph Cotten, Melvyn Douglas, William Marshall, Gerald S. O'Loughlin, Leif Erickson, Charles McGraw and Simon Scott give in-depth performances as presidential advisors and Richard Jaeckel and Morgan Paull are very believable as the defenders of the missile silo. Richard Widmark is excellent as the commanding general, and Charles Durning's character is one of textured personality nuances. The casting of Durning, however, does not appear to be historical since few heavy-set men have held the presidency, the last being William Howard Taft who was elected in 1908.

Twilight's Last Gleaming was also called *Nuclear Countdown*. For Swedish showings it was cut to 123 minutes and in France it was trimmed to 91 minutes.

Up in Smoke (1957; 64 minutes)

Producer: Richard Heermance. Director: William Beaudine. Screenplay: Jack Townley. Story: Elwood Ullman and Bert Lawrence. Photography: Harry Neumann. Editor: William Austin. Music: Marlin Skiles. Art Director: David Milton. Sound: Frank McKenzie. Production Manager: Allen K. Wood. Sets: Joseph Kish. Makeup: Emile LaVigne. Wardrobe: Sid Mintz. Continuity: Frank Remsden. Assistant Director: Jesse Corallo, Jr.

CAST: Huntz Hall (Horace Debussy "Sach" Jones), Stanley Clements (Stanislaus "Duke" Coveleskie), David Gorcey (Chuck), Eddie LeRoy (Blinky), Dick Elliott (Mike Clancy), Judy Bamber (Mabel), Byron Foulger (Mr. Bub), Ralph Sanford (Sam), Ric Roman (Tony), Joe Devlin

(Al), James Flavin (Policeman), Earle Hodgins (Friendly Frank), John Mitchum (Desk Sergeant), Jack Mulhall (Police Clerk), Fritz Feld (Dr. Bluzak), Wilbur Mack (Druggist), Benny Rubin (Bernie).

After Bowery Boys Sach (Huntz Hall), Duke (Stanley Clements), Chuck (David Gorcey) and Blinky (Eddie LeRoy) and café owner Mike Clancy (Dick Elliott) collect $90 to help pay the medical expenses of a polio victim, Sach is given a ride to the bank to deposit the funds by Sam (Ralph Sanford), who takes him to a bookie joint run by Tony (Ric Roman) and Al (Joe Devlin). The two crooks cheat Sach out of the money. When he gets back to the café he is belittled by Duke for being so stupid. Sach informs Blinky that he wants to get even with the crooks even if it means selling his soul to the Devil. Mr. Bub (Byron Foulger) appears and informs Sach that he will give him horse race winners for the next seven days in return for his soul. Sach goes along with the deal but, after being given the name of the first day's winner, he finds out the bookies will not take his bet because he has no money. He dreams up a scheme to sell the boys' old jalopy, unaware that Duke has already done so. After being paid ten cents for the jalopy by a dishonest salesman (Earle Hodgins), Sach is arrested for car theft and put in jail where Mr. Bub shows up and gives him the next winner. Tony and Al become suspicious when the horse Sach picks wins again. After the boys bail him out of jail, Sach gets the third day tip from the Devil disguised as an organ grinder's monkey. When Mike and the others see him talking to the monkey, they send Sach to Dr. Bluzak (Fritz Feld), a psychiatrist, who becomes so discombobulated trying to psychoanalyze Sach he ends up on the couch asking for the names of horse race winners. Borrowing $20 from Mike, Sach goes back to the bookies and bets on the Devil's latest tip, causing Tony and Al to do the same. Just before the race, Sach is persuaded to change his mind and the horse he bets on loses. The bookies have Tony's girlfriend Mabel (Judy Bamber) become a waitress at Mike's in order to discover Sach's system for making bets. On the seventh day, Mr. Bub gives Sach $100 and tells him to go to the race track where he will be given the name of the horse that will win the big race. Going to the race track with Mike and Mabel, Sach is followed by the bookies and Sam. In the guise of a soda peddler, Mr. Bub gives Sach the name of the winning horse and he bets the money. Chuck shows up saying that a charity is going to pay the polio victim's expenses so Sach tries to break his deal with Mr. Bub. Mabel tells Tony to bet on the same horse as Sach. Realizing the Devil will get his soul if the horse wins, Sach convinces Mike to waylay its jockey and he takes his place. Even with Sach in the saddle, the horse wins and Mr. Bub comes for his soul only to learn the horse has been disqualified because he was ridden by the wrong jockey. When the boys go back to Clancy's Café, Sach sees Mr. Bub working as the new busboy. He tells Sach he can get reinstated if he finds new clients. Sach sends him to Tony and Al, who lost all their funds on the race.

Richard Heermance, who produced *The Maze* and *World Without End* (qq.v.), took over from Ben Schwalb as the producer for the final two "Bowery Boys" productions, *Up in Smoke* and *In the Money* (1958). Released late in 1957, *Up in Smoke* is a cheap affair highlighted by an amusing performances by Byron Fougler as the Devil and Earle Hodgins as slick used car salesman Friendly Frank. Otherwise the laughs are few. *Variety* stated, "Director William Beaudine might have been nodding a little on this one." David Hayes and Brent Walker wrote in *The Films of the Bowery Boys* (1984), "Repetition characterizes *Up in Smoke*. The film cuts from the lunchroom to the bookmaking office, and back, rarely breaks the pattern.... New producer Richard Heermance kept sets sparse, and writers Elwood Ullman and Bert Lawrence simply updated the old 16th century story of Faust."

War of the Satellites (1958; 66 minutes)

Producers: Roger Corman, Jack Rabin and Irving Block. Director: Roger Corman. Screenplay: Lawrence Louis Goldman. Story: Jack Rabin and Irving Block. Photography: Floyd Crosby. Editor: Irene Morra. Music: Walter Greene. Art Director: Daniel Haller. Sound: Philip Mitchell. Production Manager: Lionel C. Place. Sets: Harry Reif. Makeup: Stanley Orr. Special Effects: Louis DeWitt, Irving Block and Jack Rabin. Assistant Director: Jack Bohrer.

CAST: Dick Miller (Dave Boyer), Susan Cabot (Sybil Carrington), Richard Devon (Dr. Pol Van Ponder), Eric Sinclair (Dr. Howard Lazar), Michael Fox (Jason Ibn Akad), Robert Shayne (Ambassador Hodgekiss), Jerry Barclay (John Compo), John Brinkley, Tony Miller (Control Room Officers), Bruno VeSota (LeMoine), Jay Sayer (Jack), Mitzi McCall (Mitzi), Roy Gordon (United Nations President), Roger Corman (Ground Control Officer), Beach Dickerson (Armed Crewman/Voice of Reporter), James Knight (Second Crewman).

Eight months after the Soviets launched the first space satellite, *Sputnik*, in October 1957, Allied Artists released *War of the Satellites* on a double-bill with *Attack of the 50 Foot Woman* (q.v.). Filmed in eight days in cramped settings, the sci-fi outing attempted to cash in on the space craze and even included a brief *Life* magazine blurb in its advertising since that periodical had made mention of it in an article on current science fiction movies. The film's chief asset is its cast, with an especially good performance by Richard Devon in three roles, the scientist behind the satellite program and his two alien clones. Susan Cabot does not have a role befitting her talents as the scientist's assistant; she is also harshly lit in several scenes. Even producer-director Roger Corman shows up as the ground control officer. A major highlight of the picture is Walter Greene's bombastic music score that gives the film the feel of an old-time serial. *War of the Satellites* is based on a story by special effects artists Irving Block and Jack Rabin, who also co-produced it with Corman. Their effects, done with Louis DeWitt, are among the tackier aspects of the production.

A satellite manned by volunteers attempts to succeed where nine predecessors failed by penetrating an energy barrier that halts further space travel and destroys the vessels. Among the United Nations representatives watching the voyage are U.S. Ambassador Hodgekiss (Robert Shayne) and foreign emissaries Ibn Akad (Michael Fox) and LeMoine (Bruno VeSota), along with Dr. Pol Van Ponder (Devon), the head of Project Sigma. Akad complains of the half-billion dollars lost in the previous futile flights and LeMoine predicts that this one will also fail. The satellite makes contact with the barrier and explodes. Akid calls for an end to the project. Two necking teenagers (Jay Sayer, Mitzi McCall) find a small missile that fell from the sky and take it the authorities. At the United Nations, Sybil Carrington (Cabot), Van Ponder's assistant, reads a message written in Latin found on the missile. It says it is from a civilization called the Spiral Nebula Ghana and it will stop low level humans from exploring space. In response Hodgekiss says no one has the right to keep people from space travel and urges the body to continue with Project Sigma. Van Ponder informs newsmen that the missive is a hoax but confides to Sybil and staff engineer Dave Boyer (Dick Miller) that the missile is harder than anything ever devised by humans and that he does not know where it came from. The next Sigma launch is planned and Hodgekiss asks Van Ponder to a UN forum to answer questions about the preparations. On his way there, the scientist is blinded by a bright light; his car crashes down an embankment. While Akad denounces the latest launch plans, Hodgekiss is told that Van Ponder has been killed. Moments later, the scientist arrives and is given an ovation. After the meeting, Van Ponder tells the ambassador a police officer was mistaken about his being killed and asks to use his office to go over some plans. When Hodgekiss leaves, Van Ponder separates into a second being, aliens having taken the form of the dead scientist. Van Ponder communicates with the aliens about his plans to thwart the space mission. Dave arrives and asks that Sybil not be included in the launch crew but his request is denied. Sybil alerts them to news of the world being blanketed in a holocaust of fires, floods and volcanic explosions which many connect with the alien message. Van Ponder phones Hodgekiss to say that Sigma should be halted and he tells Dave and Sybil the aliens are apparently so powerful they look upon humans as we look upon bacteria. He prepares a message that he asks Dave to read at the UN but instead the engineer says mankind cannot survive by abject surrender and Sigma must proceed at all costs. The members agree with him unanimously and vote to continue the project. When Dave is working with Van Ponder some time later, he notices the scientist has exactly the same growths on each arm. After taking down the license number on the scientist's car, Dave decides to look at his wrecked vehicle. As Van Ponder is talking with John Compo (Jerry Barclay), the project's astronomical engineer, he accidentally incinerates his right hand on a burner. When Compo goes for help, the alien revitalizes it by rubbing it with his left hand. When Compo returns with Dr. Howard Lazar (Eric Sinclair), the two men find Van Ponder in perfect health and Compo is told he has been working under too much pressure. Compo says Van Ponder is not human. Dave goes to a junkyard and finds the scientist's wrecked car which is so badly mangled that he realizes no one could have survived the crash. Dave calls Sybil and she tells him that Van Ponder has moved up the latest launch time. The scientist is not happy when Dr. Lazar clears Compo to be part of the crew with him and Sybil on Rocket One, with Dave following on the second rocket. Just before blast-off, Dave witnesses Van Ponder duplicate himself. Three rockets are successfully launched and after their components break apart they merge to become the Sigma satellite. Following the launch, the scientist confronts Compo and tells him the truth about being an alien and offers to make him one but the engineer refuses and is murdered. When Sybil comes into the room, Van Ponder announces that Compo died due to launch acceleration and then informs the crew of the death and his plans to blast through the Sigma barrier and destroy it. Dave tries to make Sybil believe Van Ponder is not human but she scoffs at him so he accuses the scientist of killing Compo. After the funeral for Compo, Dave asks Dr. Lazar about Compo's health which the doctor says was perfect. Dave tells the doctor that Van Ponder murdered Compo and then shows him the scientist's fingerprints which prove he isn't human. Lazar tells Van Ponder he must check his heart and, after the alien leaves to observe the formation of a distant cloud mass, he gives himself a heart to fool the medical man. Now partly human, the scientist realizes he loves Sybil and makes a date to talk to her about their future together. Going back to the doctor, Van Ponder murders Lazar as Sybil informs Dave about the scientist's strange behavior toward her. Dave tells her to stay with Lazar, not realizing the doctor has been killed. Van Ponder orders Dave's arrest for the deaths of Compo and the doctor and he is taken into custody by two crewmen (Beach Dickerson, James Knight). When Van Ponder disposes of Lazar's body, he is observed by Sybil who runs from him into the Solar Energy Room. He follows her and tells her he needs her because he is now human. As the satellite nears the barrier, the control room officers (John Brinkley, Tony Miller) call to Van Ponder for instructions and he orders them to head for it. The scientist then clones himself. One of the aliens goes to the control area while the other remains and tries to molest Sybil. Dave knocks out his guards and, taking a gun, finds one of the aliens and wounds him. Then the two engage in a struggle with Dave killing the alien. When Van Ponder dies, the other alien with Sybil collapses and both life forms disappear. Dave orders the control room officers to use solar energy to get through the barrier. As the UN representatives watch, the Sigma satellite blasts its way through the barrier and Dave announces that the whole universe is now a new frontier.

"A confusing space action melo" is how *Variety* termed *War of the Satellites*, adding, "A lesser entry for the exploitation market.... Over-talkative script ... characters are so unreal they are mere walk-throughs...." *The Hollywood Reporter* felt it was "[t]opical" while the British *Monthly Film Bulletin* commented, "Reasonably diverting science fantasy, unduly cluttered with international problems and the inevitably brainy female in the space ship. The production is generally makeshift, but the trick effects work, the atmosphere is occasionally eerie." Phil Hardy stated in *Science Fiction* (1984), "The signs of swift making are all too evident, especially in the over-talkative script and the mismatch between the special effects ... and the action.... The result is a conventional film, in which the aliens clearly represent the Russians...." In *Horror and Science Fiction Films: A Checklist* (1972), Donald C. Willis claimed it is "[o]ne of Corman's worst."

While the film's title may have suggested a battle in outer space, it apparently referred to the Sigma Project's efforts to break through the alien barrier.

The Wasp Woman (1959; 63 minutes)

Producer-Director: Roger Corman. Screenplay: Leo Gordon. Story: Kinta Zertuche. Photography: Harry Neumann. Editor: Carlo Lodato. Music: Fred Katz. Art Director: Daniel Haller. Sound: Philip Mitchell. Production Manager: Jack Bohrer. Makeup: Grant R. Keat.

CAST: Susan Cabot (Janice Starlin), Fred [Anthony] Eisley (Bill Lane), Barboura Morris (Mary Dennison), William Roerick (Arthur "Coop" Cooper), Michael Mark (Eric Zinthrop), Frank Gerstle (Private Investigator Les Hellman), Bruno VeSota (Night Watchman), Roy Gordon (Paul Thompson), Carolyn Hughes (Jean Carson), Lynn Cartwright (Maureen Reardon), Frank Wolff (Delivery Man), Lani Mars (Nurse Warren), Philip Barry (Jerry), Roger Corman (Hospital Doctor), Gene Corman (Board Member).

The first production of Gene and Roger Corman's Filmgroup, *The Wasp Woman* was filmed in five days and released on a double-bill with the brothers' *Beast from Haunted Cave* (q.v.) by Allied Artists in November 1959. It was Susan Cabot's final film; she worked for Roger Corman previously in *Sorority Girl, Carnival Rock* (both 1957), *The Saga of the Viking Women and Their Voyage to the Waters of the Great Sea Serpent, Machine-Gun Kelly* and *War of the Satellites* (q.v.) [all 1958]. As the title character she wore a black insect head mask and black hairy gloves. The monster is seen mostly in dark scenes and is more repulsive than scary. The film has a cheap, hurried look although Cabot and the rest of the cast give exemplary performances, making it a bit more interesting than it otherwise might have been. There is even some comedy repartee between goldbricking, busty secretaries (Carolyn Hughes, Lynn Cartwright) with *Beast from Haunted Cave* star Frank Wolff showing up in a bit as a delivery man. *Variety* termed it an "[u]nexciting but exploitable horror film.... [It] looks polished but it's pretty slow and not very frightening." The British *Monthly Film Bulletin* called it "[r]outine stuff" while Donald C. Willis in *Horror and Science Films: A Checklist* (1972) stated, "Terrible. The attempts at suspense are pretty silly, though a few scenes in a cosmetics firm have an air of credibility about them, and Susan Cabot is good. One of Roger's worst."

Revenue at cosmetics firm Janice Starling Enterprises has dropped over fourteen percent and during a board meeting, Bill Lane (Fred [Anthony] Eisley) tells Janice (Cabot) and the other members that the problem is the new face representing the company's products. Janice has been used for advertising for sixteen years but it was felt she was growing too old for the job. Janice talks with chemist Arthur "Coop" Cooper (William Roerick) about the possible use of enzyme extracts but he warns her against the idea. Eric Zinthrop (Michael Mark) makes an appointment with Janice and in her company's laboratory he injects guinea pigs with a youth formula he has invented from royal jelly derived from queen wasps. The aged, sickly animals are made young by the formula and she hires him to make a compound that will be safe for humans and orders him to use her for the experiments. Janice announces to the board that she has hired Zinthrop and lays out her plans to revolutionize the company as a result of his experiments. Lane informs his girlfriend, Mary Dennison (Barboura Morris), who is also Janice's private secretary, that he thinks Zinthrop is a confidence man, and Coop agrees. Both men tell Mary to keep them informed on Janice and Zinthrop's activities. After working on the formula for some time, Zinthrop shows Janice a cat he has caused to revert to a kitten and she takes the first injection of the youth enzyme. Three weeks pass and while Janice is impatient she looks five years younger. Mary locates Zinthrop's letter to Janice about the wasp enzyme and shows it to Bill and Coop, who plans to check on the man's past. One night Janice goes to the laboratory and injects herself with the formula and a few days later she comes to work looking younger; Mary tells her she appears to be in her early twenties. Janice then informs the board that her company will market Zinthrop's formula under the banner "Return to Youth with Janice Starlin." One morning Zinthrop goes to the lab and is attacked by the cat, which has returned to its normal size and gone mad. He kills the animal and disposes of it and then leaves. The disappointed Zinthrop walks in front of a car. Coop finds the man's notebook and realizes the origins of his formula. When Zinthrop does not return, Janice hires a private detective, Hellman (Frank Gerstle), and the man's assistant Jerry (Philip Barry) locates him at Central Emergency Hospital as an amnesia case.

Poster for *The Wasp Woman* (1960)

Coop returns to the lab to test Zinthrop's formula and is attacked by Janice, who has turned into a wasp woman. After she kills him and drinks his blood, Janice returns to normal and realizes that the formula which she has been injecting is nearly gone. She has Zinthrop transferred to her office and cared for by a nurse (Lani Mars). That night a watchman (Bruno VeSota) hears noises in the lab and when he enters, Zinthrop and the nurse hear a loud scream. Trying to locate Coop, Bill and Mary go to the lab where they find Zinthrop's notebook and Coop's pipe. Bill tells Mary he thinks Coop and the night watchman are dead. Suffering from severe headaches, Janice tries to get Zinthrop to concoct more of the formula. When the nurse enters the room, Janice turns back into the monster and kills her. Bill and Mary talk with Zinthrop, who tries to tell them about the attack but he becomes violent. When Mary tries to convince Janice to call the police, her boss again becomes a wasp woman and attacks her. Bill and Zinthrop hear Mary's screams and Bill runs upstairs to the lab where he sees Mary's body being dragged away. The Wasp Woman attacks him. When Zinthrop shows up, she tries to kill him. Bill holds the monster off with a chair as Zinthrop douses the creatures with carbolic acid. Using the chair, Bill pushes the Wasp Woman out of a window and she falls over forty floors to her death. Zinthrop dies from the exertion as Bill finds Mary is all right.

The Wasp Woman was written for the screen by actor Leo Gordon, based on a story by Kinta Zertuche, the wife of the film's art director, Daniel Haller. TV prints include several extra minutes of footage filmed by director Jack Hill. The scenes shot by Hill give the reason for Zinthrop contacting the Starlin company. Michael Mark reprises the Zinthrop character, who works for the Honey Fresh company as a chemist. He is fired by executive Howard Renfro (Karl Schanzer) for not turning in a report on royal jelly from bees and instead working with wasps. The scenes also feature Aron Kincaid as beekeeper Howard. Although the sequence is merely padding, it does fit in well with the rest of the movie. In 1995, director Jim Wynorski remade *The Wasp Woman* for Roger Corman's New Horizon Pictures, with Jennifer Rubin in the title role.

The Wasp Woman proved to be the first of several genre outings for Anthony Eisley, who changed his name from Fred after the movie was made. He went on to appear in *Lightning Bolt* (q.v.) and *The Navy vs. the Night Monsters* (both 1966), *Journey to the Center of Time* and *The Mighty Gorga* (both 1967), *The Witchmaker* (1969), *Dracula vs. Frankenstein* (1971), *The Mummy and the Curse of the Jackal* (made in 1971 but not released on video until 1985), *Monstroid* (1978), *Deep Space* (1987) and *Evil Spirits* (1991).

Who? (1975; 93 minutes; Color)

Producer: Barry Levinson. Co-Producer: Kurt Berthold. Director: Jack Gold. Screenplay: John Gould [Jack Gold], from the novel by Algis Budrys. Photography: Petrus Schlomp. Editor: Norman Wanstall. Music: John Cameron. Art Director: Peter Scharff. Sound: Mike Le Mare, Colin Miller and Hayo von Zuendt. Costumes: Ille Sievers. Production Manager: Frank Winterstein. Unit Manager: Peter Bergens. Special Makeup: Colin Arthur. Special Effects: Richard Richtsfeld. Continuity: Sandra Piffrader. Stunt Coordinator: Remy Julienne. Assistant Director: Siegfried Rothemund.

CAST: Elliott Gould (Sean Rogers), Trevor Howard (Colonel Azarin), Joseph Bova (Dr. Lucas Martino), Ed Grover (FBI Agent Finchley), John Lehne (FBI Agent Haller), James Noble (General Deptford), Lyndon Book (Dr. Barrister), Michael Lombard (Dr. Jacob Besser), Kaym Tomborg (Edith Hayes), Joy Garrett (Barbara), John Stewart (Frank Heywood), Bruce Boa (Miller), Fred Vincent (Douglas), Alexander Allerson (Dr. Korthu), Ivan Desny (General Sturmer), Dan Sazarino (Uncle Lucas), Craig McConnell (Tonino), Herb Andress, Del Negro, Frank Schuller (FBI Agents).

A tepid and confusing mixture of sci-fi and spy film genres, *Who?* was filmed in 1973 but did not see release in the U.S. until August 1975. Made in West Germany and Miami, Florida, by Hemisphere Productions and Lion International, the picture had numerous alternate titles. In Italy it was called *Who? I'uomo dei due Volte* and in West Germany it was entitled *Das Phantom mit der Stahl Maske* (The Man with the Steel Mask). In England it was shown as *Man Without a Face*; another U.S. title was *Prisoner of the Skull*. It was released on video as *The Man with the Steel Mask* and *Roboman*. While its advertising promised a metal man, "The Kill Machine with the Megaton Mind," *Who?* proved to be a limp Cold War melodrama that shows the similarities between Soviet brainwashing and U.S. debriefing. Its plot is hard to follow since the script calls for constant jumping from the present to the title character's stay in the U.S.S.R. and back again. Joseph Bova, a former children's TV host, manages to make a sympathetic being out of the man with a metal face but most of the cast appears confused by the proceedings. Kaym Tomborg offers a nicely etched portrayal of the woman who once loved the metal man. There is even a car chase sequence staged by Remy Julienne that looks like something out of a Charles Bronson thriller.

Dr. Lucas Mariano (Bova), the supervisor of the top secret government Neptune Project in Florida, is badly injured in a car accident near the Iron Curtain while attending a conference. Following the fiery explosion, he is rescued by the Soviets and kept by them for six months. Upon his release he is met by FBI agents Sean Rogers (Elliott Gould), Finchley (Ed Grover) and Haller (John Lehne), who are taken aback when he appears wearing a gray steel face helmet and a mechanical left arm. Rogers is in charge of debriefing Lucas, who says he was interrogated by Soviet Colonel Azarin (Trevor Howard), and not General Sturmer (Ivan Desny), as Rogers expected. He is locked in a room as the skeptical Rogers tells other agents he does not know who Lucas is or what he is but he does know who sent him. Rogers suspects the Soviets have either sent a double or have rigged Lucas to send back information to them once he returns to the Neptune project. In flashback, Azarin talks with Dr. Korthu (Alexander Allerson), who says Lucas is so badly mangled he will have to be recreated as a partially artificial man. The U.S. medical experts tell Rogers the man they examined is human and some of him used to be Lucas Mariano. Rogers questions Lucas and asks him why the Soviets let him return and he replies that he told them nothing about Neptune. Lucas' colleague, Dr. Besser (Michael Lombard), comes to see him but Rogers will not let the two converse about their work. Both Rogers in the present and Azarin in the past question Lucas about his life, including working at this Uncle Lucas' (Dan Sazarino) restaurant and his romances with Edith (Tomborg), who loved him, and promiscuous Barbara (Joy Garrett). Rogers checks on Lucas' college friend Frank Heywood (John Stewart), who is deceased, and how he came to work for Neptune and then left to work in Tokyo as a consultant. After ten days of interrogation, Rogers tells Lucas he can go home but as they get to their plane, two assassins try to kill the scientist. After Rogers chases the hit men, their vehicle overturns and explodes. When Haller tells Rogers the Soviets tried to kill Lucas, Rogers says Azarin wants them to believe they have the real scientist so he can go back to work on Neptune. In Miami, Lucas walks the streets and is stared at by everyone. He goes to see Edith and they reminisce about their time together but after he leaves, Rogers calls her and tells her to continue to work with him. When Lucas seems confused he is approached by Finchley, who has been shadowing him, and accidentally lets him know he was overheard talking with Edith. Lucas runs away and Finchley follows him only to be hit and killed by a car. At the beach, Lucas tells Rogers he wants to go back to his late parents' farm but the agent says if he is cleared he can go back to work. At Neptune, Besser informs Rogers that the project needs Lucas and that Hayward had been insecure with his work there. In flashback, when Lucas fails to cooperate with the Soviets, Azarin asks Dr. Korthu to make him another metal man and they enlist Hayward who agrees so they can find out about Neptune. As Lucas works the family farm, Rogers shows up and asks him to return to the project. In flashback, Hayward dies from post-operative shock and Azarin is forced to send Lucas home. In the present, Lucas decides to stay on the farm where he is happy.

Variety said the film, adapted from Algis Budrys's 1958 novel, "is an action-espionage thriller examining, from a science fiction perspective, the nature of identity.... Joe Bova gives a beautiful, underplayed performance as diminutive US scientist Martino." Phil Hardy in *Science Fiction* (1984) called *Who?* "a modest offering.... [Jack] Gold directs as though unimpressed by his own script, spending too much time on chases rather than concentrating on the impassive Bova who gives the film's best performance as the listless cyborg." C.J. Henderson in *The Encyclopedia of Science Fiction Movies* (2001) termed it a "competent work, but that's about all."

World Without End (1956; 80 minutes; Color)

Producer: Richard Heermance. Director-Screenplay-Story: Edward Bernds. Photography: Ellsworth Fredericks. Editor: Eda Warren. Music: Leith Stevens. Art Director: David Milton. Sound: Ralph Butler. Production Manager: Allen K. Wood. Sets: Joseph Kish. Set Sketches: Alberto Vargas. Makeup: Emile LaVigne. Special Effects: Irving Block, Jack Rabin and Milt Rice. Continuity: Kathleen Fagan. Assistant Director: Don Torpin.

CAST: Hugh Marlowe (Dr. John Borden), Nancy Gates (Garnet), Nelson Leigh (Dr. Eldon Galbraithe), Rod Taylor (Herb Ellis), Shawn Smith [Shirley Patterson] (Elaine), Lisa Montell (Deena), Christopher Dark (Hank Jaffe), Booth Colman (Mories), Everett Glass (Timmek), Stanley Fraser (Elda), William Vedder (James), Paul Brinegar (Vida), Rankin Mansfield (Beryl), Mickey Simpson (Naga), David Alpert (Major), Herb Vigran, Don Kennedy, John Close, Walter Conrad (Reporters), Bill Forman (Radio Announcer), Strother Martin (Nihka), John Bleifer (Jule), Keith Richards (Human Captive), Mimi Gibson (Jenny Jaffe), Hugh Corcoran (Master Jaffe), Nancy Howard (Mrs. Jaffe), Michael Garth (Military Officer), John Hiestand (Television Newsman).

Not only is *World Without End* the first film of the 1950s to deal with time travel, it is one of the finest sci-fi films of the decade and one the best in the genre from Allied Artists. Filmed in CinemaScope and Technicolor, it was released in March 1956 on a double bill with *Indestructible Man* (q.v.). Except for a rather puny rocketship (via footage from Monogram's *Flight to Mars* [1951]) and two tatty giant spiders, the film was visually satisfying, thanks to well-chosen exterior locations and Joseph Kish's sets as well as art direction by David Milton. The set sketches for the production were drawn by noted artist Alberto Vargas. Leith Stevens' musical score adds much to the futuristic feel of the proceedings; he earlier composed the music for *Destination Moon* (1950), *When Worlds Collide* (1951) and *The War of the Worlds* (1953). Emile LaVigne's makeup for the subhumans is very well done, although most of the mutants are seen only in background and medium shots. One exception is the one-eyed Naga (Mickey Simpson), the leader of the pack, a very fine presentation of the human race degenerated by atomic war.

The acting in the movie is above par for sci-fi efforts with Hugh Marlowe heading the cast and giving a superb performance as a scientist who must adapt to life six centuries in the future. After working in radio and stage, Marlowe began making movies in the mid–1930s and by the time he starred in *World Without End* he had been in prestige items like

Christopher Dark, Rod Taylor, Hugh Marlowe, Nelson Leigh and Keith Richards in *World Without End* (1956)

Twelve O'Clock High, *Night and the City* and *All About Eve* (all 1950), *The Day the Earth Stood Still* and *Rawhide* (both 1951), *Monkey Business* (1952) and *Garden of Evil* (1954). The same year he did *World Without End* he also headlined the equally fine sci-fi effort *Earth vs. the Flying Saucers*. He would go on to appear in *Elmer Gantry* (1960), *Birdman of Alcatraz* (1962) and *Seven Days in May* (1964); his other genre effort was *Castle of Evil* (1966). Marlowe and leading lady Nancy Gates make a good romantic team. The film also includes two other lovelies, Shawn Smith and Lisa Montell. Smith, who used the name Shirley Patterson when making "B" westerns in the 1940s with Bill Elliott, Tex Ritter, Charles Starrett, Johnny Mack Brown, Russell Hayden and Eddie Dean, went on to appear in *The Land Unknown* (1957) and *It! The Terror from Beyond Space* (1958). Nelson Leigh, who portrayed the leader of the space expedition in *World Without End*, was the screen's first Jor-El in the 1948 serial *Superman*; he also appeared in *Creature with the Atom Brain* (1955). Rod Taylor, the film's radioman, starred in one of the screen's best sci-fi features, *The Time Machine* (1960).

The main drawback to *World Without End*, filmed as *Flight to the Future*, is Edward Bernds' somewhat plodding direction. Starting out in the sound department at Columbia Pictures, Bernds went on to write and direct Three Stooges shorts for the studio before taking over directing the "Blondie" series in the late 1940s. Leaving Columbia in 1952, he went to Allied Artists where he worked with the Bowery Boys on *Private Eyes* (1953), *The Bowery Boys Meet the Monsters* and *Jungle Gents* (both 1954) and *Bowery to Bagdad* (1955) [qq.v.] before making *World Without End*, his best feature film. He also wrote the screenplay from his supposedly original story although the film is obviously influenced by H.G. Wells' 1895 novel *The Time Machine*. Bernds went on to make *Queen of Outer Space* (q.v.) for Allied in 1958 and it not only borrowed part of *World Without End*'s storyline, it used some of its footage and one of the spiders. Bernds also directed *Space Master X-7* (1958), *Return of the Fly* (1959), *Valley of the Dragons* (1961), *The Three Stooges Meet Hercules* and *The Three Stooges in Orbit* (both 1962).

The military, newsmen and the family (Nancy Howard, Mimi Gibson, Hugh Corcoran) of astronaut Hank Jaffe (Christopher Dark) await word of the fate of the first space reconnaissance mission to Mars in 1957. Radio control has been lost between mission control and spaceship XRM. The astronauts have reached Mars and completed two orbits of the planet and are about to return home. Dr. Eldon Galbraithe (Leigh) is the leader of the expedition and its other members are scientist Dr. John Borden (Marlowe) and communications officer Herb Ellis (Taylor). As they head back, the ship is caught in a turbulent red cloud and begins accelerating at a fantastic speed with the crew being unable to reverse its rockets. The men black out and eventually the ship crashlands in a mountainous area covered with snow. When the crew awakes, they find they are unharmed on a planet with Earth-like gravity and oxygen although it contains some minor radiation. Having no radio contact with Earth and unable to repair the craft, the men take food, water and weapons and walk several miles until they get below the snow line and arrive in a green valley. Hank finds a cave where the men are attacked by two giant spiders, one of which they manage to kill. Getting back outside, they make camp for the night but are attacked by human-like mutants, one of which they kill. The creature has only one Cyclopean eye. The next day the astronauts come upon a cemetery with the latest date on the headstones reading 2188. This causes Dr. Galbraithe to speculate that their rocket traveled faster than the speed of light and they are on Earth in the distant future. While John and Herb accept the verdict, Hank is upset because he realizes his wife and two children have been dead for centuries. Guessing they are in either Colorado or New Mexico, the men press onward. Dr. Galbraithe tells Hank that John's wife and children died in a plane crash on the way to join him in Hawaii. John is attacked by the mutants and the others come to his rescue. They find refuge in a cave where they discover a metal door. When it lifts, they enter a lighted hallway where a voice tells them to leave behind their paraphernalia and enter a large room. There they are greeted by an old man, Timmek (Everett Glass), who introduces them to his council, including a younger member, Mories (Booth Colman). Timmek informs them that he and his people are the descendants of survivors of a devastating atomic war that took place five centuries before. They live underground where power plants and laboratories supply all their needs since radiation destroyed most of the surface world, leaving a race of deformed mutants. Mories informs the astronauts that his people are peaceful and need no weapons. The men meet Timmek's beautiful daughter Garnet (Gates) and she and John find they are attracted to each other, much to the chagrin of Mories who feels Garnet belongs to him. Another young woman, Elaine (Smith), is attracted to Herb, as is servant girl Deena (Montell). Garnet tells John that Deena came from the surface and not all those living above ground are mutants, although those not killed in infancy are enslaved by them. Since Garnet has said that her people will not engage in warfare, John tells Hank he feels Timmek and his men will not help them repair their ship so they can explore the planet in hopes of finding other pockets of civilization. After touring the underground world, the astronauts note the vitality of the women but the anemic quality of the men and the sparsity of small children. When the astronauts make a proposal to the council to set up an outpost on the surface in order to repair their ship, it is tabled for consideration although Mories accuses the newcomers of wanting to use their weapons to seize control and start a new war. Hank tells the others that he has learned the colony is dwindling in size. That evening Garnet shows John an old tunnel that leads to a hillside where they sit in the moonlight. Mories listens in on the astronauts planning to make their own weapons to fight the mutants and also learns that their guns are being kept by James (William Vedder) in his apartment. He goes there to confiscate the weapons and when James finds him, Mories hits him with a gun butt and kills him. He then stashes the weapons under a bed in the astronaut's quarters, not realizing he has been seen by Deena, who is jealous of Elaine for kissing Herb. Garnet tries to convince Timmek to let the men have the material they need, saying she loves John, but they are interrupted by the news of James' murder. The astronauts are captured and the guns found. The council members order them exiled above ground with their guns and supplies. When Deena tries to talk to Timmek, she is beaten by Mories. Timmek and his men find the young woman who tells them it was Mories who hid the guns and an order is issued for his capture. Mories runs out of the compound into the upper world where he is surrounded and bludgeoned to death by the mutants. Timmek and the council give the astronauts permission to fashion new weapons and they fabricate a rocket launcher to fight the savages. Deena finds out that Hank is in love with her. She tells John they only need to kill the mutant leader, Naga (Simpson), to free the normal ones being held captive. Going above ground, the four men use the bazooka to kill a number of the mutants, who take refuge in a cave. One of the normal slaves (Keith Richards) begs for mercy, and John tells Hank to take him back to Deena for questioning. She returns with Hank, saying Naga will order her people killed. Hank goes to check out the cave area but is wounded by Naga with a spear. John has Deena call to Naga, offering to fight him in one-to-one combat. Although the others protest, John says he can defeat Naga, who has no depth perception because of having only one eye. The savage runs out of the cave and attacks John but after a short skirmish, John manages to kill him. Deena tells the other mutants that John is now their leader and they retreat. Months later, a colony has been established on the surface, integrating the people from the underground with the normal ones once held as slaves. As John finds love with Garnet, Hank with Deena, and Herb with Elaine, the astronauts set out to rebuild the human race.

While viewers generally deem *World Without End* a cut above most Allied Artists sci-fi offerings, reviews of the film vary. Ed Naha in *Horrors: From Screen to Scream* (1975) dubbed it a "[s]ophomoric attempt at Wellsian moralizing." Steven H. Scheuer in *Movies on TV 1969–70* (1969) said, "An interesting premise makes this sci-fi tale a bit more absorbing than some comparable films." In *Science Fiction* (1984), Phil Hardy complained, "Ironically the money spent on the film's special effects only serves to highlight the weak melodramatics of Bernds' script and the stodginess of his direction." *John Stanley's Creature Feature Movie Guide Strikes Again* (1994) termed it an "[e]ntertaining grade-B actioner.... Nothing new, but fast moving with its many fights, monsters, etc." Dennis Fischer in *Science Fiction Film Directors, 1895–1998* (2000) stated, "*World Without End* plays the hoariest of science fiction cliches to the hilt, and while it is never invigorating, it never becomes completely boring either."

Television Features

In the mid–1970s, Allied Artists Television, a subsidiary of Allied Artists Pictures Corporation, released several packages of motion pictures for television distribution. These packages included not only Monogram and Allied Artists theatrical films but also motion pictures made by other companies. Of the latter, twenty-two feature films dealing with horror, science fiction and fantasy were included in some of these packages and they are discussed here. Some of the movies were re-titled for television.

Atlas (The Filmgroup, 1961; 79 minutes; Color)

Producer-Director: Roger Corman. Associate Producer-Screenplay-Production Manager: Charles B. Griffith. Photography: Basil Maros. Editor: Michael Luciano. Music: Ronald Stein. Sound: Allen Hershey. Costumes: Barbaro Comeau. Assistant Director: Henry Yatron.

CAST: Michael Forest (Atlas), Frank Wolff (Praximedes), Barboura Morris (Candia), Walter Maslow (Garnis), Christos Exarchos (Indros), Andreas Flippides (King Talectos), Miranda Kounelaki (Ariana), Sascha Dario (Dancer), Theodoros Dimitriou (General Gallus), William Jolley (Seronikosian Rebel), Robert Hudson (Socrates), Jean Moore (Handmaiden), Dick Miller, Charles B. Griffith (Thenisian Soldiers), Roger Corman (Seronikosian Senator), James Carleton, Keith Whitley, Charles Stirling (Soldiers).

Producer-director Roger Corman's company, The Filmgroup, released *Atlas* in the spring of 1961. It was filmed the previous year in Greece. Corman originally announced it would be a big-budget road show production but when local financing fizzled it was done in ten days for $70,000. Sword-and-sandal epics were the rage at the time thanks to the Hercules films with Steve Reeves and their Continental offshoots. *Atlas* proved to be a tacky, puny effort despite some nice on-location shooting at actual Greek ruins and color filming in Vitsascope. Unable to corral more than a handful of extras as soldiers, Corman filmed the tepid battle scenes in close-ups with Filmgroup regular Dick Miller and the film's writer, Charles B. Griffith, having bits as participants. Special billing is given to Sascha Dario, the prima ballerina of the Greek National Opera. Michael Forest is a listless Atlas although Frank Wolff has a field day chewing up scenery as the wicked warlord Praximedes; the two actors previously starred in Corman's *Beast from Haunted Cave* (1960) [q.v.]. Another Filmgroup member, Barboura Morris, was the leading lady, displaying more legs than energy.

Located in the northern mountains of Greece, the city of Thenis is under siege by Praximedes (Wolff) of Seronikos, a self-proclaimed tyrant. At a meeting between Thenis' King Talectos (Andreas Flippides) and Praximedes, it is proposed that the drawn-out fight be decided with a match to the death between Talectos's son Indros (Christos Exarchos) and a warrior of Praximedes' choice. Agreeing to the proposal, Praximedes travels to the Olympic Games in Athens with his mistress Candia (Morris) and advisor Garnis (Walter

Maslow). There they see Atlas (Forest) defeat another wrestler and become the hero of the games. Praximedes asks Atlas to fight Indros for him. After falling under the spell of Candia, the mighty man agrees, although he refuses to kill his opponent if he wins. On the way back to Thenis, Praximedes and his soldiers are attacked by rebels whom he orders his men to massacre. In Thenis, Atlas engages in combat with Indros and defeats him but refuses Praximedes' command to kill the man. Keeping his word, King Talectos turns Thenis over to Praximedes and his men. During a banquet, Candia is slapped by her lover; she asks Atlas to take her with him when he leaves the city. Secretly, Praximedes has some of his men dress as Thenisian soldiers and massacre more than 800 citizens. Atlas and Candia observe the slaughter. King Talectos is arrested and charged by Praximedes with instigating the massacre. Praximedes' general, Gallus (Theodoros Dimitriou), is made the judge at Talectos' trial, with Garnis as his defender and Praximedes as the prosecutor. The king is found guilty and ordered executed with an axe. Praximedes lets a disgusted Atlas leave the city as Indros' lover, Ariana (Miranda Kounelaki), helps Candia get out of Thenis. Garnis lusts for the beautiful blonde Ariana but she refuses his offer of help. Candia and Atlas meet outside the city, but when Praximedes finds his mistress is missing he follows them and they are captured by his soldiers. Riding back to Thenis, the band is attacked by Indros, who escaped the slaughter, and his rebels. Atlas and Candia are freed as Praximedes rides back to the city. There he informs Garnis to guard Ariana who he wants to use as a hostage. Garnis tells the young woman her life is in danger and for her to go to Athens where he will meet her. When Garnis informs Praximedes that Ariana is missing, the tyrant accuses him of treachery and stabs him to death. Ariana goes to Indros as Atlas conceives a plan to sneak most of the rebels into Thenis through a secret passage since Praximedes will lead his men to ambush them. The rebels take the city as its few defenders surrender. When Praximedes finds he has been tricked, he takes his army back to Thenis where it is are defeated by the rebels. In hand-to-hand combat with Atlas, Praximedes is killed. With peace restored to Thenis, Atlas and Candia ride off to Egypt.

The year 1961 saw the release of more than a dozen sword-and-sandal costume dramas and while none of them can be considered epics, *Atlas* was certainly the runt of the litter. The *British Monthly Film Bulletin* complained, "Not one of the best Cormans.... Both script and acting leave much to be desired.... [I]t's all a bit too heavy and plodding." Joe Kane in *The Phantom of the Movies' Videoscope* (2000) claimed, "[Charles B.] Griffith's script and [Barboura] Morris' appealing presence help save the day" while *VideoHound's Complete Guide to Cult Flicks and Trash Pics* (1996) states, "The script adds wit, style, and even some political commentary to the sword and sandal shenanigans, while avoiding all the more expensive clichés." *Video Watchdog* #4 (1991) dubbed the film "amusingly undernourished" and noticed that Jack Nicholson may have played one of the battle scene warriors: "[H]is shield's in the way, but that smile is unmistakable."

Allied Artists Television included *Atlas* in its "Science-Fiction Features" package.

The Brain from Planet Arous (Howco International, 1957; 71 minutes)

Producer-Photography: Jacques Marquette. Associate Producer: Dale Tate. Director: Nathan Hertz [Juran]. Screenplay: Ray Buffum. Editor: Irving Schoenberg. Music: Walter Greene. Sound: Philip Mitchell. Makeup: Jack Pierce. Technical Advisor: J.L. Cassingham. Assistant Director: Bert Chervin.

CAST: John Agar (Steve March), Joyce Meadows (Sally Fallon), Robert Fuller (Dan Murphy), Thomas B. Henry (John Fallon), Ken Terrell (Colonel), Henry Travis (Colonel Frogley), E. Leslie Thomas (General Brown), Tim Graham (Sheriff Wally Paine), Bill Giorgio (Soviet Observer), Dale

Joyce Meadows and Thomas B. Henry in *The Brain from Planet Arous* (Howco International, 1957)

Tate (Professor Dale Tate/Voices of Gor and Vol), Kenner G. Kemp, Gil Perkins (Military Men), George (Dog).

Cinematographer Jacques Marquette made a brief foray into the production side of filming in the late 1950s when he produced and photographed *The Brain from Planet Arous*. With most of the same crew from that film, he also took over as director for *Teenage Monster*, which Howco International put out on a double-bill with *Brain*. The next year he was executive producer and did the camerawork on *Attack of the 50 Foot Woman* (q.v.) and in 1961 he had the same chores with *Flight of the Lost Balloon* (q.v.). He also photographed *Creature from the Haunted Sea* (q.v.) and *The Strangler* (1964) [qq.v.]. Billed as Nathan Hertz, Nathan Juran directed both *Attack of the 50 Foot Woman* and *The Brain from Planet Arous*. Considering the content of both sci-fers, it is no wonder he used a non de plume. Dale Tate, the associate producer of *Brain*, supplied the voices of aliens Gor and Vol so the title should have been *The Brains from Planet Arous*, although only one model was used for both aliens. Outside of the use of the caverns in Bronson Canyon, the film is pictorially arid although it packs a lot of activity into its brief running time. It was released to TV in Allied Artists Television's "Science-Fiction Features" package.

A mysterious object crashes into Mystery Mountain and a short time later scientists Steve March (John Agar) and Dan Murphy (Robert Fuller), who are experimenting with nuclear fission in the desert, notice high radioactivity with the source thirty miles away. The two men have lunch with Steve's fiancée Sally Fallon (Joyce Meadows) and her father John (Thomas B. Henry) and then go by Jeep to the origin of the disturbance. They find a huge cave recently blasted out of a mountain and when they enter it they notice that the radioactivity comes and goes. The men see a huge floating brain with two eyes coming at them and when they fire at the thing, it emits a ray that knocks out Steve and kills Dan. The thing then takes possession of Steve's body. A week later, Fallon calls his worried daughter to see if Steve and Dan have returned and a short time later Steve shows up saying Dan has gone to Las Vegas. When Steve gets too rough with Sally, her dog George attacks him. He leaves after Sally tells Steve he needs to see a doctor. When he returns to his laboratory after experiencing severe head pain, the alien arises from Steve's brain and tells him that it is Gor from the distant planet Arous. The thing says it will use Steve's body as a dwelling place and that it finds Sally to be very exciting. The next day Sally and her father go to Mystery Mountain and find the cave containing Dan's dead body. They are met by a giant brain named Vol who tells them that it too is from Arous and that it has come to Earth to capture the outlaw Gor. It says Gor is controlling Steve and it says it will meet them at their home the next day to map out a strategy to capture the criminal alien. Steve arranges with Colonel Frogley (Henry Travis) to be an observer at an atomic energy test at Indian Springs and Gor promises Steve that it will demonstrate something that will use the power of pure intellect, letting it rule the planet. Vol informs Sally and her father that Gor is insane for power and asks their permission to use George as a host so it can keep a close watch on the criminal. Ordering Steve to see Sally, Gor uses its powers to destroy an airplane, killing 38 people. As they take George along, Sally tells Steve that he seems different and he says he plans to introduce an important discovery at the atomic test, a power that will make him the most feared man on Earth. When Steve again tries to seduce Sally, she pushes him away and he apologizes, saying he got carried away. Hearing about the airplane crash, they go to the site where Frogley shows Steve a burned corpse and says the destruction was caused by some unearthly power. Back home, Sally informs her father that she thinks Gor's possession of Steve caused the tragedy. Vol tells them that Gor must leave the host body each day to get oxygen and that it can be destroyed by being struck at a spot called the Fissure of Orlando, on the top of the brain.

Sheriff Paine (Tim Graham) talks to Steve about Dan's death and when he threatens to arrest him, Steve tells him he killed Dan and caused the plane crash and then murders the lawman. At a meeting of the military and various scientists, General Brown (E. Leslie Thomas) announces that the Earth has been invaded but the atomic test will be held. Steve tells them of this powers and demonstrates by destroying the test site and another airplane. When Frogley tries to shoot him, he is slain. Steve demands to meet with world leaders that night and intends to give them a demonstration that will cause as much excitement as the bombing of Hiroshima. Exhausted, Steve later confides to Sally that after they are married they will be rich and live in Washington, D.C. Meeting with representatives of the United States, Great Britain, France, the Soviet Union, China and India, Steve says he wants these nations' resources so he can build an interplanetary fleet of rockets to return to Arous and become the master of the universe. He also says he will take over the United Nations building and meet with them again in two days. With Vol's aid, Sally finds a diagram of the brain and points out the Fissure of Orlando and leaves it in Steve's laboratory. When he returns, she hides as Gor leaves Steve's body and Steve sees the picture. Sally backs into the sheriff's body and screams and Gor attacks her but Steve comes at the alien with an axe and kills it. Vol leaves for Arous as Steve returns to normal and kisses Sally, who tries to tell him how Vol helped her.

John Agar does as well as possible in the lead role, considering he is playing a man whose body is taken over by a horny alien who not only wants to rule the universe but is hot for his woman. Joyce Meadows as the feminine interest appears worried most of the time and Thomas B. Henry seems mostly uninterested as her father. The title monster is neither intimidating or frightening. Surprisingly, Donald C. Willis in *Horror and Science Fiction Films: A Checklist* (1972) called it "the usual." While the film is not good, or even mediocre, it is hardly usual. C.J. Henderson in *The Encyclopedia of Science Fiction Movies* (2001) wrote, "It sounds awful, but it's actually fun to watch if for no other reason than Agar's performance. Trashy, but not *that* trashy." Regarding the brains, Dennis Fischer commented in *Science Fiction Film Directors, 1895–1998* (2000), "[They] were simply balloons with lit up interiors manipulated on piano wires with a pair of eyes on the front lobes, but they do make memorable menaces, especially with Dale Tate's sinister readings for Gor."

Castle of Terror (Woolner Bros., 1964; 84 minutes)

Producers: Frank Belty [Leo Lax] and Walter Sarch [Mario Vicario]. Director: Anthony M. Dawson [Antonio Margheriti]. Screenplay: Jean Girmaud [Giovanni Grimaldi] and Gordon Wilson, Jr. [Sergio Corbucci]. Photography: Richard Kramer [Riccardo Pallottini]. Editor: Othel Langhel [Otello Colangeli]. Music: Ritz [Riz] Ortolani. Art Director: Walter Scott [Ottavio Scotti]. Special Effects: E. Catalucci. Makeup: Sonny Arden. Wardrobe: Rose Lynne. Assistant Director: Roger Drake [Ruggero Deodato].

CAST: Barbara Steele (Elisabeth Blackwood), Georges Reviere (Alan Foster), Margarete Robsahm (Julia), Henry Kruger [Arturo Dominici] (Dr. Carmus), Montgomery Glenn [Silvano Tranquilli] (Edgar Allan Poe), Sylvia Sorrente (Elsi), Raoul H. Newman [Umberto Raho] (Sir Thomas Blackwood), Phil Karson [Giovanni Cianfriglia/Ken Wood] (Herbert), John Peters (William Blackwood), Merry Powers (Cynthia Blackwood), Ben Steffen [Benito Stefanelli] (Groom), Salvo Randone (Tavern Keeper), Johnny Walters (Driver).

Allegedly based on a short story by Edgar Allan Poe, *Castle of Terror* was shown theatrically in the United States in the summer of 1964 by Woolner Bros. as *Castle of Blood*. Allied Artists released it to TV in its "Cavalcade of the '60's — Group V" and "Science-Fiction Features" packages. A French-Italian co-production, it was made in Italy as *Danza Macabre* (Macabre Dance) by Vulsinia Film–Jolly Film–Ulysse Productions–Leo Lax Films. In its homeland it was also called *La Lunga Notte del Terrore* (The Long Night of Terror) and *Terrore* (Terror), while its alternate English titles include *Coffin of Horror*, *Coffin of Terror* and *Tombs of Horror* as well as *Dimensions in Death*, *Edgar Allan Poe's Castle of Blood* and *Edgar Allan Poe's Castle of Terror*. Under any title, it is a scary horror thriller, nicely paced and moody, with all of its scenes taking place at night except for the brief finale. Beautiful Barbara Steele highlights the proceedings as the specter heroine and Georges Reviere nicely handles the role of the protagonist who must spend a night in a supposedly haunted castle to win a bet. The actors manage to keep the characters believable and the gothic feel of the old castle in which most of the film takes place adds greatly to the atmosphere of endless terror.

In 1840s London, *Times* journalist Alan Foster (Reviere) arrives at a tavern to meet visiting author Edgar Allan Poe (Montgomery Glenn) on All Souls' Night. The dissipated Poe is reciting one of his tales of the living dead to Sir Thomas Blackwood (Raoul H. Newman). Alan scoffs when the author claims his works are not fiction. Sir Thomas bets Alan ten pounds he cannot spend the night in the old castle on a cliff near Providence, where honeymooners disappeared after going there on their wedding night. Sir Thomas and Poe drive Alan to the castle, agreeing to meet him there at dawn. Entering the dark abode, Alan is soon frightened by his own reflection in a mirror and later hears music, briefly seeing couples dance. He is soon met by a beautiful woman, Elisabeth Blackwood (Steele), who says she lives alone in the castle, and that each year Sir Thomas sends someone to visit her.

Barbara Steele and Georges Reviere in *Castle of Blood* (Woolner Bros., 1964)

She asks him to stay in order to spite Sir Thomas and takes Alan to a bedroom where they are joined by Julia (Margarete Robsahm), whose beauty the man earlier admired when he saw her portrait. In the hallway, Elisabeth informs Julia that Alan belongs to her and that he must never learn the truth about the castle. Elisabeth also says she loves Alan and accuses Julia of being jealous. Returning to Alan's room, Elisabeth learns he is very attracted to her and they kiss, not knowing they are being spied on by Julia. In bed, Alan rests his head on Elisabeth's breast but cannot hear her heart beat. She says it has not beat for ten years because she is dead. A shirtless man (Phil Karson) runs into the room and stabs Elisabeth and runs away as Alan shoots at him. Returning to the bedroom, Alan finds Elisabeth is gone. Hunting for her, he meets Dr. Carmus (Henry Kruger), a famous scientist the writer thought was deceased. Carmus says he saw what happened but was unable to intervene. The doctor also relates to Alan he can prove that humans can exist after death. He also claims that the castle's dead will soon relive their last five minutes of life. At midnight, Alan and Carmus see the dead dancing. Elisabeth tells the shirtless man, the castle's gardener Herbert, to go away although he reminds her she said she loved him more than her husband William (John Peters). After the guests, including William's brother Sir Thomas and his wife Cynthia (Merry Powers), leave, Elisabeth and William make love. Herbert breaks into their bedroom and strangles William. He then tries to kill Elisabeth but is struck and killed by Julia, who then tries to seduce Elisabeth; she stabs her to death. Alan searches for Carmus and demands to be let out of the castle. Alan watches as Carmus enters the castle's crypt and opens a stone coffin with the decayed corpse inside returning to life and becoming mist. Herbert murders Carmus, who tells Alan that is how he met his destiny. Two newlyweds

(Sylvia Sorrente, Ben Steffen) arrive at the castle to spend their wedding night and they too are murdered by Herbert. As Julia and Carmus tell Alan that it is his turn to die, he runs to the crypt where Elisabeth says the ghosts need his blood so they can return to life next year. She leads him through a passage to the outside but tells him she cannot go with him. Alan drags Elisabeth into the night only to see her decompose beside her tombstone. Running from the other spirits, Alan is impaled on the castle's iron gate. At dawn Sir Thomas and Poe return and find Alan dead with the castle's owner taking ten pounds from the dead man's purse. The voices of Elisabeth and Alan tell each other they are together forever.

Castle of Terror's director, Antonio Margheriti (billed as Anthony M. Dawson) had a lengthy genre career, including *Assignment Outer Space* (1960), *Battle of the Worlds* (1961), *Horror Castle* (1963), *The Long Hair of Death* (1964), also with Steele; *Wild, Wild Planet* (1965), *Lightning Bolt* (q.v.) and *The War of the Planets* (both 1966), *Mr. Superinvincible* (1970), *Seven Deaths in a Cat's Eye* (1973), *Whisky and Ghosts* (1976), *Killer Fish* (1979), *Cannibal Apocalypse* (1980), *The Hunters of the Golden Cobra* (1982), *Ark of the Sun God* (1983), *Yor, the Hunter from the Future* (1983), *Treasure Island in Outer Space* (1987) and *Alien from the Deep* (1989). In 1971 Margheriti remade *Castle of Terror* as *Web of the Spider*, starring Anthony Franciosa, Michele Mercier and Klaus Kinski (as Edgar Allan Poe). Billed as Gordon Wilson, Jr., director Sergio Corbucci receives co-writing credit for *Castle of Terror*. In an interview with Carlo Piazza in *Cine Zine Zone* (May 1989) he claims he directed more than half of the film before turning it over to Margheriti so that he, Corbucci, could work on another assignment. The film's assistant director, Ruggero Deodato, billed as Roger Drake, went on to direct such gore features as *Jungle Holocaust* (*The Last Survivor*) (1976) and *Cannibal Holocaust* (1978).

In *The Encyclopedia of Horror Movies* (1986), Phil Hardy noted, "Margheriti's direction is wonderfully atmospheric, with long, meandering sequence shots and perfectly executed gothic imagery." *The Phantom's Ultimate Video Guide* (1989) said *Castle of Terror* has an "earnestly creepy flair.... [Steele is] sepulchrally seductive.... [I]t's a good bet for Italo Gothic horror fans." James O'Neill in *Terror on Tape* (1994) thought it an "[a]bove-average Steele vehicle.... Barbara is shown to good advantage as the dreamy Elisabeth...." According to *VideoHound's Complete Guide to Cult Flicks and Trash Pics* (1996), "Cult favorite Steele enhances this atmospheric chiller" while Luca M. Palmerini and Gaetano Mistretta in *Spaghetti Nightmares* (1996) declared it to be a "classic of its kind."

Castle of Terror was issued on video in France around 1990 as *Danse Macabre* (Macabre Dance) running 87 minutes, four minutes longer than the U.S. version. *Video Watchdog* #7 (1991) said this "uncovered version contains Barbara's lesbian kiss with Margarete Robsahm, and a brief disrobing scene of newlywed Sylvia Sorrente."

Creature from the Haunted Sea (The Filmgroup, 1961; 74 minutes)

Producer-Director: Roger Corman. Associate Producer: Charles Hanawalt. Screenplay: Charles B. Griffith. Photography: Jacques Marquette. Editor: Angela Scellars. Music: Fred Katz. Production Manager: Jack Bohrer. Sound: Roberto Velasquez. Makeup: Brooke Wilkerson. Monster Costume Design: Beach Dickerson.

CAST: Antony Carbone (Renzo Capeto), Betsy Jones-Moreland (Mary Belle Monahan), Edward Wain [Robert Towne] (Sparks Moran/Agent XK150/Narrator), Edmund Rivera Alvarez (General Tostada), Robert Bean (Happy Jack Monahan/The Creature), Sonia Noemi Gonzalez (Mango Perez), Beach Dickerson (Pete Peterson, Jr.), Esther Sandoval (Carmelita Rodriguez), Terry Nevin (Colonel), Blanquita Romero (Rosina Perez), Elsio Lopez, Tanner Hunt, Armando Rowra

(Rebel Soldiers), Jaclyn Hellman (Agent XK120 in TV version), Richard Sinatra (Man Waiting To Use Pay Phone), Kay Jennings (Bar Spy).

Following the overthrow of the Batista regime in Cuba by Fidel Castro, General Tostada (Edmund Rivera Alvarez), his colonel (Terry Nevin) and a group of soldiers rob the country's treasury and make a deal with expatriate American Mafioso Renzo Capeto (Antony Carbone) to smuggle the gold out of the island country on his yacht. After escaping from government soldiers, the craft heads out to sea with Capeto's mistress, gun moll Mary Belle Monahan (Betsy Jones-Moreland), her morose younger brother Happy Jack (Robert Bean), the gangster's dim-witted but loyal associate Pete Peterson, Jr. (Beach Dickerson), who does animal imitations, and crew member Sparks Moran (Robert Towne), really U.S. government spy, Agent XK150. Renzo wants to get rid of half the Cuban contingent so he decides to use the legend of a local sea monster to cover up his eliminating the soldiers. He has Pete use a toilet plunger to make "footprints" so that it will appear as though a sea creature boarded the craft when they kill one of the soldiers, although they do not realize the real Creature (Bean) killed a second one. The general believes it was the Creature and Renzo suggests they change course to Puerto Rico. The incompetent Moran wires his superiors that the yacht is headed for Bali. As Mary Belle sings a song about the Creature from the Haunted Sea, Renzo and Pete kill the members of a Cuban military boat. Moran tells Mary Belle he wants her and she is repulsed. Renzo outlines a plan to Pete in which he will wreck the yacht on some rocks, take the gold by boat to the island but upset it, causing the treasure to sink to the bottom of the sea. He says they will return later to get the strongbox, sending Happy Jack to San Juan for supplies. The two carry out the plan and the yacht's passengers reach the island. As the others built thatch huts, Pete explores the jungle and meets a hefty middle-aged woman, Rosina Perez (Blanquita Romero), who also does animal calls, and they immediately fall in love. Pete takes Rosina back to camp. Happy Jack shows up with the boat and brings with him Carmelita Rodriguez (Esther Sandoval), a waterfront hooker he professes to love. To his dismay, Renzo learns from the general that his soldiers are actually frogmen and are ready to dive for the strongbox. Moran meets Carmelita and they fall for each other. During the dive, Renzo, Pete and Happy Jack kill several of the Cubans and blame the sea monster. After Carmelita tells Happy Jack she loves Moran, who still wants Mary Belle, Rosina takes Happy Jack into the jungle and introduces him to her beautiful daughter Mango (Sonia Noemi Gonzalez) and he is immediately smitten. When Rosina's husband objects to her playing around, he is knocked out by Pete who allies with Happy Jack in getting rid of the rest of their crew in order to stay on the island and marry Rosina and Mango. During the next dive, Renzo finds the strongbox and hides it under a wreck. After he leaves, it is retrieved by the Creature. After the monster carries off Mango, Happy Jack accuses Renzo of killing her, and Mary Belle agrees with her brother. Wanting to get rid of the rest of the Cubans, Renzo and his men dive the next day with spear guns. When the general finds the gold, he is killed by the gangster and Pete. After finding the remains of Mango's sarong, Happy Jack is attacked and killed by the sea monster. On the yacht, Mary Belle blames Renzo for her brother's death. The monster boards the craft and abducts Mary Belle and returns to attack the rest of the passengers as Moran and Carmelita escape in a lifeboat. Renzo manages to get to shore but the monster follows and kills him. As they look forward to the future together, Moran informs Carmelita that it was the Creature from the Haunted Sea who got the gold.

Producer-director Roger Corman produced *Battle of Blood Island* (1960) in Puerto Rico and followed it with *Last Woman on Earth* (1960) [q.v.], which he also directed. Using the latter film's cinematographer (Jacques Marquette) and three lead players (Antony Carbone, Betsy Jones-Moreland, Edward Wain [Robert Towne]), he quickly shot a third feature, *Creature from the Haunted Sea*, a horror comedy reworking of Charles B. Griffith's script for *Beast from Haunted Cave* (1959) [q.v.], itself refashioned by Griffith from Corman's *Naked Paradise* (*Thunder Over Hawaii*) (1956). The Filmgroup, a small company operated by Corman and his brother Gene Corman, released *Creature from the Haunted Sea* in June 1961, usually combined with *The Devil's Partner*.

Creature from the Haunted Sea is one of those films viewers either love or hate; there appears to be no middle ground. It looks, and is, cheap. Its forced humor, some of it funny, and oddball characters give the film what little entertainment value it possesses. No one is really likable, except the beautiful Mango, who ends up being a meal for the title creature. The cast seems to be having fun with the affair and the acting is uniformly good. Robert Bean, who started out as the boom operator, took over the role of Happy Jack when Roger Corman vacated it; Bean also played the title monster. Beach Dickerson, who was the pea-brained animal imitator Pete Peterson, Jr., designed the creature. It is one of the tackiest monsters ever put on film.

Creature from the Haunted Sea, which ran theatrically at 63 minutes, was too short for a 90-minute TV time slot, so 11 minutes of new additional footage was shot and interpolated, most of it directed by Monte Hellman. These scenes include a nearly six-minute segment prior to the credits where Agent XK150 (Towne) escapes from two assassins and meets his beautiful counterpart, Agent XK120 (Jaclyn Hellman, the director's wife) in a Santo Domingo bar. In another new sequence, he phones her in Havana from a pay phone on a desolate beach to report that the case is about to break wide open. *Creature* was included in Allied Artists Television's "Science-Fiction Features."

Crypt of the Living Dead (Atlas Films, 1973; 85 minutes; Color)

Producer: Lou Shaw. Executive Producer: Wolf Schmidt. Director: Ray Danton and (uncredited) Julio Salvador. Screenplay: Ricardo Ferrer, Lou Shaw and Julio Salvador. Story: Ricardo Ferrer and Lois Gibson. Photography: Juan Gelpi. Editor: David Rawlins. Music: Phillip Lambro. Art Director: Juan Alberto. Production Manager: Antonio Espinosa. Unit Manager: Ali Taygun. Sound Effects: Marv Kerner. Makeup: Mariano Garcia Rey. Special Effects: A. Molina. Assistant Director: Gil Carretero.

CAST: Andrew Prine (Chris Bolton), Mark Damon (Peter), Teresa Gimpera (Queen Hannah), Patty Sheppard (Mary), Ihsan Genik (Wild Man), Mariano [Garcia] Rey (Professor Bolton), Frank [Brana] Branya (Abdul Hamid), Edward Walsh (Ali), John Alderman (First Fisherman), Jack LaRue, Jr. (Adnan), Jem Osmanoglu (Boy), Shera Osman (Zora), Daniel Martin (John).

The Spanish production *Crypt of the Living Dead* has a puzzling history. Filmed in Turkey, it was made as *La Tumba de la Isla Maldita* (The Tomb of the Cursed Island), directed by Julio Salvador, who collaborated on the script with Ricardo Ferrer, from a story by Ferrer and Lois Gibson. Its original running time was 99 minutes. When the production was acquired for U.S. release, actor Ray Danton, who had helmed Robert Quarry's *Deathmaster* (1972), directed new scenes from script additions by the film's producer, Lou Shaw. Quite a bit of the original footage was removed and the movie, now called *Hannah, Queen of the Vampires*, ran 85 minutes. Atlas Films released it in the U.S. in the fall of 1973; it was rated PG. Allied Artists included it in its TV packages "The Golden Seventies—Group VII" and "Science-Fiction Features" a few years later as *Crypt of the Living Dead*. It was filmed in Metrocolor but some prints are black and white. The TV version was later issued on video as *Vampire Woman*, *Vampire Women* and *Young Hannah, Queen of the Vampires*.

Under any title it is very atmospheric with effective sinister locales but it is hampered by many overly dark scenes and a sometimes muffled soundtrack.

In an ancient church on a Turkish island, Professor Bolton (Mariano Rey) is searching for the tomb of Hannah (Teresa Gimpera), the wife of French King Louis VII, who had her buried alive there in 1269 for practicing vampirism. Finding Hannah's coffin, Bolton is strangled by Peter (Mark Damon) and shoved under the vault by his cohort, Wild Man (Ihsan Genik), who uses a hammer to knock loose the vault's foundation which comes crashing down on the dead man. Chris Bolton (Andrew Prine), the professor's engineer son, comes to the island to bury his father and is ignored by the local fishermen. Peter takes him to the church and shows him the place where his father lies. Peter is writing a novel about Hannah and how she came to be buried there on a return trip from the Crusades with her royal husband. Chris, who also meets Peter's schoolteacher sister Mary (Patty Sheppard), says he wants to move the tomb to remove and bury his father's body. During the night, Chris sees Wild Man and chases him. Mary later informs the engineer that the professor was researching the legend of Hannah. Rigging a hoist, Chris breaks the seal on the marble tomb in order to move it in two sections. The reluctant locals finally agree to pull the hoist ropes as the skies turn black and a storm erupts. Chris peers into the tomb and finds Hannah perfectly preserved. As Chris later talks to Peter about the corpse, Hannah returns to life, rises from the tomb as a mist and turns into a wolf that kills the dog of blind sailor Abdul Hamid (Frank Brana) for its blood. Hamid warns the locals that the vampire has returned, and that in two days she will have full strength unless her tomb is resealed. Chris goes back to the tomb as the Wild Man carries off Mary. Hearing her screams, he pursues the two and saves the young woman, using his knife to put out one of her abductor's eyes. As they sit by a bonfire on the beach, Mary informs Chris that there have been rumors of a devil cult on the island. They spend the night together; they are awakened the next morning by Hamid, who brings them wolfbane, telling them to spread it around Hannah's tomb to keep her inside. Peter secrely watches as Chris and his sister have sex. Later, Chris informs Peter that he wants to take Mary away from the island. Jubilant over Mary having found happiness, Chris says she came to the island to look after him due to his addiction to drugs and helped him put his life back together. Hamid has a young man, Adnan (Jack LaRue, Jr.), prepare a stake to drive into the vampire's heart but as he makes a crucifix he is murdered by the Wild Man. After Hamid's body is found in the tomb, Chris wants to reseal it but the others refuse to help him. Going back to the tomb alone, Chris removes the garlic, sees that Hannah has disappeared and goes to warn the villagers. The vampire attacks Adnan's father, Ali (Edward Walsh), as Chris hunts for Mary. She has gone to the tomb where she finds her brother conducting a ceremony in homage to Hannah. When he is attacked by the Wild Man, Chris uses a stake to kill him. Mary promises to stay with her brother if he will only leave the island. Peter tells her he killed Professor Bolton and plans to do the same with Chris. Hannah starts to attack a young girl (Shera Osman) but is spotted by the villagers and turns into a wolf. Tying up Mary, Peter prays to Hannah for eternal life while Ali, now a vampire, begs Chris to kill him with a stake through the heart. After doing so, Chris tries to stop Peter from sacrificing Mary to the vampire. As the two men fight, Peter falls on Chris' knife and the sight of his blood causes Hannah to attack him. Giving Mary the wolfbane for protection, Chris returns to the tomb as the villagers surround Hannah with crosses. She turns into mist as one of the men drives a stake into Peter, killing him. When Chris calls to Hannah, she attacks him in the form of a wolf. Mary uses the wolfbane to make her stop. Chris sets the vampire on fire with a lantern and her badly burned form is surrounded by the villagers. As she tries to fend them off, Chris drives a stake through her heart. Later he buries his father and leaves the island with Mary as the young girl, now fanged, attacks a playmate (Jem Osmanoglu).

Phil Hardy noted in *The Encyclopedia of Horror Movies* (1986), "Scenes of graphic violence punctuate the movie and culminate in the images of [Teresa] Gimpera set alight with an oil lamp and staked with the camera chronicling in detail the disintegration of her body and face into an unsightly mess. Script and dialogue are both rudimentary...." In *Terror on Tape* (1994), James O'Neill thought it a "low-cost vampire tale," adding, "[P]oor Hannah, sporting a paste tiara making her look like the hometown beauty queen, is given short shrift indeed, spending most of her time in her tomb before being set on fire and staked. Some days it just doesn't pay to get out of bed." [I]n *The Essential Monster Movie Guide* (2000), Stephen Jones wrote, "Atmospheric night sequences and unusual Turkish locations make this an interesting vampire thriller."

Crypt of the Living Dead was made by a number of people who were genre veterans. Besides *Deathmaster*, Ray Danton also directed *Psychic Killer* (1976) while top-billed Andrew Prine was in *Simon, King of the Witches* (1971), *Terror Circus* (*Barn of the Naked Dead*) (1973), *The Town That Dreaded Sundown* and *Grizzly* (both 1976), *The Evil* (1978) and *Amityville II: The Possession* (1982). Mark Damon was in *House of Usher* (1962), *Beauty and the Beast* (1963), *Black Sabbath* (1964), *The Young, the Evil and the Savage* (1968) and *The Devil's Wedding Night* (1973). Beautiful Teresa Gimpera appeared in the horror outings *Count Dracula* and *Aoom* (both 1970), *The Devil's Lover* and *Night of the Devils* (both 1971), *Spirit of the Beehive* (1973) and *The People Who Own the Dark* (1975). Equally gorgeous Patty Sheppard was in *The Man Who Came from Ummo* (*Assignment Terror/Dracula vs. Frankenstein*) and *La Noche de Walpurgis* (*Werewolf vs. the Vampire Woman*) (both 1970) and *Witches' Mountain* (1972). Mariano Garcia Rey, who played the role of Professor Bolton, was also *Crypt of the Living Dead*'s makeup artist. Daniel Martin, the star of several spaghetti Westerns, had a bit part as one of the villagers; his role may have been much larger in the original Spanish version of the film.

Dark Venture (First National Film Distributing, 1956; 84 minutes; Color)

Producer-Director-Screenplay-Editor: John Trevlac [Calvert]. Photography: Sven Persson. Music: Louis Palange, George Brown and Leonid Rabb. Sound: Doug Geerdts. Sets: Koos Botha. Production Manager: Jack Hall. Costumes: Hilda Combs. Special Effects: Ted Allan. Makeup: Ray Madison. Continuity: Madrian Calvert. Assistant Director: Lindsley Parsons, Jr.

CAST: John Calvert (John Kenyon), Ann Cornell (Pamela Cameron), John Carradine (Gideon), Charles Haydon (Dr. Cameron), Stuart Mitchell (MacIntyre), Paul Gordon (Cuthbert Matumba-Baobab), Bruce Meredith Smith (Harley Barlow), Jimmy the Chimp (Himself), Swazi Tribesmen (Themselves).

Produced by Expedition Epics Film Corporation and filmed in Panorama-Scope, *Dark Venture* is an obscure jungle melodrama that touches on the supernatural with its plot involving a sacred elephant burial ground and a phantom-like figure (played by horror film great John Carradine) who guards it. The movie is the work of John Calvert, who not only starred in it with his wife Ann Cornell, but also produced, directed, wrote the script and edited it under the name John Trevlac, his surname spelled backward.

Calvert, a native of Trenton, Indiana, came to fame in the 1930s as a professional magician, the Great Calvert, and began working in films in the next decade. Cinematically, he is best known for essaying the role of Michael Waring, "The Falcon," in a trio of Film Classics releases, *Devil's Cargo* and *Appointment with Murder* (both 1948) and *Search for*

Danger (1949), the latter with Cornell, who also co-starred with her husband in *Gold Fever* (1952). Filmed in 1955 in the East African areas of Kenya and Mozambique, *Dark Venture* includes the song "The Jungle" by Leonid Rabb and George Brown. It was issued to TV by Allied Artists in the mid–1970s in its "Cavalcade of the '60s — Group III" package.

John Kenyon (Calvert) comes to Africa in search of a reputed elephant burial ground rich in ivory. After searching for six months he meets Harley Barlow (Bruce Meredith Smith), a poacher, who ill treats his tracker Baobab. Barlow incites a local tribe to eliminate Kenyon by saying he killed the chief's sacred cow. Kenyon is warned by Baobab and the two men use dynamite, disguised as magic, to scare off the natives. The tracker leads Kenyon to a herd of old elephants, not realizing they are being trailed by Barlow, who kills several of the animals. When Kenyon tries to stop him, Barlow threatens to shoot him. Kenyon is forced to kill him to protect himself. The wounded Kenyon is taken to a remote village where Dr. Cameron (Charles Haydon), a Canadian whose licensed has been revoked by the British, lives; he is away but his daughter Pamela (Cornell) tends to Kenyon's injuries. As he recovers, Kenyon falls in love with the young woman. Her father, near death, asks Kenyon to take Pamela out of Africa. While exploring the local grasslands, Kenyon meets a mysterious man, Gideon (Carradine), who guards a series of caves. Gideon becomes hostile when Kenyon asks about them. Back in the village, Kenyon saves a child from a crocodile but has a falling-out with Dr. Cameron, who later throws himself to the reptiles. After an attempt is made on his life because of the doctor's death, Kenyon returns to the village and takes Pamela away before the angry tribe destroys it to get rid of evil spirits. When Pamela accuses Kenyon of being responsible for her father's death, he tells her of their pact about taking her out of the jungle. The next day the young woman is stalked by a lion that is killed by Kenyon. When Baobab locates elephant tracks, Pamela convinces Kenyon to follow them. They are nearly killed in an animal stampede instigated by Gideon. Marauding elephants decimate the area, destroying Baobab's village and killing his wife and children. Kenyon manages to shoot three of the elephants and badly wounds a fourth when it attacks Pamela. Hoping the dying beast will lead them to the elephant graveyard, Kenyon, Pamela and Baobab follow it, not knowing that the burial grounds are guarded by Gideon. Pamela slips and nearly falls off a ledge but is rescued by Kenyon as Gideon tries to push a boulder onto them. The tremor from the crashing boulder causes Gideon to tumble to his death as molten lava shoots out of a crater created by the jolt. Kenyon and Pamela manage to make it to safety.

In 1985, John Calvert fashioned a new alternate version of *Dark Venture* called *Beyond the Sahara*, in which he and Ann Cornell recreated their roles as John Kenyon and Pamela Calvert. Here Kenyon relates his African adventures to a newsman named Clayton, with the film's story being told in flashback. Twelve years later Calvert added new opening and closing sequences to *Dark Venture* with Cornell again appearing in new footage; this time it was called *The Great Expedition to the Elephant's Graveyard*. This version includes a brief appearance by David Carradine discussing his father John Carradine's role in the original footage. In 2004 it debuted at the Williamsburg Film Festival and was introduced by Calvert, who continued to do his magic act well into his nineties.

Death Curse of Tartu (Thunderbird International Pictures, 1967; 84 minutes; Color)

Producers: Joseph Fink and Juan Hidalgo-Gato. Director-Screenplay: William Grefe. Photography-Editor: Julio C. Chavez. Music: Al Jacobs. Songs: Al Greene and Al Jacobs. Sets: Tom

Spanish lobby card for *Death Curse of Tartu* (Thunderbird International, 1966) picturing Maurice Stewart and Gary Holtz

Casey. Sound: Armando Fernandez. Makeup: Marie Del Russo. Assistant Director: Earl Wainwright.

CAST: Fred Pinero (Ed Tison), Babette Sherrill (Julie Tison), Bill [William] Marcus (Billy), Mayra Gomez (Cindy), Sherman Hayes (Johnny), Gary Holtz (Tommy), Maurice Stewart (Joann), Fred Weed (Sam Gunter), Doug Hobart (Tartu), Brad F. Grinter (Explorer).

Deep in the Florida Everglades, an explorer (Brad F. Grinter) locates the hidden entrance to a cave but after he enters its stone door closes, trapping him inside. He is killed by a mysterious figure who takes the parchment he was carrying. Hunter Sam Gunter (Fred Weed) and his Indian guide Billy (Bill Marcus) travel by canoe through the swamp and land near an ancient native burial ground. Billy does not want to go any further, for despite being educated, he believes in evil spirits and the legends of his people. Gunter tells Billy to bring back Ed Tison (Fred Pinero) and his party in air boats. Going through the marshes, Gunter finds a skull. Making camp, Gunter digs up a large rock with writing on it. The long-dead Indian Tartu (Doug Hobart) returns to life, becomes a snake and kills the explorer. Ed and his wife Julie (Babette Sherrill) arrive at Billy's wildlife haven with four archaeology students, Cindy (Mayra Gomez), Johnny (Sherman Hayes), Tommy (Gary Holtz) and Joann (Maurice Stewart), who are going on a field trip to the burial grounds. Billy tells the Tisons that the area is haunted and that four hundred years ago the witch doctor Tartu had the power to turn into wild beasts; when he died, he promised to return to take revenge on anyone who desecrated his burial place. Disregarding Billy's warnings, the six people take two air boats into the Everglades, locate the spot where Gunter landed and find the skull. After making camp, they come upon the tablet and Ed translates it, telling his wife it contains Tartu's prophecy. Tommy and Joann go swimming in the swamp and are devoured by a shark, a creature that does not live in fresh water. Hearing jungle drums, the others break camp and prepare to leave but Johnny brings word that their air boats have been sunk. Ed says the only explanation is Tartu's curse. He sends Johnny for help but the young man is stalked and killed by a deadly snake. Cindy dreams that Johnny has been killed. Ed says they must find Tartu's burial place and destroy him. As they search, the three hear chanting coming from under the ground and Julie finds the opening to the cave. When they see Gunter's body, Cindy runs away and Ed and Julie find themselves locked inside. Cindy is chased by an alligator and runs back to the cave but cannot get in and takes refuge by clinging to a tree limb. Ed uses gunpowder to jar loose the cave's stone door but by the time they get to Cindy she has fallen from the tree. The young student dies after the alligator bites off her left arm. Ed and Julie return to the cave but cannot move the stone lid on the coffin. As they talk, the mummified Tartu rises from his grave and turns into a warrior who attacks them. Julie runs away as Ed and Tartu fight. After knocking out Ed, the witch doctor goes after the woman. Ed revives and follows them carrying an axe. Tartu pushes Julie into quicksand but Ed jumps him and the two men struggle as Julie slowly sinks into the mire. Ed manages to shove Tartu into the quicksand and pull out Julie. Tartu disappears, fulfilling his prophecy that only nature can destroy him.

Death Curse of Tartu was released theatrically early in 1967 by Thunderbird International Pictures on a double-bill with *Sting of Death*; both films were directed by William Grefe. Produced by Falcon International Pictures and filmed on location in Florida's Everglades National Park, *Tartu* is a fairly entertaining independent horror outing that would have benefited from a shorter running time. Too much of the movie is taken up with slow-moving scenes and long, drawn-out chase sequences. It is quite scenic with good photography by Julio C. Chavez, who also edited the production. Marie Del Russo's makeup for the half-decayed corpse of Tartu is well done. One amusing scene has four college students dancing to rock 'n' roll tunes while the camera lingers lovingly on the two scantily clad coeds' posteriors. James O'Neill in *Terror on Tape* (1994) thought it "[m]inor but imaginative.... Poor acting, but bleak locations and effective makeup make it a passable time-killer." *VideoHound's Cult Flicks and Trash Pics* (1996) termed it "a low-budget flick so bad it's funny," and Stephen Jones opined in *The Essential Monster Movie Guide* (2000), "Writer-director Grefe pads out the slim storyline with interminable treks through the undergrowth, accompanied by an irritating music score and numerous screams."

Allied Artists released *Death Curse of Tartu* to television in its "Science Fiction Features" package. In 1990 the home video company American Video issued the movie in France, where it never had a theatrical release, as *Cobra Woman* and credited its direction to Jess Franco.

Brad F. Grinter, who had a bit part as the murdered explorer at the beginning of the film, went on to co-produce and direct Veronica Lake in *Flesh Feast* (1970), also filmed in Florida. A later feature dealing with vengeful Indian spirits is *The Dark Power* (1985) starring Lash LaRue.

Flight of the Lost Balloon (American International, 1961; 91 minutes; Color)

Producer: Bernard Woolner. Executive Producer–Photography: Jacques Marquette. Associate Producer-Director-Screenplay-Story: Nathan Juran. Editor: Rex Lipton. Title Song Sung by Marcella Wright. Sound: Tom Ashton. Sound Editors: Bill and Terry MacDonald. Makeup: Charles Gemora. Properties: Richard Rubin. Miniatures: Projects Unlimited. Assistant Directors: Howard Alston and Jack Bohrer.

Advertisement for *Flight of the Lost Balloon* (Woolner Bros., 1960)

CAST: Mala Powers (Ellen Burton), Marshall Thompson (Dr. Joseph Farady), James Lanphier (The Hindu), Douglas Kennedy (Sir Hubert Warrington), Robert W. Gillette (Sir Adam Burton), Felippe Birriel (Golan), A.J. Valentine (Giles), Blanquita Romero (The Malkia), Jackie Danois (Native Dancer).

Flight of the Lost Balloon was a W-M-J Production, a collaboration between producer Bernard Woolner, executive producer and cinematographer Jacques Marquette and associate producer–director–writer Nathan Juran. Filmed in Eastman Color and SpectraScope in Puerto Rico, the film had brief release by Woolner Bros. before being distributed nationally by American International Pictures. A promotional gimmick involved handing out motion sickness pills to patrons as they bought tickets to see the film. Mainly an adventure outing, *Flight of the Lost Balloon* does have some genre elements, including the search for Cleopatra's mummy and her lost treasure; a tall, grotesque henchman, two vicious gorillas and an attack by a flock of giant condors. Allied Artists Television included it in its "Science-Fiction Features" package.

In 1878, the London Geographical Society finances a balloon expedition to Lake Victoria in Africa to rescue one of its members, Sir Hubert Warrington (Douglas Kennedy), who is being held prisoner in an old castle. Word of Sir Hubert's plight is brought by the Hindu (James Lanphier), who will accompany the rescue leader, Sir Adam Burton (Robert W. Gillette) and navigator Dr. Joseph Farady (Marshall Thompson), on the flight. The expedition moves to its starting point in Niger where the natives are unfriendly because they believe the men are going to the Moon, which they worship. As Joe is preparing the craft for ascent, Sir Adam's beautiful daughter Ellen (Mala Powers) comes aboard to wish him well in freeing Sir Hubert, her fiancé. She is followed by the Hindu, who gives orders to the natives to let go of the ropes. The balloon rises, leaving Sir Adam behind. With a storm coming up and no hope of a safe landing, Joe informs Ellen that they will have to travel across Africa with the Hindu. When they land in the Congo jungle to replenish their water supply, the trio is surrounded by cannibals. The Hindu tells the locals they are gods from the Moon who have come to honor their village and they are asked to attend to the tribe's queen (Blanquita Romero), who is ill. Joe determines she is only drunk and, after reviving her with smelling salts, the trio watch a native celebration and then sneak back to the balloon. When the locals see the Moon rise, they realize they have been duped and follow the strangers who escape and fly to Lake Victoria. After the Hindu says Sir Hubert is on a nearby island, the balloon is attacked by a flock of giant condors. In order for the craft to be able to descend, Joe jumps overboard as Ellen and the Hindu land on the island. Ellen is escorted to the Hindu's castle while he tells his gaunt, mute henchman Golan (Felippe Birriel) to take his men and find and kill Joe. They locate the navigator when he swims to shore but he manages to elude them. The Hindu informs Ellen that Egyptian queen Cleopatra visited the headwaters of the Nile River during her reign and he also warns her not to wander around the castle because of its many dangers. Joe locates Ellen and tells her that Golan has been trying to kill him. The Hindu informs the chained Sir Hubert (who, despite torture, has refused to tell him the location of Cleopatra's treasure) that Ellen is on the island. Sir Hubert scoffs at the Hindu's plan to torture the young woman to make him talk, saying he only romanced her to get the financial support of her father in searching for the treasure. In an underground cavern, Joe and Ellen find two chained gorillas. The Hindu informs Ellen that Cleopatra, after the death of Marc Antony, buried her nation's treasure on the island before killing herself. He spent thirteen years looking for it only to have Sir Hubert make the discovery; he tells Ellen that until the explorer reveals the treasure's location, he will torture her. Joe overhears the conversation and, after the Hindu and Ellen leave, he sets Sir Hubert free and they plot their escape. The next day the Hindu brings Ellen back to the torture chamber to put her on the rack but first he demonstrates it on a native. As Golan begins to torture Ellen, Joe gets his attention and Sir Hubert knocks the giant out with a maul. Joe frees Ellen and tells her to scream to make the Hindu think she is being tortured. Joe, Ellen and Sir Hubert make their way to the underground cavern where they lock themselves in a cage and set the gorillas free. When Golan revives, he goes after the trio but ends up being killed by the beasts. Sir Hubert and Ellen run for the balloon as Joe stays behind as a decoy. The young woman prepares the craft for takeoff while Sir Hubert goes to the grotto where the treasure is hidden and brings back chests filled with jewels. He goes back again and Ellen follows him, realizing he would have let her die so he could keep the secret of the treasure. As Sir Hubert tries to open the coffin containing Cleopatra's mummy, several heavy chests fall on him, crushing the explorer among the treasure he sought. Joe returns to the balloon, followed by the Hindu and his minions. He and Ellen board the craft but are forced to throw over most of the treasure chests in order to ascend. The Hindu manages to climb the rope to the balloon's basket but Joe throws a box at him and he falls into the lake. Realizing they cannot get over the mountains to land in Zanzibar, Joe and Ellen throw off the remainder of the treasure, although she keeps one large jewel for a wedding band.

A fast-moving, entertaining romp, *Flight of the Lost Balloon* is minor compared to some of director Nathan Juran's other efforts, including *The Deadly Mantis* and *20 Million Miles to Earth* (both 1957), *The 7th Voyage of Sinbad* (1958), *Jack the Giant Killer* (1962) and *First Men in the Moon* (1964). As Nathan Hertz he helmed *Attack of the 50 Foot Woman* and *The Brain from Planet Arous* (both 1958) [qq.v.]. The former film was also produced by Bernard Woolner; Juran worked on both features with co-producer and cinematographer Jacques Marquette. Top-billed Mala Powers appeared in *The Unknown Terror* (1957), *The Colossus of New York* (1958) and *Doomsday Machine* (1972), while co-star Marshall Thompson had a number of genre credits: *Cult of the Cobra* (1955), *It! The Terror from Beyond Space* (1958), *Fiend Without a Face* (1958), *First Man into Space* (1959), *Around the World Under the Sea* (1966) and *The Formula* (1980), as well as the TV series *World of Giants* (Syndicated, 1961). James Lanphier, who gave the film's best performance as the erudite and sinister Hindu, was also in *The Deadly Mantis* (1957).

Gun Riders (Independent-International Pictures, 1969; 81 minutes; Color)

Producer-Director: Al Adamson. Associate Producers: Robert Dix and John "Bud" Cardos. Story-Screenplay: Robert Dix. Photography: Vilmos Zsigmond. Editors: William Faris and Pete Perry. Sound: Robert Dietz. Production Manager: John "Bud" Cardos. Unit Manager: Rick Jackson. Wardrobe: Leona Grosz. Sound Effects: Jim Farris. Titles: Bob Lebar. Script Supervisor: Ray Doyle. Production Advisor: Fred Saletri. Music Editor: Ed Norton.

CAST: Robert Dix (Ben Thompson), Scott Brady (Jim Wade), Jim Davis (Clay Bates), John Carradine (Preacher Boone Hawkins), Paula Raymond (Kansas Kelly), John "Bud" Cardos (Joe Lightfoot/Satago), Gene Raymond (Voice of Death), Tara Ashton (Althea Richards), Kent Osborne (Dave Miller), Vicki Volante (Nora Miller), Denver Dixon [Victor Adamson] (Rawhide), Ray Young (Horace Higgins), Julie Edwards (Lavinia), Fred Meyers (Driver), Maria Polo (Little Fawn), Jill Moelfel (Vi), Keith Murphy, Ray Goldrup, Tom Goldrup (Yaquis), Al Adamson (Yaqui with Knife).

Gun Riders was the title Allied Artists Television gave *Five Bloody Graves* when it was syndicated in its TV package "The Golden Sixties — Group VI." The film was toned down (deleting excessive violence and nudity) for the small screen; eight minutes of footage was cut from its original running time of 89. Filmed at Capitol Reef, Utah, as *Lonely Man* and *Five Bloody Days to Tombstone*, the film was made by Dix International Pictures in 1968 and was one of the first movies to be distributed by Independent-International Pictures, which released it theatrically late in 1969. Like most I-I product it played mainly to smaller venues and drive-ins. A very violent western, its horror content had Death (voice of Gene Raymond)

Tara Ashton, Julie Edwards and John Carradine in *Five Bloody Graves* (Independent-International, 1969)

narrating the affair. Populated by a fine cast, *Five Bloody Graves* was photographed by future Academy Award winner Vilmos Zsigmond and its outstanding feature is beautiful desert locales. Robert Dix, son of actor Richard Dix, co-produced and wrote the film in addition to playing the lead, a gunman known as the Messenger of Death, based on a real character. Tara Ashton, who was one of the saloon girls in the movie, later married Dix.

In the Old West, Death (Raymond) rides alongside his messenger, Ben Thompson (Dix), who wants to kill Satago (John "Bud" Cardos), who murdered his wife Mary on their wedding night. Satago is the leader of the Yaquis, renegade Apaches, out to rid the area of whites, and his half-brother Joe Lightfoot (Cardos), who is riding with his squaw Little Fawn (Maria Polo), informs Ben that the Indians have been getting weapons from gunrunners. When a Yaqui (Al Adamson) attacks Ben's old flame Nora Miller (Vicki Volante), he fights and kills the renegade. Nora's husband Dave (Kent Osborne) returns from Tucson and orders Ben off his land. Dave is warned to leave since the area is crawling with Yaquis. When Dave goes to check his traps, the Indians attack their home and kill Nora. He returns in time to try and fight them off but Satago kills him, burns their cabin and scalps Nora. Gun riders Clay Bates (Jim Davis) and Horace Wiggins (Ray Young) trade guns for gold with Satago and are given two days to get out of the territory or be fed to the ants. Ben finds Joe, who has been ambushed; after Ben removes an arrow from his shoulder, they ride on in search of Satago, who has captured Little Fawn and staked her to the ground. Clay and Horace come upon the young woman and Clay rapes and shoots her with Horace taking a pendant from her neck. Ben and Joe find Little Fawn's body and Joe vows vengeance on her killer. A wagon overturns and its passengers fight off their Yaqui attackers. The travelers are gambler Jim Wade (Scott Brady) and saloon girl Lavinia (Julie Edwards), whom he won in a poker game; loquacious preacher Boone Hawkins (John Carradine), madam Kansas Kelly (Paula Raymond), saloon girl Althea (Ashton), old cowboy Rawhide (Denver Dixon) and a driver (Fred Meyers). As the Indians retreat, Ben and Joe ride to help the travelers and Jim informs them they were run out of Tucson and are headed for Tombstone. Lavinia becomes jealous of Althea's attentions to Jim and the two fight. After they are separated, Boone watches Althea change clothes before he is surprised by Ben. When a Yaqui tries to kill Althea, Ben shoots him. She tells Ben her man got gold fever and left her. That night Ben and Joe sneak into the Yaqui camp and kill several of the braves, although Satago gets away. The next day Clay and Horace find the group traveling across the plains and join them. Clay spies Lavinia bathing in the river and tries to entice her with the pendant, which is seen by Joe. When Lavinia screams, Jim comes to her rescue and knocks out Clay, but the young woman is killed by an arrow. Boone preaches a sermon over Lavinia when they bury her and the group continues its journey. Horace suggests to a drunken Clay that they take the others' rifles and sell them to Satago to save their own skins. When he tries to do so, Horace is shot by Boone. Joe goes after Clay for killing Little Fawn. After catching the gun rider, he stakes him out to be eaten by ants. Satago shoots Joe but before he dies he knifes Clay. When Joe does not return, Jim informs Ben they have to move on. Boone is shot with an arrow, Kelly is stabbed and Jim is killed. With all of their party gone, Ben and Althea try to escape but she is killed by a Yaqui arrow. After he kills her attackers, Ben fights with Satago. When they fall into the river, the current carries off the half-breed, drowning him. Burying the members of the wagon party, Ben rides away.

Gun Riders was directed by Al Adamson, whose father Victor Adamson (billed as Denver Dixon) plays one of the wagon defenders; after a few scenes he disappears, apparently done in by the Yaquis. Al also produced and directed the Independent-International releases *Man with the Synthetic Brain (Blood of Ghastly Horror)* and *Vampire Men of the Lost Planet (Horror of the Blood Monsters)* [qq.v.] (both 1969), that were issued to TV by Allied Artists.

Phil Hardy in *The Western* (1984) stated, "Despite its violence and sexual excesses, this is a surprisingly traditional Western.... The film is cheaply, but imaginatively made."

The Hand of Power (Constantin Film/Rialto, 1968; 83 minutes; Color)

Producer: Horst Wendlandt. Director: Alfred Vohrer. Screenplay: Ladislas Fodor, from the novel by Edgar Wallace. Photography: Karl Lob. Editor: Jutta Hering. Music: Peter Thomas. Production Designers: Walter Kutz and Wilhelm Vorwerg. Sound: Gerhard Muller. Production Manager: Fritz Klotsch. Costumes: Irms Pauli. Makeup: Charlotte Kersten and Will Nixdorf. Assistant Director: Eva Ebner.

CAST: Joachim Fuchsberger (Inspector Higgins), Siw Mattson (Peggy Ward), Wolfgang Kieling (Sir Cecil Rand), Pinkas Braun (The Stranger), Hubert von Meyerinck (Sir Arthur), Claude Farell (Sister Adela), Peter Mosbacher (Ramiro/Sir Oliver Ramsey), Siegfried Rauch (Dr. Brand), Otto Stern (Mr. Merryl), Renate Grosser (Mrs. Potter), Hans Krull (Vicar Potter), Lil Lindfors (Sabrina), Ilse Page (Miss Finley), Edith Schneider (Professor Bound), Wolfgang Spier (Mr. Bannister), Ewa Stromberg (Librarian), Jimmy Powell (Casper), Thomas Danneberg (Captain Winscott), Max Wittmann (Elderly Laboratory Attendant), Dietrich Behne (The Zombie), Eva Ebner (Secretary), Michael Miller (Mechanic), Al Pereira (Mourner), Alfred Vohrer (Voice of the Laughing Corpse).

Allied Artists Television released *The Hand of Power* to the small screen as part of its "The Golden Sixties—Group VI" and "Science-Fiction Features" packages. This was the first time the movie had showings in the United States since it was never released here theatrically. Circa 1990 it was brought back to TV syndication by Independent-International Pictures as *The Zombie Walks*. The production was a West German *Krimi* (a mystery-horror outing) based on the works of British thriller writer Edgar Wallace, said to be the most filmed of all fiction authors. During the 1960s and early 1970s the *Krimis* were the biggest moneymaking movies in West Germany and they were also popular worldwide. In the U.S. they mostly were shown on television. Produced by CCC-Rialto Film as *Im Banne des Unheimlichen* (In the Thrall of the Sinister One), the film was based on Wallace's 1927 novel *The Hand of Power* although its action-filled, fast-moving, complicated storyline had little resemblance to the literary work. Wallace's voice (probably via recordings he made for English Columbia in the late 1920s) is heard at the beginning and end of the movie. The Laughing Corpse, the phantom who uses poison from a scorpion ring to eliminate his victims, sports a black costume with a skull face and skeleton hands. Much of the action takes place in a spooky castle, a dark old church and its environs and a dismal hospital. The horror mood is also enhanced by foggy, windswept terrain presented mainly in night sequences.

During a funeral service at the church in Crowfield for Sir Oliver Ramsey, who was killed in a plane crash, a demonic laugh is heard, and the deceased's half-brother, Sir Cecil Rand (Wolfgang Kieling), claims it is his sibling who has come back to haunt him. Reporter Peggy Ward (Siw Mattson) of the *London Star* learns that Rand has inherited most of the dead man's estate which is also sought by the local vicar, Potter (Hans Krull), for his church, and Dr. Brand (Siegfried Rauch), for the hospital he operates with Sister Adela (Claude Farell), who took care of Sir Oliver when he was injured many years before. In a nearby tavern, half-caste stonemason Ramiro (Peter Mosbacher) claims that Sir Oliver has returned from the grave as a zombie. At New Scotland Yard, Inspector Higgins (Joachim Fuchsberger) finds secretary Miss Finley (Ilse Page) upset because he broke a dinner date with her. Later, his boss Sir Arthur (Hubert von Meyerinck) who has taken over from the equally incompetent Sir John, consults with him regarding the "Case of the Laughing Corpse." At the family castle, Rand sees a skeleton face at a window and is told by his lawyer Merryl (Otto Stern) that his sibling is dead; his scorpion ring has not been found. On the way home, the lawyer is forced off the road and accosted by a figure in black wearing a skull mask and skeleton hands. Peggy finds his body and calls Higgins, who is dining with Miss Finley. Merryl died of shock. Potter says that Rand saw his dead brother and was found unconscious in the cemetery. Dr. Brand tends to Rand while Sister Adela brings Ramiro and relates seeing a shadow in the graveyard. Higgins questions Rand who claims his brother killed the lawyer. In her dressing room, singer Sabrina (Lil Lindfors) opens an envelope containing £10,000, not knowing she is being spied on by Rand. The hooded figure shows up and kills the young woman with poison from a scorpion ring. When the phantom leaves, Rand takes back the money but is forced to share it with his blackmailing chauffeur Casper (Jimmy Powell). While London newspapers claim that the two murders were committed by a zombie, Higgins gets a report saying both victims died from a poison that caused heart failure without leaving any traces. He goes to the library to get a book on the subject only to find out from the librarian (Ewa Stromberg) that the only copy was checked out by Peggy. When he goes to her apartment, the inspector hears the reporter screaming and breaks in and sees she has been attacked by the phantom, who steals the book and escapes. Finding out the work was written by scientist Professor Bound (Edith Schneider), Higgins goes to her laboratory and is told that the only volume, a proof copy, was just sent to her by Mr. Bannister

(Wolfgang Spier), the undertaker who buried Sir Oscar. The zombie kills Bannister whose corpse is found by his friend, Dr. Brand. The vicar informs his wife (Renate Grosser) that they will get the bulk of Sir Oscar's estate if Rand dies within one year. When Higgins confronts Rand, he says Sister Adela dropped him for Sir Oscar because he would inherit most of the family money and she responds that Sir Oscar left England eighteen years before because of his brother. Higgins sees the skeleton face at the window and goes after it but is knocked out and brought in by Casper and revived by Peggy. In Sabrina's dressing room, Higgins finds a picture of Captain Woodridge, the pilot of the plane that crashed killing Sir Oscar, and learns he was engaged to the singer, who then worked as a stewardess, Miss Winslow. He also finds a record of the Laughing Corpse's laugh and has it played at the vicar's next sermon, causing Rand to collapse; at Dr. Brand's hospital, he is attended by Sister Adela. When he is strapped to a table for x-rays, Rand is frightened by the appearance of the phantom as Dr. Brand is murdered. Higgins arrives with Sir Arthur, and Rand tells them he is afraid of Sister Adela who is named in Sir Oscar's will. The inspector and Sir Arthur break into the hospital's record room to look at Sir Oscar's medical reports only to beaten to them by Peggy. Casper is murdered and Rand is the main suspect as Higgins tries to locate Ramiro to help him open Sir Oscar's grave. He finds the stonemason deathly ill. Sister Adela takes him to the hospital where he dies. Higgins finds Sir Oscar's coffin has been moved and the vicar claims it was done by Ramiro. When Rand escapes from the hospital, Sir Arthur informs Higgins that the man is insane. Higgins goes to the mortuary where he hears the organ being played and finds out it is Peggy who says she was brought there after being kidnapped by a man who stole Sir Oscar's medical records from her. The two find Rand in the burial vault raging hysterically that his brother wants to kill him. They take him back to the castle where he is placed under special police guard. Sir Arthur is knocked out by the phantom. When he is revived, Sir Arthur and Higgins question Rand, who states he gave Sabrina money because she told him she was pregnant. Sister Adela informs the policemen that Rand did not want her to marry Sir Oscar since their children would have inherited the family fortune and not him. Hearing a noise in the attic, Higgins investigates and is confronted by a man who identifies himself as Captain Winscott (Thomas Danneberg), a friend of the dead pilot. He is also working for Dr. Bound, the pilot's sister. Peggy identifies him as the man who kidnapped her and took Sir Oscar's medical records. The phantom uses the scorpion ring to murder Rand. When the others hear his cries, they chase the killer onto the castle grounds where he steals a police car. Higgins and the others follow him to the vicarage in another vehicle and there they confront Potter. The phantom gets the drop on them and calls Adela to his side. He has her hold them at gunpoint as he opens a valve that emits poison gas. As a fire starts, Higgins chases the phantom and unmasks him as Ramiro. The inspector shuts off the gas as Sister Adela attempts to save Ramiro with an antidote for an inflection from which he suffers, but fails. She admits that Ramiro was really Sir Oscar who was out to eliminate all those who tried to kill him. She then takes her own life.

 Between 1961 and 1968 Alfred Vohrer directed fourteen Edgar Wallace *Krimis* and in *The Hand of Power* he also provided the voice of the Laughing Corpse. Joachim Fuchsberger portrayed Inspector Higgins in two earlier Wallace thrillers helmed by Vohrer, *Der Hexer* (The Hexer) (1964), shown on TV as *The Mysterious Magician*, and *Der Monch mit der Peitsche* (*The Monk with the Whip*) (1967), released to television and on disc as *College Girl Murders*. Ilse Page also played Miss Finley in the latter movie as she did in a total of five *Krimis*.

In *The Video Watchdog Book* (1992), Tim Lucas termed *The Hand of Power* an "entertaining film ... is noteworthy for several reasons," including director Vohrer and cinematographer Karl Lob "working deliberately against their usual stylistic grain, delivering a film shot in subdued earthtones to compliment its central, monochromatic (and wonderful!) villain."

Portions of the soundtrack of *The Hand of Power* are included on the compact disc *Peter Thomas — Film Musik: Die Original Musik aus den Edgar Wallace und Jerry Cotton Filmen* (Polydor 517 096-2), although it does not have the song "Feel My Heartbeat" sung in the film by Lil Lindfors.

Last Woman on Earth (The Filmgroup, 1960; 71 minutes; Color)

Producer-Director: Roger Corman. Associate Producer: Charles Hanawalt. Screenplay: Robert Towne. Photography: Jacques Marquette. Editor: Anthony Carras. Music: Ronald Stein. Sound: Beach Dickerson. Production Manager-Assistant Director: Jack Bohrer. Properties: Stanley Watson.

CAST: Betsy Jones-Moreland (Evelyn Gern), Antony Carbone (Harold Gern), Edward Wain [Robert Towne] (Martin Joyce).

A variation of Arch Oboler's post-nuclear holocaust drama *Five* (1951), *Last Woman on Earth* is so sparse in budget and plot it could have been called *Three*. Released theatrically on a dual bill with *The Little Shop of Horrors* (q.v.), this dour affair no doubt disappointed its audience by being filled with seemingly endless talk. It was filmed in color and VitaScope in Puerto Rico, following producer Roger Corman's winding up *Battle of Blood Island* (1960). Corman spent so little money on the second film that he was able to follow it with *Creature from Haunted Sea* (1960) [q.v.] with the same trio of leading players, Betsy Jones-Moreland, Antony Carbone and Edward Wain, a pseudonym for the writer of *Last Woman on Earth*, Robert Towne. Allegedly Towne had not finished the script when shooting began so Corman brought him to Puerto Rico and had him play the tertiary role in the film while he also completed the screenplay. Towne went on to script *The Tomb of Ligeia* (1965) for Corman, *Chinatown* (1974), for which he won an Academy Award, *The Yakuza* (1975), *Shampoo* and *Marathon Man* (both 1976). He also directed *Personal Best* (1982) and *Tequila Sunrise* (1984). As an actor he is badly miscast in *Last Woman on Earth*, coming off as a nerd. He projected the same kind of manner in *Creature from the Haunted Sea* but it fit better in that comedy. The underwater wreck shown in *Last Woman on Earth* also appears in *Creature from the Haunted Sea*.

Indicted in a million dollar housing scandal, wealthy businessman Harold Gern (Carbone) is staying in Puerto Rico with his wife Evelyn (Jones-Moreland). During a cockfight his lawyer, Martin Joyce (Towne), shows up to confer with him. After Harold gambles and tries to pick up two women in a bar, he tells Martin to get their legal papers from his hotel room. The lawyer runs into a tipsy Evelyn who becomes coy and dangerously walks on a banister railing before telling Martin that her marriage is a sham. In the bar, Evelyn wants Harold to be more affectionate but he leaves her for his dates, saying they will go fishing the next day. Taking Martin with them, the Gerns go scuba diving. When a manta ray gets too close, Evelyn fires at it with a spear gun and slightly wounds the lawyer. When they surface, the trio find they cannot breathe and continue to use their oxygen tanks. On board Harold's yacht they find Manuel, the skipper, dead. When the boat will not start and they cannot get a radio signal, they take a small boat and row to shore. As they trek through the jungle toward town, their oxygen supply runs out; taking off their masks, they find the air is thin but breathable. In the city they find corpses in the streets. Taking a car, they drive to the Caribe Hotel, where they had been staying. As they drink at the bar, Harold asks Martin what happened and the lawyer says the world found a bigger and better bomb, or it was an act of God. Unable to stay in the same locale with dead bodies, the three drive to the end of the island to a home owned by Harold's business partner. The next day they find they have enough supplies to survive for a long time but both Evelyn and Martin are morose and cynical about their situation, while Harold wants to devise a survival plan. When Harold spies an insect, he realizes they cannot stay on the island due to the pestilence its kind will bring and suggests they take the yacht and go north to colder terrain. While Harold teaches the others to fish and navigate a boat, he notices that his wife and Martin are becoming more affectionate. Both Evelyn and Martin resent Harold's controlling their lives. The lawyer finds a dead young girl on the beach and the two men verbally spar over Evelyn. When Harold goes fishing, Martin invites Evelyn to go with him to the beach where they kiss and go back to the house and have sex. Harold returns home to find his wife embracing Martin. The next day the two men go fishing, and Martin informs Harold that he will not take orders from him. They fight, fall out of the boat and get to shore where Harold hits Martin near the right eye with a rock. Martin says Harold wants to exile him and the businessman says he and Evelyn are going to leave the island without him. Evelyn finds out about Harold's ultimatum and objects. When he refuses to reverse his decision, she asks Martin to take her with him. He agrees to drive with her to the yacht and the two take the car, along with the keys to a van, the only other vehicle. As they drive away, Harold says he will not go after them but later hotwires the van. Martin's eye bothers him to the point he wrecks the car. Evelyn and Martin cut through a forest and when they get to town she asks him if they can have a baby but he says the world is finished. Leaving Evelyn in a church, Martin goes to find Harold. The two men meet on a pier where Harold hits Martin in the head with a rifle butt. The two continue to fight but the exertion takes its toll on Martin and he begins to lose his sight. He returns to the church, followed by Harold, and dies. Harold tells Evelyn he killed Martin and says he wants to go home. He holds out his hand to her and asks his wife to help him.

Variety found *Last Woman on Earth* to be a "[s]lim lower-berth melodrama.... Corman's direction is generally lackluster." The British *Monthly Film Bulletin* thought it "frankly dull, burdened with pretentious dialogue." Phil Hardy in *Science Fiction* (1984) found deeper meaning in the scanty production: "A fascinating minimalist film.... [D]espite its tacky surface, [it] has the vision of the best of Science Fiction writing, a rare occurrence in American Science Fiction films of the period."

Although it was filmed in color, most prints of *Last Woman on Earth* are in black and white. Some sources claim director Monte Hellman added footage to make the film fit a ninety minute TV time slot but this appears to be one film that made it to the small screen without any additional scenes incorporated into it. Allied Artists Television included it in its "Science-Fiction Pictures" package.

Lightning Bolt (Woolner Bros., 1966; 94 minutes; Color)

Producers: Alfonso Balcazar, Giuseppe De Blasio and Cleto Fontini. Director: Anthony M. Dawson [Antonio Margheriti]. Story-Screenplay: Alfred [Alfonso] Balcazar. Photography: Riccardo Pallottini. Editor: Juan Oliver. Music: Riz Ortolani. Art Director: Antonio Visone. Sets: Juan Alberto Solar. Sound: Alesandro Sarandrea. Production Manager: Luigi Millozza. Production Supervisor: Dino Mercuri. General Manager: Francisco Balcazar. Costumes: Paolo Moschi. Makeup: Romolo de Martino. Assistant Directors: Luis Martin and Nino Fruscella.

CAST: Anthony Eisley (Lieutenant Harry Sennett), Wandisa [Guida] Leigh (Kary), Diana Lorys (Captain Pat Flanagan), Ursula Parker [Luisa Rivelli] (Sylvia), Folco Lulli (Rehte), Paco Sanz (Dr. Rooney), Barta Barry (Flacccus), Tito Garcia (Fidel), Jose Maria Caffarel (Archie White), Luciana Petri (Sea Plane Hostess), Goffredo Unger (Wilkes), Rene Montalban, Oreste Palella.

Woolner Bros. released *Lightning Bolt* in the U.S. in 1966 with Allied Artists including it in its "Cavalcade of the 60's — Group V" and "Science-Fiction Features" TV packages a decade later. A Spanish-Italian co-production from Seven Films–B.G.A.–Balcazar, it was originally called *Operazione Goldman* (Operation Goldman) in Italy, where it ran 96 minutes, with a four-minute-longer running time in Spain. Its U.S. prints clocked in at 94 minutes. Made at the height of the James Bond craze, the film is a tongue-in-cheek action spoof of the spy genre with the smooth hero (Anthony Eisley) surrounded by a bevy of beautiful woman as he fights a supervillain (Folco Lulli) out to control the world. Both the hero and the bad guy have red hair and Eisley drives an orange Jaguar. *Variety* noted, "Unfoldment of the film's incredible plot premise is professional and rapid, if still standard and uninspired spy fare.... [Eisley] makes a more than adequate hero...." Matt Burke and David Deal in *The Eurospy Guide* (2004) wrote, "This is one cheesy movie.... The special effects are as to be expected — not very special.... Though the movie has a few charms, they are outweighed by too much silliness, a weak villain, and the sense that the time spent watching it is worth more than the budget spent to make it."

Following the sabotage of six Cape Kennedy Moon rockets, the Federal Security Investigation Commission has nuclear scientist Dr. Rooney (Paco Sanz) investigate but he turns up missing after diving into a lagoon with his assistant Wilkes (Goffredo Unger), following the discovery of a ray station. Captain Patricia "Pat" Flanagan (Diana Lorys) is named chief of Operation Lightning Bolt (the recovery of Dr. Rooney), and she enlists the aid of Lieutenant Harry Sennett (Eisley), who masquerades as a playboy and buys a seaplane complete with a sexy hostess (Luciana Petri). At his rented house near Hotel Florida, a spa for spies, Harry finds Pat in the shower and washes her back. They observe Archie White (Jose Maria Caffarel) searching the place but his young blonde wife Sylvia (Ursula Parker) shows up, shoots him and drives away. The injured man escapes. Harry and Pat go to his place and along they way see a number of silos belonging to a local brewery. A radio signal leads them into one of the silos where they get locked in and deluged by water. Harry stops the rising water by plugging an air hole but a panel is opened, he is carried outside and then returns to rescue Pat. He sends Pat for security as he goes back home and finds Sylvia, who holds him at bay with an acid-shooting pistol. Pat shoots Sylvia and the silos explode. Harry decides to check out Dr. Rooney's apartment and sees a beautiful woman, Kary (Wandisa Leigh), leaving the place, which has been ransacked. Harry finds a secret room filled with recording equipment and listens to a tape the scientist made before he went to check out the lagoon. When Pat informs Harry that the latest rocket launch has been moved up and is scheduled to take place in the next few minutes, he rushes to the site in his Jaguar and is followed by Kary. He is too late and gets caught in the fiery debris of the exploding rocket but makes it to the shore where he is stopped by the military police. Harry knocks out the MPs, takes their Jeep and follows a Rehte Beer Company truck he saw near the launch site. He fights with the driver and takes the truck into the company's warehouse where he runs into White, whom he disables with a gas-filled fountain pen. White is electrocuted when he tries to kill Harry with a wrench but hits a high voltage pipe. Harry tries to escape in the Jeep but is captured. Kary has him put in a capsule that is dropped into the sea and sent to an underwater city. When he awakes, Harry meets Dr. Rooney who shows him a laser he was forced to develop for Rehte (Lulli). He also sees the madman's hibernation chamber where Rehte freezes people who are no longer of use to him. Taking Harry to Rehte, Kary tells him her father is in one of the chambers and will be killed unless she does the tyrant's bidding. Rehte informs Harry that his underground city is mostly automated and that he plans to launch a lava cannon to the Moon and with the laser he will be able to destroy any city on Earth and rule the planet. Harry tells Rehte he is insane. The agent is ordered to the hibernation chamber as the madman tells Dr. Rooney to have positive results with the laser in forty-eight hours. Kary informs Dr. Rooney that Harry is their only hope and she helps the agent to escape but is captured and taken to Rehte, who kills her father and then her with one of his rays. Dr. Rooney shuts down the city's generator as Harry eludes the guards and causes an explosion that triggers a deluge of lava. All the prisoners in the hibernation chambers die. Rehte plans to launch his rocket manually. Dr. Rooney orders Harry to stop Rehte and the two men climb to the top of a catwalk and fight with Rehte falling to the floor and engulfed in the lava. Harry and Dr. Rooney take refuge in the rocket cannon that launches them to the surface of the water as the subterranean city is destroyed. His seaplane (carrying Pat) picks up Harry and the scientist, and Harry and Pat retire to one of its bedrooms.

An inside joke in the dubbed U.S. version of the film has one of the Senators investigating the rocket explosions called Woolner, the name of the movie's releasing company.

Lisa and the Devil (Peppercorn-Wormser, 1975; 91 minutes; Color)

Producer: Alfred [Alfredo] Leone. Director: Mickey Lion [Mario Bava] and (uncredited) Alfred Leone. Screenplay: Alberto Cittini and Alfred Leone. Photography: Cecillio Paniagua. Editor: Carlo Reall. Music: Carlo Savina; Rodrigo's "Concerto d'Aranjuez." Conducted by Paul Muriat. Art Director: Nedo Azzini. Sets: Rafael Ferri. Production Manager: Faustino Ocaria. Makeup: Franco Freda. Special Effects: Franco Tocci. Assistant Director: Lamberto Bava.

CAST: Telly Savalas (Leandro), Elke Sommer (Lisa Reiner), Silva [Sylva] Koscina (Sophia Lehar), Robert Alda (Father Michael), Alida Valli (The Countess), Alessio Orano (Max), Gabriele Tinti (Chauffeur George), Kathy Leone (Tour Companion), Eduardo Fajardo (Frank Lehar), Carmen Silva (Anna), Franz von Treuberg (Shopkeeper), Espartaco Santoni (Carlo), Andres Esterhazy (Tourist).

Filmed in Italy as *Lisa e il Diavolo* (Lisa and the Devil) by director Mario Bava in 1972, this surreal horror film failed to please its producer, Alfredo Leone, after it did not get picked up by a U.S. distributor. He had Bava shoot new footage in order to have it appeal to fans of *The Exorcist* (1973), and when it was released stateside in 1975 as *The House of Exorcism* it made little sense plot-wise. Filmed in Technicolor by Leone International Films, *The House of Exorcism* added new footage of Robert Alda as a priest who tries to rid Elke Sommer's character of its demonic inhabitant and juxtaposed scenes from the original film with the new footage to make a farrago with some striking and horrifying scenes sewn together with others that are starkly mediocre and filled with foul language. When Allied Artists Television included it in the TV package "The Golden Seventies -Group VII," it reverted to the title *Lisa and the Devil* but it lost several minutes of theatrical footage containing nudity, bad language and violence. It was not until the early 1980s that Bava's original 116-minute version of the movie was released.

Two young women, Lisa Reiner (Sommer) and a new friend (Kathy Leone), are members of a tour group in the Italian city of Toledo. They view a fresco in which the Devil carries off the dead. Lisa wanders away from the group and finds a curio shop whose proprietor (Franz von Treuberg) is talking to a man, Leandro (Telly Savalas), who looks like the Devil in the fresco. On the street, Lisa has a fit and is aided by Father Michael (Alda), a priest, and is taken to a hospital by ambulance. She wakes up in the street and sees Leandro carrying a dummy; and he points her to the square containing the fresco. She meets a man, Carlo (Espartaco Santoni), who calls her Elena; when she pushes him away, he falls down a flight of stone steps and she runs away. In the hospital Lisa becomes violent and speaks in a masculine voice, ordering the priest to go away. She tells him she is not Lisa but then asks for his help. That night Lisa gets a ride in a car with Frank Lehar (Eduardo Fajardo) and his much younger wife Sophia (Sylva Koscina). The car overheats, forcing George (Gabriele Tinti), the chauffeur, to stop in front of an decaying villa where she sees Leandro, the butler. The place belongs to the blind countess (Alida Valli) who wants the people to leave but her son Max (Alessio Orano) begs her to let them stay and she relents. At the hospital the doctors find nothing physically wrong with Lisa and tell Father Michael that her problems are psychiatric but he suspects something supernatural. George and Sophia make love. The doctors inform the priest that Lisa has a split personality. She breaks her bonds, causes a light fixture to explode and goes berserk. The countess meets her guests at dinner. Father Michael prays for Lisa but she throws up on him. He demands to know who she is and her reply is "Elena." Max asks Lisa to stay at the villa when the others depart; the countess says it is too late because she is the likeness of Carlo's lover. Lisa informs Father Michael that she took Carlo from his wife, the countess, because her husband Max was impotent. The Lehars find George murdered in their car, his throat slashed. When Frank tries to make Sophia leave, she runs over him with the auto as Leandro watches. Lisa sees someone staring at her through a window and runs outside, pursued by the man, who turns out to be Carlo. In the villa, Lisa watches Leandro break a corpse's ankles to make it fit in a coffin, and Carlo calls her Elena as she faints. Father Michael sees visions of his dead

Poster for *The House of Exorcism* (Peppercorn-Warmser, 1976), which Allied Artists released to television under its original title, *Lisa and the Devil*.

lover Anna (Carmen Silva), who was killed in a car crash, and she reveals her naked body and begs him to have sex with her before turning into Lisa, who taunts the priest. Carlo is bludgeoned to death. Sophia sees the killing and runs into the villa where she is murdered by Max. Father Michael demands to know the whereabouts of Lisa's soul. Lisa awakens to find Leandro measuring her. He informs her that Carlo is dead and she finds the countess hovering over Sophia's bloody corpse. Running to Max, Lisa is told they will run away together and start a new life, adding that his mother is jealous beyond reason. He also tells Lisa she is more beautiful than Elena, who deceived him. Max shows Lisa a bed containing Elena's decayed corpse and he uses chloroform on the young woman and undresses her. Max tries to have sex with Lisa but is impotent. Later he tells his mother that Elena ran away with her husband and that he avenged her and himself at the same time by killing his lover. He also says he killed George and Sophia because they were going to take Lisa away. The countess tells her son he can only be saved if Lisa disappears and he kills her. Going to the dining room, Max sees all the dead ones sitting at the table. when his mother's corpse comes toward him, he backs out of a window and falls to his death. The countess' corpse is being pushed by Leandro. Father Michael demands to know where the events took place as Lisa spews toads from her mouth. In the city, Lisa walks toward the square with the fresco while the shopkeeper complains to Leandro that she got away. Father Michael goes to the vacant villa and fights with Satan, who attacks him with snakes. The priest orders the Devil and his accursed souls back to Hell and exorcises the villa.

Richard Meyers wrote in *For One Week Only: The World of Exploitation Films* (1983), "Now this one is a hoot. Savalas makes all sorts of casual demonic speeches to the innocent Sommer while sucking on a lollipop, exactly as his television character *Kojak* had done.... It is all extremely absurd, but very funny." In *The Encyclopedia of Horror Movies* (1986), Phil Hardy opined that the U.S. release's new scenes "not only destroy the rhythm of Bava's picture but no doubt also remove the most poetic sequences since they wouldn't contribute to the action." Regarding the original footage, Hardy notes, "The overwhelmingly morbid sense of necrophilia exuded by the movie, with Bava's camera lovingly caressing draperies and corpses, is punctuated by flamboyantly eerie exterior night scenes in which the director's morbid romanticism achieves intensely beautiful effects." Perhaps the contrast between the two versions of the movie is best described in *Video Watchdog #2* (1990), deriding producer Alfredo Leone's "transforming Mario Bava's twilight masterpiece *Lisa and the Devil* into the execrable pea soup paen, *House of Exorcism*."

The role of Lisa's tour friend is well played by Kathy Leone, the daughter of producer Alfredo Leone, who took over the direction from Bava for some of the new scenes added to *Lisa and the Devil* to become *The House of Exorcism*.

The Little Shop of Horrors (The Filmgroup, 1960; 71 minutes)

Producer-Director: Roger Corman. Screenplay: Charles B. Griffith. Photography: Arch Dalzell. Editor: Marshall Neilan, Jr. Music: Fred Katz. Art Director: Daniel Haller. Sound: Phillip Mitchell. Properties: Carl Brainard. Assistant Director: Richard Dixon.

CAST: Jonathan Haze (Seymour Krelboin), Jackie Joseph (Audrey Fulquard), Mel Welles (Gravis Mushnik), Dick Miller (Burson Fouch), Myrtle Vail (Winifred Krelboin), Tammy Windsor, Toby Michaels (High School Girls), Leola Wendorff (Mrs. Siddie Shiva), Lynn Storey (Hortense Feuchtwanger), Wally Campo (Detective Sergeant Joe Fink), Jack Warford (Detective Frank Stoolie), Merri Welles (Leonora Clyde), John Shaner (Dr. Phoebus Farb), Jack Nicholson (Wilbur Force), Dodie Drake (Waitress), Jack Griffin (Drunk), Robert Cogan (Hobo), Charles B. Griffith (Drunk Patient/Burglar/Voice of Audrey, Jr.).

Jonathan Haze and Audrey, Jr., in *The Little Shop of Horrors* (The Filmgroup, 1961)

Allied Artists Television released *The Little Shop of Horrors* to the small screen as part of its "Science-Fiction Features" package. Made as *The Passionate People Eater* on a budget of less than $30,000 in three days, the film is a minor classic in the field of horrific comedy. Although Roger Corman receives solo producer and director credit on the production, some sources claim scriptwriter Charles B. Griffith and co-star Mel Welles directed some of the footage. *The Little Shop of Horrors* developed such a cult following over the years that it spawned the 1982 award-winning musical of the same title by composers Alan Menken and Howard Ashman. In 1986 the musical came to the big screen starring Rick Moranis, Ellen Greene, Vincent Gardenia, Steve Martin and Bill Murray with direction by Frank Oz. An animated cartoon series, *Little Shop*, was telecast by Fox Kids Network in 1991.

Detective Sergeant Joe Fink (Wally Campo) relates how a homicide on L.A.'s Skid Row turned into the most horrifying period of his career. Gravis Mushnik (Welles) runs a florist shop in a downtrodden area of the city along with bumbling employee Seymour Krelboin (Jonathan Haze), who he pays ten dollars a week. A new customer, Burson Fouch (Dick Miller), orders carnations to eat and puts the cost on his tab. After Seymour messes up still another order, Mushnik wants to fire him but another employee, Audrey Fulquard (Jackie Joseph), defends him, not knowing Seymour is smitten with her. Seymour offers to give Mushnik a new plant he has grown from seeds obtained from a Japanese gardener and Fouch points out that small shops with exotic plants do better business. Mushnik sends Seymour to his apartment to get the plant, which he has named Audrey Jr. Upon his arrival, the young man delights his mother Winifred Krelboin (Myrtle Vail), a hypochondriac, with a tonic that is 98 percent alcohol. Taking Audrey Jr. back to the flower shop, Seymour finds his boss is not impressed but he is given ten days to turn it into an acceptable display. Sitting up with the sickly plant, Seymour notices it has opened up and when he goes to get it water he accidentally cuts his finger on a thorn and finds out Audrey Jr. is nourished by blood. The next day the plant has doubled in size and brought in a large crowd, causing Mushnik to give Seymour a two dollar raise and make plans to adopt him. Two Cocamonga High School students (Tammy Windsor, Toby Michaels) want the plant for their school's float in the Rose Bowl Parade and Mushnik is overjoyed when they agree to consider a $2,000 flower purchase. Audrey Jr. begins wilting. Seymour promises to make the plant healthy again. That night it talks and demands to be fed. Not knowing what to do, the young man walks through Skid Row and over to the railroad yards where he throws a rock at a bottle and accidentally knocks out a drunk (Jack Griffin), who falls on the tracks and is decapitated by a train. Seymour takes the body back to the flower shop and, when the plant demands food, he gives it the drunk's body parts. Mushnik sees Seymour feeding Audrey Jr. and vows to inform the law. The next morning the plant is huge and the shop is swarming with customers so Mushnik holds his tongue. A dentist, Dr. Farb (John Shaner), is angry with Seymour for messing up one of his flower orders and tries to take out more than one tooth. The two get into a fight and Seymour mortally wounds Farb with a dental instrument but is unable to remove the body because of the intrusion of pain-loving undertaker Wilbur Force (Jack Nicholson). Pretending to be the dentist, Seymour yanks out several of Wilbur's teeth. Seymour gives Audrey Jr. Dr. Farb's body and later informs his boss that the plant is through eating because it has been fed three times, the most required of a cross between a Venus Fly Trap and a butterwort. Due to the two disappearances on Skid Row, Fink and his partner, Detective Frank Stoolie (Jack Warford) interrogate a nervous Mushnik but learn nothing. Hortense Feuchtwanger (Lynn Storey) of the Society of Silent Flower Observers of Southern California shows up at the shop and says she will give Seymour a trophy for Audrey Jr. when it blooms in two days. As Mushnik sits with the plant that night and refuses its demand for food, Seymour takes Audrey to his home for a dinner prepared by his mother, made up of health foods and medications. When the two young people talk about getting married, the old sot chastises Seymour for not getting her an iron lung first. A burglar (Charles B. Griffith) breaks into the flower shop and demands money from Mushnik, who tells him it is hidden inside Audrey Jr. The crook goes to retrieve the money and is devoured by the plant. The next night Seymour and Audrey have a picnic in the flower shop but when the plant calls out to be fed, the young woman thinks it is Seymour talking, becomes disgusted with him and leaves. The dejected Seymour roams Skid Row where he is enticed by a hooker (Merri Welles) whom he accidentally kills and then feeds to Audrey Jr. The special ceremony for the plant's blooming takes place at sunset the next day and is attended by Mushnik, Audrey, Mrs. Krelboin, Hortense and the two policemen. Just as Seymour arrives, the blooms open showing the faces of the murder victims. The young man runs out of the shop, chased by the detectives and Mushnik. He leads them through a junkyard filled with hundreds of semi-truck tires and bathroom appliances before hiding in a commode. Seymour goes back to the shop where Audrey Jr. demands to be fed. He picks up a knife and dives into the plant, promising to kill it. When Mushnik, the detectives, Audrey and Mrs. Krelboin return, the last bloom opens, revealing Seymour's face.

Variety reported that the film was a "serviceable parody of a typical screen horror number.... *Little Shop of Horrors* is kind of one big sick joke, but it's essentially harmless and good natured.... The acting is pleasantly preposterous." The *Motion Picture Herald* called it "[h]orrifically funny," adding, "The deft production-directional touches of the resourceful redoubtable Roger Corman are very much present...." The British *Monthly Film Bulletin* termed it "the best full-length horror comedy ever made in two days." Mark Thomas McGee reported in *Roger Corman: The Best of the Cheap Acts* (1988), "Over the years, *Little Shop of Horrors* has developed a cult following and is probably better and more fondly remembered than any of Roger's more prestigious productions. It was one of two American films to be shown at the Cannes Film Festival the years of its release.... No picture ever gave Roger a better return."

While Corman may get most of the praise for turning out such an amusing film on so little money in such a short time, the actors also deserve much credit. Jonathan Haze is top-notch as the half-witted, well-meaning Seymour, and Jackie Joseph is able to bring off the difficult role of his addled love interest. The film's best performance is that of Mel Welles as the harried Gravis Mushnik and he is almost matched by Myrtle Vail as Seymour's batty, health-conscious mother. (Vail, who was scripter Charles B. Griffith's grandmother, for many years starred on the radio serial "Myrt and Marge.") Dick Miller adds a nice touch as the flower eater and Wally Campo and Jack Warford nicely carry off their Joe Friday–Frank Smith imitation of "Dragnet." Jack Nicholson makes the most of his outrageous part as the masochistic dental patient.

Lost Women (Howco International, 1953; 69 minutes)

Producers: G. William Perkins and Melvin Gordon. Directors: Herbert Tevos and Ron Ormond. Screenplay: Herbert Tevos. Photography: Karl Struss and Gilbert Warrenton. Editors: Hugh Winn and Ray H. Lockert. Supervising Editor: W. Donn Hayes. Music: Hoyt Curtin. Sound: Harry Smith. Sets: Theodore Offenbecker. Makeup: Paul Stanhope and Harry Ross. Special Effects: Ray Mercer. Properties: Oscar Lau and Ernest Johnson. Dialogue Supervisor: Orville H. Hampton. Dialogue Director: Herb A. Lightmann. Script Supervisor: Sam Freedle. Assistant Director: Theodore Joos.

CAST: Jackie Coogan (Dr. Arana), Richard Travis (Dan Mulcahey), Allan Nixon (Dr. Tucker), Mary Hill (Doreen Culverson), Robert Knapp (Grant Phillips), Chris-Pin Martin (Pepe), Harmon Stevens (Dr. Leland J. Masterson), Nico Lek (Jan van Croft), Samuel Wu (Wu), John Martin (Frank), Tandra Quinn (Tarantella), George Barrows (George), Dean Riesner (Henchman), Kelly Drake, Candy Collins, Doris Lee Price, Mona McKinnon, Sherry Moreland, Ginger Sherry, Chris Randall, Diane Fortier, Karna Greene, June Benbow, Doris Hart (Spider Women), Katina Vea [Katherine Victor] (Spider Woman Guide), Dolores Fuller (Blonde Spider Woman in Woods), Margia Dean (Brunette Spider Woman in Woods), Fred Kelsey (Cantina Bartender), Angelo Rossitto (Dwarf), John George (Mute Assistant), Julian Rivero, Suzanne Ridgeway, Jack Low (Cantina Customers), Lyle Talbot (Narrator).

Herbert Tevos wrote and directed footage for a film called *Lost Women of Zarpa* and *Tarantula* for Joy M. Houck and J. Francis White, Jr., the owners of Howco International Pictures. When Houck and White deemed the production too short and incoherent for release, they called in Ron Ormond to finish the film. Ormond had previously directed westerns starring Lash LaRue for the two producers' Western Adventure company and he helmed new footage written by Orville H. Hampton, who got screen credit as dialogue supervisor for the finished product, *Mesa of Lost Women*, which Howco issued theatrically in the summer of 1953. The film was shown in Great Britain as *Lost Women*, the title used by Allied Artists Television when it was included in its "The Golden Sixties — Group VI" and "Science-Fiction Features" packages. Under any title, it is an insipid mess, although it contains lots

Spanish lobby card for *Mesa of Lost Women* (Howco International, 1953). Contrary to the advertising, Jack Holt does not appear in the film.

of eye candy via the sexy spider women that included Ed Wood actresses Dolores Fuller and Mona McKinnon, and Jerry Warren's perennial leading lady, Katherine Victor. Hoyt Curtin's constantly annoying flamenco music soundtrack was later used in Wood's *Jail Bait* (1954) with Fuller, McKinnon and Lyle Talbot, the narrator of *Mesa of Lost Women*.

In Mexico's Muerto Desert, surveyor Frank (John Martin) and his sidekick Pepe (Chris-Pin Martin) find Grant Phillips (Robert Knapp) and Doreen Culverson (Paula Hill) near death from dehydration. They take them to the Amer-Exico Field Hospital, where they are treated by Dr. Tucker (Allan Nixon). Grant comes to and begins raving about super-sized deadly bugs and begs camp foreman Dan Mulcahey (Richard Travis) to use oil to burn off the top of Zarpa Mesa. Grant tells the story of how, a year before, the renowned scientist Dr. Leland J. Masterson (Harmon Stevens) traveled to Zarpa Mesa to meet Dr. Arana (Jackie Coogan) to discuss scientific theory. Masterson is led to Arana's hidden cave laboratory by a mysterious woman (Katherine Victor); Arana informs Masterson that he has been able to control the interior pituitary gland's growth hormone and in working with spiders has created beings with the properties of both species. He laments that his main success has been with females while his experiments with males have only resulted in creating dwarfs. Arana shows Masterson the beautiful Tarantella (Tandra Quinn), who he says can grow new limbs and will lives for centuries, along with a giant spider. The horrified Masterson tells Arana he is evil and that he and his creations must be destroyed. As Masterson tries to escape, he is given a shot by Tarantella that makes him lose consciousness. After being confined in a mental ward for a year, Masterson escapes and is trailed for two days by his nurse, George (George Barrows). Masterson winds up in a cantina in a small Mexican town where Doreen is stranded with her wealthy older fiancé Jan von Croft (Nico Lek) as their pilot, Grant, tries to repair Jan's plane so the couple can fly to Mexico City to be married. Masterson, whose mind has snapped, sits with Doreen and Jan and as George joins them they watch Tarantella dance. Jan is unaware that his servant Wu (Samuel Wu) has been mesmerized by the spider woman. Masterson shoots Tarantella and then forces the others to go with him to Jan's plane; after they leave, the dancer revives. Although the plane is not totally repaired, Masterson tells Grant to fly them out of the town as the police approach. Flying over the Muerto Desert, an engine fails and Grant is forced to make a landing on Zarpa Mesa. After Grant fires a flare, Wu makes a fire and George decides to explore. He is attacked and killed by a giant spider. During the night, Doreen hears a rustling noise and starts talking to Grant, who makes her admit she is marrying Jan for his money. Doreen is frightened when she sees the spider women and dwarfs watching them. Wu goes to Arana and informs him that he has brought Masterson back to the mesa; as he leaves, he is killed by the spider women. Jan is killed by the giant spider. The other members of the party are captured by Arana's creatures and taken to his underground laboratory where he gives Masterson a serum that restores his sanity. The scientist again refuses to aid Arana in his mad schemes. When Tarantella tries to kill Masterson, she is restrained by Doreen as Grant subdues Arana. Masterson mixes together volatile chemicals and orders Doreen and Grant to run from the laboratory as he causes a conflagration that destroys Arana and his creations. Except for Pepe, all the listeners at the hospital doubt Grant's story, even though it is confirmed by a revived Doreen. Dan refuses Grant's request to set fire to Zarpa Mesa where one of the spider women keeps watch.

Needless to say, *Lost Women* garnered little praise. *Variety* called it "for laughs only" while *John Stanley's Creature Features Movie Guide Strikes Again* (1994) dubbed it "[t]urgidly written-directed-acted sci-fi thriller.... So incompetent you won't believe your eyes." Phil Hardy said in *Science Fiction* (1984), "The special effects are grim." In *The Psychotronic Encyclopedia of Film* (1983), Michael J. Weldon declared it "[g]reat grade-Z nonsense" while *The Phantom's Ultimate Video Guide* (1989) thought it "[u]ndeservedly underrated classic dreck...." James O'Neill in *Terror on Tape* (1994) termed it "[o]ne of the very worst.... [T]he two guys who helmed this mess make Ed Wood look like John Ford."

Co-director Ron Ormond went on to make exploitation films, including westerns, country music and religious movies. Among them were the genre efforts *The Exotic Ones* (*The Monster and the Stripper*) (1968) and *The Grim Reaper* (1976).

The Magic Voyage of Sinbad (The Filmgroup, 1962; 79 minutes; Color)

Producer: Joseph Moss [Art Diamond]. Associate Producer: Jack Woods. Director: Alfred Posco [Aleksandr Ptushko]. Screenplay: Karl Isar [Konstantin Isayev]. Photography: Frank Provor [Fyodor Provorov]. Editor: George Stein. Music: Nikolai Rimsky-Korsakov. Music Director: Grigori Gamburg. Song: John Smich, sung by Gino Marsili. Choreography: Sergei Koren. Art Directors: Edward Kuman and Eva Disel. Sound: Victor [Viktor] Zorin. Costumes: O. Kruchinina. Makeup: Jose Malar. Special Effects: Sidney Mulin [Sergei Mukhin].

CAST: Edward Stolar [Sergei Stolyarov] (Sinbad), Anna Larion [Alla Larionova] (Luberia), Ellen Mysova [Yelena Myshkova] (Princess Morgiana), Maurice Troyan [Mikhail Troyanovsky] (Trifon), Norman Malish [Nadir Malishevsky] (Tanus), Robert Surow [B. Surovtsev] (Hadabad),

William Leon [Yuri Leonidov] (Cassim), Laurence Astan [M. Astangov] (Prince Lal Bahari Day), Irving Perev [Ivan Pereverzev] (Abdalla), Eugene Krikol [Nikolai Kryuchkov] (Old Merchant), Stanley Martinson [Sovol Martinson] (Money Lender), Nord [Lev] Fenin (Viking Leader), Arnold Kaylor [Stepan Kayukov] (King Neptune), Olivia Viklandt (Queen Neptuna), Lucille Vertisya [Lidiya Vertinskaya] (The Phoenix), Julian Burton (Voices of Sinbad and King Neptune), Luana Anders (Voice of Princess Morgiana), Francis Ford Coppola (Voice of Cassim).

The Filmgroup, headed by producer-director Roger Corman, purchased the English-language rights to the 1953 Soviet film *Sadko*, directed by Aleksandr Ptushko, based on the 1867 symphonic poem by Nikolai Rimsky-Korsakov. Corman assigned Francis Ford Coppola and James Landis the task of turning the movie into a dual bill release item and they changed the musical fantasy into a Sinbad film thanks to the continuing success of Columbia Pictures' *The 7th Voyage of Sinbad* (1958). The new dubbed version deleted ten minutes of running time, added a title song, and was released theatrically in March 1962 as *The Magic Voyage of Sinbad*. Allied Artists Television brought it to the small screen in its "Science-Fiction Features" grouping.

Sadko was first released in the United States in 1953 by Artkino Films, the company that seven years later sold it to Corman. That year it received the Venice Film Festival's Silver Lion award and was widely screened throughout the world. Issued in its homeland in 1952, *Sadko* was the final film of Soviet director Aleksandr Ptushko, who died that year. Known for his direction and special effects, Ptushko imbued the feature with his trademark sumptuous production values that included exotic and impressive sets, well-staged battle scenes, a fascinating underwater world and the Phoenix, a bird woman who entices men to sleep forever. As to be expected from a Soviet production, politics involving class struggle dominates the first third of the movie. While Corman's U.S. reworking glosses over the political overtones and excises music that would have slowed down a feature destined for kiddie matinees, *The Magic Voyage of Sinbad* retains the topnotch fantasy elements like Sinbad's magic harp, the water nymph who changes goldfish into bullion, a tiny living White Horse chess piece, the Phoenix and her mysterious lair and the aquatic world of Neptune with a dancing octopus and a lobster-drawn chariot.

After completing his famous seven voyages, legendary sailor Sinbad (Edward Stolar) returns to the coastal city of Covosan. Having given all his treasure to the poor of other lands, he comes home with only his magic harp. He is disappointed to find the city run down with all the wealth in the hands of greedy merchants. Sinbad meets a beautiful working girl, Luberia (Anna Larion), who gives him water. Trying to rally the citizens to bring the city back to its former glory, Sinbad tells them of the bird of happiness and vows he will build boats and sail around the world to bring it back to Covosan. At a feast given by a wealthy old merchant (Eugene Krikol), Sinbad is derided when he asks the rich to use their money to build a fleet of ships; he vows to construct the boats himself. A young boy, Hadabad (Robert Surow), asks to come along on the voyage and Sinbad agrees. That night the sailor plays his harp at the water's edge and is kissed by Princess Morgiana (Ellen Mysova), the daughter of King Neptune (Arnold Kaylor), who agrees to help him by providing golden fishes. Sinbad summons the townspeople and makes a bet with the merchants that he will get the golden fishes or they can have his head. He is joined in his efforts by strongman Cassim (William Leon), who outwrestles a bear, and old wise man Trifon (Maurice Troyan). Sinbad makes two unsuccessful attempts to bring up the golden fishes in his net but on the third try the princess keeps her promise and he obtains his prize. The impressed merchants agree to open their warehouses and a celebration takes place. At the end of the day Sinbad

Edward Stolar and Ellen Mysova in *The Magic Voyage of Sinbad* (The Filmgroup, 1962), a reworking of the Soviet film *Sadko* (1952).

realizes he has given the city's wealth to the poor and that he has no money to build his fleet. Luberia tells Sinbad that her mother forbids their being together. Princess Morgiana again comes to his rescue and turns the golden fishes into gold coins, giving Sinbad the funds he needs to construct three ships. Bidding goodbye to Luberia, Sinbad sets sail with his men to find the bird of happiness. They sail north and land on a desolate coast where they are attacked by Viking warriors. Sinbad and his men win the battle and take the Viking leader's (Nord Fenin) white stallion as a prize. They sail to the exotic cities of Abadu, Banagalor and Nashapur but are unable to find the bird of happiness. Sinbad next leads his men to India where Trifon learns that a maharajah (Laurence Astan) has a phoenix of happiness kept in a tall tower surrounded by seven walls. When the ruler arrives on an elephant, he is insulted when Sinbad, riding the white stallion, will not bow to him. The monarch wants the horse and Sinbad suggests they play a game of chess with the prize being either the stallion or the Phoenix. Outsmarting the maharajah, Sinbad wins the game and enters a hidden staircase with Trifon, Hadabad and Cassim. They arrive in an ornamental tower where they find the Phoenix (Lucille Vertisya) perched. The evil bird begins singing a siren song that puts Trifon, Hadabad and Cassim to sleep but Sinbad uses his harp to resist her; awakening his friends, they go back into the palace. The maharajah orders his army to attack the strangers as they try to return to their ships but Sinbad uses the Phoenix to put the soldiers and their elephants to sleep. Sailing on to Egypt, Sinbad realizes he cannot find the bird of happiness and decides to return to Covosan and Luberia. The ships are hit by a great storm because no homage was paid to King Neptune. Sinbad decides to give up his life to save his crew: He dives to the bottom of the sea and finds the coral gates to Neptune's palace where he serenades the king and his argumentative wife, Queen Neptuna (Olivia Viklandt). Claiming he must return to land to replace his broken harp strings, Sinbad tries to leave the kingdom but Neptune orders him to marry one of his seven beautiful daughters. He chooses Morgiana, although he tells her he really loves Luberia. She provides him with a seahorse so he can escape. Sinbad is followed by the king, who drives a chariot pulled by a giant lobster. Sinbad outraces Neptune and gets back to Covosan where he is reunited with Luberia. When the three vessels return unharmed, Sinbad tells the people happiness is not a bird and that it has always been in Covosan.

Tim Lucas in *Video Watchdog #9* (1992), provides an insightful summary: "*The Magic Voyage of Sinbad* may be a foolish translation of a wonderful film, but it is too feeble a disguise to fully desecrate Ptushko's original production. Ptuschko's most splendid scenes ... all remain essentially intact. *The Magic Voyage of Sinbad* cannot help but be a remarkable viewing experience ... in spite of itself." Michael J. Weldon in *The Psychotronic Encyclopedia of Film* (1983) noted, "No Sinbad here.... It's really pretty impressive.... The only real low point is a silly-looking octopus." In *Movies on TV 1975–76* (1974), Steven H. Scheuer said, "No magic here. Hokum swashbuckling adventure."

Man with the Synthetic Brain (Independent-International, 1972; 86 minutes; Color)

Producer-Director: Al Adamson. Executive Producers: Charles McMullen and Zoe Phillips. Associate Producers: Samuel M. Sherman and J.P. Spohn. Screenplay: Dick Poston and Chris Martino. Story: Al Adamson and Samuel M. Sherman. Photography: Louis Horvath and William [Vilmos] Zsigmond. Editor: Samuel M. Sherman (uncredited). Music: Jimmie Roosa and Don McGinnis. Sound: Robert Dietz. Makeup: Lee James. Production Manager: J.P. Spohn. Titles: Bob Le Bar. Script Supervisor: Sandy Portelli.

CAST: John Carradine (Dr. Howard Van Ard), Kent Taylor (Dr. Elton Corey), Tommy Kirk (Police Lieutenant Cross), Regina Carrol (Susan Van Ard), Roy Morton (Joe Corey), Arne Warda (Sergeant Grimaldi), Tacey Robbins (Linda Clarke), Richard Smedley (Acro), Kirk Duncan (David Jordan Clarke), Tanya Maree (Vicky), Barney Gelfan (Detective Pete), John Aimond (Nick), Lyle Felice (Vito), Joey Benson (Police Lieutenant Ward), John Talbert (Curtiss), K.K. Riddle (Nancy Clarke), Al Adamson (Murdered Gang Member), Robert Dietz (Policeman), J.P. Spohn (Head in Box).

Allied Artists Television released *Man with the Synthetic Brain* to the small screen in its "The Golden Sixties — Group VI" and "Science-Fiction Features" packages in the mid–1970s. At the same time it was still getting theatrical showings under its 1972 Independent-International Pictures release title, *Blood of Ghastly Horror*. The feature's history dates back to 1963 when Victor Adamson Productions made the tawdry jewel heist thriller *Two Tickets to Terror* in Hollywood and Lake Tahoe. Adamson, better known as Denver Dixon, produced this cheap effort and his son Al Adamson made his directorial debut with it (and also played one of the robbers). Also called *Echo of Terror*, it was released to theaters in 1965 as *Psycho A-Go-Go* with added songs by the Vandells. In 1967, new footage with John Carradine was interpolated, giving the movie a science fiction subplot, and it was shown as *Fiend with the Electronic Brain* by Hemisphere Pictures. In the early 1970s, more scenes were

Roy Morton and John Carradine in *Man with the Synthetic Brain*, the TV title of *Blood of Ghastly Horror* (Independent-International, 1971).

spliced in with Kent Taylor, Tommy Kirk and Regina Carrol; Independent-International released it as *Blood of Ghastly Horror*. The final result is one of the worst films ever patched together. It is incredibly dull and lacks the redeeming quality of being fun to watch. Much of the latter-day footage is lensed in tight facial close-ups, barely matching the older material.

A disfigured fiend, Acro (Richard Smedley), goes on a killing spree, murdering a hooker and her doper customer, a female pedestrian and two cops. Lieutenant Cross (Kirk) is put in charge of the case and he receives a box in the mail containing a severed head and a note signed by Joe Corey (Roy Morton). Cross relates to his associate, Sergeant Grimaldi (Arne Warda), Corey's history of being a shell-shocked Vietnam War veteran who was treated by brain surgeon Dr. Howard Van Ard (John Carradine). Van Ard is visited by Police Lieutenant Ward (Joey Benson) and says Corey died during an operation two years before. Benson notes the dead man's fingerprints were found at the scene of a jewel robbery. Corey takes part in the heist but his briefcase containing the gems ends up in the back of a pickup truck owned by David Clarke (Kirk Duncan). The sadist Corey murders one of his cohorts (Al Adamson) as Clarke drives home where his little daughter, Nancy (K.K. Riddle), finds the jewels. Corey goes to an office building, kills a secretary, gets Clarke's address and invades the man's home with three other gang members, Vito (Lyle Felice), Curtiss (John Talbert) and Nick (John Aimond). When Clarke denies knowing about the diamonds, Corey beats him and is sent by Vito to find the man's wife Linda (Tacey Robbins), who sings at a club. Ward goes back to see Van Ard, who tells him he has been experimenting on the rehabilitation of damaged brain cells and has built an artificial brain component which he put in Corey's head, causing him to become a psychopathic homicidal maniac. Corey goes to the bar where

Linda sings and picks up a hooker who tells him the woman and her daughter took a bus to Lake Tahoe where they are to meet her husband. Corey strangles the young woman and then goes to Van Ard's office, straps him to some equipment and fills him full of electricity. Cross informs Grimaldi that everyone involved in the Corey case is dead except himself. The lieutenant receives a visit from blonde Susan Van Ard (Carrol), the late neurosurgeon's daughter, who tells him she fells she is being contacted telepathically. After she leaves, Cross informs Grimaldi that Corey once said his missing father, Dr. Elton Corey (Taylor), was involved in voodoo experiments. At his laboratory, Dr. Corey keeps his zombie slave Acro in a cage and vows to avenge the death of his son. He telephones Susan, saying he once worked with her father and he has some papers for her. Susan sends word about the call to Cross, who is out of the office. As Dr. Corey and Acro go to meet Susan, Detective Pete (Barney Gelfan), who took Susan's message, drives to the meeting place. As Dr. Corey carries off Susan, Acro attacks Pete, who writes part of a license plate number in his own blood before dying. Cross and Grimaldi see Pete's note from Susan and go to the area where they find Pete's body and the partial number. At his laboratory, Dr. Corey informs Susan that he plans to turn her into his slave and that he blames her father for making his son an electronic freak. He also relates how his son followed Linda Clarke and her daughter to Lake Tahoe with he and Curtiss taking them into the desert where he demands the jewels. When Linda says she knows nothing about the robbery, she and her daughter are taken to a motel where Corey tries to rape Linda but is stopped by Curtiss. The two men fight and Corey shoots Curtiss. Linda and Nancy take his car and drive away. Corey steals a another car and follows them as the police are alerted to their whereabouts. Clarke and Ward also follow. Linda stops her car in snow country and she and her daughter try to elude Corey on foot as they are trailed by her husband and Ward. Corey corners Linda and Nancy but he is shot by Ward and plunges off a cliff. Corey finds the jewels in Nancy's doll. Dr. Corey starts to give Susan an injection when Grimaldi arrives; he is murdered by the dying Acro. The madman turns Susan into a hideous crone and says she will serve him. Acro breaks out of his cell and kills Dr. Corey before collapsing. Susan takes an antidote that returns her to normal as Cross arrives on the scene.

In *Schlock-O-Rama: The Films of Al Adamson* (1998), David Konow said, "*Blood of Ghastly Horror* is the perfect example of Al [Adamson] and Sam's [Samuel M. Sherman] diehard mentality to do whatever it takes to complete a movie.... With so many films of this era promising so much in their ads yet delivering so little, at least *Blood of Ghastly Horror* delivered. As Sam says, 'It had blood, it was ghastly and it was horrible.'"

John Carradine in *The Man with the Synthetic Brain*, which was derived from *Fiend with the Electronic Brain* (Hemisphere, 1968).

Mermaids of Tiburon (The Filmgroup, 1962; 76 minutes; Color)

Producer-Director-Screenplay-Underwater Photography: John Lamb. Associate Producer: Ron Graham. Photography: Brydon Baker and Hal McAlpin. Editor: Bert Honey. Music: Richard LaSalle. Music Editor: Lloyd Young. Sound: Del Harris.

CAST: George Rowe (Dr. Samuel Jackson), Diane Webber (Mermaid Queen), Timothy Carey (Milo Sangster), Jose Gonzalez-Gonzalez (Pepe Gallardo), John Mylong (Ernst Steinhauer), Gil Baretto (Baquero), Vicki Cantenwine, Nani Morrissey, Judy Edwards, Jean Carroll, Diana Cook, Karen Goodman, Nancy Burns (Mermaids).

While working at his job at Marineland, Dr. Samuel Jackson (George Rowe), a marine biologist, is approached by pearl expert Ernst Steinhauer (John Mylong) with a business proposition. Steinhauer wants Jackson to go with him to Tiburon Island to dive for large pearls. Jackson agrees to join the expedition and flies to Mexico to meet Steinhauer, who is missing. Jackson charters a boat and sails to Tiburon as does adventurer Milo Sangster (Timothy Carey), who has hired a craft owned by Pepe (Jose Gonzalez-Gonzalez). Jackson arrives at Tiburon which he notes is untouched since the beginning of time. After going ashore, he finds sea otters, a species thought to be extinct. Sangster informs Pepe that they are going to Tiburon to dive for pearls and makes him a gift of one of them. Finding Tiburon to be an amazing marine sanctuary, Jackson spies a strange sea creature that turns out to be a mermaid (Diane Webber). Following her underwater, he finds several others like her

Spanish lobby card for *The Mermaids of Tiburon* (The Filmgroup, 1962)

and determines that they are water-breathing mammals. Sangster and Pepe locate the island as Jackson picks a bouquet of water flowers which the mermaid readily accepts. She leads him into a grotto where he sees many more mermaids who flee from him, but some return due to curiosity. The mermaids take him to a bed of giant oysters and one of them leads a killer shark away from Jackson. Sangster throws dynamite into the water in an effort to kill Jackson, who manages to recover and return to shore. Sangster and Pepe search for the pearls as Jackson boards their boat and finds evidence that Sangster robbed and murdered Steinhauer. Sangster returns and the two men fight. When Pepe tries to stop Sangster from shooting Jackson, he is pushed into the sea and devoured by the shark. A fire is started by Sangster's flare gun and the dynamite explodes, destroying the craft. Sangster escapes in a rowboat and returns to the oyster bed; Jackson goes after him. After taking two of the huge oyster shells to shore, Sangster sees the mermaids, follows them and ends up in a grotto where he is caught between boulders and dies. Jackson decides to return home as the mermaids disappear; he promises to someday go back to Tiburon Island.

Basically an undersea photo essay in the Gulf of California, *Mermaids of Tiburon* had a piddling adventure plot highlighted by producer-director-writer John Lamb's outstanding underwater photography. The subplot of mermaids gives the film a fantasy theme. Issued theatrically in June 1962 by the Filmgroup, it was produced by Pacifica Productions. The original version was included by Allied Artists Television in its movie package "Science-Fiction Pictures." Lamb removed most of the mermaid footage and re-shot it with topless women, including Gaby Martone, and the film was shown in adult and art theatres as *The Aqua Sex* and *The Virgin Aqua Sex* in 1964. In 1985 Lamb again re-edited the feature and it was issued as the nude version of *The Mermaids of Tiburon*.

"Foolish undersea adventure concerning 'unclassified' fish women" is how Michael J. Weldon wrote in *The Psychotronic Encyclopedia of Film* (1983). R.G. Young in *The Encyclopedia of Fantastic Film* (2000) said it was a "[s]tandard semi-fantasy." Steven H. Scheuer in *Movies on TV 1969–70* (1968) thought it "[p]retty fishy, despite good camera work." Donald C. Willis in *Horror and Science Fictions: A Checklist* (1972) called it "[d]ull."

Mermaids of Tiburon footage appeared in the "Mermaid" episode of "Voyage to the Bottom of the Sea" (ABC-TV, 1964–68) and the 1968 Mexican film *La Mujer Murcielago* (The Batwoman).

Satanik (Interfilm/Hispamex, 1968; 84 minutes; Color)

Producer: Romano Mussolin. Director: Piero Vivarelli. Story-Screenplay: Eduardo Manzanos Brochero, from the comic strip by Magnus [Roberto Raviola] and Max Bunker [Luciano Secchi]. Photography: Silvano Ippoliti. Editor: Gianmaria Messeri. Music: Manuel Parada. Art Directors: Cubero and Galicia. Sound: Romano Pamplona and Alessandro Sarandrae. General Production Manager: Giancarlo Marchetti. Production Manager: Mario Barboni. Production Secretary: Mario Villani. Sets: Cimino. Wardrobe: Berniece Sapanaro. Makeup: Gianni Ornadi. Assistant Director: Giuseppe Avati.

CAST: Magda Konopka (Dr. Marnie Bannister), Julio Pena (Inspector Trent), Umi [Umberto] Raho (George Van Donan), Luigi Montini (Dodo La Roche), Armando Calvo (Inspector Gonzalez), Mimma Ippoliti (Stella Dexter), Isarco Ravaioli (Commissaire La Duc), Nerio Bernardi (Professor Graves), Joe Atlanta (Albert), Antonio Pica (Louis La Roche), Piero Vivarelli (Max), Gaetano Quartararo (Sergeant Ortega), Mirella Pamphilli (Dancer), Gustavo Simone (Frank), Giancarlo Prete (Pedro), Pedro Fenollar (Janitor), Luis de Tejada (Gang Member).

Also called *Satanic*, this Italian-Spanish co-production's major asset is its presentation of star Magda Konopka's body, mainly in exotic costumes. Otherwise it is a listless, mundane effort offset somewhat by some scenic Swiss scenery. The star's monster makeup is tacky and no explanation is given for her facial deformity although its temporary remedy fills her with bloodlust. Outside of Konopka's striptease in a black Diabolik-like suit, *Satanik* has little claim to fame, except for being based on the popular comic strip of the same name, published by Corno of Milan, and must rate as one of Europe's lesser excursions into the horror-sci-fi film field. With its brief nude scenes snipped out, the film was included by Allied Artists Television in its "The Golden Sixties — Group VI" and "Science-Fiction Features" packages.

On a stormy night in Madrid, facially grotesque Dr. Marnie Bannister (Konopka) goes to see her associate, Professor Graves (Nerio Bernardi), a world-famous biochemist who has been working on a cell regeneration serum. He has had success with animals but notices a ferocity in their behavior after the injections. Marnie wants him to experiment on her but he refuses and she kills him. She mixes his formula with a crystal and drinks the concoction, becoming a very beautiful woman. She takes the dead man's money and medical papers and leaves. Local police inspector Gonzalez (Armando Calvo) calls in Scotland Yard Inspector Trent (Julio Pena) to work with him on the case, since Marnie, who has disappeared, is a British citizen. At a hotel bar, Marnie meets diamond dealer George Van Donan (Umi Raho) and she goes back with him to his apartment where he buys her clothes as she takes them off. She extracts information from him about gambler Louis La Roche (Antonio Pica) and gives it to the police. Louis has transferred a large amount of money to a Geneva bank in the name of his mistress, Stella Dexter (Mimma Ippoliti). The police raid Louis' club and he and his men, excepting Albert (Joe Atlanta), are killed in the shootout. When Marnie meets Van Donan that night, she turns into a hag and kills him before going back to the laboratory, murdering the guard (Pedro Fenollar) and restoring her youth with the serum. The police find that Van Donan has been murdered and trace his car to the laboratory. After Marine lets them in, she kills Sergeant Ortega (Gaetano Quartararo) and takes the vehicle but is pursed by Trent and Gonzalez. She manages to elude them and goes to Stella's apartment, drowns the young woman in her bath tub and assumes her identity. Landing in Geneva, she is taken to Louis' brother, night club owner Dodo La Roche (Luigi Montini), who never met Stella. Trent traces the dead Stella's airline ticket to Geneva and goes there, joining forces with Commissaire La Duc (Isarco Ravaioli). The two policemen go to Dodo's club and watch Marnie perform a striptease. Albert arrives and tells Dodo that Stella double-crossed his brother. After her dance is finished, Marnie sees the two lawmen and flees with Dodo and Albert also after her. She takes a boat, the *Major Davel*, to escape to France, but Trent and La Duc and the gangsters also board the craft. Dodo and Albert confront Marnie but Albert says he is not Stella. The policemen get the drop on them and a shootout ensues. The gangsters are killed and Trent receives a leg wound. Marnie escapes to shore and is followed by La Duc, who lets her go because she has reverted to a hag. Having lost the crystals on the boat, Marnie steals a car from a garage, not knowing its brakes are faulty. She speeds along a curving road and drives over an embankment. The car catches fire and Marnie is killed but in death her beauty is restored.

In *The Encyclopedia of Horror Movies* (1986), Phil Hardy summarized the film as "a routine potboiler derived from gangster clichés, science fiction and horror movies with the odd musical number thrown [in] and totally lacking in style." James O'Neill in *Terror on Tape* (1994) called it "[f]amiliar-looking…. Visually interesting but dramatically hollow." "Yet another variation on Robert Louis Stevenson's [*Dr. Jekyll and Mr. Hyde*]" is how Stephen Jones described it in *The Essential Monster Movie Guide* (2000).

Terror in the Haunted House (Howco International, 1961; 80 minutes)

Producer: William S. Edwards. Executive Producer: Robert Corrigan. Associate Producer: Michael Miller. Assistant Producer: Taggart Cassey. Director: Harold Daniels. Screenplay: Robert C. Dennis. Photography: Frederick E. West. Editor: Tholen Gladden. Music: Darrell Calker. Art Director: A. Leslie Thomas. Sound: Alfred J. Overton. Sets: Tom Oliphant. Production Manager-Assistant Director: Lester D. Guthrie. Makeup: Harry Thomas. Wardrobe: Joyce Rogers. Properties: Al Hurley.

CAST: Gerald Mohr (Philip Justin Tierney), Cathy O'Donnell (Sheila Wayne Justin), Bill Ching (Mark Snell), John Qualen (Jonah Snell), Barry Bernard (Dr. Victor Forel).

Terror in the Haunted House premiered under that title in 1962 (it was made in 1958) but soon became *My World Dies Screaming*. When Allied Artists Television included it in its "Science-Fiction Features" grouping, shorn of five minutes running time, it reverted back to its original title. Theatrically the feature advertised itself as the first movie to be made in "Psycho Rama," using subliminal communications techniques. This gimmick no doubt came about thanks to producer-director William Castle's successful stratagem in features like *Macabre* (1958), *House on Haunted Hill* (1959) [qq.v.], *The Tingler* (1959), *13 Ghosts* (1960) and *Homicidal* (1961). When shown in theaters, the movie had a prologue and epilogue with star Gerald Mohr discussing and demonstrating the techniques of subliminal imagery that had quick exposures of skulls and snakes; he orders the audience to scream. When the movie came to TV, these shots were replaced by animation. *Terror in the Haunted House* has some genuine scares but overall it is a mediocre production saddled with bland characters and dingy, oppressive settings. In *Horror and Science Fiction Films: A Checklist* (1972), Donald C. Willis called it "[t]horoughly routine mystery-horror."

Sheila Justin (Cathy O'Donnell) tells Lausanne, Switzerland, psychiatrist Dr. Forel (Barry Bernard) about her recurring dream of being in a silent, malignant, deserted mansion, a place of unspeakable horror. She sees the name *Tierney* on a mailbox and enters the house, goes up a flight of stairs and opens the door to an attic where she knows death in its most hideous form is waiting for her. The doctor is unable to unravel the source of her nightmare as she recalls a mundane life spent mostly in a sanitarium recovering from insipid tuberculosis. He notes that her dream has resumed in the past six weeks since her whirlwind courtship and marriage to fellow American Philip Justin (Mohr). Sheila and Philip fly to the United States and on the plane he informs her that he has no family. The couple drive to Florida where Philip wants his wife to have a two-week rest but when they reach the remote house he has rented, she becomes upset when it looks like the one in her dream. Sheila has reservations about going into the house and when they do so they are met with hostility by the caretaker, Jonah (John Qualen), and his snarling white dog, Jacob. He tells them the owners of the place left seventeen years ago and he is taking care of it as he awaits their return. When Sheila sees that the inside of the house is also like her nightmare, she begs to leave and Philip agrees but their car will not start since some wires have been pulled and the distributor cap is gone. Jonah tells the young woman that the owners of the house are named Tierney and she has a vague recollection of playing there as a child with a boy who carved their initials on a palm tree. The caretaker says the neighbors called the house's owners "the mad Tierneys." He disappears when Philip returns. Sheila asks her husband if he brought along a gun and he assures her he did. During the night she hears a scream and wakes up to find Philip gone and then sees an inhuman face at the window. Sheila runs downstairs, opens the door to the cellar and is confronted by Jacob. She goes back to her bedroom where she is comforted by Philip. Philip informs

Sheila that he thinks Jonah is trying to scare them away and goes to have a talk with the old man. Finding the gun in her husband's suitcase, Sheila also sees the distributor cap. Going down the hall, she opens the door to the attic and faints; Philip carries her back to bed. The next day Sheila tells Philip she did not have a nightmare and asks him why he brought her to the house; he says he wants to rid her of the bad dream. Not finding the distributor cap, Sheila explores the yard and locates the tree with the carved initials. While her husband goes for a walk, Mark Snell (Bill Ching) drives up and informs Sheila that he owns the house and tells her to leave. She says her husband rented it but he declares it is not safe to live in and he does not want the cost of liability if anyone should get hurt. Philip returns and it is obvious the two men are acquainted as Mark decides to stay for a few days although he again warns Sheila to leave. Mark later informs her that she lived in the house before and that her husband's real name is Tierney. When she asks him about what Mark told her, Philip says they both lived in the house as children and she realizes he was the older boy she loved as a little girl. He also says she was never ill but was sent to a Swiss sanitarium at age seven after suffering a nervous collapse. When she peruses the Tierney family bible, Sheila learns that Philip's father, Samuel, his brother Lawrence and their father Matthew all died on the same day, April 11, 1939. When she questions Jonah about the family, he tells her that Matthew saw signs of insanity in his sons and killed them with an axe before dying himself. He also informs her that Philip, who was away at the time of the slaughter, is tainted with insanity and for her to go away before it is too late. As Sheila walks down the hall, Jonah warns her of a falling chandelier that nearly kills her. Thinking Philip tried to kill her, Sheila locks herself in the their bedroom; when Mark brings her dinner, he informs her he and Philip are cousins and he is the son of Matthew's daughter Lydia, who died giving birth to him. He says he was raised by his grandfather who felt he had escaped the Tierney curse and that is why he was not murdered. When Sheila hears a scream that night, she opens the bedroom door and sees Jonah falling to his death over the banister. Mark says the old man's neck is broken. Philip drives for the police but comes back and places Jonah's body in the cellar. Mark tells Sheila to lock herself in the bedroom with the gun while he goes to a neighbor's house to call the police. Philip breaks into the room and tells his wife to shoot him but she refuses, saying she wants to help him. He makes her go to the attic, where she faints. When she comes to, Sheila recalls being in the room the night of the murders and says Jonah was the killer. Philip informs her that Jonah was married to Lydia and was Mark's father and he murdered the Tierneys so that his son could have the family plantation, money and estate. He also says the old man may have come to regret what he did and, in saving Sheila from the falling chandelier, he caused his son to murder him to keep him quiet. Mark returns and confronts Philip and tries to kill him with an axe. The two men fight, and Mark falls on the weapon and dies. Philip tells Sheila her nightmare is over as they leave the house where no one else will ever live again.

Gerald Mohr appeared in several genre outings like *Charlie Chan at Treasure Island* (1939), *Jungle Girl* and *The Monster and the Girl* (both 1941), *The Catman of Paris* (1946), *Invasion U.S.A.* and *Son of Ali Baba* (both 1952) and *The Angry Red Planet* (1960). Cathy O'Donnell, who was billed here as Kathy O'Donnell, was in *The Spiritualist (The Amazing Mr. X)* (1948), while Bill Ching was in *Scared Stiff* (1953). Director Harold Daniels also helmed *Port Sinister* (1953) and *House of the Black Death* (*Blood of the Man Devil*) (1965).

This Is Not a Test (Modern Films, 1962; 72 minutes)

Producers: Fredric Gadette and Murray De'Atley. Executive Producers: James Grandin and Art Schmoyer. Director: Fredric Gadette. Screenplay: Peter Aberheim, Betty Lasky and Fredric Gadette. Photography: Brick Marquard. Editor: Hal Dennis. Music: Greig McRitchie. Production Manager: Gordon Gadette.

CAST: Seamon Glass (Deputy Sheriff Dan Colter), Thayer Roberts (Jake Saunders), Aubrey Martin (Juney Saunders), Mary Morlas (Cheryl Hudson), Mike Green (Joe Baragi), Alan Austin (Al Weston), Carol Kent (Karen Barnes), Norman Winston (Sam Barnes), Ron Starr (Clint Delaney), Don Spruance (Peter Crandall), James George, Jr., Norm Bishop, Ralph Manza, Jay Della, William Flaherty, Phil Donati, Doyle Cooper (Looters).

While on night patrol, Deputy Sheriff Dan Colter (Seamon Glass) receives orders to set up an emergency roadblock on a mountain road. He first pulls over elderly Jake Saunders (Thayer Roberts) and his pretty granddaughter Juney (Aubrey Martin), who are carrying crates filled with chickens in their old truck. Colter is nearly run down by tipsy Cheryl Hudson (Mary Morlas), who is with her gambler boyfriend Joe Baragi (Mike Green), who has just won $175,000. The deputy also stops trucker Al Weston (Alan Austin), a driver for Discount World, who has picked up hitchhiker Clint Delaney (Ron Starr). As Dan gives Cheryl a speeding ticket, his car radio alerts him to a worsening situation. A married couple, Sam (Norman Winston) and Karen Barnes (Carol Kent), drive up with their little poodle, Timothy. When Dan and Al go to check on the hitchhiker, the young man runs away and the deputy recognizes him as an escaped killer. The police radio announces a yellow alert for an impending air raid. When the others try to use their car radios, Jake tells them there is no regular radio reception in the area due to the mountains. When a condition red and martial law is announced, the trucker says the group is caught between a military base and missile silos. Joe announces he is going to a local bar so Dan knocks him out and handcuffs him to the bumper of his car. Some of the people begin to panic; Dan announces they will work together to unload the truck so it can be used as a bomb shelter in case of an attack. Juney is afraid of being locked up in the truck and runs away, followed by her grandfather. She finds the killer but he lets her go as motorcycle rider Peter Crandall (Don Spruance) shows up and helps unload the truck. Dan sets Joe free when he agrees to help with the work. Al flirts with Karen and gives her merchandise from his truck's cargo. Dan destroys all the liquor on the truck. When Clint tries to steal food, the deputy shoots at him but the killer gets away. Al agrees to stand lookout as orders come from the police radio to shoot all looters. When Sam sees Karen and Al making love, he walks away. Clint decides to move the truck further up the road and orders Sam to get his wife and Al. When he confronts them, Sam backs down and the trio return to the others as Karen deserts her husband for Al. After Al drives the truck away and the rest go with Dan, Clint returns for his suitcase and goes berserk when he cannot get any of the cars to start. When the police radio reports that missiles have been launched, Jake, Juney and Peter break away and Sam shoots himself. As Dan, Cheryl, Joe, Al and Karen stay in the truck, Jake tells his granddaughter and Peter to take refuge in an old mine shaft while he plans to climb to a mountaintop and watch the bomb blast. Dan kills Karen's dog in order to conserve oxygen. A distraught Karen opens the truck door and is confronted by a group of looters as the police radio announces a missile strike is three minutes away. The looters overpower Dan, takes his keys, steal his car and take Karen with them. Al locks Dan out of the truck. As Clint shows up, the deputy begs to be let in and the blast hits.

Made in the early 1960s at the apex of fears of a nuclear attack from the Soviets, *This Is Not a Test* is a cheaply made but competently presented look at the reactions of a group of people caught in pre-holocaust frenzy. It takes place in a few hours at night on a lonely mountain road. While top-billed Seamon Glass is stoic as the lawman, the rest of the cast handles their parts well and the plot holds viewer interest, although it looks more like a lengthy television episode than a theatrical feature. Made by GPA Productions, it apparently had some big screen showings from Modern Films although *The Film Buff's Checklist of Motion Pictures (1912–1979)* (1979), edited by D. Richard Baer, claims it was an Allied Artists release. This is unlikely although Allied Artists Television did put it in its small screen packages "Cavalcade of the '60's — Group III" and "Science-Fiction Features." Reviews of the movie tend to be contemporary since it has been included in releases like Mill Creek Entertainment's 50 Movie Pack "Nightmare Worlds." Joe Kane in *The Phantom of the Movies' Videoscope* (2000) called it a "truly bizarre desert-set cheapie," adding, "The ending's a minor classic." *VideoHound's Sci-Fi Experience* (1997) declared, "The effectiveness of the film's social commentary is hindered by its small budget," while C.J. Henderson in *The Encyclopedia of Science Fiction Movies* (2001) complained, "Those who expect humankind to end this way will be bored; those who think people are too smart to end this way will be offended and bored." Bill Warren in *Keep Watching the Skies! The 21st Century Edition* (2010) noted, "It's a modest film with modest goals, but some of those are attained."

Vampire Men of the Lost Planet (Independent-International, 1970; 85 minutes; Color)

Producer-Director: Al Adamson. Executive Producers: Charles McMullen and Zoe Phillips. Associate Producer-Supervising Editor: Ewing Brown. Screenplay: Sue McNair. Photography: William Zsigmund [Vilmos Zsigmond], William G. Troiano and (uncredited) Gary Graver. Editor: Peter Perry. Music: Mike Velarde. Sound: Bob Dietz and Jerry Hansen. Makeup: Jean Hewitt. Special Effects: David L. Hewitt. Effects Editor: Fred Badiyan. Production Consultant: Samuel M. Sherman. Script Supervisor: Joyce King. Second Unit Director: George Joseph.

CAST: John Carradine (Dr. Rynning), Robert Dix (Colonel Manning), Vicki Volante (Valerie), Joey Benson (Willy), Jenifer Bishop (Lian Malian), Bruce Powers (Commander Steve Bryce), Fred Meyers (Captain Bob Scott), Britt Semand (Linda), Brother Theodore [Theodore Gottlieb] (Narrator), Al Adamson, John "Bud" Cardos, Gary Graver, Gus Peters, Irv Saunders (Vampires), John Andrews (Vampire Victim), Sean Graver (Young Boy).

This Tal Production was first released theatrically early in 1970 by Independent-International Pictures as *Horror of the Blood Monsters*. It was still playing under that name in movie houses when Allied Artists Television included it in its "The Golden Seventies — Group VII" and "Science-Fiction Features" packages as *Vampire Men of the Lost Planet* later in the decade. In some locales it was released as *Space Mission to the Lost Planet*. Its working titles included *Creatures of the Prehistoric Planet, Creatures of the Red Planet* and *Horror Creatures of the Prehistoric Planet*. It was shown in Italy as *7 Per L'Infiniti Contro I Mostri Spaziali* (7 for Infinity Against the Space Monster). Advertised with color effects in Spectrum X, "A New Dimension in Terror," the movie was made up of footage from a 1965 black-and-white Philippines horror film *Tagani*, directed by Rolf Bayer, with new color footage added for U.S. release by producer-director Al Adamson. In this new release, the Filipino footage was tinted in various hues. The rocket ship used in the new scenes is obviously a cheap toy. The fight scenes from *Tagani* are realistic and brutal. The film also contains monster footage from *One Million B.C.* (1940) and *Unknown Island* (1948).

In the near future, a series of vampire attacks spark a space probe to a remote galaxy where the virus was thought to originate millions of years ago. Noted scientist Dr. Rynning (John Carradine) is the head of the expedition to the galaxy in the ship XB-13 along with

Britt Semand, Bruce Powers and John Carradine in *Horror of the Blood Monsters* (Independent-International, 1970)

Commander Steve Bryce (Bruce Powers), Captain Bob Scott (Fred Meyers), astronaut Willy (Joey Benson) and laboratory assistant Linda (Britt Semand). Ground control, lead by Colonel Manning (Robert Dix) and Valerie (Vicki Volante), coordinate the ship's takeoff but later contact is lost with the vessel. When he is finally able to communicate, Rynning says the ship was involved in a collision and the crew is shaken but all right. With the XB-13's power system damaged, Rynning declares they will have to land on a nearby planet to make repairs. Steve informs Linda that he thinks they are on a suicide mission. After several days, a planet is spotted and the craft safely lands. The orb is identical to Earth except for a red haze. Rynning has suffered a minor coronary and stays aboard the ship while the others explore the planet and see dinosaurs, mammoths, snake men and a battle between two gigantic lizards. As the explorers pick up samples of rock, flora and fauna, they view two rival tribes doing battle and save a young woman (Jenifer Bishop) from tribesmen with fangs. Placing a communicator device behind the right ear of the girl, the explorers are able to talk to her and find out her name is Lian Malian. She tells them she is a member of the Tagani tribe who are peaceful cave dwellers at odds with the bloodthirsty Tubetons. Back at Earth's Ground Control, Manning and Valerie have sex using electrodes. Lian Malian relates how she killed two Tubeton tribe members who were vampirizing a young boy. On Earth, Manning informs Valerie that the XB-13 is lost on an uncharted planet that houses chromatic radiation and then the two again make love electronically. The Tagani hole up in a cave and a young brave is sent to bring back more warriors to fight the Tubeton vampires; Lian Malian sneaks out to go with him. As the explorers follow her back to the cave, they see the Taganis attacked by lobster men but the tribesmen manage to get to shore. The warriors go to a mountain cave to get fire water to keep their eternal flame alive and there they are attacked by bat demons which they kill. As the warriors go to help the rest of her people, Lian Malian leads the Earth people to the mountain cave and Steve realizes the fire water is actually petroleum. He sends Bob back to the ship for cans so they can use the oil to get their rocket re-launched. Along the way he sees three dinosaurs. After the cans are filled, Steve and Linda take them back to the ship as Willy and Bob return Lian Malian to her people. On the way to the rocket, Steve finds a metal container and Rynning orders him to bring it back with him. After avoiding a huge lizard, Steve and Linda make it back to the ship as the two tribes fight. After a brutal battle, the Tagani win. While Willy, who has fallen in love with Lian Malian, goes to say goodbye to the girl, Bob is killed by a surviving Tubeton warrior, who is shot by Willy. Steve and Linda return to the spot where they found the metal container for rock samples but after analyzing the artifact, Rynning orders the astronauts to return to the ship. Willy collapses. Lian Malian finds Steve and Linda and tells them Bob is dead. Steve carries Willy back to the ship where Rynning informs the crew they have entered a poisonous atmosphere that contains the deadly vampire virus. Saying it was caused by the careless use of nuclear weapons, the scientist announces that the virus cannot live on Earth and orders a takeoff. As Lian Malian, who loved Willy, watches from a distance, the ship begins its return flight.

A "paste-up science-fiction atrocity" is how Michael J. Weldon accurately described *Horror of the Blood Monsters* in *The Psychotronic Encyclopedia of Film* (1983), adding, "Ten points for the title." While supposedly a straight science fiction affair, the movie has "many funny moments" according to David Konow in *Schlock-O-Rama: The Films of Al Adamson* (1998). He notes, "The women of the vampire tribe are cave babes with the bottoms of their loin-cloths cut like miniskirts. But the best scene in *Horror* offers a sex machine." The writer is probably referring to the character played by Jenifer Bishop when he talks about the feminine outfits. When first introduced in the movie she is called Malian but later on is identified as Lian. Apparently Bishop was hired to match scenes with the Filipino actress in *Tagani* who played that part and the two women look enough alike to give some cohesion to their diverse scenes.

Reissues

In 1963 Allied Artists acquired the theatrical rights to *The Blob* (Paramount, 1958) and *Dinosaurus!* (Universal-International, 1960), both produced by Jack H. Harris and directed by Irvin S. Yeaworth, Jr. Released as a double bill, the movies proved to be very successful, no doubt in part due to the fact that Steve McQueen, the star of *The Blob*, had become an international box office draw.

The Blob (Paramount, 1958; 82 minutes; Color)

Producer: Jack H. Harris. Associate Producer: Russell Doughten. Director: Irvin S. Yeaworth, Jr. Screenplay: Kate Phillips [Kay Linaker] and Theodore Simonson, from an idea by Irvine H. Millgate. Photography: Thomas Spalding. Editor: Alfred Hillman. Music: Ralph Carmichael. Song: Burt Bacharach and Mack David. Art Directors: William Jersey and Karl Karlson. Sound: Gottfried Buss and Robert Clement. Makeup: Vin Kehoe. Special Effects: Barton Sloane. Continuity: Travis Hillmann. Assistant Director: Bert Smith.

CAST: Steve McQueen (Steve Andrews), Aneta Corsaut (Jane Martin), Earl Rowe (Lieutenant Dave), Olin Howlin (Old Timer), Stephen Chase (Dr. T. Hallen), John Benson (Sergeant Jim Bert), George Karas (Officer Ritchie), Lee Payton (Nurse Kate), Elbert Smith (Henry Martin), Hugh Graham (Mr. Andrews), Vince Barbi (Diner Owner George), Audrey Metcalf (Elizabeth Martin), Jasper Deeter (Elderly Fireman), Tom Ogden (Fire Chief Phil), Elinor Hammer (Mrs. Porter), Pamela Curran (Kissing Teenager), Ralph Roseman (Mechanic), Charlie Overdorff (Marty), David Metcalf (Drunk), George Gerbereck (Bartender), Julie Cousins (Waitress Sally), Kieth Almoney (Danny Martin), Eugene Sabel (Projectionist), Robert Fields (Tony Gressette), James Bonnet (Mooch Miller), Anthony Franke (Al), Josh Randolph, Molly Ann Bourne, Diane Tabben (Teenagers), Howard Fishlove, Jack H. Harris, Theodore Simonson (Theater Patrons).

Considered one of the classic low-budget sci-fi features of the 1950s, *The Blob* was filmed at Valley Forge Film Studios in Pennsylvania under the auspices of local film distributor Jack H. Harris' Tonylyn Productions. Budgeted at $147,000, Harris sold the film to Paramount and it grossed more than ten times its cost at the box office. The rights to the movie reverted back to Harris in the early 1960s and he leased it to Allied Artists who kept it in cinemas for the rest of the decade. Made mostly of silicone, the title monster was not frightening and (except for one vague scene when it apparently assimilates a doctor) its ability to absorb humans is only stated and not shown. What is impressive about *The Blob* is that it is so well made considering its non–Hollywood origins and that its interesting plot moves swiftly, nicely supported by its cast. The film also reflects the restless youth syndrome of the period, exemplified by Steve (billed as Steven) McQueen in his first starring role. The only drawback is that the "teenagers," including McQueen, appear a bit too old for their parts. So successful was *The Blob* that its title became a part of the nation's culture, an umbrella term for low-budget movie monsters. The film's title song, composed by Burt Bacharach and Mack David, was recorded by the Five Blobs for Columbia Records (41250)

Aneta Corsaut, Stephen Chase, Olin Howlin and Steve McQueen in *The Blob* (Paramount, 1958), reissued theatrically in 1963 by Allied Artists.

and appeared on the pop music charts for two months in the fall of 1958. The recording can be heard during the film's credits. In 1971 Harris produced a comedy sequel to *The Blob*, *Beware! The Blob*, which had video release as *Son of Blob*. Thirty years after the first film, *The Blob* was remade in 1988 by director–co-writer Chuck Russell; the result was graphic but vapid.

As teenager Steve Andrews (McQueen) tries to get to first base with Jane Martin (Aneta Corsaut) while they are parked in his jalopy, they see what looks like a shooting star. It lands nearby and they try to locate it. A rustic recluse (Olin Howlin) finds a crater-covered ball-shaped object in a small pit near his shack and when he pokes it with a stick the shell cracks and a glob-like substance attaches itself to his hand. The teenagers find the old man and take him to Dr. Hallen (Stephen Chase) who is about to leave for Johnsonville for a medical conference. Unable to determine what plagues the oldtimer, the doctor asks Steve and Jane to go back to Old North Road where they found the man and look for clues. As Steve and Jane are about to leave, they are met by teens Tony (Robert Fields), Mooch (James Bonnet) and Al (Anthony Franke). The trio challenge Steve to a race. He accepts, but his antics are spotted by policeman Lieutenant Dave (Earl Rowe) and he is lectured. The doctor calls in his nurse, Kate (Lee Payton), saying he may have to amputate the old man's arm since the substance continues to spread. At the pit, Steve and Jane and the three teen boys locate the meteor's shell and at the old man's shack they find his small dog which Jane takes with her. Kate shows up to assist Dr. Hallen but when she goes to take the old man's pulse rate she finds he is gone and she is attacked and absorbed by the ever-growing blob. The doctor shoots at the thing, to no effect. He locks himself in his study and tries to call for help. Steve and Jane return to the doctor's house and looking in through a window Steve sees the physician assimilated by the monster. The two teens go to the police station but the story is derided by Sergeant Bert (John Benson). Steve and Jane's parents are called; while Steve's father (Hugh Graham) stands up for his son, Jane's father, Henry Martin (Elbert Smith), the local high school principal, forbids Steve to see his daughter again. The teenagers agree to meet later. While slipping out of her house, Jane is confronted by her little brother Danny (Kieth Almoney) whom she tells to go back to bed. Steve and Jane go to the local movie theater's midnight spook show and get the other teens to help them locate the blob, which has devoured a mechanic (Ralph Roseman) and drinkers at a bar. Steve and Jane see the dog outside his father's grocery store but when Steve discovers the door is unlocked they go inside and are accosted by the monster. They take refuge in a meat locker; the monster slides in under the door but quickly retreats. Telling the other teens what happened, Steve orders them to wake up the town with car horns and sirens. When a crowd gathers in the center of town, Steve implores Dave to listen to him while Bert searches the Andrews store and finds it empty. As Dave tries to break up the mob, the blob attacks the patrons in the movie house and they run screaming into the street. As the blob approaches, Danny shoots at it with his cap pistol. Jane grabs him and goes with Steve into the Downingtown Diner. With the owner (Vince Barbi) and a waitress (Julie Cousins), they take refuge in the basement as the monster envelopes the place. Dave attempts to destroy the blob by having Bert shoot down an electric line that lands on it but to no effect. The power line causes the diner to catch on fire and the owner tries to put out the fire with an extinguisher which causes the blob to retreat. Steve realizes the thing can be stopped with cold and calls to Dave to use fire extinguishers. Martin leads the teens to the high school where they collect 22 extinguishers and take them downtown and use them to subdue the blob. As Steve, Jane and Danny get out of the diner, Dave contacts the government. A plane flies the frozen monster to the Arctic, the film ending with a question mark.

Variety said *The Blob* "will tax the imagination of adult patrons," adding, "Neither the acting nor direction is particularly creditable.... Star performers ... are the camerawork of Thomas Spalding and Barton Sloane's special effects. Production values otherwise are geared to economy." Joe Kane in *The Phantom of the Movies' Videoscope* (2000) declared that it "shapes up as *the* quintessential late–50s monster movie. The gaudy color, lightly self-mocking tone, and memorable title creature likewise add to the fun.... *The Blob* remains a must for the uninitiated and a musty delight for the rest." In *Films of Science Fiction and Fantasy* (1988), Baird Searles said *The Blob* "epitomizes the low-budget, high-grossing film that combined adolescents and aliens and singlehandedly convinced producers that there was no need to pour money into big productions when the same public would turn out for cheaper ones."

Many consider the Blob's invasion of the movie theater spook show the highlight of the movie. Scenes from the 1953 horror outing *Daughter of Horror* (*Dementia*) are shown. In one quick sequence the teens can be seen standing before a movie poster for *The Vampire and the Robot* with Bela Lugosi. This is a re-title of the British feature *Mother Riley Meets the Vampire* (1952), which was also released as *Vampire Over London*. It also got stateside showings in 1964 as *My Son, the Vampire*.

Dinosaurus! (Universal-International, 1960; 85 minutes; Color)

Producers: Jack H. Harris and Irvin S. Yeaworth, Jr. Director: Irvin S. Yeaworth, Jr. Screenplay: Dean E. Weisburd and Jean Yeaworth, from an idea by Jack H. Harris. Photography: Stanley Cortez. Editor: John A. Bushelman. Music: Ronald Stein. Art Director: Jack Senter. Sound: Jack Cornall and Jack Wheeler. Sets: Herman Schoenbrun. Makeup: Don Cash. Wardrobe: Bill Edwards. Underwater Sequences: Paul Stader. Special Photographic Effects: Tim Baar, Gene Warren and Wah Chang. Script Supervisor: Sam Freedle. Assistant to Producer: S. Robert Zanger. Assistant Director: Herbert Mendelson.

CAST: Ward Ramsey (Bart Thompson), Paul Lukather (Chuck), Kristina Hanson (Betty Piper), Alan Roberts (Julio), Fred Engelberg (Mike Hacker), Wayne Treadway (Dumpy), Luci Blain (Chica), Howard Dayton (Mousey), Jack Younger (Jasper), James Logan (T.J. O'Leary), Wilhelm Samuel (Lou), Gregg Martell (The Neanderthal Man), Jack H. Harris (Tourist).

Poster for *Dinosaurus!* (Universal-International, 1960), re-released by Allied Artists in 1963.

"Movie junk" is how the *New York Times* termed *Dinosaurus!*, not realizing the film's intended audience or its genre appeal. Following the success of *The Blob* (1958) (q.v.) and *4D Man* (1959), producer Jack H. Harris re-teamed with director Irvin S. Yeaworth, Jr., to make this sci-fi effort for their Fairview Productions; it was issued in the summer of 1960 by Universal-International. Filmed near St. Croix in the Virgin Islands, the film greatly benefited from Stanley Cortez's cinematography and a likable cast that included Ward Ramsey, Paul Lukather and lovely Kristina Hanson. Gregg Martell adds much to the film as a caveman and he has some amusing sequences involving culture shock such as his trying to eat fake fruit, seeing his reflection in a mirror and trying on a dress. He even gets a chance to throw a pie at the villain. For the youngsters and teens, the film's main draw is its two dinosaurs whose models were constructed by uncredited Marcel Delgado, whose films included *The Lost World* (1925), *King Kong* and *The Son of Kong* (both 1933), *Mighty Joe Young* (1949), *The War of the Worlds* (1953) and *Jack the Giant Killer* (1962). The photographic effects for these creatures are mostly mediocre.

American contractor Bart Thompson (Ramsey), his foreman, Chuck (Lukather) and bulldozer operator Dumpy (Wayne Treadway) are building a port at a Caribbean island which will bring commerce to the area. Island manager Mike Hacker (Fred Engelberg) keeps the natives from working on the project since he will not see any profit from it. He is also the cruel guardian of young Julio (Alan Roberts), who has ingratiated himself with Bart and Chuck. When some underwater explosives fail to detonate and Bart's girlfriend Betty Piper (Hanson) dives into the water, Bart goes after her. The young woman swims face to face with a prehistoric creature and faints with Bart bringing her to safety. Bart has two frozen dinosaurs brought on shore and hires T.J. O'Leary (James Logan), an alcoholic, to watch them during the night until paleontologists can arrive to examine them. Hacker finds the body of a caveman (Martell) on the shore and stashes it nearby with plans to sell for exhibition. He goes to the local café, which is run by pretty Chica (Luci Blain), and roughs up Julio for not doing his chores, causing the boy to run into the jungle. Hacker tells Chica he will have her put in jail unless she becomes his girlfriend. After she leaves, Hacker hires Mousey (Howard Dayton) and Jasper (Jack Younger) to help him take the body of the prehistoric man away the next day. A storm hits the island and lightning strikes the two dinosaurs, reviving them and the caveman. O'Leary is killed by the T-Rex. Chuck suggests that a safe haven for the people of the island might be an old abandoned fortress and he sets out to build a moat around it as the citizens are evacuated there. The caveman goes to Betty's house and frightens away her mother as Julio watches the T-Rex destroy a Jeep and its occupants. The boy goes to the Piper home and is confronted by the caveman but the two become friends. When Hacker and his cohorts show up, the caveman and Julio manage to get away. Betty sees Julio and the caveman riding on the neck of the Brontosaurus. When the T-Rex comes after the other dinosaur, Bart, Betty and Dumpy try to save Julio who jumps off his ride (as does the caveman). Betty is captured by the T-Rex but the caveman drives an axe into the beast's foot and then carries the young woman to the safety of a mine shaft. The T-Rex attacks and mortally wounds the Brontosaurus as Betty fends off the caveman's mild romantic overtures and tries to cook him some food. When Julio is attacked by the T-Rex, the caveman carries him into the mine shaft. Hacker uses a rope to get into the mine and holds Betty, Julio and the caveman at bay with a pistol and shoots the prehistoric man in the arm when he tries to defend his new friends. The T-Rex attacks the mine shaft as Bart and Dumpy try to hold it at bay by tossing homemade bombs. Just as Hacker plans to feed Julio to the T-Rex, Bart manages to throw a bomb into its mouth, causing the beast to dislodge timbers in the shaft. The frightened Hacker tries to escape and is killed by falling rocks and timber. The caveman holds up some of the timbers so Betty and Julio can get away but is crushed under them before Bart can bring him to safety. Bart, Betty, Dumpy and Julio drive to the fort which Chuck has prepared for an attack from the monster. The dying Brontosaurus falls into quicksand. When the T-Rex arrives, the moat is set on fire but there is only enough fuel to burn for five minutes. Bart gets into one of the bulldozers and does battle with the creature, eventually pushing it into the sea.

Dinosaurus!, like *The Blob*, ends with a question mark, but in this case no sequel followed.

Theatrical Films in Chronological Order

• 1952 •
The Ghost of Crossbones Canyon (November)
Crow Hollow

• 1953 •
Jalopy (February)
The Maze (July)
Jennifer (October)
Private Eyes (December)

• 1954 •
The Golden Idol (January)
Paris Playboys (March)
The Bowery Boys Meet the Monsters (June)
Jungle Gents (September)
Target Earth (November)
Port of Hell (December)

• 1955 •
Bowery to Bagdad (January)
Phantom Trails (May)
Dig That Uranium (December)

• 1956 •
Invasion of the Body Snatchers (February)
The Atomic Man (March)
Indestructible Man (March)
World Without End (March)
Crashing Las Vegas (April)
Fright (June)

• 1957 •
Attack of the Crab Monsters (February)
Not of This Earth (February)
Hold That Hypnotist (March)
Destination 60,000 (May)
Spook Chasers (June)
The Cyclops (July)
Daughter of Dr. Jekyll (July)
The Disembodied (August)
From Hell It Came (August)
The Hunchback of Notre Dame (November)
Sabu and the Magic Ring (November)
Up in Smoke (December)

• 1958 •
The Bride and the Beast (February)
Macabre (March)
Hell's Five Hours (April)
Attack of the 50 Foot Woman (May)
War of the Satellites (May)
Frankenstein 1970 (July)
Spy in the Sky! (July)
Queen of Outer Space (September)

• 1959 •
The Cosmic Man (February)
House on Haunted Hill (February)
The Giant Behemoth (March)
Face of Fire (August)
The Bat (September)
Beast from Haunted Cave (October)
The Wasp Woman (October)
The Atomic Submarine (December)

• 1960 •
The Hypnotic Eye (February)
Bluebeard's Ten Honeymoons (April)

Sex Kittens Go to College (August)
Caltiki the Immortal Monster (September)
Tormented (September)

• 1962 •
Hands of a Stranger (April)
Confessions of an Opium Eater (June)
The Day of the Triffids (July)

• 1963 •
Black Zoo (May)
Shock Corridor (September)

• 1964 •
The Strangler (April)
The Human Vapor (May)

• 1965 •
The Human Duplicators (March)
Mutiny in Outer Space (March)
Oh! Those Most Secret Agents! (March)
Blood and Black Lace (April)
Frankenstein Meets the Space Monster (September)
Curse of the Voodoo (September)
The Magic Weaver (September)

• 1966 •
Moonwolf (May)
Nightmare Castle (July)

• 1967 •
Island of the Doomed (November)
The Sorcerers (November)

• 1968 •
Mission Mars (February)

• 1969 •
The Body Stealers (April)

• 1970 •
Eugenie (August)
Blood Rose (September)

• 1971 •
Beyond Love and Evil (March)
Shinbone Alley (April)
Fright (May)

• 1974 •
Deborah

• 1975 •
Who? (August)

• 1976 •
Communion (November)

• 1977 •
Twilight's Last Gleaming (February)

Bibliography

Books

Alvarez, Max Joseph. *Index to Motion Pictures Reviewed by Variety, 1907–1980*. Metuchen, NJ: Scarecrow Press, 1982.

Blake, Matt, and David Deal. *The Eurospy Guide*. Baltimore: Luminary Press, 2004.

Bleiler, David, ed. *TLA Video and DVD Guide 2004*. New York: St. Martin's Griffin, 2003.

Bojarski, Richard. *The Films of Bela Lugosi*. Secaucus, NJ: Citadel Press, 1980.

_____, and Kenneth Beale. *The Films of Boris Karloff*. Secaucus, NJ: Citadel Press, 1974.

Brooks, Tim, and Earle Marsh. *The Complete Directory of Prime Time National TV Shows from 1946 to the Present*. New York: Ballantine, 1988.

Everman, Welch. *Cult Horror Films*. New York: Carol, 1995.

_____. *Cult Science Fiction Films*. New York: Carol, 1995.

Fischer, David. *Science Fiction Film Directors 1895–1998*. Jefferson, NC: McFarland, 2000.

Frank, Alan. *The Films of Roger Corman*. London: BT Batsford, 1998.

_____. *Horror Movies*. London: Octopus, 1974.

Gifford, Denis. *Karloff: The Man, the Monster, the Movies*. New York: Curtis, 1973.

Glut, Donald F. *Classic Movie Monsters*. Metuchen, NJ: Scarecrow Press, 1978.

_____. *The Dracula Book*. Metuchen, NJ: Scarecrow Press, 1975.

_____. *The Frankenstein Legend*. Metuchen, NJ: Scarecrow Press, 1973.

Hardy, Phil. *The Encyclopedia of Horror Movies*. New York: Harper & Row, 1986.

_____. *Science Fiction*. New York: William Morrow, 1984.

Hayes, David, and Brent Walker. *The Films of the Bowery Boys*. Secaucus, NJ: Citadel Press, 1984.

Henderson, C.J. *The Encyclopedia of Science Fiction Movies*. New York: Checkmark, 2001.

Herx, Henry, and Tony Zaza. *The Family Guide to Movies on Video*. New York: Crossroad, 1988.

Hickerson, Jay. *The New, Revised Ultimate History of Network Radio Programming and Guide to All Circulating Shows*. Camden, CT: Jay Hickerson, 1996.

Jones, Stephen. *The Essential Monster Movie Guide*. New York: Billboard, 2000.

Kane, Joe. *The Phantom of the Movies' Videoscope*. New York: Three Rivers Press, 2000.

Katz, Ephraim. *The Film Encyclopedia*. New York: Harper Perennial, 1994.

Konow, David. *Schlock-O-Rama: The Films of Al Adamson*. Los Angeles: Lone Eagle, 1998.

Lee, Walt. *Reference Guide to Fantastic Films*. 3 vols. Los Angeles: Chelsea-Lee Books, 1972–74.

Leonard, William Torbert. *Theatre: Stage to Screen to Television*. 2 vols. Metuchen, NJ: Scarecrow Press, 1981.

Lucas, Tim. *The Video Watchdog Book*. Cincinnati: Video Watchdog, 1992.

Maltin, Leonard. *Leonard Maltin's 2004 Movie and Video Guide*. New York: Signet, 2003.

Martin, Len D. *The Allied Artists Checklist: The Feature Films and Short Subjects 1947–1978*. Jefferson, NC: McFarland, 1993.

Mavis, Paul. *The Espionage Filmography*. Jefferson, NC: McFarland, 2001.

Mayo, Mike. *Videohound's Horror Show*. Detroit: Invisible Ink Press, 1998.

McGee, Mark Thomas. *Roger Corman: The Best of the Cheap Acts*. Jefferson, NC: McFarland, 1988.

Meyers, Richard. *For One Week Only: The World of Exploitation Films*. Piscataway, NJ: New Century, 1983.

Minton, Lynn. *Movie Guide for Puzzled Parents*. New York: Delta, 1984.

McGee, Mark Thomas. *Roger Corman: The Best of the Cheap Acts*. Jefferson, NC: McFarland, 1988.

Naha, Ed. *Horror: From Screen to Scream*. New York: Avon, 1975.

O'Neill, James. *Terror on Tape*. New York: Billboard, 1994.

Palmer, Randy. *Paul Blaisdell: Monster Maker*. Jefferson, NC: McFarland, 1997.

Palmerini, Luca M., and Gaetano Mistretta.

Spaghetti Nightmares. Key West: Fantasma Books, 1996.
Parish, James Robert. *Ghosts and Angels in Hollywood Films*. Jefferson, NC: McFarland, 1994.
_____. *The Great Movie Series*. Cranbury, NJ: A.S. Barnes, 1971.
_____, and Michael R. Pitts. *The Great Science Fiction Pictures*. Metuchen, NJ: Scarecrow Press, 1977.
_____, and _____. *The Great Science Fiction Pictures II*. Metuchen, NJ: Scarecrow Press, 1990.
Peary, Danny. *Guide for the Film Fanatic*. New York: Fireside, 1986.
The Phantom's Ultimate Video Guide. New York: Dell, 1989.
Pirie, David. *A Heritage of Horror: The English Gothic Cinema 1946–1972*. New York: Avon, 1973.
Pitts, Michael R. *Radio Soundtracks: A Reference Guide, 2nd Ed*. Metuchen, NJ: Scarecrow Press, 1986.
_____. *Western Film Series of the Sound Era*. Jefferson, NC: McFarland, 2009.
Pym, John, ed. *Time Out Film Guide 9th Ed*. London: Penguin, 2000.
Quinlan, David. *British Sound Films: The Studio Years 1928–1959*. Totowa, NJ: Barnes & Noble, 1985.
_____. *Quinlan's Film Directors*. London: BT Batsford, 1999.
_____. *Quinlan's Film Stars, 5th Ed*. Washington, DC: Brassey's, 2000.
Roat, Richard. *Hollywood's Made-to-Order-Punks: The Complete History of the Dead End Kids, Little Tough Guys, East Side Kids and the Bowery Boys*. Albany, GA: BearManor Media, 2010.
Ross, Jonathan. *The Incredibly Strange Film Book*. London: Simon & Schuster, 1995.
The Scarecrow Movie Guide. Seattle: Sasquath Books, 2004.
Searles, Baird. *Films of Science Fiction and Fantasy*. New York: Harry N. Abrams, 1988.
Scheuer, Steven H., ed. *Movies on TV 1969–70*. New York: Bantam, 1969.
_____. *Movies on TV 1975–76*. New York: Bantam, 1974.
_____. *TV Movie Almanac and Ratings 1958 & 1959*. New York: Bantam, 1958.
Senn, Bryan. *Drums O' Terror: Voodoo in the Cinema*. Baltimore, MD: Luminary Press, 1998.
Stanley, John. *John Stanley's Creature Feature Movie Guide Strikes Again*. Pacifica, CA: Creatures at Large Press, 1994.
Strick, Philip. *Science Fiction Movies*. London: Octopus, 1976.
Tohill, Cathal, and Pete Tombs. *Immoral Tales: European Sex and Horror Movies*. New York: St. Martin's Griffin, 1994.
TV Feature Film Sourcebook. 2 vols. New York: Broadcast Information Bureau, 1978.
VideoHound's Complete Guide to Cult Flicks and Trash Pics. Detroit: Invisible Ink Press, 1996.
VideoHound's Sci-Fi Experience: Your Quantum Guide to the Video Universe. Detroit: Invisible Ink Press, 1997.
VideoHound's Vampires on Video. Detroit: Invisible Ink Press, 1997.
Warren, Bill. *Keep Watching the Skies! The 21st Century Edition*. Jefferson, NC: McFarland, 2010.
Weldon, Michael J. *The Psychotronic Film Guide*. New York: St. Martin's Griffin, 1996.
_____, with Charles Beasley, Bob Martin and Akira Fitton. *The Psychotronic Encyclopedia of Film*. New York: Ballantine, 1983.
Williams, Lucy Chase. *The Complete Films of Vincent Price*. New York: Citadel/Carol, 1995.
Willis, Donald C. *Horror and Science Fiction Films: A Checklist*. Metuchen, NJ: Scarecrow Press, 1972.
_____. *Horror and Science Fiction Films II*. Metuchen, NJ: Scarecrow Press, 1982.
Worth, D. Earl. *Sleaze Creatures*. Key West: Fantasma Books, 1995.
Young, R.G. *The Encyclopedia of Fantastic Films*. New York: Applause, 2000.

Periodicals

Billboard (Los Angeles, CA)
Castle of Frankenstein (Bergen, NJ)
Cine Zine Zone (St. Maur, France)
Ecco (Washington, DC)
Filmfax (Evanston, IL)
Horror Monsters (Derby, CT)
Little Shoppe of Horrors (Waterloo, IA)
Mad Monsters (Derby, CT)
Psychotronic Video (Chincoteague, VA)
Screen Facts (Kew Gardens, NY)
Variety (New York, NY)
Video Watchdog (Cincinnati, OH)

Websites

American Film Institute (www.afi.com)
Creepy Classics (www.creepyclassics.com)
Internet Movie Database (www.imdb.com)

Newspaper Archive (www.newspaperarchive.com)
YouTube (www.youtube.com)

Index

Abtcon Pictures 162
Ackerman, Bettye 66
Adams, Brooke 108
Adams, Casey 102
Adams, Lillian 165
Adams, Mason 134
Adams, Nick 123, 124
Adamson, Al 215, 216, 217, 224, 226
Adamson, James 81
Adamson, Victor *see* Dixon, Denver
Addobbati, Giuseppe *see* MacDouglas, John
The Adventures of Wild Bill Hickok 77, 78, 137
Agar, John 183, 184
Aherne, Brian 85
Ahlstrand, Linne 17
Ahn, Philip 43
Aimond, John 216
Albert Zugsmith Productions 145
Alcazar Studios 65
Alda, Robert 205
Aldrich, Robert 167
Alese, John D. 68
Alexander, Jim 138
Alice, Sweet Alice see *Communion*
Allen, Patrick 29
Allerson, Alexander 176
Allied Artists Industries 2
Allied Artists Pictures Corporation 2
Allied Artists Productions 2
Allied Artists Television 181, 182, 183, 195, 197, 199, 203, 205, 208, 210, 213, 215, 219, 224
Allied Artists Video Corporation 2
Almoney, Kieth 229
Almquist, Dean L. 72
Alper, Murray 111, 113
Altayskaya, Vera 118
Alvarez, Edmund Rivera 188
Amanti d'oltretomba (Lovers Beyond the Tomb) see *Nightmare Castle*
American International Pictures 6, 24, 43, 162
American Releasing Corporation 162
Ames, Michael *see* Andrews, Tod
Anders, Merry 99, 101
Anders, Rudolph 69, 114
Anderson, Leona 90
Andre, Victor (Vittorio) 37, 38
Andrews, Tod 75, 77
Angel Eyes 113
Anglo-Amalgamated Films 4

Ankers, Evelyn 164
Anwar, Gabrielle 108
The Aqua Sex see *Mermaids of Tiburon*
Arden, Mary 23
Argento, Dario 24
Arlen, Richard 91, 92
Arnold, Newton 85
Arson for Hire 77
Art Cinema Corporation 14
Artkino Films 213
Ashman, Howard 208
Ashton, Tara 198, 199
Associated British-Pathe 46
Astan, Laurence 214
The Astounding Giant Woman see *Attack of the 50 Foot Woman* (1958)
Atlanta, Joe 220
Atlas 181–82
The Atomic Man 3–5, 104, 233
The Atomic Submarine 1, 5–7, 233
Attack of the 50 Crab Monsters 7–10, 131, 233
Attack of the 50 Foot Woman (1958) 1, 10–13, 171, 183, 273, 233
Attack of the 50 Foot Woman (1993) 10
Attack of the Spider Women see *Lost Women*
Austin, Alan 223
Austin, Charlotte 34, 35, 69, 70
Austin, Gene 25
Avallone, Michael 152

Bacharach, Burt 227
Backus, Jim 116
Bakewell, William 14
Bamber, Judy 170
Bannen, Ian 73, 75
Barbi, Vince 229
Barclay, Jerry 172
Bardones, Elizabeth 134
Bardot, Brigitte 146
Bardot, Mijanou 146
Barnes, Rayford 32
Barrett, Minnie 16
Barron, Baynes 75, 160
Barrow, Janet 48
Barrows, George 212
Barry, Don "Red" *see* Barry, Donald
Barry, Donald 69, 70
Barry, Philip 174

Bartlett, Bennie 31, 33, 61, 62, 111, 114, 136, 140
Bartok, Eva 23
Barton, Anne 60
The Bat (1926) 15
The Bat (1959) 1, 13–17, 65, 233
The Bat Whispers 15
Bates, Jeanne 160
Battaglia, Rik 128, 129, 131
Bauer, Steven 134
Bava, Mario 24, 36, 38, 205, 207
Bayer, Rolf 224
Bean, Robert 188, 189
Beast from Haunted Cave 17–19, 173, 181, 189, 233
Beaudine, William 110, 170
Beaumont, Charles 141
Beaumont, Hugh 91, 92, 93
Beauty and the Robot see *Sex Kittens Go to College*
Becker, Ken 6
Beebe, Ford 83
Behemoth the Sea Monster see *The Giant Behemoth*
Belasco, Leon 111
Bellucci Productions 119
Belmont Books 152
Bender, Russ 160
Benedict, Richard 110
Bennett, Bruce 44, 45
Benson, Joey 216, 225
Benson, John 229
Bergerac, Jacques 99, 100, 101
Berke, Irwin 70, 146
Bernard, Barry 221
Bernardi, Nerio 220
Bernds, Edward 31, 32, 115, 141, 178–79, 180
Bernstein, Morey 72, 88
Besserer, Eugenie 13
Best, James 150, 151
The Betsy 2
Beware! The Blob 228
Beyond Love and Evil 19, 64, 234
Beyond the Sahara see *Dark Venture*
Bice, Robert 33, 181
The Big Circus 2
Birch, Paul 132, 134, 142
Birriel, Felippe 196
Bishoff, Samuel 159
Bishop, Ed 31
Bishop, Jenifer 225, 226
Bissell, Whit 163

237

A Black Ribbon for Deborah see *Deborah*
Black Sunday (1960) 24, 36, 38
Black Zoo 1, 20–22, 234
Blackman, Honor 73, 75
Blain, Luci 231
Blair, Nicky 47
Blaisdell, Paul 27, 134
Blake, Matt 135, 204
The Blob (1958) 2, 227–29, 231
The Blob (1988) 228
Bloch-Woodfield Productions 100
Block, Irving 171
Blood and Black Lace 1, 22–24, 36, 234
Blood of Ghastly Horror see *Man with the Synthetic Brain*
Blood Rose 1, 24–26, 234
Blore, Eric 33
Bluebeard (1944) 26
Bluebeard (1963) see *Landru*
Bluebeard (1972) 27
Bluebeard's Ten Honeymoons 26–29, 156, 233
Bobby Breen Quintet 50
Boccardo, Delia 58
Body Snatchers 108
The Body Stealers 29–30, 234
Boisgel, Valerie 25
Bojarski, Richard 102
Boleslavsky, Jan 133
Bomba 1, 81–83
Bomba and the Golden Idol see *The Golden Idol*
Bond, Lillian 121, 122
Bonnet, James 228
Borello, R. 158
Bosche, Peter 40
Bova, Joseph 176, 177
The Bowery Boys 1, 31, 33, 46, 48, 61, 63, 88, 110, 114, 136, 140, 155, 170
The Bowery Boys Meet the Monsters 30–32, 179, 233
Bowery to Bagdad 32–33, 179, 233
Brack, Claudia 22
Bracken, Eddie 149
Bradford, Lane 81
Bradley, Leslie 8
Brady, Scott 199
The Brain from Planet Arous 11, 182–85
Brana, Frank 190
Branco Pictures 94
Brendel, Mike 108, 109
Brent, Earl 113
The Bride and the Beast 1, 33–35, 70, 233
Brinkley, John 172
Bristow, Gwen 89
Britannia-British Lion 84
Broadway Television Theatre 14
Brodie, Steve 157, 158
Broidy, Steve 1, 2
Bronson, Charles 176
Brooke, Hillary 121, 122
Brooks, Mel 149
Brown, George 192
Brown, Johnny Mack 178

Browne, Roscoe Lee 167
Bruton Film Producers 49
Bryant, John 16
Budry, Algis 177
Buono, Victor 159, 161
Burke, Paul 62
Burton, Richard 27

Cabaret 2
Cabot, Susan 171, 173
Cacao, Johnny 25
Caffarel, Jose Maria 204
Caiano, Mario 131
Caltiki—I monstro immortale see *Caltiki The Immortal Monster*
Caltiki The Immortal Monster 1, 24, 35, 38, 164, 234
Caltiki The Undying Monster see *Caltiki The Immortal Monster*
Calvert, John 191, 192
Calvert, Steve 31, 34, 35
Calvet, Corinne 28, 29
Calvo, Armando 220
Campo, Wally 17, 18, 160, 208, 210
Canby, Vincent 167
Cannon, Esma 48
Carbone, Antony 188, 189, 202
Cardos, John "Bud" 198
Carey, Timothy 218
Carlson, Richard 120, 122, 164, 166
Carmen, Jewel 14
Carminati, Tullio 14
Carol, Sheila 17, 18
Carr, Marian 102
Carr, Trem 1
Carradine, David 192
Carradine, John 1, 26, 45, 46, 146, 149, 150, 191, 192, 198, 199, 215, 216, 217, 224, 225
Carrol, Regina 216, 217
Carroll, Anne 133
Cartwright, Lynn 173
Carver, Tina 76, 77
Castellato, Gigi 59
Castle, Mary 47
Castle, William 2, 39, 43, 88, 89, 115–16, 221
Castle of Blood see *Castle of Terror*
Castle of Terror 185–87
Cavanagh, Paul 63
CCC Productions 125
Central Park Films 2
Chandler, Chick 140
Chaney, Lon, Jr. 1, 51, 52, 53, 101, 102
Chaney, Lon, Sr. 97, 98
Channing, Carol 149, 150
Chaplin, Charles 26
Chaplin, Charles, Jr. 146
Charlton Publications 22
Chase, Frank 10, 11
Chase, Steven 228
Chavez, Julio C. 194
Ching, Bill 222
Christine, Virginia 105
Christopher, Robert 62, 63, 155
The Circular Staircase 13
Citadel Films 39
Clark, Bobby 60, 105
Clark, Dane 137, 138, 139

Clark, Fred 135
Clay, Phillipe 97
Clements, Stanley 31, 48, 87, 88, 155, 170
Clift, Lawrence 129
Clinton, Mildred 40
Clive, Colin 84
Close, John 18
Cobb, Edmund 6
Cohen, Herman 20, 164
Cole, George 73, 75
Cole, Nat (King) 113
Cole, Phyllis 100
Cole, Selette 159
College Confidential 148
Collinson, Peter 75
Collinson, Tara 73, 75
Colman, Booth 179
Columbia Pictures Corporation 31, 32, 33, 89, 213
Columbia Records 227
Communion 38–41, 234
Condon, David 31, 33, 47, 61, 87, 111, 114, 136, 140; *see also* Gorcey, David
Confessions of an Opium Eater 41–44, 81, 234
Connery, Neil 29
Consolidated Film Industries 1
Continental Talking Pictures 1
Conway, Pat 60
Conway, Tom 6, 28, 63
Coogan, Jackie 146, 147, 211
Cook, Clyde 120
Cook, Elisha, Jr. 22, 90
Cooper, Jeanne 21
Copeland, Jack L. 86
Coppola, Francis Ford 213
Corby, Ellen 31, 116, 159, 160
Corcoran, Hugh 179
Cording, Harry 114
Corman, Gene 18, 173, 189
Corman, Roger 9, 18, 19, 110, 131, 132, 134, 162, 171, 173, 175, 181, 182, 188, 189, 202, 203, 208, 210, 213
Cornell, Ann 191, 192
Corrigan, Lloyd 31
Corrigan, Ray "Crash" 35
Corsaut, Aneta 228
Cortez, Stanley 230
The Cosmic Man 1, 44–46, 233
Cosmos Aventuras 144
Cotten, Joseph 167, 169
Coulouris, Joseph 28, 157
Cousins, Julie 229
Cowan, Jerome 20, 21
Craig, Carolyn 90
Craig, James 51, 52
Craig, John 151
Crane, Stephen 65
Cranford, Robert 160
Crashing Las Vegas 46–48, 233
Crawford, Joan 5
Creature from the Haunted Sea 183, 187–89, 202
Creature of the Maze see *The Maze*
Creatures of the Red Planet see *Vampire Men of the Lost Planet*

Crosby, Floyd 20
Crow, Carl 126
Crow Hollow 1, 48–49, 233
Crowley, Kathleen 162
Crypt of the Living Dead 189–91
Culver, Michael 39
Cuny, Alain 97
Curiel, Herbert 157
Curran, Pamela 126
Curse of Simba see *Curse of the Voodoo*
Curse of the Voodoo 49–51, 68, 234
Curtis, Tony 101, 159
Curtiz, Gabriel 127
Cutell, Lou 67, 68
Cuthbertson, Allan 29
Cutting, Richard H. 8
The Cyclops 51–53, 54, 233

Dahlberg, Uta 64
Dahlke, Paul 125
Daly, Toni 153
Damon, Mark 190, 191
Danet, Jean 97
Daniels, Danny 50
Daniely, Lisa 50
Danneberg, Thomas 201
Dano, Royal 66
Danse Macabre see *Castle of Terror*
Danton, Ray 189, 191
La danza macabre see *Castle of Terror*
Dario, Sascha 181
Darion, Joe 149
Dark, Christopher 178, 179
The Dark Power 194
Dark Venture 191–92
Darrow, Barbara 142
Daughter of Dr. Jekyll 1, 52, 53–55, 71, 233
Daughter of Horror 229
David, Hal 227
Davies, Humphrey 71
Davis, Jim 198
Davis, Lisa 142
Davis, Owen 84
Davison, Davey 159, 160
Dawson, Anthony M. *see* Margheriti, Antonio
The Day of the Triffids (1963) 55–58, 234
The Day of the Triffids (1981) 58
The Day of the Triffids (2009) 58
Dayton, Howard 231
Deacon, Richard 105
Deal, David 135, 204
Dean, Eddie 178
Dean, Ivor 154
Death Curse of Tartu 192–94
De Beausset, Michael 123
Deborah 58–59, 234
Dehner, John 31
De Lange, Bob 157
Delannoy, Jean 99
Delevanti, Cyril 144
Delgado, Marcel 231
Del Russo, Marie 194
Demara, Fred 100, 101
De Marney, Terence 42

Dementia see *Daughter of Horror*
Denmer, Charles 27
Denning, Doreen 66
Denning, Richard 162, 164
Dennis, John 70
Dennis, Matt 113
DeNoble, Alphonso 40
Deodato, Ruggero 187
De Paolo, Dante 22
De Quincy, Thomas 43, 43
Desny, Ivan 176
Destination 60,000 59–60, 233
Devine, Andy 77, 78, 137
Devlin, Joe 170
Devon, Richard 171
De Vries, George 123
De Witt, Louis 171
Dickerson, Beach (Beech) 9, 172, 188, 189
Dierkes, John 54
Dig That Uranium 60–62, 233
Dillman, Bradford 58, 59
Dimitriou, Theodoros 182
Dinosaurus! 2, 85, 227, 229–31
The Disembodied 1, 62–63, 77, 233
The Distant Cousins 67
Distinction Films 64
Dix, Richard 199
Dix, Robert 198, 199, 225
Dix International Pictures 197
Dixon, Denver 199, 215
Dmytryk, Edward 27
Dobson, James 126
Dodsworth, John 121
Domberg, Andrea 158
Domergue, Faith 3, 5
Dominici, Arturo 36, 38
Domino Pictures Corporation 156
Don Post Studios 77
Donahue, Jill 166
Donnell, Jeff 60
Donovan, King 105, 106, 107–08
Dorian, Leon 157
Doucette, John 77
Douglas, Don 72
Douglas, George 11
Douglas, Jerry 22
Douglas, Melvyn 167, 169
Dow Hour of Great Mysteries 14
Drake, Allan 146
Drake, Frances 84
Drake, Tom 52
Druxman, Michael B. 56
Dubov, Paul 5, 7, 151
Duel of the Space Monsters see *Frankenstein Meets the Space Monster*
Duff, Howard 111, 112
Dufilho, Jacques 98
Duggan, Tom 69
Dumke, Ralph 106
Dumont, Daniella 98
Duncan, Kirk 216
Duncan, Pamela 8
Duperey, Anny 25
du Pont, Michael 84
Durant, Ted 92
Durant, Theo 115
Durning, Charles 167, 168, 169
Dwyer, Hilary 29

Easton, Jane 111
Eburne, Maude 14
Echo of Terror see *Man with the Synthetic Brain*
Eden, Dorothy 49
Edwards, Elaine 15, 16
Edwards, Julie 198, 199
Edwards, Vincent 66
Eisley, Anthony 173, 175, 204
Eisley, Fred *see* Eisley, Anthony
Elliott, Bill 178
Elliott, Dick 170
Elliott, Ross 102
Ellis, Edward 14
Ellis, Marvin 102
Ellser, Effie 14
Elstree Studios 27
Emery, Katherine 120
Engel, Roy 103, 133
Engleberg, Fred 231
Ercy, Elizabeth 153
Erickson, Leif 167, 169
Eros Films 80
Eugenie 1, 20, 64–65, 234
Evans, Gene 78, 79, 150, 151
Evans, Maurice 29, 30
Everman, Welch 7, 143
Evils of Chinatown see *Confessions of an Opium Eater*
Exarchos, Christos 181
Expedition Epics Film Corporation 191
Exploitation Films 72

Face of Fire 65–66, 233
The Faceless Monster see *Nightmare Castle*
Fadden, Tom 105
Fair, Jody 148
Fairman, Paul W. 162
Fairview Productions 230
Faith, Dolores 91, 92, 126, 128
Fajardo, Eduardo 204
Fantale Films 73
Farell, Claude 200
Fawcett, Charles 66
Faye, Janina 57
Fazenda, Louise 14
Feld, Fritz 170
Felice, Lyle 216
Felleghy, Tom 37
Fenin, Mort 214
Fennelly, Libby 40
Fenollar, Pedro 220
Ferrell, Ray 86
Ferrer, Mel 84
Ferrer, Ricardo 189
Ferris, Peter 153
Feyisetan, Nigel 50
Fields, Darlene 155
Fields, Robert 228
Fields, W.C. 146
Fiend with the Electronic Brain see *Man with the Synthetic Brain*
55 Days at Peking 2
Film Ventures Productions 54
The Filmgroup 18, 173, 187, 213, 219
Fine, Michael 74
Fine Arts Films 149

Index

Finney, Jack 107
Un fiocco nero per Deborah (A Black Ribbon for Deborah) see *Deborah*
Fischer, Dennis 12, 53, 122, 180
Fisher, Kay (Kai) 108
Fitzgerald, Ella 113
Fitzroy, Emily 14
The Five Blobs 227
Five Bloody Graves see *Gun Riders*
Flaherty, Pat 113
Flaherty, Robert 194
Fleer, Harry 45, 164
Fleischman, A.S. 156
Fleming, Eric 71, 72, 142
Flesh Feast 194
Flight of the Lost Balloon 183, 194–97
Flight to Mars 177
Flippides, Andreas 181
Fluellen, Joel 114
Flynn, Joe 102
Flynn, Pat 133
Foam, John see Bava, Mario
Fong, Harold 133
Foran, Dick 5, 6
Ford, Carol Ann 57
Ford, John 212
Forest, Michael 17, 18, 181
Forrest, William 140
Foster, Preston 60
Foulger, Byron 170
Foulk, Robert 86, 87
Fox, Michael 171
Franchi, Franco 134, 135
Franciosa, Anthony 187
Francis, Freddie 56, 57
Francis, Sandra 157
Franco, Jess 25, 64, 65, 194
Franke, Anthony 228
Frankenstein Meets the Space Monster 1, 50, 67–69, 234
Frankenstein 1970 1, 35, 55, 69–71, 141, 233
Franz, Arthur 5, 6
Fraser, Harry L. 34
Fraser, Stanley 120
Freda, Riccardo 36
Frederic, Norman 62, 63
Fredericks, Dean see Frederic, Norman
Frees, Paul 29
Friendly Persuasion (1956) 2
Fright (1956) 27, 71–72, 73, 88, 156, 233
Fright (1971) 72–75, 234
From Hell It Came 1, 62, 75–77, 233
Frye, Gil 35
Fuchsberger, Joachim 200, 201
Fulci, Lucio 135
Fuller, Dolores 34, 211
Fuller, Lance 34, 35
Fuller, Robert 183
Fuller, Samuel 150, 151, 152
Futura Pictures 46
Futurama 67
Futurama Entertainment Corporation 67

Gabor, Zsa Zsa 28, 141–42
Ganley, Gail 132
Gardenia, Vincent 208
Gardett, Robert 27
Garland, Beverly 132, 134
Garland, Richard 8, 126
Garrett, George 68
Garrett, Joy 176
Garriba, Mario 59
Gas Ningen Dai Ichigo (The First Gas Human) see *The Human Vapor*
Gates, Larry 105, 106
Gates, Nancy 72, 178, 179
Gates, Tudor 74, 75
Gelfan, Barney 217
Gemora, Charles 85
Gene Autry's Melody Ranch 82
Geni, Ihsan 190
George, Susan 73, 75, 153, 154
Geray, Steven 136
Gerie Productions 166
Gerson, Jeanne 35
Gerstle, Frank 151, 174
The Ghost of Crossbones Canyon 77–78, 137, 233
The Giant Behemoth 1, 77, 78–81, 233
Gibson, Lois 189
Gibson, Mimi 179
Gillette, Robert W. 197
Gimpera, Teresa 190, 191
Giroux, Charles A. 1
Glass, Everett 106, 179
Glass, Ned 112, 114
Glass, Seamon 223, 224
Glasser, Albert 53
Glenn, Montgomery 185
Glenn, Roy 81, 82, 114
Glenwood-Neve Productions 85
Glover, Bruce 67
Glut, Donald F. 55, 68, 70
Godsell, Vanda 4
Gold, Jack (John) 177
Golden Era 38
The Golden Idol 81–83, 233
Gollin, Albert E. 157
Gomez, Mayra 193
Gonzales, Sonia Noemi 188
Gonzalez-Gonzalez, Jose 146, 218
Gorcey, Bernard 31, 32, 46, 61, 62, 111, 113, 136, 140, 155
Gorcey, David 155, 170; *see also* Condon, David
Gorcey, Leo 31, 32, 46, 47, 48, 61, 62, 88, 110, 111, 114, 136, 140, 141
Gordon, Alex 5
Gordon, Barry 84
Gordon, Bernard 55
Gordon, Bert I. 52, 53, 164, 166
Gordon, Flora 166
Gordon, Gavin 15, 16
Gordon, Leo 175
Gordon, Richard 50, 51
Gordon, Robert 20
Gordon, Roy 12, 136
Gordon, Susan 164
Gorham Productions 7
Gorini, Arianna 23
Gough, Michael 20, 21
Gould, Elliott 176
GPA Productions 224

Grabowski, Norman "Woo Woo" 146, 148
Graeff, Tom 133
Graham, Hugh 229
Graham, Tim 184
Grant, Lee and The Capitols 153
Grassby, Bertram 13
Grauman, Walter 63
Gray, Coleen 60, 86
Gray, Donald 3
The Great Expedition to the Elephant Graveyard see *Dark Venture*
Green, Mike 223
Greene, Angela 45
Greene, Ellen 208
Greene, Otis 63
Greene, Rita 54, 103
Greer, Dabbs 106
Grefe, William 194
Gregson, John 73
Grey, Virginia 20, 21, 163
Gribbon, Eddie 14
Griffin, Jack 209
Griffith, Charles B. 181, 182, 189, 208, 209, 210
Grimaldi, Hugo 93, 127
Grimes, Tammy 149
Grinter, Brad F. 193, 194
Grover, Ed 176
Guderman, Linda 116
Guerin, Lenmana 76
Guifoyle, Paul 81, 82
Gun Riders 197–99
Gynt, Greta 28

Haddon, Larry 84
Haerter, Gerard 36, 37
Hafner, Ingrid 28
Hagemeyer, H.J. 158
Haggerty, Don 47
Hall, Huntz 31, 32, 47, 48, 61, 62, 87, 88, 110, 111, 113, 136, 155, 170
Haller, Daniel 175
Hallett, Neil 80
Halliday, Bryant 50, 51
Halsdorf, Serge 19
Halsey, Brett 6
Hamilton, Alean "Bambi" 92
Hamilton, Margaret 14
Hammer Films 57, 74
Hampton, Grace 4
Hampton, Orville H. 210
Hampton, Robert see Freda, Riccardo
Hamton, Robert see Freda, Riccardo
Hanawalt, Chuck 9
The Hand of Power 2, 199–202
Hands of a Stranger 83–85, 234
The Hands of a Strangler see *The Hands of Orlac*
The Hands of Orlac 84, 85
Hanna, Mark 11
Hannah, Daryl 10
Hannah, Queen of the Vampires see *Crypt of the Living Dead*
Hanold, Marilyn 67, 68
Hanson, Kristina 230, 231
Hardmuth, Paul 4

Index

Hardstark, Michael 40
Hardy, Phil 12, 20, 32, 38, 41, 46, 62, 74, 85, 89, 93, 110, 122, 123, 125, 131, 163, 173, 177, 180, 187, 191, 199, 203, 207, 212, 220
Harris, Jack H. 227, 230
Harvey, Don C. 82
Harvey, Joan 83, 84, 85
Hatton, Raymond 61
Haukoff, Ralph 108
Hauser, Gilgi 57
Haussler, Richard 125
Hayden, Russell 178
Haydon, Charles 192
Hayes, Allison 10–12, 62, 63, 99, 101
Hayes, Chester 76
Hayes, David 32, 47, 62, 110, 136, 141, 170
Hayes, Helen 14
Hayes, Sherman 193
Hayward, Louis 72
Haze, Jonathan 132, 133, 208, 210
He Walked by Night 102
Healey, Myron 61, 62, 140
Hecht, Ben 141
Heermance, Richard 170
Hellman, Jaclyn 19, 189
Hellman, Monte 18, 19, 189, 203
Hell's Five Hours 85–87, 137, 233
Helton, Percy 155
Hemisphere Pictures 215
Henderson, C.J. 68, 146, 163, 177, 224
Henderson, Douglas 22
Henderson, Marcia 99, 101
Henry, Bill 155
Henry, Thomas B. 183, 185
Henry, Victor 153
Herrick, Abbie 135
Hertz, Nathan *see* Juran, Nathan
Herx, Henry 150
Hewitt, Heather 123
Hidarki, Bokuzen 95
Hill, Jack 175
Hill, Linda Lee 14
Hill, Marianna 21
Hill, Mary 211
Hirsch, Robert 97
Hitchcock, Alfred 39
Ho, Linda 43
Hobart, Doug 193
Hodgins, Earle 170
Hoffman, Howard 90, 117
Hold That Hypnotist 48, 87–88, 233
Holden, Joyce 140, 141
Holt, Jack 211
Holtz, Gary 193
Holy Terror see Communion
Honda, Ishiro 94
Honore, J.P. 25
Hood, Darla 15, 16
Hopwood, Avery 13–14
Horror Monsters Presents Black Zoo 22
Horror of the Blood Monsters see Vampire Men of the Lost Planet
Horrors of the Black Zoo see Black Zoo
Horton, Louisa 40

Houck, Joy M. 210
The House of Exorcism see Lisa and the Devil
House on Haunted Hill (1959) 1, 2, 46, 88–91, 116, 221, 233
House on Haunted Hill (1999) 89
Houston, Donald 48, 49
Howard, Nancy 179
Howard, Trevor 176
Howco International Pictures 183, 210
Howlin (Howland), Olin 228
Huart, Gerard 25
Hubbard, Tom 138
Huc, Nicole 19
Hudson, William 10, 11
Hughes, Carolyn 173
Hughes, Ken 5
Hughes, Mary Beth 61, 62
Hughes, Robin 120, 136
Hugo, Victor 97
Hugo Grimaldi Productions 127
The Human Duplicators 91–93, 127, 234
The Human Vapor 94–96, 234
The Hunchback of Notre Dame (1923) 97
The Hunchback of Notre Dame (1939) 97
The Hunchback of Notre Dame (1957) 96–99, 233
Hunter, Arline 146, 148
Hurst, Veronica 120
Huxley, Aldous 107
Hyer, Martha 136
HypnoMagic 100
The Hypnotic Eye 99–101, 233

I'm Alone and I'm Scared see Fright (1971)
Im banne des Unheimlichen (In the Thrall of the Sinister One) *see The Hand of Power*
Imelda 17
The Immortal Monster see Caltiki The Immortal Monster
Independent-International Pictures 197, 215, 216, 224
Independenti Regionali 93
Indestructible Man 53, 101–03, 177, 233
Indrisano, John 92
Ingrassia, Ceccio 134, 135
Interstate Television Corporation 2
Invasion 108
Invasion of the Body Stealers see The Body Stealers
Invasion of the Body Snatchers (1956) 1, 4, 29, 103–08, 233
Invasion of the Body Snatchers (1978) 108
Ippoliti, Mimma 220
Irving, George S. 149
La isla de la muerte (The Island of the Dead) *see Island of the Doomed*
Island of the Doomed 1, 108–10, 234
The Isotope Man see The Atomic Man
Iverson Ranch 62

Jackson, Selmer 6
Jackson, Thomas E. 12
Jaeckel, Richard 167, 168
Jaffe, Carl 4
Jaffe, Sam 66
Jalopy 110–11, 233
Jaws of the Alien see The Human Duplicators
Jeffries, Herb 113
Jenks, Frank 61
Jennifer (1953) 111–13, 233
Jerry Fairbanks Studios 102
Jewell, Austen 88
Johns, Mervyn 57
Johnson, Edith 13
Johnson, Russell 8
Johnston, W. Ray 1
Joint, Alf 154
Jones, Carolyn 106
Jones, Morgan 133
Jones, Stephen 74, 102, 191, 194, 220
Jones-Moreland, Betsy 188, 189, 202
Joseph, Jackie 208, 210
Jostyn, Jay 14
Julienne, Remy 176
Jungle Gents 113–15, 179, 233
Juran, Nathan 183, 196, 197
Justice, William 35

Kalvex, Inc./PSP, Inc. 2
Kane, Joe 7, 167, 182, 224, 229
Kaplan 64
Karen, James 67
Karloff, Boris 1, 69–71, 102, 153, 154
Karson, Phil 186
Kaufmann, Maurice 80
Kaylor, Arnold 213
Keaton, Buster 135
Keays, Vernon 85
Keel, Howard 56, 57
Keene, Tom *see* Powers, Richard
Kellerman, Sally 85
Kemper, Doris 47
Kennedy, Douglas 196
Kent, Carol 223
Kent, Jean 28
Kerman, David 67
Kerridge, Mary 50
Khadhapuridze, Olya 119
Khoury, George 145
Kidd, Jonathan 116
Kiel, Richard 91, 92
Kieling, Wolfgang 200
Kilgore, Charles 166
Kim, June 42
Kimbell, Anne 81, 82
Kincaid, Aron 175
Kinski, Klaus 189
Kirk, Tommy 216
Kish, Joseph 177
Kishkon, Nina 118
Kiss Me Deadly 86, 137
Kitt, Eartha 149
Klavun, Walter 72
Kleinsinger, George 149
Kling Studios 162
Knapp, Robert 211
Knight, James 172
Knox, Mona 111

Koch, Howard W. 69
Konopka, Magda 219, 220
Konow, David 217, 226
Korda, Susan *see* Miranda, Soledad
Koscina, Sylva (Silva) 206
Kounelaki, Miranda 182
Kramer, David 85
Kramer, Siegfried 108
Krikol, Eugene 213
Kruger, Henry *see* Dominic, Arturo
Kruger, Lea 23
Krull, Hans 200
Kubatsky, Anatoli 118
Kupcinet, Karyn *see* Windsor, Tammy
Kurlick, Daniel 22
Kuznetsov, Michael (Mikhail) 118

Lacey, Catherine 153
Lackteen, Frank 6
Lake, Veronica 194
Lamb, John 219
Lamble, Lloyd 80
Lancaster, Burt 167, 168, 169
Landis, James 213
Landru 27
Landru, Henri Desire 26
Lane, Lenita 13–15
Lane, Mike 69
Langan, Glenn 127, 128
Langton, Paul 44, 45
Lanphier, James 196, 197
Lansing, Joi 6
Larion, Anna 213
LaRue, Jack, Jr. 190
LaRue, Lash 194, 210
Last Woman on Earth 188, 202–03
Latell, Lyle 134
Laughton, Charles 97, 98
Lauren, Rod 20, 21
Lauter, Harry 61, 62
La Vigne, Emile 177
Lawrence, Bert 170
Lawrence, Sheldon 28
Lee, Christopher 64, 65, 84
Lee, Rudy 140
Leggatt, Alison 57
Lehne, John 176
Leigh, Nelson 178, 179
Leigh, Wandisa 204
Leigh-Hunt, Ronald 50
Lek, Nico 212
Lemaire, Phillippe 25
Leon, William 213
Leonard, William Torbert 15, 150
Leone, Alfredo 205, 207
Leone, Kathy 205, 207
Leonetti, Tommy 91, 92
Le Roy, Eddie 155, 170
Le Saint, Edward J. 13
Leslie, Bethel 14
Leslie, William 126, 128
Liberty Pictures 1
Lieb, Herbert 14
Lightning Bolt 203–05
Liljedahl, Marie 64, 65
Lindfors, Lil 200, 202
Line, Helga 128, 130, 131
Lipton, Lawrence 100, 101

Lisa and the Devil 205–07
The Little Shop of Horrors (1960) 202, 207–10
The Little Shop of Horrors (1986) 208
Lloyd, Harold, Jr. 127, 128, 146
Lob, Karl 202
Lodge, Jean 50
Logan, James 231
Lollobrigida, Gina 97, 99
Lombard, Michael 176
London, Babe 146
Long, Richard 90
Loo, Richard 42
Lopez, Manuel 52
Lord, Marjorie 138
Lords, Traci 134
Lorimar Productions 2
Lorre, Peter 84
Lorys, Diana 204
Lost Women 210–12
Lost Women of Zarpa see *Lost Women*
Lourie, Eugene 80–81
Love, Lucretia 58
Love in the Afternoon 2
Lowe, Edmund 121
Lowery, Robert (Bob) 110
Lowry, Jane 40
Lu, Alicia 43
Lucas, Tim 202, 215
Luez, Laurette 114
Lugosi, Bela 1, 77, 101, 155, 229
Lukather, Paul 83, 84, 85, 230, 231
Lulli, Folco 204
Lund, Jana 69, 70
Lundh, Borje 66
Lung, Charles 32
Lupino, Ida 111, 112
Lydon, James 99
Lynd, Eva 99
Lynn, DanI 21
Lytton, Herbert 45

Macabre 1, 2, 86, 115–17, 221, 233
MacDouglas, John 130
MacGowran, Jack 80
MacKaye, Norman 71
Macready, George 91, 92
Mad Love 84
Madison, Guy 77, 78, 137
Madison, Leigh 79
The Magic Voyage of Sinbad 212–15
The Magic Weaver 1, 117–20, 234
Mahoney, Louis 51
Majestic Pictures 1
Malfatti, Marina 58
Malone, Nancy 71
Maltin, Leonard 89, 145, 150
Mamakos, Peter 140, 144, 155
Man Eater of Hydra see *Island of the Doomed*
The Man Who Would Be King 2
Man with the Steel Mask see *Who?*
Man with the Synthetic Brain 199, 215–17
Mangano, Vittorio 58
Manku, Vivianne 13
Manning, Bruce 89
Manson, Maurice 87
Maraschal, Launce 3

Marcus, Bill 193
Margheriti, Antonio 187
Marion, Paul 32
Mark, Michael 174, 175
Marlowe, Hugh 177, 178, 179
Marquette, Jacques 183, 189, 196, 197
Marquis, Don 159
Marr, Eddie 103
Marrill, Alvin J. 98
Mars, Lani 175
Marsh, Vera 164
Marshal, Alan 90
Marshall, Mort 163
Marshall, Nancy 67, 68
Marshall, William 144, 167, 169
Marston, John 62
Martell, Gregg 230, 231
Marth, Frank 71
Martin, Audrey 223
Martin, Chris-Pin 211
Martin, Daniel 191
Martin, George 108
Martin, John 211
Martin, Ross 149
Martin, Steve 208\
Martin, Tony 126
Martin Nosseck Productions 125
Martone, Elaine 84
Martone, Gaby 219
Marya-Iskusnitsa (Maria, The Wonderful Weaver) see *The Magic Weaver*
Mascot Pictures 1
Maslow, Walter 45, 181–82
Mason, Laura 31
Mason, Pamela 146, 148
Massey, Athena 134
Massey, Daria 144
Matsumoto, Sensho 95
Matsumura, Minosuke 94
Mathews, Carole 138
Mathews, Grace 76
Matthews, Geoffrey 57
Matthews, John 151
Mattson, Siw 200
Maude, Beatrice 105
Maurey, Nicole 57
Mavis, Paul 135
Maxim Gorky Studios 119
Mayo, Mike 41
The Maze 1, 120–22, 170, 233
McCall, Mitzi 171
McCalla, Irish 84
McCard, Mollie 54
McCarthy, Kevin 105, 107, 108
McDonald, Francis 61
McGavin, Darren 123, 124
McGee, Mark Thomas 10, 210
McGraw, Charles 167, 169
McHugh, Kitty 112
McKim, Robert 114
McKinnon, Mona 211
McLean, David 159
McMaster, Niles 40
McNally, Stephen 86
McNamara, John 75
McQueen, Steve (Steven) 227, 228
Meadows, Joyce 183, 184

Medin, Harriet White 23
Melchers, W.R. 158
Melies, Georges 26
Menken, Alan 208
Menzies, William Cameron 121–22
Mercier, Michele 187
Merivale, John 36
Merkel, Una 14
Mermaids of Tiburon 218–19
Merton Park Studios 4, 49
Mesa of Lost Women see *Lost Women*
Meyers, Andy 50
Meyers, Fred 199, 225
Meyers, Richard 207
Michaels, Toby 209
Migliano, Adriano Amidei 59
Miller, Arnold L. 154
Miller, Dick 132, 133, 171, 181, 208, 210
Miller, Linda 39
Miller, Tony 8, 172
Mills, Mort 47
Millyar, Georgi 118
Milner, Martin (Marty) 146, 147
Milner Bros. 77
Milton, David 177
Minton, Lynn 167
Miranda, Soledad 65
Mission Mars 1, 122–24, 234
Mistretta, Gaetano 24, 38, 59, 131, 187
Mitchell, Cameron 23, 24, 66, 108
Mitchell, Laurie 142
Mitchum, Julie 90
Modern Films 2, 224
Moehner, Carl 125
Mohr, Gerald 221, 222
Monogram Pictures 1, 2, 31
Monsieur Verdoux 26
The Monster (1959) see *Face of Fire*
Montell, Lisa 178, 179
Montes, Elisa 108
Montini, Luigi 220
Moonwolf 1, 124–26, 234
Moore, Eva 14
Moore, Kieron 56, 57
Moorehead, Agnes 13–15
Moranis, Rick 208
Moray, Yvonne 43, 44
Morell, Andre 79, 80
Morlas, Mary 223
Morricone, Ennio 131
Morris, Barboura 174, 181, 182
Morris, Chester 14
Morris, Dorothy 116
Morris, Wayne 137, 138
Morrison, Ann 14
Morrow, Byron 22
Morrow, Scotty 45
Morrow, Susan 116
Morrow, Vic 86
Morse, Robin 144
Morton, Roy 216
Mosbacher, Peter 200
Mother Riley Meets the Vampire 229
Mudie, Leonard 81, 82
Mulhall, Jack 6
Muller, Paul 64, 65, 128, 129–30
Munday, Penelope 48

Munshin, Jules 149
Murakami, Fuyuki 94
Muriel Corporation 86
Murphy, Jimmy 47, 87, 155
Murray, Bill 208
Mutiny in Outer Space 91, 93, 126–28, 234
My Son, the Vampire 229
My World Dies Screaming see *Terror in the Haunted House*
Mylong, John 218
Mysova, Ellen 213, 214

Nader, George 91, 92, 93
Naha, Ed 5, 7, 32, 46, 62, 66, 89, 101, 102, 180
Naschy, Paul 65
Nash, Robert 127
Nehlsen, Hermann 108
Nelson, Ed 8, 9
Nelson, Gene 35
New Horizon Pictures 175
Newby, Valli 50
Newman, Raoul H. 185
Nicholson, Jack 182, 209, 210
Nicholson, James H. 162
Nicholson, Nora 48
Nicolai, Bruno 65
Nigh, Jane 87
Night Legs see *Fright* (1971)
Night of the Doomed see *Nightmare Castle*
Nightmare Castle 128–31, 234
The Ninth Guest 89
Nixon, Allan 211
Noonan, Sheila see Carol, Sheila
Nord, Eric "Big Daddy" 100, 101
Norman, Jett see Walker, Clint
Norvo, Red 85
Not of This Earth (1957) 1, 9, 10, 11, 131–34, 233
Not of This Earth (1988) 134
Not of This Earth (1995) 134
Not of This Earth (1998) 134
Not of This Earth: The Film Music of Ronald Stein 10, 13, 134
Notre-Dame de Paris see *The Hunchback of Notre Dame* (1959)
Nurmi, Maila see Vampira
Nye, Louis 146, 147

002 Agenti Segretissimi see *Oh! Those Most Secret Agents!*
Ober, Robert 14
Oboler, Arch 202
O'Brien, Willis 80
O'Connolly, Jim 5
O'Donnell, Cathy (Kathy) 221, 222
Ogilvy, Ian 153
Oh! Those Most Secret Agents! 134–35, 234
O'Higgins, Brian 4
Ohmart, Carol 90
Okuda, Ted 31, 33
Old Mother Riley Meets the Vampire 229
Oliver, Guy 12
O'Loughlin, Gerald S. 167, 169
One Million B.C. 226

O'Neill, James 24, 38, 131, 161, 166, 187, 191, 194, 212, 220
Oorthuis, Dity 158
Operazione Goldman (Operation Goldman) see *Lightning Bolt*
Orano, Allesio 206
Ordung, Wyott 162
Orlacs Haende (The Hands of Orlac) 84
Ormond, Ron 210, 212
O'Rourke, Patrick 114
Orwell, George 107
Osborn, Lyn 45
Osborne, Kent 198
Oscard, Miko 66
Osman, Shera 190
Osterloh, Robert 107, 140
Oswald, Marianne 98
Otis, Ted 84
Ott, Warrenne 21
Owens, Pat (Patricia) 48, 49
Oz, Frank 208

Pacifica Productions 219
Padula, Vicente 52
Page, Ilse 200, 201
Page, Manuel 54
Palmer, Gregg 75
Palmer, Randy 77, 134
Palmer, Robert 127
Palmerini, Luca M. 24, 38, 59, 131, 187
Paolo Film 59
Papillon 2
Paramount Pictures 227
Parish, James Robert 31, 44
Paris Playboys 135–36, 233
Parker, Shirley 123
Parker, Ursula 204
Parkin, Duncan (Dean) 53
Parnell, Emory 113
Parry, Natasha 48, 49
Pate, Michael 120
Patridge, Joe 99, 101
Patterson, Kenneth 105, 106
Patterson, Shirley see Smith, Shawn
Paul, Eugenie 62
Paull, Morgan 167
Payton, Lee 228
Pearce, Alice 14
Peary, Danny 38, 41, 151
Peary, Harold 138
Pena, Julio 220
Pepper, Barbara 146
Perello, Michelle 25
Pereva, Vito 118
Perrault, Charles 26
Perri, Luciana 204
Perry, Vic 4
Peters, Dennis Alaba 50
Peters, John 186
Petkovich, Anthony 67
Phantom Trails 78, 137, 233
Phillips, William (Bill) 140
La Philosophie dans le boudoir see *Beyond Love and Evil*
Philosophy in the Boudoir see *Eugenie*
Photoplay Associates, Inc. 145
Pica, Antonio 220

Pickford, Jack 14
Pickford, Mary 14
Pieral 98
Pierce, Thomas 141
Pigozzi, Lucinao 23
Pinero, Fred 193
Pirie, David 154
Pitts, ZaSu 14
The Plague of the Zombies 73
Platt, Edward 72
Poe, Edgar Allan 185
The Poets 67
Pollexfen, Jack 53–54
Polo, Maria 198
Port of Hell 86, 137–39, 233
Poston, Tom 149
Powell, Jimmy 200
Powers, Bruce 225
Powers, Mala 197, 198
Powers, Merry 186
Powers, Richard 61, 62
Prescott, Guy 99
Price, Dennis 50
Price, Vincent 14, 15, 42, 43, 88, 89, 90, 153
Prince, William 116
Prine, Andrew 190, 191
Private Eyes 140–41, 233
Psycho-A-Go-Go see *Man with the Synthetic Brain*
Psycho Rama 221
Ptushko, Aleksandr 120, 213, 215
Purdy, Jon 134
Pyle, Denver 60

Qualen, John 221
Quarry, Robert 189
Quartaro, Gaetano 220
Queen of Outer Space 1, 71, 72, 141–44, 179, 233
Queen of Spades 2
Queen of the Gorillas see *Bride and the Beast*
Quinlan, David 4, 49
Quinn, Anthony 97, 98, 99
Quinn, Tandra 211

Rabb, Leonid 192
Rabin, Jack 171
Raho, Umi (Umberto) 220
Rains, Claude 14
Ramsey, Ward 230, 231
Randall, Stuart 103
Rauch, Siegfried 200
Ravaged see *Blood Rose*
Ravaioli, Isarco 220
Ray, Aldo 124
Rayart Productions 1
Raymond, Gene 198, 199
Raymond, Paula 199
Raytone Pictures 1
Razetto, Stella 12
The Red Norvo Quintette 85
Red Ram Productions 123
Reding, Judi 164, 166
Reed, Alan 149, 150
Reed, Ralph 132
Reeves, Michael 153
Reeves, Richard 163

Reeves, Steve 181
Reilly, Robert 67
Reiner, Thomas 23
Renard, Maurice 84
Rennie, Guy 106
Republic Pictures Corporation 1
Republic Pictures Home Video 108
Ressel, Franco 23
Reviere, Georges 185, 186
Rey, Mariano Garcia 190, 191
Reynolds, Tom 72
Rhodes, Erik 149
Rhodes, Hari 150, 151
Rich, Bernard 145
Rich, Kathy 40
Richards, Keith 178, 180
Richmond, Susan 48
Riddle, K.K. 216
Ridgeway, Suzanne 75
Righi, Massimo 23
Rimsky-Korsakov, Nikoli 213
Rinehart, Mary Roberts 13
Ritter, Tex 178
Rivera, Chita 149
RKO Radio Pictures 52, 97
Roark, Robert 163
Robbins, Tacey 216
Roberson, Chuck 150, 151
Roberto 25
Roberts, Alan 231
Roberts, Arthur 134
Roberts, Ewan 56
Roberts, Thayer 223
Robin, Olivia 25
Robinson, Christopher (Chris) 17, 18
Roboman see *Who?*
Robsahm, Margarete 186, 187
Roc, Patricia 27, 28
Rocca, Antonino 39
Rocca, Daniela 37
Roerick, William 132, 173
Rohm, Maria 64, 65
Roman, Ric 170
Romero, Blanquita 188, 196
La Rose écorchée (The Burnt Rose) see *Blood Rose*
Roseman, Ralph 229
Ross, Mike (Michael) 11, 32
Rossi-Stuart, Giacomo 38
Roth, Gene 138, 165
Roth, Johnny 35
Roth, Lillian 39, 41
Rou, Aleksandr 119, 120
Row, Alexander see Aleksandr Rou
Rowe, Earl 228
Rowe, George 218
Royce, Riza 15, 16
Rubin, Jennifer 175
Ruick, Mel 92
Russell, Chuck 228
Ryan, Michael 161
Ryan, Tim 140
Rye, Michael 83, 84

Sabu 144
Sabu and the Magic Ring 144–45, 233
Sadko see *The Magic Voyage of Sinbad*
Sagittarius Productions 29, 123

Saint-James, Fred 19
Salvador, Julio 189
Sampredo, Matilda 108
Sanders, George 27, 28, 29, 30, 65
Sanders, Lugene 164
Sandoval, Esther 188
Sanford, Ralph 170
Santoni, Espartaco 206
Sanz, Paco 204
Sasaki, Takamaru 96
Sata, Keiko 95
Satana, Tura 91
Satanic see *Satanik*
Satanik 219–20
Sattin, Lonnie 91, 92
Savalas, Telly 205, 207
Savo, Ann 125
Sawaya, George 84
Sayer, Diane 159, 160
Sayer, Jay 171
Sazarino, Dan 176
Schanzer, Karl 175
Scheuer, Steven H. 7, 53, 72, 85, 110, 125, 144, 146, 180, 215, 219
Schiller, Norbert 69–70
Schmidt, Helmut 125
Schneider, Edith 200
Schoeller, Ingrid 135
Schwalb, Ben 63, 100, 110, 141, 170
Scorpio International 2
Scott, Jacqueline 115, 116
Scott, Janette 56, 57
Scott, Simon 167, 169
The Screaming Sleep see *The Hypnotic Eye*
The Search for Bridey Murphy 72, 88
Searles, Baird 229
Secret of the Telegian 94
Secrets of a Soul see *Confessions of an Opium Eater*
Sei donne per l'assassino (Six Women for the Assassin) see *Blood and Black Lace*
Seiler, Jacques 26
Sekeley, Steve 56, 57
Selig Pictures 13
Selwin 1
Selwin on Saturday 1
Semand, Britt 225
Sendry, Albert 126
Sen Yung, Victor 138
The 7th Voyage of Sinbad 213
Sex Kittens Go to College 42, 145–48, 234
Shafo, Robert 144
Shaner, John 209
Shaughnessy, Mickey 146, 148
Shayne, Robert 102, 155, 171
Sheeler, Mark 76
Sheffield, Johnny 81, 83
Sheffield, Reginald 83
Sheppard, Patty 190, 191
Sheppard, Paula 39
Shepperton Studios 29, 73
Sheridan, DanI 163
Sherman, Samuel M. 217
Sherpix Pictures 135
Sherrill, Babette 193
Shields, Arthur 54

Shields, Brooke 39, 40, 41
Shinbone Alley 148–50, 234
Shipp, Mary 112
"Shock!" 1
Shock Corridor 81, 150–52, 234
Shonteff, Lindsay 51
Showalter, Max *see* Adams, Casey
Siegel, Don 104, 108
Signorelli, Tom 40
Sigoloff, Marc 167
Sikking, James 161
Silva, Carmen 207
Simon, Robert F. 66
Simpson, Mickey 177, 180
Simpson, Russell 77
Sinatra, Frank 113
Sinatra, Richard 17, 18
Sinclair, Eric 172
Sitka, Emil 141
Ski Troop Attack 18
Slavin, Susan 21
Sloane, Barton 229
Smedley, Richard 216
Smith, Bruce Meredith 192
Smith, Queenie 87
Smith, Shawn 178, 179
Smith, William 167, 169
Snowden, Eric 114
Sojin 14
Sokoloff, Vladimir 145
Solon, Ewen 48
Sommer, Elke 205
Son of Blob see Beware! The Blob
Son of Dr. Jekyll 54
"Son of Shock!" 1
The Sorcerers 1, 152–54, 234
Sorrente, Sylvia 187
Souchka 19
Souls for Sale see Confessions of an Opium Eater
Space, Arthur 163
Space Mission to the Lost Planet see Vampire Men of the Lost Planet
Spalding, Thomas 229
Speed, F. Maurice 26
Spell of the Hypnotist see Fright (1956)
Spier, Wolfgang 201
Spook Chasers 48, 155–56, 233
Spruance, Don 223
Spy in the Sky! 156–58, 233
Stanley 18
Stanley, John 24, 85, 102, 110, 123, 180, 212
Stapleton, James 83, 84
Stapp, Marjorie 55, 103
Star-Cine Cosmos 38, 58, 194
Star Portal 134
Starr, Ron (Ronald) 223
Starrett, Charles 178
Steele, Barbara 128, 129, 130, 131, 153, 185, 186, 187
Steele, Bob 6
Steele, Mike 16
Steffen, Ben 187
Stein, Ronald 10, 13, 134
Stephens, Harvey 16
Stephens, Susan 68
Stern, Otto 200
Stevens, Eileen 12

Stevens, Harmon 211
Stevens, Leith 177
Stevenson, Robert Louis 52, 55, 220
Stewart, John 176
Stewart, Maurice 193
Sting of Death 194
Stoker, Ron 127
Stolar, Edward 213, 214
Stone, Merritt 165
Storey, Lynn 209
The Strangler 1, 158–61, 234
Stribling, Melissa 48, 49
Strudwick, Shepperd 14
Style, Michael 74
Sullivan, Deirdre 38
Sullivan, Didi 36
Superbug 2
Surow, Robert 213
Sutherland, Donald 108
Sutton, John 15, 16
Svensk Filmindustries 65
Swan, Robert 75
Swenson, Ingrid 64
Switzer, Carl "Alfalfa" 61
Syndicate Film Exchange 1

Taft, William Howard 169
Tagani 224, 226
Tal Production 224
Talbert, John 216
Talbot, Lyle 211
Talbott, Gloria 51, 52, 54
Tanaka, Tomoyuki 94
Tannen, William 82
Target Earth 161–64, 233
Tate, Dale 11, 183, 185
Taylor, Jack 64, 65
Taylor, Kent 216, 217
Taylor, Rod 178, 179
Teele, Margot 92
Teissier, Elisabeth 25
Tenser, Tony 30, 153
Terrell, Ken (Kenneth) 12, 102
Terror in the Haunted House 221–22
Tessier, Valentine 97
Tevos, Herbert 210
Thawnton, Tony 50
Thayer, Lorna 112
Thin Air see The Body Stealers
This Is Not a Test 2, 223–24
Thomas, E. Leslie 184
Thomas, Peter 202
Thompson, Howard 64
Thompson, Marshall 138, 139, 197, 198
Thompson, Paul 62
Thon, Doris 19
The Three Stooges 31, 32, 68, 141
Thurston, Carol 100
Tiemeyer, Hans 156, 157
Tieri, Aroldo 135
Tigon Pictures 29, 153
Tilly, Meg 108
Time Warner 2
Timeslip see The Atomic Man
Tinling, Ted 40
Tinti, Gabriele 206
Tissier, Jean 97
Titra Sound Corporation 36

Tobey, Kenneth 72
Tohill, Cathal 64
Toho Company 94
Tomborg, Kaym 176
Tombs, Pete 64
Tomelty, Joseph 3
Tonge, Philip 115, 116
Tonlyn Productions 227
Topper, Burt 159, 161
Torey, Hal 45
The Torment (1974) *see Deborah*
Tormented 164–66, 234
The Torturer! Master of "The Hypnotic Eye" see The Hypnotic Eye
Towers, Constance 150, 151
Towers, Harry Alan 65
Towne, Robert 188, 189, 202
Travis, Henry 184
Travis, Richard 211
Treadway, Wayne 231
Trevlac, John *see* Calvert, John
Troyan, Maurice 213
Tsuburaya, Eiji 94
Tsuchiya, Yoshio 94
Tucker, Larry 151
Tucker, Richard 14
La tumba de la isla maldita (The Tomb of the Cursed Island) *see Crypt of the Living Dead*
Turkel, Joe 165
Turner, John 79
Twilight's Last Gleaming 166–69, 234
Twitty, Conway 146, 148
Two Tickets to Terror see Man with the Synthetic Brain
Tyler, Richard 6

Ullman, Elwood 115, 170
Ulmer, Edgar G. 26, 53, 55
...Und immer ruft das Herz see Moonwolf
Ungaro, Francesca 22
Unger, Goffredo 204
Unger, Gustaf 66
United Artists 14, 86
Universal-International Pictures 230
Unknown Island 226
Up in Smoke 48, 169–70, 233

Vail, Myrtle 209, 210
Valle, Ricardo 108
Valley Forge Film Studios 227
Valli, Alida 206
Vallin, Rick 32, 82
Vampira 146
Vampire Men of the Lost Planet 199, 224–26
Vampire Over London 229
Van Doren, Mamie 145, 146, 147, 148
Varconi, Victor 6
Vargas, Alberto 177
Vargas, Daniele 36
Vaz Dias, Selma 28
Vea, Katina *see* Victor, Katherine
Vedder, William 180
Veidt, Conrad 84
Vejar, Harry 107
The Vendells 215
Vernon, Howard 25

Vernon-Seneca Films 67
Vertisya, Lucille 214
Ve Sota, Bruno 171, 175
Vickers, Yvette 10, 11
Victor, Katherine 211
Victor Adamson Productions 215
Video-International 64
Vidon, Henri 79
Viklandt, Olivia 215
The Virgin Aqua Sex see *Mermaids of Tiburon*
Vohrer, Alfred 201, 202
Vokes, May 14
Volanti, Vicki 198, 225
von Meyerinck, Hubert 200
Vonn, Veola 136
von Seyffertitz, Gustav 14
von Theumer, Ernst 110
von Treuberg, Franz 205
Voodoo Blood Bath see *Curse of the Voodoo*

W. Lee Wilder Productions 156
Waggner, George 60
Wain, Edward *see* Towne, Robert
Wake in Fright see *Fright* (1971)
Waldis, Otto 12, 138, 139
Walker, Bill 81
Walker, Brent 32, 47, 62, 110, 136, 141, 170
Walker, Clint 114
Wallace, Edgar 200, 201, 202
Walsh, Edward 190
Walter Wanger Pictures 104
Waltz, Patrick 142
War of the Satellites 156, 171–73, 233
Ward, Dervis 4
Warford, Jack 209, 210
Warner Bros. 69, 77
Warner Bros. Entertainment, Inc. 2
Warren, Bill 12, 102, 104, 164, 224
Warren, Jerry 18, 63, 66, 211
The Wasp Woman (1960) 19, 173–75, 233
The Wasp Woman (1995) 175
Waterman, Dennis 73
Watkins, Linda 75, 77
Watson, Lucille 14
Watts, Elizabeth 72
Way, Guy 105

Wayne, David 149
Web of the Spider 187
Webb, Denis 48
Webb, Harry S. 34
Webber, Diane 218
Weed, Frank 193
Weiler, A.H. 151
Weiss, Adrian 34
Weiss, Louis 34
Weiss, Samuel 34
Weld, Tuesday 146
Welden, Ben 155
Weldon, Michael J. 26, 64, 68, 102, 211, 215, 219, 226
Welles, Mel 8, 87, 110, 208, 210
Welles, Meri 209
Welles, Orson 26
Wells, H.G. 179
Wengraf, John 62, 63, 136
Wentworth, Martha 54
Wessell, Dick 33
West, Roland 14
West London Studios 153
Wexler, Paul 31
White, Christine 116
White, J. Francis 210
White, R. Meadows 48
White, Robb 115
Whitfield, Smoki 81
Whitney, Steven 44
Whitsun-Jones, Paul 28
Who? 175–77, 234
Widmark, Richard 167, 169
Wiene, Robert 84
Wilbur, Crane 15
Wilde, Lorna 29
Wilder, Billy 27
Wilder, Myles 27, 72, 156
Wilder, W. Lee 27, 28, 72, 73, 156
Willes, Jean 33, 105
Williams, Leonard 3
Williams, Robert B. 17
Willis, Donald C. 4–5, 26, 38, 41, 46, 53, 62, 75, 77, 85, 101, 122, 131, 143, 163, 166, 219, 221
Willock, Dave 142
Willrich, Rudolph 40
Wilson, Ian 56
Windsor, Tammy 209
Winfield, Paul 167, 168, 169

Winkless, Terence H. 134
Winston, Norman 223
Winwood, Estelle 14
Wise, Robert 46
Wittey, John 50
W-M-J Productions 195
Wolf, Emanuel L. 1
Wolff, Frank 17, 18, 173, 181
Wong, Arthur 42
Wontner, Arthur 14
Wood, Edward D., Jr. 34, 211, 212
Wood, Ken *see* Karson, Phil
Woolner, Bernard 195, 197
Woolner Bros. 91, 127, 185, 196, 204
World Without End 1, 102, 141, 170, 177–80, 233
Worth, D. Earl 10, 77
Wright, Teresa 22
Wu, Samuel 212
Wyndham, John 55, 58
Wynorski, Jim 134, 175
Wynter, Dana 105

Xanadu Books 152

Yachigusa, Kaoru 95
Yamamoto, Ren 95
Yates, George Worthing 164
Yates, John 160
Yeaworth, Irvin S., Jr. 230
Yordan, Philip 55
York, Francine 127, 128
York, Michael 134
Young, Burt 167, 169
Young, Gig 58, 59
Young, Ray 198
Young, R.G. 219
Young, Victor 131
Young Dillinger 23, 124
Younger, Jack 231

Zaza, Tony 150
Zertuche, Kinta 175
ZIV Studios 115
Zoet, Antonie 157
The Zombie Walks see *The Hand of Power*
Zuckert, William (Bill) 150

www.ingramcontent.com/pod-product-compliance
Lightning Source LLC
Chambersburg PA
CBHW060259240426
43661CB00060B/2835